Rebel Watchdog

Rebel
Watchdog
The Confederate States
Army Provost
Guard

Kenneth Radley

Louisiana State University Press

Baton Rouge and

London

Designer: Barbara Werden
Typeface: Linotron Times Roman
Typesetter: The Composing Room of Michigan, Inc.
Printer: Thomson-Shore, Inc.
Binder: John H. Dekker & Sons, Inc.

Library of Congress Cataloging-in-Publication Data

Radley, Kenneth, 1943–
    Rebel watchdog: the Confederate States Army provost guard/Kenneth Radley.
    p.   cm.
    Bibliography: p.
    Includes index.
    ISBN 0-8071-1468-5 (alk. paper)
    1. Confederate States of America.   Army—Military police.
    2. United States—History—Civil War, 1861–1865.   I. Title
UB825.U54R33   1989
973.7′42—dc19   88-30338
                                                                              CIP

The author is grateful to Doubleday and Company for permission to quote from William
C. Davis, *The Orphan Brigade* (1980), and to Kraus Reprints for permission to quote
from the *Southern Historical Society Papers*. Passages are reprinted by permission of the
University of South Carolina Press from *A Carolinian Goes to War: The Civil War
Narrative of Arthur Middleton Manigault, Brigadier General, C.S.A.*, edited by R.
Lockwood Tower.

*In memory of the officers and men
of the Confederate States
Army Provost Guard*

If we only act for ourselves to neglect the study of history
is not prudent; if we are entrusted with the care of others it
is not just.

SAMUEL JOHNSON

Contents

Illustrations

following page 109

Figures

Colonel (Brigadier General) Benjamin Jefferson Hill
Colonel Charles G. Livenskiold
Brigadier General John H. Winder
Castle Thunder, Richmond, Virginia
Libby Prison, Richmond, Virginia

Maps

Movements of Bragg's Army from Tupelo, Mississippi, to Chattanooga,
Tennessee, June–August, 1862

Railroads Used to Transport the First Corps of the Army of Northern
Virginia to Chickamauga, September, 1863

Battle of Fredericksburg

Abbreviations

CWTI Civil War Times Illustrated

OR   The War of the Rebellion: A Compilation of the Official Records of the Union and Confederate Armies. 130 vols. Washington, D.C., 1880–1901. All citations are to Series I unless otherwise indicated.

SHSP Southern Historical Society Papers

Preface

Tell it as you may—
It never can be told—
The story of the glory
Of the men who wore the gray.

ALICE BAXTER,
"Battle Flag of the Third Georgia"

This study of the provost guard of the Confederacy during the American Civil War stems from an interest in the war as a whole and a desire to explore a little-known aspect of Confederate military history. Throughout history organizations have inevitably attracted nicknames, laudatory or otherwise. In more recent times the introduction of radio communications into armies necessitated a system of code words for ease in referring to the various arms and services of an army. Armored units, for example, became known as "Ironsides." Provost, or military police, in British and Canadian radio parlance are referred to as "Watchdog." A distinctive dress or visual symbol identified those who served as military policemen. Thus the British army adopted the red cap or beret whereas German military police were easily recognizable by the chain and metal gorget worn around the neck. Because of their unpopularity among the troops of the Third Reich they were often called "chained dogs," a reference to their wearing of the gorget. Provost were, and are, similarly unpopular in other armies. Former members of any service can no doubt recall numerous vivid and impolite descriptive terms for the military policeman. Because most of these could not reasonably grace the cover of any book, I have chosen the term "Watchdog" for my title.

Many readers on the Civil War are probably familiar with Douglas Southall Freeman's summary of the difficulties historians of the war must face: the volume of testimony to be interpreted; the relationship of time, weather, and terrain to particular incidents; and, most important, the conflicting evidence on any aspect of the war. Freeman admits that regardless of the time spent in considering and surmounting these difficulties, "the more you probe, the less confident you are that you know precisely what occurred."[1]

1. Address by Douglas Southall Freeman to the Civil War Round Tables in Richmond on May 7, 1953, published as "An Address," *Civil War History,* I (rpr. 1963), 10.

I share Freeman's uncertainty. For example, in seven years of research I found no evidence of insignia for provost, yet a nagging feeling persisted that they *must* have worn some distinguishing badge or device. Then I read Tom Wicker's marvelous *Unto This Hour,* which described a provost sergeant wearing a yellow armband. Alas, a letter to Wicker requesting the source of this information drew the response that in his years of research he had found nothing on insignia so he invented the armband. Such a tactic is permissible in a first-rate novel, but I must adhere to the facts. I cannot use what I cannot prove.

An even more immediate difficulty in the research for *Rebel Watchdog* was highlighted by one reader, who, referring to the exhaustive published literature, noted that the author "must have had to read most of these works verbatim to glean what he has found, for the word 'provost' is not usually indexed." It is in fact virtually never indexed.

Nor did the research problems end there. On top of Freeman's difficulties and the one just described it was soon apparent that there were weaknesses in the information available on the Confederate provost. Many secondary works contained brief references to the provost, but most gave only names of persons or dates and were not particularly informative. Fortunately, some provided substantial information.

The situation in regard to manuscripts was similar. Although these often served to confirm, or less frequently to correct, statistical information, only one source, the Major I. H. Carrington Papers in the William R. Perkins Library, Duke University, Durham, North Carolina, contained substantial and detailed data. Most of the material therein, however, was well covered in the secondary sources.

It is certainly possible to speculate on and suggest additional manuscripts that might have been examined, and some readers may. One criterion should be kept in mind: manuscripts by individuals who did *not* serve as provost tend to be general and unspecific regarding such duty, even less specific than manuscripts by those who did serve as provost. After reading a number of manuscripts I concluded that additional manuscript research was unlikely to yield significant data. Further, I found that the primary sources are entirely supportive of the published literature.

These cautions aside, I am pleased to say that a great deal of significant data emerged from study of the *Official Records of the Union and Confederate Armies* and more than four hundred other books about the war. Many of these latter, mostly memoirs and personal recollections of officers and men, described personal and unit experiences, revealing details on the provost in the Confederate army. The sources highlight that the provost presence had far-reaching effects on the battles and on the war and that the successes and failures of the military police had considerable impact on the South's bid for independence. That finding in itself is justification for this book. Of particular interest to the genealogist is the annex listing more than three hundred individuals who were employed for various periods of time as provost guards. A compilation of units—regiments, battalions, and companies—that were engaged at one time or another in provost duty is provided in the Appendix.

It is probable, indeed certain, that a volume such as this will contain errors despite my best efforts to ensure accuracy. Many of these are inevitable because this is, to my knowledge, the first study of the Confederate provost guard. Like Thucydides in his *History of the Peloponnesian War,* perhaps I too may claim "to have used only the plainest evidence and to have reached conclusions which are reasonably accurate."[2] Reconciling the often fragmentary and contradictory evidence presents a major challenge in any study of the life of the Confederacy. Losers are never as well documented as winners.

I am grateful to Hubert Leroy and several members of the Confederate Historical Association of Brussels, Belgium, for making available numerous books from their libraries. Thanks also to Tom Broadfoot and Robert Bridgers of Wilmington, North Carolina, who provided references from the reprint of *Confederate Veteran.* I am grateful also to Jack Dumican of Bournemouth, England, for her help with various periodicals. *Merci beaucoup,* thank you very much.

I should particularly like to express my deep gratitude to my wife, Lillian. Little did she suspect that in marrying into the Canadian army she would also don Confederate gray "for three years or the war." Her conscription into the latter uniform has in no way lessened her enthusiasm for and interest in the book. Her repeated readings of the manuscript resulted in many useful comments that greatly improved the text. In addition, much of her free time was devoted to the tedious task of compiling the index. She has done a first-class job.

Finally, my thanks to all those authors whose works on the war have included even the most marginal information on the Confederate provost. Their assistance is gratefully acknowledged.

2. Thucydides, *History of the Peloponnesian War,* trans. Rex Warner (Harmondsworth, Eng., 1954), 47.

Rebel Watchdog

Introduction

Trust is good, control is better.

LENIN

Although the Confederate provost system was initially designed to maintain military discipline in the very large armies the South raised, eventually it assumed a degree of control over civil life unique in American history. The performance of just one provost responsibility, the suppression of disloyalty and subversion, entailed the imposition of ever wider and more stringent controls over many civilian activities.

A provost system largely based on British precedent had existed since the Revolution, but it had been restricted to purely military police functions. General Albert Pike, commanding the Indian Territory in July, 1862, complained vigorously about Confederate military regulations that had no authority in law and was adamant in his opinion that provost powers could not extend beyond the army.[1] His concern was that if internal security of the Confederacy became a provost responsibility, the authority of the states would be abrogated.

The South's preparation for war was a complex and demanding process. One of the first tasks, the formidable one of fielding an army, commenced in February, 1861, with the establishment of the War Department, the raising of provisional forces, and the organization of a general staff. During March further legislation created and organized the Confederate States Army.[2] The urgency with which these matters were negotiated through Congress is evident in that the first act, creating the War Department, was passed the day before the provisional government was established.

In theory, all provost activities were sanctioned by the Articles of War, which, as adopted on March 6, 1861, provided for provost marshals and for military courts to try army personnel charged with offenses against military law. A subsequent act in October, 1862, authorized a military court for each army corps and gave each court a provost marshal to execute its orders. Jurisdiction of these courts included offenses against the Articles of War and customs of war and against Confederate and state laws.[3]

1. *OR*, Ser. I, Vol. XIII, pp. 856, 900–902. Unless otherwise indicated, all citations are to Series I.

2. *OR*, Ser. IV, Vol. I, pp. 106, 114, 117, 127–31.

3. Henry Putney Beers, *Guide to the Archives of the Government of the Confederate States of America* (Washington, D.C., 1968), 142; *OR*, Ser. IV, Vol. II, pp. 202–203.

1

Across the new national border the Federal army was rapidly expanding. Union military leaders, especially that brilliant organizer General George B. McClellan, saw the need for an apparatus to enforce discipline, and police units were soon on duty both in Washington and with the Union forces concentrating south of the Federal capital. On assuming command McClellan formalized the provost system in Washington, established military prisons, and took steps to control vice and the movement of the masses of citizen soldiers.

In February, 1862, McClellan appointed a provost marshal for the Army of the Potomac and announced the creation of the Provost Marshal's Department. Army divisions and later corps were directed to designate provost marshals and provost guards.[4] From March, 1863, military police duties in the Federal army were performed by the Provost Marshal's Department; previously these duties had been left to army provost marshals and line units detailed for the purpose.[5]

The onerous roles and tasks that were given to the Confederate provost were, as we shall see, much the same as those assigned to the Union provost. This is not surprising because many Confederate regulations and orders, including the Articles of War, were almost exact copies of Union regulations.[6]

Rudyard Kipling's comment regarding the unsaintly behavior of single men in barracks is also appropriate for the Confederate army. There was a pressing need to ensure the discipline and efficiency of thousands of untrained men. It was obvious that Richmond, the new national capital, must have provost to control the many volunteers hastening to the defense of the young Confederacy. Similarly, military law and order would be vital in northern Virginia, where the fledgling Confederate army was deploying in the spring of 1861. References to brigade provost marshals make it clear that a provost system was in place in the army even before the first Battle of Manassas.[7]

4. E. B. Long, *The Civil War Day By Day: An Almanac, 1861–1865* (New York, 1971), 271; *OR*, Vol. LI, Pt. 1, p. 532; Vol. V, 30. Brigadier General Andrew Porter was appointed on February 19, 1862. He was replaced by Brigadier General M. R. Patrick after the Battle of Sharpsburg.

5. Francis A. Lord, "Badges of Civil War Provost Guards," *Military Collector and Historian,* XXIII (1971), 91–92.

6. *Index: A Weekly Journal of Politics, Literature and News; Devoted to the Exposition of the Mutual Interests, Political and Commercial, of Great Britain and the Confederate States of America* I (May 15, 1862), 75.

7. The provost marshal of the 1st Brigade as of July 10, 1861, is named as Major W. P. Butler in William C. Davis, *Battle at Bull Run: A History of the First Major Campaign of the Civil War* (New York, 1977), xi. The provost marshal on Longstreet's staff (4th Brigade) as of July 23, 1861, is identified as G. Moxley Sorrel in Wilbur D. Thomas, *General James "Pete" Longstreet, Lee's "Old War Horse," Scapegoat for Gettysburg* (Parsons, W.Va., 1979), 26.

In due course the Confederacy would have divisional and corps provost and a headquarters provost with the Army of Northern Virginia. Such police troops would be present, although perhaps not as extensively or formally, in all her field armies, and she too would have a provost marshal general. As well, the rear areas of the nation would eventually have provost; these areas were divided into departments, districts, and subdistricts, each with a provost marshal and each with troops to act as a provost guard.

The departmental commands instituted by the War Department in time became virtually autonomous, based in part on the premise that where and when necessary departmental commanders could lend or borrow resources to meet the enemy threat.[8] At first the system was simple and the departments were small in size, but as new fronts were created to counter new menaces, their size increased. By 1863 General P. G. T. Beauregard, for one, found himself commanding a department that covered three states. As the departments went, so went the provost, and a dramatic increase in their duties and the number of men devoted to them was inevitable.

Certainly in the Confederate army the provost were needed largely because Johnny Reb was not noted for his acquiescence to military authority. The provost's success in combating this military failing is debatable. No less a leader than Robert E. Lee himself would say: "I could always rely on my army for *fighting,* but its discipline was poor."[9] Indiscipline was the root cause of many of the shortcomings of the Confederate army: the tendency to straggle and the attendant evils, and the trickle of desertion that near the end of the war became a flood, blunted the edge of Confederate offensive power.

Understanding how the provost strove to combat these weaknesses presupposes some knowledge of its status in the army. The South chose not to have a separate provost corps, preferring instead to detail officers and men to such duties for extensive periods of time, in many cases because of ill health or wounds that rendered them unfit for combat. Units employed as provost generally spent only limited periods on such duties. Regardless of the time they were so employed, individuals and units quickly discovered that policemen had unique and often infamous status.

8. The department system is outlined in Emory M. Thomas, *The Confederate Nation, 1861– 1865* (New York, 1979), 109. A full list of departments is in William Frayne Amann (ed.), *The Confederate Armies* (New York, 1961). Many departments are described in Patricia L. Faust (ed.), *Historical Times Illustrated Encyclopedia of the Civil War* (New York, 1986).

9. E. P. Alexander, "Sketch of Longstreet's Division," *SHSP,* IX (rpr. 1977), 512–18. General Lee made the comment at Appomattox.

Genesis

*The safety of the people must be
the supreme law.*
ROMAN PROVERB

As the war raged on, the provost became an increasingly controversial organization. The initial issue of whether it would be under the control of state or national government was complicated and exacerbated by the question of its existence outside of the operational areas near the fronts. This question was the subject of protracted and acrimonious correspondence between military, state, and national leaders starting shortly after the outbreak of war and persisting until late in March, 1865, when the Confederacy toppled into ruin.

One of the responses of the military commanders to the supreme test of war was to urge the appointment of a national chief of military police endowed with radical powers sufficient to put every available man into the field. Such powers would not likely have remained confined to conscription or purely military matters. The attitudes of Governors Zebulon Vance of North Carolina and Joseph E. Brown of Georgia, neither of whom was particularly receptive to the wishes of Richmond, are indicative of strong state opposition to such measures as conscription.

In the Confederate Senate two diametrically opposed attitudes toward military authority emerged early in the war and festered throughout. The following exchange neatly delineates both ends of the spectrum:

> Mr. Orr said it was known that he and the Senator from Texas (Mr. Wigfall) differed widely upon the question of military authority. The Senator believed in strong military measures, which he (Mr. Orr) called despotism. He (Mr. Wigfall) introduced the law for conscribing everybody; he voted for the bill to suspend the *habeas corpus* act, putting the military above the civil power. He (Mr. Orr) would say . . . that there was not the shadow of authority for any of the provost marshals in the country beyond the limits of a camp or army. Every provost guard to be

4

met between this city and Atlanta was an outrage . . . it was time that
the legislature should put a curb on the unbridled will of military power.[1]

Even semantics, or what appears at first sight to be semantics, entered the
controversy. In July, 1862, Major General Leonidas Polk, then commanding a
corps in the Army of the Mississippi, advised Secretary of War George W.
Randolph of controversy over what name to give an officer responsible for the
military police of a city or town. Should this officer be known as the provost
marshal or as the chief of police? Polk also advised the secretary of war that
General Gideon Pillow, an officer he would later propose as chief of police in a
much wider sense, was opposed to the term "provost marshal."[2] It is easy to see
why because this term implied military control over civilians. Nevertheless, the
term entered into general use.

Polk had raised one of those matters on which specifics are sometimes best
avoided. In September, however, Randolph tutored the Senate on an essential
element of the military use of provost marshals: because commissioned officers
acting as provost marshals were *employed,* not *appointed,* they need not hold a
second and distinct appointment from the government. He agreed completely
with a prominent senator's comment that there was no law authorizing the
appointment of provost marshals. What was the point of legislation on nonexistent appointments? Moreover, the secretary of war agreed that provost
authority did not extend over civilians, except in areas where martial law was in
force.[3]

Some state governors, steeped in states' rights and to varying degrees reluctant to accept even the necessity for provost, rejected the idea that the central
government should exercise the police mandate. Nor was contention limited to
which level of government should be responsible. From the very beginning
many prominent Confederates, particularly state governors, had opposed formation of any provost apparatus. Eventually their persistent agitation, with the
urging of senators and representatives, led to a motion in December, 1863,

1. "Proceedings of Second Confederate Congress, First Session, Second Session in Part, 2
May–14 June 1864, 7 November–14 December 1864," *SHSP,* LI (rpr. 1980), 28.

2. *OR,* III, 319. Pillow was later assigned to the volunteer and conscript bureau and was briefly
commissary general of prisoners after the death of General John H. Winder in February, 1865.

3. "Proceedings of First Confederate Congress, Second Session in Part," *SHSP,* XLVI (rpr.
1980), 103; "Proceedings of First Confederate Congress, First Session Completed, Second Session
in Part," *SHSP,* XLV (rpr. 1980), 249.

aimed at abolition of the provost.[4] This motion, which also sought to transfer control of the provost to the state governors, was defeated on Christmas Eve.

Having failed to eliminate or gain direct control of the provost, the governors attempted to limit provost authority, especially its existence outside the operational areas of the armies. Such limitations were pursued in the belief that military jurisdiction must be strictly defined to prevent any abuses against the civilian population. Congressional records reveal that as early as September 9, 1862, the House of Representatives wanted a report prepared on the measures necessary to prevent such abuses.[5] In one debate a prominent Texan, Senator William S. Oldham, stated that the War Department had no right to give provost marshals any power over civilians, nor did the provost have legal authority to police towns or cities.[6] The evidence indicates that these civilian fears regarding the extension of provost power were justified.

Inevitably the original purpose of the provost—to preserve order in the armies—was widened by the pressures of war. For example, the provost was compelled to monitor transportation services such as stage lines and trains if it was to have even a fighting chance of decreasing the surging rate of desertion and inhibiting the movement of the many Yankee spies who were presumed to be everywhere. A system of passes to regulate travel was soon in effect and proved an annoyance to citizens and soldiers alike.[7]

Later that month Senator Oldham raised the subject of the provost again. He proposed to allow the general in chief or divisional commanders (in the rank of general) to appoint a provost marshal with a suitable guard or police force to take charge of prisoners, but under no circumstances would they have authority over civilians or the towns and cities. The secretary of war was specifically admonished that he could not limit or otherwise restrict the jurisdiction of civil courts. In effect, provost marshal powers could not extend beyond the army.[8] The last part of the resolution, regarding the maintenance of civilian jurisdic-

---

4. *Journal of the Congress of the Confederate States of America, 1861–1865* (7 vols.; Washington, D.C., 1904–1905), VI, 529, 564.

5. *Ibid.*, V, 360.

6. Frank L. Owsley, *State Rights in the Confederacy* (1925; rpr. Gloucester, Mass., 1961), 167; Jon L. Wakelyn, *Biographical Dictionary of the Confederacy* (Westport, Conn., 1977), 333–34; "Proceedings of First Confederate Congress, Second Session in Part," 225. Oldham, an outspoken champion of states' rights, was consistently opposed to conscription and suspension of the writ of *habeas corpus*.

7. E. Merton Coulter, *The Confederate States of America, 1861–1865* (1950; rpr. Baton Rouge, 1968), 395–96.

8. *Journal of the Confederate Congress*, II, 325–26; *OR*, XIII, 902; "Proceedings of First

tion, hit directly at the imposition of martial law in various parts of the Confederacy, which had proceeded apace with the institution of the provost apparatus.

On October 3 Oldham's resolution was defeated, but it was passed, after some amendment, by Congress eleven days later.[9] Nevertheless, as the war intensified and the Confederacy's military fortunes declined, the army often ignored these provisions. Obviously, military necessities had more weight than the political niceties of catering to the strict constitutionalism of state and other officials.

Operation of the passport system fell to the provost. The widespread unpopularity of passports conferred both a high profile and a large measure of odium on the provost. Eventually, as the battle fronts expanded, virtually every Confederate citizen was subject to the provost's control of his or her right to travel. By late 1864 such controls were heatedly debated in Congress. In November Representative Henry S. Foote of Tennessee—never a strong supporter of the Confederate administration and President Jefferson Davis—proposed abolition of both the passport system and the provost. To him both were a source of increasing "oppression and annoyance," and he requested action to correct this "overgrown and intolerable" situation. In December the House Committee on Military Affairs was directed to consider the effects of abolishing the provost in areas outside the actual fields of military operations.[10]

On February 21, 1865, the House of Representatives was advised that the Senate had passed Bill S.191, "An act to abolish the office of all officers engaged in discharging the duties of provost-marshals, except within the lines of an army in the field." Many members of Congress, no doubt responding to military pressure, felt that this was going much too far. An amendment to S.191 by the House of Representatives on February 28 permitted carefully controlled appointments of provost marshals in rear areas when they were judged by generals commanding armies and departments as essential to the public ser-

---

Confederate Congress, Second Session in Part," 226; "Proceedings of First Confederate Congress, End of Second Session, Third Session in Part," *SHSP,* XLVII (rpr. 1980), 31–32.

9. The resolution, in *Journal of the Confederate Congress,* II, 368, was considered with amendments on October 1, 1862 (394–96) but received a negative vote on October 3 (404); *Index,* II (November 27, 1862), 69; "Proceedings of First Confederate Congress, End of Second Session," *SHSP,* XLVII (rpr. 1980), 75–76.

10. *Journal of the Confederate Congress,* VII, 312, 402; Wakelyn, *Biographical Dictionary,* 188. Foote was expelled from Congress in 1864 and in 1865 was called a traitor for his espousal of peace.

vice. Aware of the precarious military situation, the House had provided for the harsh realities associated with continued prosecution of the war.[11] The amendment also stipulated that provost marshals could not be appointed in places lying outside the lines of the army. Once again much debate had produced an amendment that although confusing and contradictory would lean toward granting of wide discretionary powers to army and department commanders. In effect, the amendment gave *carte blanche* to the army.

The amendment further stated that, except for provost marshals at army or department headquarters, only commissioned officers over forty-five years of age, or retired officers, or those unfit for active field service could be appointed as provost marshals. This proviso aimed to return to the field officers who had been able to shirk combat by employment with the provost, essentially a noncombatant organization.

An additional amendment on March 3 stated that provost guards must be composed of either reserve soldiers or men who had been disabled but were still fit for light duty. The hope was to permit the return of fit men to the various fronts. On March 9, 1865, President Davis signed the bill into law.[12]

The military had consistently urged a general strengthening of provost authority in the belief that this would increase army combat power and the chance of achieving military victory. Any device that would lead to military success was deemed appropriate and necessary.

The military's position is reflected in extensive correspondence between Lieutenant General Leonidas Polk, Adjutant General Samuel Cooper, and President Davis on the subject of the appointment of a "chief of police" for the Confederacy. The initial conclusion to be reached from this correspondence, which went on from July, 1863, to May, 1864, is that Polk was forced to act as he saw fit. Little or no action or direction was forthcoming from a government preoccupied in mid-1863 with the twin disasters of Gettysburg and Vicksburg and a year later with the struggle between Robert E. Lee and Ulysses S. Grant in the Wilderness.

General Polk, in July, 1863, commanding a corps in the troubled Army of Tennessee, started the flow of letters by reminding General Cooper of their discussion of a program to increase the armies and accumulate reserves and

11. *Journal of the Confederate Congress,* VII, 618, 625, 663–64; "Proceedings of Second Confederate Congress, Second Session in Part, December 15, 1864–March 18, 1865," *SHSP,* LII (rpr. 1980), 334–35, 372, 416–17.

12. For agreement to the bill and its subsequent amendment by the Senate on March 3, 1865, see *Journal of the Confederate Congress,* VII, 688, 707, 734.

their mutual agreement that it was essential to get every possible man into the field. Polk proposed to establish a national organization to be entitled the Bureau or Department of Reserves, either as a separate unit or under the wing of the Adjutant and Inspector General's Department. The general officer heading this bureau would control the entire machinery of conscription, including the recovery of absent volunteers, personnel absent without leave, and deserters. To carry out this mandate the bureau chief would have to be entrusted with wide and discretionary powers; he would function as the chief of military police for the nation. Polk's nominee for the position was General Gideon Pillow. Cooper was told that a similar system was proving highly successful in General Braxton Bragg's department.[13]

The proposal did not receive the approval of the secretary of war because it roughly duplicated the already existing Bureau of Conscription. Polk, no admirer of that organization, complained to Cooper in March, 1864, of its weakness and inefficiency and pointed out the detrimental effects of absenteeism on his department. A glaring example was the murder of a conscript officer and the routing of his troops by a band of deserters in Mississippi.

In another initiative Polk proposed to merge the duties of overseeing conscription and arresting deserters, both to be a direct responsibility of department commanders. This proposal was also rejected because it was felt that it would increase Polk's responsibilities without any significant savings in manpower or increase in efficiency. Stymied in his bid to gain control of the mechanism of conscription, Polk determined to ensure the efficient internal organization of his department. On March 10 he promulgated a general order dividing the Department of Alabama, Mississippi, and East Louisiana into nine districts: four in Mississippi and four in Alabama, with Louisiana east of the Mississippi River as a single district. A chief provost marshal was appointed at each district headquarters. Major Jules C. Denis, Polk's provost marshal general, was authorized to assign additional marshals to each district.[14]

On March 31 Polk advised Cooper of the reorganization and reiterated that where possible he had used only officers unfit for field service. He went on to say that these measures were designed to prevent disorder, ensure the arrest and return of stragglers and deserters, and maintain both the security of the citizens

13. *OR*, Vol. XXIII, Pt. 2, pp. 921–22.

14. *OR*, Vol. XXXII, Pt. 3, pp. 580–581, 611. Some of these district provost marshals have been identified: Third District of Mississippi, Lieutenant Colonel J. Hanlon; First District of Alabama, Lieutenant Colonel John W. Estes; and Second District of Alabama, Lieutenant Colonel T. H. Baker. See Appendix I.

and the discipline of the army. Polk then requested authority to raise companies of exempt men to be used by the provost marshals to enforce his orders. The request was denied on the grounds that commanders in the field had no legal means to enroll or conscript men. In lieu it was suggested that companies of reserves could be supplied by the secretary of war. Clearly, commanders were not going to be allowed to raise what would amount to private armies.

Other commanders were expressing interest in the steps Polk had taken. In response to one query Colonel George Brent, Braxton Bragg's assistant adjutant general, advised Bragg in late April, 1864, that Polk's provost staff consisted of a provost marshal in the rank of lieutenant colonel in each of the nine districts and a captain provost marshal in each of the eighteen subdistricts, all under the command of a provost marshal general at department headquarters. All twenty-seven officers had either been wounded or were supernumerary. Brent also stated that provost guards were supplied by detachments from the army, but Polk hoped to replace these with local defense companies raised specifically for police duties.[15]

In May, Colonel George B. Hodge, an officer on the adjutant general's staff, submitted a report on his inspection of Polk's department. An estimated ten thousand men were absent from their commands, there was widespread disaffection with the Confederate cause in many areas (Jones County, Mississippi, being a prominent example), swarms of deserters ravaged the counties bordering the Mississippi, and the Bureau of Conscription was unable to cope with the situation.[16] Although Polk had acted without authority in raising troops to restore law and order, Hodge considered the step "expedient." The situation was improving, and there was "promising prospect of greater and more decided results." Hodge stressed that all officers on provost duty were unfit for field service. The provost guards also consisted of more than three hundred men who were not fit for field service. From being exclusively engaged in police duties, they had acquired a proficiency that temporary details of men could not be expected to achieve.

Three days later Polk advised President Davis that he had raised companies of exempts to act as guards. Local defense companies had also been organized from the reserves (men between seventeen and eighteen and forty-five and fifty years of age), but these would be used for infantry purposes only.[17]

15. *OR*, Vol. XXXII, Pt. 3, pp. 723–26, 817; Ser. IV, Vol. III, pp. 294–95.

16. James Street based his 1946 novel *Tap Roots* on the situation in Jones County. His portrayal was much exaggerated.

17. *OR*, Vol. XXXIX, Pt. 2, pp. 570, 579–80.

In summary, in at least one major department a provost organization had been formalized on a district and subdistrict basis and the necessary police officers had been appointed, presumably disabled officers when possible. Polk had done his best to use exempt personnel as provost, but some fit men and detachments from the army continued to be employed in that duty. In many areas the absence of any other manpower made use of these classes of men inevitable.

In the departments the provost chain of command was from subdistrict to district and finally to department provost marshals. In the field armies as well a chain extended up through the levels of command from brigade through division and corps to army. Staff responsibilities were largely well defined and, much like today, provost received their orders either directly from formation commanders or through the appropriate staff officers. Considerable documentation shows that even in the most remote commands the provost machinery was firmly in place.

One of the earliest references to the provost chain of command in the field is found in the correspondence of the Army of the Mississippi early in 1861. In March a general order directed that disciplinary matters were the concern of the adjutant general of the army. Another report, this time of a corps provost marshal (Stonewall Jackson's 2d Corps), refers to his acting under authority of Jackson's assistant adjutant general in January, 1863. Another such reference in June, 1864, notes that the provost marshal of Nathan Bedford Forrest's cavalry reported directly to Forrest's assistant adjutant general on prisoners of war. These reports and many others like them show that provost marshals were reporting to the appropriate staff officer, the adjutant general, at the various levels of command.[18] In addition, provost officers reported to the next senior level of provost officer, as is apparent in an order of the Army of Tennessee dated April 9, 1863: "A provost marshal general will be assigned to duty at army headquarters with one assistant. Corps commanders will detail a field officer, with one assistant, for duty at corps headquarters, a captain for division headquarters, and a lieutenant for brigade headquarters. These officers will . . . report regularly to the provost marshal of the army."[19] The anomaly of all provost marshals reporting directly to the provost marshal general was

18. *OR,* Vol. LII, Pt. 2, p. 25; XXI, 641–42; Vol. XXXIX, Pt. 1, p. 227. The *OR* contain many references to the system, and the geographical spread of these reports indicates that this reporting procedure was the general practice.

19. *OR,* Vol. XXIII, Pt. 2, p. 744.

corrected by Order No. 36 in November, 1864, specifying that brigade provost marshals would report through division and corps provost marshals.[20]

Some provost establishments may have been allowed direct access to the provost marshal general of the Confederacy. One example is a letter addressed directly to General John H. Winder by Captain G. H. Hammond, the provost marshal of Williamsport, Maryland, in February, 1864.[21] More likely, this junior provost officer ignored the chain of command. Winder quickly passed the letter to General Jubal Early, who was operating in the area; the irascible Early would not have been averse to reminding Winder of proper channels of communication. Moreover, the correspondence contravened an order by the adjutant general of January, 1863, prohibiting such direct communication.[22]

Deliberate or inadvertent flouting of orders or inability to adhere to them would not have impressed this young officer's superiors. The incident, moreover, indicates that provost personnel, like those in the rest of the army, were of varying competence and caliber.

20. *OR*, Vol. XLV, Pt. 1, p. 1227.

21. *OR*, XXXIII, 1160.

22. War Department, Collection of Confederate Records, Record Group 109, Chap. IX, Vol. 199½.

2

What Manner of Men Are These?

Though the provost guard surround me,
Prompt to do their master's will.

ALBERT ROBERTS,

"I'm Conscripted, Smith, Conscripted,"

Confederate Veteran

The need for manpower became so insatiable that volunteers alone could not suffice. This shortage led to two conscription bills, which, among other things, restricted the classes of men eligible for use as provost. At first, the caliber of the men assigned to the provost was high, and throughout the war, when regular units could be spared or when from sheer necessity they were diverted from fighting to policing, the performance of rear area provost remained creditable. As more and more men were required at the front, however, provost guards in rear areas increasingly consisted of unfit men, militia, and under- and overage men. Their use for the provost function allowed fit soldiers to return to the regiments, where they were desperately needed, but there was a corresponding decline in the efficiency of the provost in the rear areas. At the front, though, where the provost guards consisted of detailed units, mainly seasoned battalions integral to the army, their performance remained high. The experiences of the 1st Virginia and 5th Alabama battalions show what these veteran troops could do for the army when they were employed as policemen.

It was realized from the start that if provost were to be truly effective in maintaining good order and discipline, their own conduct had to be exemplary. One of the first expressions of the desire to ensure a high caliber of military policeman was a general order of the Department of Northern Virginia on June 5, 1862, directing that provost guards be chosen for their reliability and efficiency.[1] General Lee considered this need so important that shortly after suc-

---

1. *OR*, Vol. XI, Pt. 3, pp. 576–77. This order directed that each divisional provost guard would consist of one officer, one noncommissioned officer, and ten men from each regiment in the division. Disregarding battalions, the total number of infantry regiments in the Army of Northern Virginia after the Seven Days' Battle was 66 in Longstreet's Corps and 67 in Jackson's for a total of

ceeding Joseph E. Johnston during the Seven Days' Battle, he directed that officers entrusted with provost commands be "efficient, energetic and firm."[2] The advantage of using high-caliber officers and men as provost was recognized in even the most remote areas of the Confederacy. In late 1864, for example, General Sterling Price, commanding the Army of Missouri, ordered his provost marshal to organize guards of picked officers and men.[3] Meantime, in South Carolina, General Joseph Wheeler directed that "Each division commander will select a regiment, under a strict officer, which shall be used as a provost guard of the division. This regiment will be selected for its general good conduct and will be retained on this duty only while its conduct is exemplary."[4]

Another illustration of the desire to ensure that competent personnel were assigned to the provost also demonstrates how good intentions can sometimes be perverted. In September, 1862, Major General J. P. McCown, commanding the Department of East Tennessee, complained to Secretary of War Randolph that regulations requiring the provost marshal and his deputies to be officers in service were injuring the army both by withdrawing good officers from their commands and by preventing him from having the best men in provost positions. In recommending that *ex-officio* rank be granted provost marshals and their deputies, McCown appears to have been prepared to risk civilian appointees using their *ex-officio* rank to avoid conscription. It was difficult to conscript an individual who was already serving *ex-officio* in a provost capacity.[5]

Numerous instances may be found of men using provost duty to avoid the rigors of active service. This evasion reached such serious proportions that in January, 1864, a loyal supporter of the administration, Congressman Robert

---

133 ("Organization of the Army of Northern Virginia, [General R. E. Lee Commanding], August 28 to September 1, 1862," *SHSP,* X [rpr. 1977], 555–60). Assuming that each regiment furnished the requisite number of men, total provost strength would have been 1,330 men, 133 noncommissioned officers, and 133 officers. The order stipulated that those selected would remain on provost duty unless relieved for inefficiency.

2. *OR,* Vol. XIX, Pt. 2, pp. 618–19. These criteria for selection, contained in a letter dated September 22, 1862, were presumably applied most especially to the provost marshal who would have had the most contact with Lee—Major D. B. Bridgford, provost marshal of the Army of Northern Virginia.

3. *OR,* Vol. XLI, Pt. 1, p. 648. Price's provost marshal general received this directive about September 27, 1864, and organized a guard of fifty men and four officers in each brigade.

4. *OR,* XLIV, 1002. This order was published by the headquarters of Wheeler's cavalry corps, Beaufort District, South Carolina, December 29, 1864.

5. *OR,* Vol. XVI, Pt. 2, pp. 794–95.

Johnson of Arkansas, raised the matter in Congress, asking that steps be taken to prevent enrolling officers from abusing their power to grant exemptions from conscription. Limits should be set on the time such officers could serve in one area and on the number of men they could enroll in their provost guards. Johnson thought enrolling officers who remained too long in one locality became overly familiar with the local citizens and were guilty of "keeping men out of the army in the field who should be there and putting in some who ought not to be put in."[6] Once admitted to the provost guard, a "favorite" was guaranteed exemption from active service.

Officers, too, were frequently averse to hard service in the trenches. In March, 1864, a post commander in Georgia advised his superiors of a blatant example of such behavior. Apparently, the local provost marshal, Major T. B. Howard, claimed that his battalion of boys aged fourteen to eighteen had been recognized by the War Department as the 27th Georgia Battalion. The battalion, on police duty and guarding public property at Columbus, consisted of 161 boys and a full quota of officers. The latter, all apparently over eighteen and therefore subject to conscription, were claiming exemption by virtue of their commissions. These officers were avoiding front-line service by their attachment as provost officers. These "skulkers" or "bomb-proofs,"[7] as they were called, may well have been favorites of Major Howard or had family connections that made him feel it expedient to favor them.

Initially many provost duties were performed by civilians. One of the first instances occurred late in February, 1862, when President Davis placed Norfolk and Portsmouth, Virginia, under martial law.[8] By appointing the mayor of Norfolk provost marshal of that city, Davis clearly indicated his wish to quiet civilian fears of military control of the city. In the eyes of the populace, the mayor—the civilian authority—would still have control. A civilian, H. M. Spofford, was appointed provost marshal of New Orleans in April, 1862, and in fourteen of sixteen counties and parishes of Mississippi and Louisiana placed under martial law in September, 1862, civilians received the appointments of provost marshal.[9] The commanders of armies or forces in the field were also cognizant of civilian fears of military usurpation. In June, 1862, Brigadier General George Steuart, commanding at Winchester, Virginia, appointed as

6. *Index,* IV (February 4, 1864), 70.
7. *OR,* Ser. IV, Vol. III, p. 460; John C. Walker, "Reconstruction in Texas," *SHSP,* XXIV (rpr. 1977), 46.
8. Owsley, *State Rights,* 151–52; *OR,* IX, 46, 56.
9. *OR,* XV, 805–806.

provost marshal "Mr. Brooke, a gentleman of Prince George's County, Maryland."[10]

Civilian provost marshals were probably never really satisfactory to military commanders, who would have considered civilians ignorant of military requirements and ill-equipped to meet them. In mid-1863 the problem was resolved by Congress, quite possibly at the behest of the army, which was no longer so concerned with civilian dislikes or apprehensions. On June 3 the War Department published a general order advising that because Congress had not recognized civilian provost appointments, henceforth no more would be made.[11] Department commanders were also directed to recommend suitable officers to replace civilians, giving preference to competent officers who were unfit for active field duty because of wounds or ill health. The order closed with a deadline: by July 1, 1863, those posts without army provost marshals would lose the right to have a provost marshal.

No doubt the army was pleased when Congress abolished civilian provost marshals. Civilians without military knowledge and experience had, in most cases, lacked the full confidence of commanders, and in any event, there had not been sufficient numbers of the right caliber of civilians available to act as provost marshals.

Over a year earlier in March, 1862, it was apparent that the Confederate army would soon face a severe decrease in strength. Very few of the twelve-month volunteers wished to continue on active service, and since their enlistment terms would expire in April, it appeared that the Southern armies would begin to disintegrate just as the massive Union army under General McClellan began to surge forward. Something had to be done quickly to find sufficient men to stop the enemy and maintain the Confederacy.

The state of Virginia had already made a start by ordering a general enrollment of all men eighteen to forty-five years of age into the state militia to replace men whose enlistments in Virginia regiments had expired. President Davis proposed to do Virginia one better. In late March he recommended outright conscription of men aged eighteen to thirty-five throughout the Confederacy. After heated but mercifully short debate, Congress responded on April 9, 1862, with the first national conscription act in the Western Hemisphere. On April 16 President Davis approved the act, which called for the

---

10. McHenry Howard, *Recollections of a Maryland Confederate Soldier and Staff Officer Under Johnston, Jackson and Lee* (1914; rpr. Dayton, 1975), 178.

11. *OR*, Ser. IV, Vol. II, pp. 573–74.

conscription of every white male between eighteen and thirty-five for three years' service.[12] This act was to have a dramatic impact on the Confederacy, on the war, and on the military policeman. The act, of course, had its weaknesses: the provisions for substitution and election of officers were ill-advised and proved contentious and divisive. Election of officers in particular had potential for "a most disorganizing and deleterious effect," and there would soon be evidence that "almost all of the good officers have been thrown overboard." Provision for substitution was in the long run even more fraught with peril: loud were the cries of "rich man's war . . . poor man's fight."[13]

A third weakness, the lack of exemptions to ensure the Confederacy of producers as well as fighters, was corrected by an amendment on April 21. Exemption from military service was provided for many occupations, including government officials, ferrymen, pilots, employees in iron mines and foundries, telegraph operators, ministers, printers, educators, hospital staff, and druggists. Other occupations were added later.

The act was a decided turn from the states' rights dogma on which the Confederacy had been founded. Many saw it as a repudiation of the principles for which the South had gone to war, and some prominent officials, notably Governor Joseph Brown of Georgia, remained implacably opposed to the act. Still, it was generally seen as vital to the prosecution of the war. On April 28, 1862, a general order notified the Confederate war machine of the new measure for the defense of the nation.[14] In theory, passage of the act meant that many of the men who had been detailed from their commands to serve as teamsters, employees of various military bureaus, and, of course, provost, could now return to the army. The gaps thus created would have to be filled by militia and disabled officers and men.

Even before passage of the act, militia apparently were performing provost duties, at least in Virginia. In March, 1862, one Confederate soldier, while passing through Fredericksburg, was escorted to the local provost marshal by "two old reserves with muskets."[15] The city authorities in Richmond were taking advantage of legislation passed in the summer of 1861 that had allowed

12. The full text of the act is in *Index*, I (August 28, 1862), 286–87.

13. Robert Manson Myers (ed.), *The Children of Pride: A True Story of Georgia and the Civil War* (New Haven, 1972), 894; Albert Burton Moore, *Conscription and Conflict in the Confederacy* (New York, 1924), 49.

14. *OR*, Ser. IV, Vol. I, pp. 1094–1100.

15. William Lyne Wilson, *A Borderland Confederate*, ed. Festus P. Summers (Pittsburgh, 1962), 91.

the use of local troops for immediate defense and other purposes by authorizing the president to accept volunteers for the defense of exposed localities or for special service at his discretion.[16] No age limitations had then been prescribed, but following passage of the Conscription Act men over forty-five or those not liable to conscription could serve in local defense companies.[17] In mid-May of 1862, as Confederate troops massed to defend Richmond against McClellan, the City Council requested that a local defense unit, the Tredegar Battalion, be detailed as military police in the city.[18] Either the battalion was not available or it was considered inadequate for the task, for on May 19 it was proposed that a force be organized to assist in the preservation of order. A week later Mayor Joseph Carrington Mayo was authorized to accept recruits over the age of thirty-five for the purpose of forming a regiment, to be styled the "Home Guard for the defence of Richmond," to keep order in the city and guard public property, prisons, and bridges. Every regular soldier could then join General Joseph E. Johnston for the impending Seven Days' Battle. By May 28 it was evident that a regimental strength of ten companies would be very difficult to attain; it was decided that only a battalion of five companies of one hundred men each could be formed. On August 15 the Richmond City Battalion, Virginia Local Defense Troops, officially designated as the 25th Virginia Battalion of Volunteers, mustered five companies for six months' service in and around Richmond. Four additional companies were raised later. Also in May an additional eighty men of the second-class militia reported to the provost marshal for the purpose of guarding the city.[19]

Elsewhere, too, the militia were being used as provost when possible. On May 7, 1863, Governor Vance of North Carolina reported to the secretary of war that General D. H. Hill was gathering together all available troops in the state so he would furnish militia for provost duties. A week later, in response to Hill's query on the status of local defense troops, Adjutant General Cooper advised that the terms of enlistment of such troops must be strictly adhered to, and if they had not proved useful, they must be replaced by either militia or

---

16. "An Act to provide for local defense and special service," August 21, 1861, *OR*, Ser. IV, Vol. I, p. 579.

17. "An act to authorize the formation of volunteer companies for local defense," October 13, 1862, *OR*, Ser. IV, Vol. II, pp. 206–207.

18. Louis H. Manarin (ed.), *Richmond at War: The Minutes of the City Council, 1861–1865* (Chapel Hill, 1966), 176.

19. *Ibid.*, 179, 182, 185 and n. 107 on 186–87.

disabled soldiers. Cooper also made it clear that any such men who were discharged were subject to conscription and immediate enrollment, as were the guards at the Salisbury prisoner of war compound.[20] By May, 1864, even such units as the Georgia Military Institute Cadet Battalion were being used as provost.[21]

Disabled officers and men, no longer fit for active service, were another source, and a good one, of provost manpower. One of the earliest documented examples occurred in 1862 shortly after the Battle of Shiloh. Colonel R. C. Tyler, commanding the 15th Tennessee Infantry, was badly wounded during the battle and subsequently served as provost marshal general of Braxton Bragg's army in the field.[22] In the Kentucky Orphan Brigade there were also officers whose incapacitating wounds led them to provost service. Lieutenant Thomas L. Dodd, who had served with Forrest during his East Tennessee campaign, ended the war as provost marshal of Covington, Georgia. He was recommended for the position of provost marshal general of the state, but the recommendation was not acted upon before the end of the war. Another brigade officer, Colonel Martin H. Cofer, was appointed provost marshal general of the Army of Tennessee after Chickamauga in September, 1863. One of his provost marshals, Captain David C. Walker, lost an arm at Resaca in May, 1864, and spent the rest of the war as provost marshal of Americus, Georgia. Ed Porter Thompson, in *History of the Orphan Brigade,* lists five other men who because of wounds received during the Atlanta campaign were assigned to provost duty with the Army of Tennessee and Wheeler's cavalry.[23]

Another famous brigade that contributed its share of disabled men to the provost was Hood's Texas Brigade. Harold Simpson, in his study of the brigade, lists thirty-four men who were detached to provost duty between the spring of 1862 and the end of the war. These detachments were for varying periods and in all but thirteen cases were because of wounds or chronic sickness. One other reference gives an account of a wounded soldier who was

---

20. *OR,* Vol. LI, Pt. 2, p. 703; XVIII, 1061–62.

21. Robert L. Rodgers, "Roster of the Battalion of the Georgia Military Institute Cadets in the Confederate Army Service in the Civil War from May 10th, 1864, to May 20th, 1865," *SHSP,* XXXIII (rpr. 1979), 307, 318. The cadet battalion was on provost at Marietta, Georgia, in May, 1864, and at Augusta in May, 1865.

22. Ezra J. Warner, "Who Was General Tyler?" *CWTI,* IX (October, 1970), 15; *OR,* Vol. XX, Pt. 2, p. 404.

23. Ed Porter Thompson, *History of the Orphan Brigade* (1898; rpr. Dayton, 1973), 119–20, 423–27, 504, 631, 639, 688, 793, 838. See Appendix I.

ordered to report directly to General John H. Winder, provost marshal general of the Confederacy.[24]

An interesting example of the effort expended in ensuring that disabled men were used as provost in rear areas is an 1863 special order of the Army of Tennessee, issued just before the November 23 fiasco at Missionary Ridge. It directed Lieutenant Colonel H. W. Walter, assistant adjutant general, to visit all rear area quartermaster and commissary establishments, post commandant offices, provost marshal offices, and hospitals, with the aim of returning to the front any officers and men who were in the rear without authority or as a result of unnecessary details. When possible such personnel were to be replaced by disabled officers and men. This combing of the rear area for every available man was a desperate attempt to strengthen Bragg's attenuated army in the face of an imminent and fierce Federal attack. Even Confederates under arrest for various military offenses were dispatched posthaste to the front. Bragg was indeed in dire straits.[25]

The success of the program to replace fit men with unfit men is debatable. E. Merton Coulter, in *Confederate States of America, 1861–1865,* refers to the great extension of provost functions and powers to the point that provost were virtually everywhere: on trains and stages, at stations, and any other place where they could monitor travel. Inevitably their all too obvious presence led to complaints from civilians, who were quick to point out that many seemingly able-bodied men were employed as provost. One letter to Jefferson Davis suggested that provost marshals were "ten times healthier than you are my dear President." The word *ubiquitous* was increasingly used to describe the provost presence; travel passes, for example, were scrutinized by the "ten thousand provost marshals who line all the highways and byways of the country." Complaints were so frequent and so vociferous that eventually they culminated in a joint request by the governors of the states east of the Mississippi for the return of the provost to the front. In the opinion of many, "large numbers of able-bodied young men, in spite of the effort to substitute disabled soldiers and limited service conscripts for them, were kept in the non-fighting branches."

24. Colonel Harold B. Simpson, *Hood's Texas Brigade: A Compendium* (Hillsboro, Tex., 1977), *passim;* Captain Robert Emory Park, "The 12th Alabama Infantry, Confederate States Army, Its Organization, Associations, Engagements, Casualties, etc.," *SHSP,* XXXIII (rpr. 1979), 241.

25. Special Order 301, promulgated November 19, 1863 (*OR,* Vol. XXXI, Pt. 3, p. 717). Earlier, the Army of Tennessee had ordered a similar roundup to replace the losses sustained at Chickamauga. A circular issued on September 21 (see *OR,* Vol. XXX, Pt. 4, p. 680) ordered all details for provost guards and other organizations to report to their commands.

Governor Brown of Georgia suggested putting into the army "the almost countless swarm of young, able-bodied officers, who are to be seen on all our railroad trains and in all our hotels." The media were quick, as always, to seize on any issue that had potential to embarrass the government. A Florida paper suggested that guards be withdrawn from towns and cities where they were unnecessary. The paper reported that every railroad station had enough guards to do picket duty for a brigade.[26]

Like any organization the provost had its share of soldiers and even officers who were not prepared to die in the last ditch for the Confederacy. Many were decidedly reluctant to exchange safe and comfortable rear area provost billets for the hazards of life at the front, and they were castigated severely by the public for this preference. The provost probably drew more than its fair share of venom because its enforcement of conscription had brought the power of the military authorities into the open. Very few had liked the taste of it. The extent of provost power was all too clear, particularly the passport system, which affected every citizen's right to travel, and the searches and arrests deemed necessary to ensure that those conscripted actually reported for service. These measures struck directly at the citizen, who then expressed anger at both the measures and the provost who had to enforce them.

Front-line commanders, who did what they could to prod the reluctant ones forward, had their position weakened by the dilution of the Conscription Act. In September, 1862, the Second Conscription Act had extended the maximum eligible age for conscription from thirty-five to forty-five. This measure was timely in view of Lee's repulse at Sharpsburg, which dashed hopes for immediate foreign recognition. There was now no doubt that prodigious effort would be necessary to win peace for Dixie. Within a month, however, Jefferson Davis found he had no choice but to add to the list of exempted occupations, a process that once started was difficult to limit. A notorious example was the exemption of owners or overseers of more than twenty slaves. Once again there were cries of "rich man's war . . . poor man's fight." In May and then in July, 1863, Congress, in belated reaction to such accusations, tightened some of the exemptions. At the end of the year Congress voted to abolish the right of an individual to provide a substitute for service at the front.[27] Many loopholes, however, remained in the act.

26. Coulter, *Confederate States,* 395–96; Moore, *Conscription and Conflict,* 94, 111, 305–306.

27. Paul D. Escott, *After Secession: Jefferson Davis and the Failure of Confederate Nationalism* (Baton Rouge, 1978), 85; Long, *Civil War Day by Day,* 271, 278, 449.

The deteriorating military situation and the ever-lengthening list of casualties led to yet more demands for additional fighting men. These demands received further impetus from the Federal draft calls of February and March, 1864, which would add seven hundred thousand men to the Union colors. In the face of this staggering enemy call-up something had to be done to bolster the fighting strength of the Confederate armies. The only means left was to extend the basis of conscription since another alternative, the use of Negroes as fighting soldiers, could not yet be countenanced.

On February 17, 1864, Congress enacted a further Conscription Act requiring the enrollment of every white Southern male between the ages of seventeen and fifty. This measure greatly saddened President Davis, who in referring to the necessity for seventeen-year-olds to shore up the South's valiant but tattered legions spoke of "grinding the seed corn of the nation." Once the last seed corn had gone to the mill, what then?[28] The inevitable result was the use of more militia, more disabled officers and men, and more under- and overage men as provost guardsmen. In rear areas these classes of men were often all that was available to perform police duties. The limited effectiveness of sixteen-year-olds and pensioners in controlling the hardened veterans of the South's proud regiments can well be imagined.

The military wasted no time in implementing the new regulations. Lieutenant Colonel John W. Estes, provost marshal of the First District of Alabama, proposed the use of every available man aged sixteen to fifty for local defense. Inevitably many of these would be reserved for police duties.[29] Leonidas Polk ordered the provost to release all fit men between the ages of eighteen and forty-five for active service in the field. The only exceptions were those employed in the Secret Service.[30] Polk also reminded President Davis of the provost organization he had instituted in his department in March, and he reiterated that only disabled or supernumerary officers would serve as provost officers. He would raise companies of exempts to enforce military order and use local defense units from the age groups seventeen to eighteen and forty-five to fifty. Both types of units were designated by law as reserve troops. Such companies were raised very quickly. As an example, on May 15 the headquarters of the Department of Alabama, Mississippi, and East Louisiana issued a special order directing that a

28. Shelby Foote, *The Civil War: A Narrative* (3 vols.; New York, 1958, 1963, 1974), III, 125–26; Long, *Civil War Day by Day,* 519.

29. Brent's proposal, April 14, 1864, *OR*, Vol. XXXII, Pt. 3, pp. 782–83.

30. War Department, Collection of Confederate Records, Record Group 109, Chap. II, Vol. 196.

cavalry company report to the post commander at Aberdeen, Mississippi, for provost duty. The company commander, Captain F. M. Armstrong, declared that the company was composed of men between seventeen and eighteen and between forty-five and fifty. In the same department in April the 1st Mississippi Battalion Infantry Reserves was formed for provost duty. A sergeant of the new unit recalled that it consisted mainly of "youngsters." Far to the east, Virginia youths were also joining the army. Joe Barham, one of the Virginia Military Institute cadets who participated in the Battle of New Market in May, 1864, joined a company of underage boys that later formed part of the 44th Virginia Battalion. B Company of this battalion, along with the 1st Virginia Battalion, formed the provost guard of the Army of Northern Virginia.[31]

In Richmond, too, the letter of the law was being observed as much as possible. Of forty-seven men employed in the Provost Marshal's Office in April, 1864, sixteen were disabled, overage, or underage. In June the Adjutant and Inspector General's Office ordered the disbandment of the 25th Georgia Battalion (Atlanta Provost Battalion). Of the discharged men, those liable to conscription were to be sent to the nearest enrolling officer, and those subject to militia service were to be handed over to Howell Cobb, then a major general commanding reserves.[32] It is not clear what troops immediately replaced the 25th Georgia, but on January 26, 1865, Governor William Smith placed the 19th Virginia Militia and the 1st Regiment, Second Class Militia, on guard duty in Richmond, thus freeing regular soldiers for service at a front line menaced by vastly superior enemy forces. A short time later the 3d Regiment, Local Defense Troops, reported to the city commandant for guard duty. The commandant, Lieutenant General Richard Ewell, was hard-pressed to maintain order in Richmond. As the fall of the city drew closer, it appears that only the 2d Battalion, Virginia Reserves, and a few men from the Local Defense Brigade were available to keep order.[33]

31. *OR,* Vol. XXXIX, Pt. 2, pp. 579–80, 611–12; Obituaries, *Confederate Veteran,* XXXIV (rpr. 1983), 104, 109.

32. List of Officers and Employees in Provost Marshal Office, Richmond, April 5, 1864, Department of Archives and Manuscripts, Louisiana State University, Baton Rouge; *OR,* Vol. XXXVIII, Pt. 4, p. 789. *OR,* Vol. XLII, Pt. 2, pp. 1237–40, refers to a battalion known as the "City," or 25th Battalion. This was the 25th Virginia Battalion, raised in 1862 (Manarin [ed.], *Richmond at War,* 186, n. 7). It was replaced by the 60th Alabama (*OR,* Vol. XLII, Pt. 2, pp. 1237–40), which was on provost duty in Richmond from May 22 to June 19, 1864 (*OR,* Vol. XL, Pt. 2, p. 670; Lewellyn A. Shaver, *A History of the Sixtieth Alabama Regiment* [1867; rpr. Gaithersburg, Md., 1983], 54–55).

33. *OR,* Vol. XLVI, Pt. 2, pp. 1140, 1237; Dallas D. Irvine, "The Fall of Richmond: Evacua-

Conversely, at least during 1864, it seems that many of the men assigned to provost guards in Georgia were subject to conscription. The August, 1864, return, for example, shows that out of 35 men assigned to the provost 29 were subject to conscription. Out of a cumulative total of 158, 137 were subject to conscription. By 1865, though, reserves were being used whenever possible. On March 29 a detachment of the 55th Georgia guarding prisoners at Salisbury, North Carolina, and at Andersonville, Georgia, was relieved by reserves and ordered to report to General Johnston at Bentonville.[34]

Nor was the effectiveness of the militia as provost limited only by the scarcity of militiamen. Their ability to perform provost duty drew considerable skepticism. From the start they were hindered by the contempt in which they were held by regular troops, a viewpoint common to all ranks from general officer down to private soldier. General D. H. Hill's caustic comments about the militia are particularly indicative of the prevailing attitude: "Others are warlike militia officers, and their regiments cannot dispense with such models of military skill and valor. And such noble regiments they have!—3 field officers, 4 staff officers, 10 captains, 30 lieutenants, and 1 private with a misery in his bowels." An equally instructive passage occurs in Alexander Hunter's *Johnny Reb and Billy Yank*. Hunter recalled that a pass he had was challenged by militia provost in Richmond. The tenor of the exchange between Hunter and his comrade and a provost patrol clearly illustrates the regular soldier's contempt for the "Melish," especially provost "Melish":

> "This pass ain't no'count," said the officer.
>
> "No 'count?" repeated my comrade, mechanically, forgetting his grammar in his amazement.
>
> "No!"
>
> "Don't you know that pass is from General Lee, Commander-in-Chief of the Army?". . .
>
> "We have received commands from the provost marshal to take up all officers and soldiers in the city of Richmond unless they have a passport signed by himself." . . .

---

tion and Occupation," in *Military Analysis of the Civil War: An Anthology by the Editors of Military Affairs* (New York, 1977), 386. According to *OR,* Vol. XLVI, Pt. 2, pp. 1262–63, the 2d Battalion consisted of seven companies under Major J. H. Guy.

34. *OR,* Ser. IV, Vol. III, p. 872; Vol. XLVII, Pt. 3, p. 713.

"You had better let us go, Melish", we said. "If you don't respect this pass there will be the Old Scratch to pay in the army".

"I must obey my instructions", he replied. . . .

"O for a squadron of Black Horse Cavalry," I sighed, "just to run this riff-raff provost guard out of the city!"[35]

Other general officers were also less than complimentary about the militia; one comment by inference is less than laudatory about the provost itself. In June, 1864, Major General Lafayette McLaws, commanding at Savannah, Georgia, remarked that reserve troops were fit only for provost guards and could not be relied upon for anything else. Likewise, in Richmond in the fall of 1864, Brigadier General William M. Gardner, then commanding in the city, pointed out the difficulties associated with using militia as provost. According to Gardner, the 1,250 men needed to maintain guard posts in Richmond and prevent the escape of the Federal prisoners on Belle Isle had to include sufficient men to operate a shift system; he stressed that the reserves were "old and in many cases infirm men," who could not be expected to perform their duties indefinitely without relief. The guard force was reported to consist of the 1st Battalion, Virginia Reserves; the President's Guard consisting of two officers and thirty-eight men, all disabled; a detachment of one officer and sixteen men from the 25th Virginia Battalion; and sixteen disabled soldiers from the Confederate States Barracks in the city. Gardner stated a pressing requirement to reinforce the guard by two or more battalions of reserves.[36]

Regulations for the use of disabled men as provost had been published in the 1864 Conscription Act. The act was repeated in a general order by Adjutant General Cooper on March 1, 1864. The pertinent section of the act, Section 8, stated in part: "The duties of provost and hospital guards and clerks . . . shall be performed by persons who are within *the ages* of 18 and 45 years, and . . . *unable to perform active service in the field.*" Section 8 also cautioned that men between seventeen and eighteen years of age would not be assigned to provost duty. The intent was clearly to use disabled men only; all others, including seventeen-year-olds, the president's "seed corn," would thus be freed for active war service. Penalties were provided for those who might ignore or

---

35. Moore, *Conscription and Conflict*, 71n; Alexander Hunter, *Johnny Reb and Billy Yank* (New York, 1905), 599.

36. *OR*, Vol. XXXV, Pt. 2, p. 522; Vol. XLII, Pt. 2, pp. 1237–40.

violate the provisions of the act. Section 9 warned that provost marshals convicted of violation of the regulations would be cashiered. Nor would punishment stop there. Department and district commanders who failed to relieve and try miscreant provost marshals would be dismissed from the service. According to the *Official Records,* in just six states 633 men were assigned to provost commands under the provisions of Section 8.[37]

References abound on details of disabled men to the provost guards. John A. Sloan in his *Reminiscences* refers to two private soldiers, one severely wounded, who were detailed to the provost in the spring of 1864. Edwin H. Fay in *This Infernal War* lists a private transferred to the provost guard of Jackson's cavalry division in 1864. Ephraim Anderson in his *Memoirs* lists a first lieutenant who was assigned to the provost because of his wounds. Joseph B. Polley's *Hood's Texas Brigade* mentions a Captain Chilton, who, on being disabled for active service during the 1864 Louisiana campaign, was appointed provost marshal of Navasota, Texas. John M. Hubbard in *Notes of a Private* ascribes his assignment to provost in March, 1865, to "the fact that I had not entirely recovered my health and would have more privileges on the road, though no less responsible service."[38] The last phrase is somewhat indicative of the soldiers' attitudes toward the provost and their duties, which will be discussed in Chapter 14. Judging by these references and many more like them, it seems that after February, 1864, the assignment of disabled officers and men to provost duties became a general practice in virtually all parts of the South. Leonidas Polk claimed to have returned more than three hundred fit men to the front and noted the added bonus that disabled men permanently detailed as provost gained an intimate knowledge of the units they were required to police, which engendered a dramatic increase in police efficiency.[39]

It would appear from extant correspondence that some commanders were continuing to use fit men as provost in violation of the Conscription Act. They may have done so out of ignorance of the act and published army orders relating

37. *OR,* Ser. IV, Vol. III, pp. 178–81, italics added; *ibid.,* 1101.

38. John A. Sloan, *Reminiscences of the Guilford Grays, Co. B, 27th N.C. Regiment* (1883; rpr. Wendell, N.C., 1978), 77, 121, 128; Edwin Hedge Fay, *"This Infernal War" : The Confederate Letters of Edwin H. Fay,* edited by Bell Irvin Wiley (Austin, 1958), 456; Ephraim McD. Anderson, *Memoirs: Historical and Personal; Including the Campaigns of the First Missouri Confederate Brigade* (1868; rpr. Dayton, 1972), 578; J. B. Polley, *Hood's Texas Brigade, Its Marches, Its Battles, Its Achievements* (1910; rpr. Dayton, 1976), 292; John Milton Hubbard, *Notes of a Private* (1909; rpr. Bolivar, Tenn., 1973), 183.

39. *OR,* Vol. XXXIX, Pt. 2, p. 570.

to it, or they may have chosen not to comply. It may also have been a matter of commanders being unable to assemble large enough groups of disabled men to carry out provost tasks. In any event, Richmond published an adjutant and inspector general's circular on July 1, 1864, to remind all concerned that provost guards could be composed only of disabled men between eighteen and forty-five, but when that age group had been exhausted, men between forty-five and fifty could be used as military policemen. Warning was also given that the period of grace during which details of able-bodied men had been allowed to continue, until April 10, had expired.[40] The need for a reminder indicates that able-bodied men were still serving as provost in the summer of 1864. There is evidence that this situation continued to the end of the war.

The Bureau of Conscription in the Trans-Mississippi Department specifically addressed this problem in July, 1864, ordering the arrest by enrolling officers of all able-bodied men between the ages of eighteen and forty-five serving as provost marshals, ordnance officers, and in other nonmilitary capacities. The only fit men not liable to arrest were artisans, mechanics, and those with scientific skills. Any men arrested were to be sent to their commands or to camps of instruction. Nor did the order apply only to the men; any person liable to conscription who was acting as a provost marshal was also to be enrolled and sent to a camp of instruction. In the Indian Territory, either because no provost officers were available or because the territory had already sent off its provost officers for enrollment, the district commander ordered that enrolling officers would also act as provost marshals. Lieutenant Samuel R. Mebane, the chief enrolling officer of the district, was subsequently appointed chief provost marshal. Commanding officers in the district were ordered to provide provost guards upon request of the provost marshals.[41]

The program to replace fit men with disabled men when possible may have been enjoying some small success. As an example, the post commander at Auburn, Alabama, reported in September, 1864, that the Texas hospital was under guard of a provost composed of convalescents from the wards, indicating that at least one hospital was complying with the adjutant and inspector general's circular of July, 1864. Efforts also continued to return detailed men to the front; in the fall of 1864 the Army of Tennessee ordered all teamsters back to the

40. *OR,* Ser. IV, Vol. III, pp. 523–24.

41. *OR,* Vol. XLI, Pt. 2, pp. 1002–1004. This order was subsequently repeated on July 23, 1864, as General Order 57, Headquarters, Trans-Mississippi Department. General Order 30, March 15, 1864, *OR,* Vol. XXXIV, Pt. 2, pp. 1045–46.

front and their replacement by Negroes. The army provost marshal general was given the task of ensuring that these men actually returned to their commands.[42]

These minor successes, however, were very much the exception. Generally, the provisions of the Conscription Act governing the classes of men who could be used as provost were still being violated. Fit men continued to avoid the front, either with the connivance of their commanders or by means of various "dodges." In October, 1864, the governors of the states east of the Mississippi urged the Confederate government to return to the front every able-bodied man who could be replaced by a disabled soldier, a senior reserve, or a Negro. It was strongly suggested that most of the provost and post guards be dispensed with, except in important cities and on railroads in immediate proximity to the armies. In the governors' view, the provost were "an unnecessary annoyance . . . and of no possible benefit to the country." They promised to make every effort to increase the effective strength of the armies, a statement difficult to reconcile with reports showing the inordinate numbers of men listed on the state exempt rolls.[43]

The problem was not only the waste caused by the use of fit men on light duties in rear areas but also the faulty deployment of the units of disabled men. These laboriously collected forces were often dispersed to relatively unimportant posts that had no real requirement for provost. This practice was uneconomic and ineffective. The only solution was to abolish unimportant posts or at least try to consolidate the large numbers of posts into more central ones in more important areas. Consolidated posts could then be properly officered, and the saving in manpower would allow the establishment of efficient guard forces composed of men who, although not fit for field duty, could usefully perform provost tasks. The precarious military situation made it obvious that the plethora of quartermaster and other supply depots would have to be guarded by disabled men or not be guarded at all. Correspondence of the Department of Alabama, Mississippi, and East Louisiana in October, 1864, specifically en-

---

42. *OR,* Vol. XXXVIII, Pt. 3, p. 974; General Order 19, September 14, 1864, *OR,* Vol. XXXIX, Pt. 2, pp. 835–36.

43. *OR,* Vol. XLII, Pt. 3, p. 1150; Ser. IV, Vol. III, p. 735. According to Moore, *Conscription and Conflict,* 95, in the states east of the Mississippi the following numbers of men were listed as exempt: North Carolina, 14,675; Georgia, 8,229; Virginia, 1,422; Alabama, 1,223; South Carolina, 233; Mississippi, 110; and Florida, 109. These figures add up to a staggering total of roughly 26,000 men kept out of the fighting by the state governors. The figure for North Carolina is not surprising considering the attitude of Zebulon Vance. In June, 1864, Grant reported 122,000 men present for duty; Lee had 66,000. What Lee could have done with 26,000 more!

joined that only disabled officers and men unfit for field duty would be assigned to guard such posts.[44]

In January and February, 1865, although disabled men were used extensively, rear area policing was still being done by fit men in some places. An inspection of the post of Danville, Virginia, in January, for example, revealed that the provost guard consisted "*almost* entirely" of disabled men. Similarly, in February officers of the Invalid Corps were being assigned to duty as provost marshals. These instances are counterbalanced by indications that as late as February 24, trains in Mississippi were still being guarded by fit men.[45]

Finally, on February 28, 1865, Congress proposed that provost appointments be filled only by officers who were disabled, retired, or over forty-five years of age. The only exception was to be the provost marshal general of an army or department. Provost appointments could be authorized only by army or department commanders. Further, provost officers not within the stated categories would be relieved and granted the right to volunteer for any arm of the service, provided they did so within thirty days of the passage of the act. All other provost marshal positions throughout the Confederacy were declared to be abolished. An amendment of March 3 stipulated that provost guards could consist only of reserves or disabled soldiers. President Davis approved and signed the bill on March 9, too late to help resuscitate a dying Confederacy.[46] Lee's last attack, the night assault on Fort Stedman, failed on March 25. Congress had adjourned—forever, it proved—on March 18.

Another source of provost manpower was under- and overage men. In 1864, at Columbus, Georgia, for example, Major T. B. Howard and his 27th Georgia Battalion consisting of boys aged fourteen to eighteen were on provost duty. "Nearly all" the officers were over eighteen. Similarly, the provost guard at Aberdeen, Mississippi, consisted of men between seventeen and eighteen and between forty-five and fifty. And in Georgia the provost strength return for August, 1864, shows twenty-seven under- and overage men on the rolls.[47]

Whether to use fit or unfit men as provost posed a dilemma to Confederate political and military authorities. The retention of able-bodied men as provost guards maintained the guard's effectiveness but at the price of reducing front-line fighting strength. This put the life of the Confederacy at risk and could not be countenanced. There was therefore no option but to use the unfit, the very

44. *OR*, Vol. XXXIX, Pt. 3, pp. 848–49.
45. *OR*, Vol. XLVI, Pt. 2, pp. 1151, 1240; Vol. XLIX, Pt. 1, p. 1011.
46. *Journal of the Confederate Congress*, VII, 663–64, 684, 688, 734.
47. *OR*, Ser. IV, Vol. III, pp. 460, 872.

young, the old, and the militia as provost. To paraphrase Ulysses S. Grant, the Confederacy had no choice but to rob the cradle and the grave. In so doing, a large measure of efficiency was lost and the side effects on military discipline and order were severe. Without efficient means of checking disorder, straggling, and desertion and of enforcing conscription, it was almost impossible to increase or maintain the strength of the army. It was a vicious and self-destructive cycle.

The return of many fit men to the front inevitably resulted in disorder in the rear areas. In September, 1864, the Department of Alabama, Mississippi, and East Louisiana ordered all fit officers and men connected with the provost to rejoin their commands and unfit officers to report to department headquarters. Unfit men were directed to report to post commandants. As well, men who had been employed as detectives, except for those directly authorized by the War Department, were declared liable to enrollment.[48] Post commanders were charged with maintaining provost services, but without the necessary guards the system was defunct. Its absence would be sorely felt. In Georgia, too, all fit men had been ordered to the front. The District of Northeast Georgia reported in 1865 that following the battle of Jonesboro in September, 1864, the only provost guard available at Athens consisted of one officer and fourteen men. Understandably, the district commander felt that he could not possibly enforce order in that city. He reported the guard there as constantly engaged in bearing dispatches, arresting deserters, and guarding prisoners at Augusta.[49] Athens must pretty well have been left to fend for itself. Indeed, much of the Confederacy was without provost and fending for itself.

The general rule appears to have been that infantry troops were used as provost, probably because there were more of them, but there are documented references to artillery, cavalry, and engineers serving as provost. For example, in Wilmington, North Carolina, in 1864, General W. H. C. Whiting had to use two or three heavy artillery companies as provost to maintain order in the city. Likewise, during the fall of 1864, General Richard Ewell had increased the provost guard on Belle Isle in Richmond by adding a detachment of two hundred men from the heavy artillery battalions present in the city. Field artillery was also used as provost. Captain John Thompson of the Portsmouth Light Artillery was assigned to the Richmond Provost Marshal's Office.

48. General Order 120, September 27, 1864, *OR*, Vol. XXXIX, Pt. 2, p. 870.
49. *OR*, Vol. XLIX, Pt. 1, pp. 974–76.

Thompson was not overly enthusiastic about the assignment.[50] In 1864 engineer troops were also on guard duty in Richmond. Lieutenant Colonel T. M. R. Talcott's 1st Regiment of Engineers was listed as being on duty with the City Guard forces in March.[51] In the West, too, noninfantry personnel were reported on provost duty at Macon, Georgia, after Chickamauga.[52]

Confederate horse soldiers also had more than a passing acquaintance with provost tasks in many parts of the Confederate States. Their use for this function appears to have been quite general, particularly in the far West, where cavalry often outnumbered infantry. Anderson in his *Memoirs* stated, "Our duties as provost guard became very heavy, and a company was detached from the Third Texas cavalry (then dismounted) to assist us." Other cavalry units on provost duty for varying periods in the West were Waller's Texas Battalion during the 1864 Red River campaign, Griffin's Cavalry Battalion in the Trans-Mississippi, D Company of the 4th Mississippi Cavalry with General Stephen D. Lee, and cavalry companies at Jackson, Mississippi, and Winchester, Kentucky.[53] In Richmond it was necessary to reinforce the provost guard by adding special "flying squads" of cavalry to arrest drunken soldiers and return absentees to their commands.[54] In the Army of Northern Virginia General J. E. B. Stuart's cavalry rendered valuable assistance as provost guards. In the fall of 1863 General Wade Hampton was ordered to establish provost guards at Spotsylvania Court House, Guiney's Station, and Bowling Green, with particular attention to the railroad cars.[55] The unique advantage of employing cavalry as

50. John Johns, "Wilmington During the Blockade," *CWTI*, XIII (June, 1974), 36; *OR*, Vol. XLII, Pt. 2, pp. 1237–40; Captain John H. Thompson, "Historical Address of the Former Commander of Grimes Battery," *SHSP*, XXXIV (rpr. 1979), 154.

51. *OR*, XXXIII, 1217.

52. I. Hermann, *Memoirs of a Veteran Who Served as a Private in the 60's in the War Between the States* (1911; rpr. Lakemount, Ga., 1974), 191.

53. Anderson, *Memoirs*, 207; Theophilus Noel, *A Campaign from Sante Fe to the Mississippi: Being a History of the Old Sibley Brigade . . . 1861–1864*, ed. Martin Hardwick Hall and Edwin Adams Davis (1904; rpr. Houston, 1961), 140. Two companies of Griffin's battalion were on provost duty at Houston (*OR*, IX, 723). The two companies of the 4th Mississippi were on provost at least between July and September, 1863, and possibly until January, 1864 (*OR*, Vol. XXIV, Pt. 3, p. 1042; Vol. XXX, Pt. 4, pp. 517, 656; Vol. XXXI, Pt. 3, p. 865. *OR*, Vol. XVII, Pt. 2, p. 819; Vol. XVI, Pt. 2, p. 867).

54. Martin Schenck, *Up Came Hill: The Story of the Light Division and Its Leaders* (Harrisburg, 1958), 22; *OR*, Vol. XI, Pt. 3, pp. 576–77.

55. *OR*, Vol. LI, Pt. 2, pp. 785–86. The order was issued November 14, 1863, by Lieutenant G. M. Ryals, provost marshal of the cavalry corps.

provost was its mobility. Later in the war the cavalry's mobility was much reduced because lack of fodder weakened the horses.

Even this relatively cursory look at the composition of the provost and how it was deployed throughout the Confederate States indicates that the provost apparatus was highly expensive in manpower, the commodity the Confederacy could least afford. Large numbers of men, and often entire battalions, were tied up on provost duties and were thus left out of the fighting.

3

A Matter of Organization

Generally, management of the many is the same as
management of the few. It is a
matter of organization.

SUN TZU

In the Introduction it was stressed that the Confederacy did not have a separate provost corps. Instead, provost duties were carried out by officers and men and by units detailed for that purpose. In accordance with Confederate law, most individuals were detailed as provost because of ill health or wounds that rendered them incapable of performing active field service.

Most units were employed as provost for limited periods of time. Provost marshals, under the authority of army commanders, appear to have appropriated units for policing purposes and assigned them to tasks such as guarding prisoners, chasing deserters and stragglers, or maintaining good order and discipline in the armies. Information about specific units that did nothing but provost duty is hard to come by, probably because there were few such units. The designation of one unit, the 25th Georgia Battalion (Atlanta Provost Battalion), clearly indicates the reason for its existence. Three other battalions were employed as provost throughout most of the war. These were the three infantry battalions that made up the provost guards of the Army of Northern Virginia and its 2d and 3d Corps. No specific unit could be identified as being the guard of the 1st Corps, nor is there any conclusive identification of units expressly designated as provost in the other major field army, the Army of Tennessee.

Both the Union and the Confederacy had a provost marshal general, the supreme military policeman in each country. In the case of the Union, the appointment was made on September 24, 1862, but the Confederacy did not appoint a similar official until very late in the war. General John H. Winder, provost marshal general of Richmond in 1861 and 1862 and commissary general of prisoners east of the Mississippi in 1864, seems to have functioned as *de facto* provost marshal general of the Confederate States of America. The February, 1861, act of Congress authorizing a general staff allowed for an adjutant and inspector general, a quartermaster general, and subsistence and medical officers, but made no mention of a provost marshal general.[1]

It was not until February 20, 1865, that a bill providing for the appointment of a provost marshal general was introduced in the Confederate Senate.[2] The purpose of the bill was to replace General Winder, who had died on February 7. General Daniel Ruggles was subsequently appointed.

An overview of the units that were used as provost is best achieved by a geographical approach, starting with the two premier field armies of the South, the Army of Northern Virginia and the Army of Tennessee, then a look at the provost in the departments east of the Mississippi, across the river in the Trans-Mississippi, and finally, a close scrutiny of three specific provost units: the 1st North Carolina, the 1st Virginia, and the 5th Alabama battalions. Only a few examples will be given for each command. Many more units acted as provost, but because these more naturally illustrate specific provost duties, they are discussed in other chapters.

In the Army of Northern Virginia there are numerous examples of units detailed to serve as provost. One of the earliest of these is mentioned in *I Rode with Stonewall,* in which Henry Kyd Douglas refers to a provost guard being left at Winchester, Virginia, during the Valley campaign in May, 1862. The unit left behind was the 2d Virginia Regiment.[3] Entire brigades were sometimes placed on provost duty. In September, 1862, during Lee's first invasion of the North, an entire brigade acted as a provost guard in Frederick City, Maryland.[4] At the other end of the scale, a guard sometimes consisted of a single company of a regiment, as, for example, during the October, 1862, occupation of Chambersburg, Pennsylvania, when General Wade Hampton established a "rigid provost guard" under Captain J. P. Macfie of the 2d South Carolina Cavalry.[5] These last two reports indicate that responsibility for the control of enemy civilians in areas occupied by Confederate troops devolved on the provost. Another example of a regiment being detailed to provost duty occurred shortly

1. Long, *Civil War Day by Day,* 271; *OR,* Ser. IV, Vol. I, pp. 114, 117.

2. *Journal of the Confederate Congress,* IV, 581.

3. Henry Kyd Douglas, *I Rode with Stonewall* (1940; rpr. Chapel Hill, 1968), 64; Howard, *Recollections,* 112. On May 28 General Charles Winder's brigade left Winchester, leaving behind the 2d Virginia as provost guard. According to Howard, the regiment was only on provost guard on May 28 and 29.

4. *OR,* Vol. XIX, Pt. 1, pp. 1006–1007. The brigade, Jones's, reached Frederick City on September 7. This information was included in Brigadier General J. R. Jones's report on the Sharpsburg campaign. Jones was commanding Jackson's old division.

5. *OR,* Vol. XIX, Pt. 2, p. 57.

before Gettysburg, when the 6th Alabama Infantry was placed on provost guard at Martinsburg, Virginia, on June 16 and 17.[6] In 1864, too, there are references to units being used as provost. In May of that year A Company, 1st Confederate Battalion, which was on provost duty at Atlanta, Georgia, was ordered to rejoin the battalion in Virginia.[7] Correspondence of December, 1864, notes that a cavalry company was serving as a brigade provost guard.[8]

Similarly, in the Confederacy's major western army, the Army of Tennessee, many types and sizes of units were employed as provost. One of the first was the 1st Tennessee Regiment under Colonel George Maney, who reported that before the Battle of Shiloh in April, 1862, a shortage of transportation forced him to leave one "wing" of his regiment at Chattanooga, where it carried out provost duties. Another unit in Tennessee that furnished provost guards was the 1st Missouri Cavalry. During the February, 1862, evacuation of Nashville, the Tennessee capital, the 1st Missouri, a Kentucky squadron led by John Hunt Morgan, and Nathan Bedford Forrest's regiment of Tennessee cavalry were the only organized troops available to maintain order in a city torn by rioting and looting perpetrated by a rabble of retreating troops and panicky civilians. Forrest's hard-bitten troopers were forced to make liberal use of the flat of their sabers to discourage those who attempted to loot government warehouses. These looters and the swarms of deserters and stragglers were driven from the city by the provost rear guards as the evacuation drew to a close. After the evacuation, the 1st Missouri was involved in provost guard duties elsewhere. E Company of the regiment spent the week from April 19 to 26 in Memphis and then a short period in June, 1862, at Tupelo, Mississippi, as provost.[9] The 1st Tennessee and an unidentified unit were on provost duty at Shelbyville, Tennessee. The 1st Tennessee was relieved of duty there on May 25, 1862, and ordered to report to its parent brigade. As relief, the 28th Tennessee was moved to Shelbyville.[10]

Throughout 1864 the practice of detailing units to provost tasks continued in the Army of Tennessee. In April the 29th Tennessee Regiment was ordered to

6. *OR,* Vol. XXVII, Pt. 2, p. 599.

7. *OR,* Vol. XXXVI, Pt. 3, p. 850.

8. *OR,* Vol. XLII, Pt. 3, p. 1276. The company was commanded by Captain W. E. Hinton. Appendix II lists numerous units identified as being on provost service with Lee's army.

9. A. S. Horsley, "Reminiscences of Shiloh," *Confederate Veteran,* II (rpr. 1983), 234; Richard Wormser, *The Yellowlegs: The Story of the United States Cavalry* (Garden City, N.Y., 1966), 270–71; Foote, *Civil War,* I, 216; Homer L. Calkin, "Elk Horn to Vicksburg," *Civil War History,* II (March 1956; rpr. 1963), 14, 22.

10. Special Order 115, May 25, 1862, *OR,* Vol. XXIII, Pt. 2, p. 851.

Demopolis, Alabama, to place the town under provost control. A soldier of the regiment wrote that the unit remained there for about a week.[11] On May 8 a divisional provost guard was assigned to duty with the 29th Mississippi Infantry at Dalton, Georgia. The guard may well have been used to bolster the fighting strength of the 29th for on May 8 the Federals were reported to be pressing hard against Joseph E. Johnston's positions near Dalton.[12] On September 12 the 24th South Carolina Regiment was ordered to Jonesboro, Georgia, to act as provost guard of the town in place of "the provost guard of Cheatham's Division," which was ordered to rejoin General Benjamin Cheatham. Cheatham's provost guard may have been the 28th Tennessee, which in May, 1862, had been the provost guard of Leonidas Polk's corps. The March, 1864, returns of the Army of Tennessee indicate that the 28th and the 8th Tennessee were on detached duty at Atlanta. It seems reasonable to assume that this detached duty was in fact provost duty.[13] It is possible too, that the 28th Tennessee was a provost battalion from May, 1862, on.

After the fall of Atlanta, General John B. Hood struck north into Tennessee in an ill-fated attempt to pull General William T. Sherman's army away from Atlanta. General Order 36 of November 20 outlined the reporting procedure for the provost marshals of Hood's army. The day after the Battle of Franklin, Tennessee (November 30), it was reported that the 20th Tennessee had been placed on provost duty.[14] In view of the Confederate disaster at Franklin, it is likely that the 20th had been reduced to a small provost guard and was incapable of further combat.

A western provost guard for which strength returns are fairly complete is the Atlanta Provost Battalion, whose strength during July and August, 1863, was reported as 13 officers and 155 men. One of the companies of this battalion was present in Atlanta until May 30, 1864, when it was ordered to the Army of Northern Virginia.[15]

A look at the deployment of provost in the various department commands is equally instructive. Five of these departments were east of the Mississippi,

11. C. D. M'Amy, "Brave P. E. Drew and His Fate," *Confederate Veteran*, II (rpr. 1983), 85.

12. *OR*, Vol. XXXVIII, Pt. 3, p. 806.

13. *OR*, Vol. XXXIX, Pt. 2, p. 831; Vol. XXXII, Pt. 3, p. 657; Vol. XXIII, Pt. 2, p. 851.

14. *OR*, Vol. XLV, Pt. 1, p. 1227; W. J. McMurray, *History of the Twentieth Tennessee Regiment Volunteer Infantry C.S.A.* (1904; rpr. Nashville, 1976), 144.

15. *OR*, Vol. XXIII, Pt. 1, pp. 585–86, Pt. 2, pp. 920, 941, 957; Vol. XXX, Pt. 4, p. 519; *OR*, Vol. XXXVI, Pt. 3, p. 850.

while the last, the Trans-Mississippi, functioned separately from the remainder of the Confederate States after the fall of Vicksburg.

The Department of Henrico/Richmond in Virginia, established on October 21, 1861, under the command of Brigadier General John H. Winder, was extended to include Petersburg in March, 1862, and finally was merged with the Department of Richmond on May 5, 1864.[16] Strength returns of the department in May, 1862, indicated that two companies of the 20th Virginia were on provost duty in Richmond. By October Winder had 40 officers and 1,742 men, including the City Guard personnel and those at Camp Lee, a local camp of instruction. No breakdown of the figures is given, but in all probability only the City Guard was available for provost tasks. By May, 1863, General Winder's command consisted of seven companies of Lieutenant Colonel W. M. Elliott's City Battalion (25th Virginia Battalion) and seven companies of Colonel H. H. Walker's guard force.[17]

Strength returns for March and April of 1864 show an average of fourteen hundred men available to Winder. Of these, about half were from the City Guard and the remainder consisted of men undergoing training at Camp Lee and the guards at the various military prisons. Prison guard strength was fairly constant at around four hundred, but the figures for Camp Lee declined drastically as trained men were sent to the Army of Northern Virginia.[18]

During March the City Guard was commanded by Lieutenant Colonel W. M. Elliott. The troops were provided by the 1st Regiment of Engineers under Lieutenant Colonel T. M. R. Talcott. Units present at Camp Lee, under the command of Colonel J. C. Shields, were detachments of the 46th North Carolina and 36th Virginia, D Company of the 39th Battalion Virginia Cavalry, A Company of the 9th Virginia Infantry, engineer troops, and Maryland recruits. The 39th Virginia Battalion is listed as the headquarters escort of the Army of Northern Virginia in 1865.[19] It may well have been that from time to time escort companies also performed provost duty. The returns also show that the

16. Amann (ed.), *Confederate Armies*, 183. After May 5 the combined department consisted of all of Virginia north of the James River, Drewry's Bluff, and Manchester, and the old Department of Henrico. Department headquarters included a provost marshal's department consisting of a passport office and a police organization.

17. *OR,* Vol. XI, Pt. 3, p. 542; XVIII, 749, 751; Vol. XLII, Pt. 2, pp. 1237–40.

18. *OR,* XXXIII, 1216–17, 1247, 1300.

19. Philip R. N. Katcher, *The Army of Northern Virginia* (Reading, Berkshire, Eng., 1975), 34.

troops listed as serving at Confederate States prisons consisted of one company each of the 32d and 53d North Carolina, two companies of the 45th North Carolina, and one company from each of the 3d, 12th, 18th, and 28th Virginia.

For April, 1865, the returns give the composition of the City Guard, now commanded by Colonel W. M. Watts, as one company of the 18th Virginia, all of the 28th Virginia, the Camp Winder guard, and an unattached company. The force at Camp Lee by this time had shrunk to one company of the 9th Virginia and the post band. One would have thought that at this point in an increasingly hopeless war the Confederacy would have preferred "shooters not tooters."

In May, 1864, the 60th Alabama served as provost in Richmond but only briefly, for in the face of Grant's offensive it was urgently required at the front. It was soon replaced by a battalion of reserves. A final example of a unit employed as provost in the Department of Richmond is the 41st Virginia, which was ordered to provost duty along the Blackwater River a few miles south of Richmond.[20] The Blackwater was an ideal spot for the 41st to halt and arrest deserters trying to pass from the battle line, via Richmond and Petersburg, into North Carolina. By this stage of the war, desertion, especially from Tar Heel regiments, had dramatically increased. Lee's urgent desire to decrease the outflow is clearly indicated by his willingness to detach the 41st Virginia, a loss of fighting power he could ill afford.

The Department of North Carolina, which had been established in mid-1861, was abolished, expanded, and reestablished several times during the course of the war. Generally it consisted throughout of all of North Carolina and at times included that portion of Virginia south of the James River.[21]

The Blackwater River also features in correspondence of this department. In October, 1863, the department headquarters ordered the 9th Virginia to Ivor Station on the Norfolk and Petersburg Railroad to carry out provost guard duties along the Blackwater. Presumably these duties were the same as those assigned to the 41st Virginia. The same order appointed Lieutenant John R. Gossett provost marshal of the department. Another unit in this department that experienced provost service was the 64th Georgia of Alfred Colquitt's brigade. In June, 1864, the department, rechristened the Department of North Carolina and

20. *OR,* Vol. XL, Pt. 2, p. 670; Shaver, *History of the Sixtieth Alabama Regiment,* 54–55; *OR,* Vol. XLII, Pt. 3, p. 1136.

21. For a full description of the organizational changes in the department see Amann (ed.), *Confederate Armies,* 190.

Southern Virginia, ordered the 64th to Petersburg for service as a provost guard under Brigadier General Henry A. Wise.[22]

Field returns of the department are disappointing in that generally units are not identified and only total numbers are given. There appear to have been more or less permanent provost guards at Weldon, Goldsboro, and Kinston in North Carolina from June, 1863, on. All three towns were located along railroads—the first two are rail junctions—so it is obvious that the guards were present to monitor civilian and military rail traffic. This very important provost duty is comprehensively covered in Chapter 7. In the case of Goldsboro, at least from September, 1864, a senior reserve company under Captain John B. Griswold policed the town. At Kinston the average strength of the guard between November, 1863, and February of the next year was six officers and seventy-two men present for duty.[23] The Weldon guard in all probability was also at company strength.

In the Department of South Carolina, Georgia, and Florida few provost units can be identified. This department, established in November, 1861, initially included only the territory on the Atlantic coast, but by the close of the war it consisted of virtually the whole of the three states.[24] During May and June, 1862, while Charleston, South Carolina, was under martial law, the 1st South Carolina Regiment and a battalion of cavalry (later part of the 2d South Carolina Cavalry) were on provost duty in the city. Somewhat later these units were ordered to the front in Virginia and the regiment of Charleston Reserves took over. Throughout the war various other unattached companies were employed as provost in several cities and areas of the department.[25]

Immediately to the west the large Department of Alabama, Mississippi, and East Louisiana, established on January 28, 1864, under the command of Lieutenant General Leonidas Polk, encompassed the two states and Louisiana east of the Mississippi, boundaries that remained unchanged throughout the department's existence. One of the earliest references to a specific unit detailed as provost in this department is contained in the *Confederate Veteran*. The 4th Florida Regiment, ordered to Mississippi in May, 1862, was instead diverted to

22. *OR*, Vol. LI, Pt. 2, p. 771; Vol. XL, Pt. 2, p. 669.

23. *OR*, Vol. XXVII, Pt. 3, pp. 946, 1068; Vol. XXIX, Pt. 2, pp. 851, 906; XXXIII, 1201; Vol. XLII, Pt. 2, pp. 1225–26; Vol. XLVI, Pt. 2, pp. 1186–87.

24. Amann (ed.), *Confederate Armies*, 196–97.

25. Johnson Hagood, *Memoirs of the War of Secession* (Columbia, S.C., 1910), 80; *OR*, Vol. XXXV, Pt. 2, pp. 441–42; XLIV, 876; Vol. XLVII, Pt. 2, p. 1073.

Mobile, Alabama, where it remained on provost duty until July. During that month the regiment was no doubt busy assisting with the rail move of Braxton Bragg's army as it transited Mobile en route to Chattanooga. It is possible that the 4th Florida had been ordered to Mobile to organize and maintain a control system for moving the army. Another unit on provost duty in 1862 was the 2d Missouri Infantry, which in May was provost guard of the Army of the Mississippi near Tupelo, Mississippi. The 2d Missouri remained on provost guard until the end of July. Another unit with documented provost service was the 4th Mississippi Cavalry, which provided a company-sized provost guard for Stephen D. Lee's cavalry for the last half of 1863.[26]

Although no specific provost units are named, Polk's division of his department into nine districts in March, 1864, would have entailed the allocation of provost guards. Each district was to have a chief provost marshal, all reporting to Major Jules C. Denis, who was named provost marshal general of the department. Promulgation of this appointment was accompanied by instructions that all commanding officers were to furnish troops at the request of Major Denis or any provost marshal in the department. In June Major Denis, relieved at his own request, was replaced by Colonel Thomas H. Taylor.[27]

In August, 1864, Polk forwarded a return listing all the posts that had been established in his department and naming the post commandants, who in many cases also served as the local provost marshals.[28] A partial strength return in September is indicative of the high manpower cost of maintaining the provost system. At just six posts an average of thirteen officers and forty-six men were present for duty.[29] Within the same department the field returns of Nathan Bedford Forrest's cavalry further illustrate the commitment to maintaining

26. Amann (ed.), *Confederate Armies*, 173; W. M. Ives, "History Fourth Florida Regiment," *Confederate Veteran*, III (rpr. 1983), 102; Anderson, *Memoirs*, 203, 212, 500; *OR*, Vol. XXIV, Pt. 3, p. 1042; Vol. XXX, Pt. 4, pp. 517, 656; Vol. XXXI, Pt. 3, p. 865.

27. The provost organization was announced on March 10 in General Order 43 (*OR*, Vol. XXXII, Pt. 3, p. 611). The order regarding provision of troops came out the same day (*ibid.*, p. 612). *OR*, Vol. XXXIX, Pt. 2, p. 664.

28. *OR*, Vol. XXXIX, Pt. 2, p. 811; Vol. XLV, Pt. 1, p. 1235.

29. *OR*, Vol. XXXIX, Pt. 2, p. 886. Averaging the "aggregate present and absent" figures, the total manpower commitment for all the posts in the August list would be about 2,200 men. If half were actually present for duty there would have been about 1,000 men on provost duty in the department, not including provost with the armies. There would have been, of course, wild fluctuations in the figures depending upon the military situation. The post at Columbus, for example, had a strength of only 25 in September, quite a drop from the 15 officers and 151 men present for duty in May (*OR*, Vol. XXXVIII, Pt. 4, p. 691).

provost strength. Figures for May and June of 1864 show about one hundred officers and men on provost duty with Forrest.[30]

The last department east of the Mississippi was the Department of East Tennessee, which was established in March, 1862. Although initially it included only the area implicit in its name, eventually it took in adjoining counties in Georgia, North Carolina, and Virginia. Colonel William M. Churchwell, the provost marshal general who organized the department into ten districts in the spring of 1862, assessed the provost system to be working as well as could be expected in view of the disaffection with the Confederate cause in East Tennessee. By September, 1862, Churchwell had been replaced by Colonel John E. Toole. This officer signed an order during that month listing the deputy provost marshals in each of the ten districts.[31]

The Trans-Mississippi, or "Kirby Smithdom," as it became known after the fall of Vicksburg, was established in May, 1862, and encompassed the Confederacy west of the Mississippi. The earliest references to unit provost guards in the department note that in August, 1861, Major General Sterling Price, commanding the Missouri State Guard, ordered the recruitment of a provost force for service with his army. Presumably this force came exclusively from the State Guard. Another unit detailed as provost was the 3d Louisiana Infantry, which was ordered to Fayetteville, Arkansas, early in December and spent the winter there. From other correspondence it is apparent that provost organizations also existed in Arizona and New Mexico during the brief period when Confederate prospects were bright in those areas.[32]

Three infantry battalions spent almost the entire war on provost duty with the Army of Northern Virginia. These were the 1st North Carolina Battalion, provost guard of the 2d Corps; the 5th Alabama Battalion, provost guard of the 3d Corps; and the 1st Virginia Battalion, which, together with B Company of the 44th Virginia Battalion, was the provost guard of the Army of Northern Virginia.

In his *War Memoirs* Jubal Early described the 1st North Carolina as a battalion of two companies belonging to Robert Hoke's brigade. Early gave the brigade order of battle in May, 1863, as the 6th, 21st, 54th, and 57th North Carolina regiments and Rufus Wharton's North Carolina Battalion. According

---

30. *OR*, Vol. XXXIX, Pt. 2, pp. 592, 630, 648, 675.

31. *OR*, Ser. II, Vol. III, p. 876; Ser. II, Vol. IV, pp. 899–900.

32. *OR*, LIII, 728; W. H. Tunnard, *A Southern Record: The History of the Third Louisiana Infantry* (1866; rpr. Dayton, 1970), 110; Martin Hardwick Hall, *The Confederate Army of New Mexico* (Austin, 1978), 187, 337, 355.

to Early, the battalion was permanently detached from Hoke's brigade in June, 1863, to become the provost guard of the 2d Corps. This detachment apparently took place before June 20.[33] The Appomattox parole roster shows the battalion, under First Lieutenant R. W. Woodruff, as part of Robert D. Johnston's brigade, Early's division, 2d Corps.[34] Parole lists of the 2d Corps in the *Official Records* show under "Major General John B. Gordon and staff" 28 officers and 115 men, including provost guard, couriers, escort, and hospital attendants.[35] This documentation leaves no doubt that the battalion served for at least twenty months and probably longer as provost in the Army of Northern Virginia.

The 5th Alabama Battalion, provost guard of the 3d Corps, has a very noteworthy history. When formed in December, 1861, it consisted of six companies. There was apparently some confusion regarding the designation of the battalion for in October, 1862, Adjutant General Samuel Cooper published a special order stating that "the battalion of Alabama Volunteers under the command of Captain A. S. Van De Graaff, heretofore known . . . as the 8th, will be hereafter known as the 5th Alabama Battalion Volunteers."[36]

In June, 1862, the 5th Alabama fought as part of James Archer's brigade at Mechanicsville and Gaines' Mill. Captain Albert S. Van De Graaff, commanding the battalion, was wounded during the former action. Casualties in the battalion during these engagements were reported as very heavy. At Gaines' Mill the 5th Alabama lost its colors to the 2d Maine, and the two senior captains successively in command were casualties. At Second Manassas the battalion was heavily engaged, losing yet another commanding officer, Captain Thomas Bush.[37]

33. Jubal Early, *War Memoirs* (1867; rpr. Bloomington, 1960), 185, 188. Philip J. Haythornwaite, *Uniforms of the American Civil War* (Poole, Dorset, Eng., 1975), 190, 253, includes the 1st North Carolina in the brigade at Gettysburg. See also J. A. Early, "Relative Numbers—General Early's Reply to Count of Paris," *SHSP*, VI (rpr. 1977), 36.

34. R. A. Brock (ed.), *Paroles of the Army of Northern Virginia, R. E. Lee, Gen., C.S.A., Commanding, Surrendered at Appomattox C. H., Va., April 9, 1865, to Lieutenant-General U. S. Grant, Commanding Armies of the U.S.,"* *SHSP*, XV (rpr. 1977), 204–205. Sixty-five men were listed as present in the battalion.

35. *OR*, Vol. XLVI, Pt. 1, p. 1277.

36. *OR*, Vol. LI, Pt. 2, p. 401. On December 2 the adjutant general ordered the companies of Captains E. T. Smyth, A. S. Van De Graaff, Dickinson, Davis, Smith, and Thomas Bush to Dumfries, Virginia, to be organized into a battalion to be designated the 5th Battalion of Alabama Volunteers under the command of Lieutenant Colonel F. B. Shepherd (*OR*, Vol. LII, Pt. 2, pp. 378–79).

37. Joe Bennett McBrien, *The Tennessee Brigade* (Chattanooga, 1977), 27, 29–30, 45; M. T. Ledbetter, "With Archer's Brigade," *SHSP*, XXIX (rpr. 1978), 349–54. Ledbetter, a private in the 5th Alabama, reported on the battalion's part in the battle.

After the surrender of the Federal garrison at Harpers Ferry in September, 1862, the battalion remained there to guard captured artillery while the rest of A. P. Hill's Light Division marched to assist Lee at Sharpsburg. At Fredericksburg in December the indefatigable Van De Graaff was again wounded, presumably not too seriously, because in July, 1863, he was a major commanding the battalion when it led the advance of Hill's corps toward Gettysburg.[38] During Pickett's charge the battalion lost another set of colors and half of its two hundred men. It then became the provost guard of the 3d Corps.

At the Battle of the Wilderness in May, 1864, the 5th Alabama functioned both as provost and as fighting infantry. During the early morning of May 5 the battalion, still under Van De Graaff, was detached from its brigade and the men were deployed in line in the rear of Hill's corps. Such deployments, designed to cut down straggling, were a frequent experience for provost units. By late afternoon the 5th Alabama was required to perform quite a different task. Federal troops, in their last attack of the day, were attempting to exploit a gap that had opened between the 2d and 3d Corps. With all other units committed, A. P. Hill was forced to throw in his last reserve, the 5th Alabama, which meantime had been guarding Federal prisoners. The 5th, down to 125 muskets, surged forward with a wild Rebel yell and, thanks mainly to surprise, sealed off the Federal penetration.[39] The élan of the 5th had averted a potential disaster to Lee's army.

August, 1864, strength returns of the Army of Northern Virginia show the battalion as "unattached" and with a strength of 14 officers and 157 men. The return for the next month indicates a loss of 6 men. Apparently, the unit spent the winter of 1864–65 west of Petersburg operating a receiving station for conscripts. At the turn of the year Captain Wade Ritter was in command of the battalion, now listed as provost guard of the 3d Corps.[40]

One of the battalion's final tasks of the war was the recovery of the body of A. P. Hill, killed at Petersburg on April 1 while attempting to rejoin his corps after conferring with General Lee. At the surrender the strength of the battalion, Captain Ritter commanding, was given as 125 officers and men.[41]

The third provost battalion in the Army of Northern Virginia, the 1st (Irish)

---

38. McBrien, *Tennessee Brigade*, 48, 55, 71.

39. William Woods Hassler, *A. P. Hill: Lee's Forgotten General* (Richmond, 1962), 191.

40. *OR*, Vol. XLII, Pt. 2, pp. 1219, 1243; Vol. XLVI, Pt. 2, p. 1182; Katcher, *Army of Northern Virginia*, 35, lists the battalion as provost guard as of April, 1865.

41. Walter H. Taylor, *General Lee His Campaigns in Virginia, 1861–1865, with Personal Reminiscences* (1906; rpr. Dayton, 1975), 274; G. W. Tucker, "Death of General A. P. Hill,"

Virginia Battalion, is perhaps the best documented of the three. It served as provost for virtually the entire war. An article written by an officer of the battalion reveals that in June, 1861, it was the provost guard of Jackson's 2d Corps. According to this officer, the battalion's initial period as provost was "quite an easy time." The 1st Virginia had been mustered into Confederate service earlier in June as a battalion of five companies.[42]

There is some doubt as to exactly when the battalion left Jackson to become the provost guard of the Army of Northern Virginia. An addendum to a letter from General Lee to Adjutant General Cooper dated December 20, 1862, shows the battalion as part of the 2d Brigade of Jackson's old division. According to a report dated January 9, 1863, by Major David B. Bridgford, commanding officer of the battalion, the unit had been engaged in provost duty from December 12 on. This report was signed "D. B. Bridgford, Major and Chief Provost Marshal, Second Corps." Other sources, however, indicate that about December 17 the battalion was detached from its brigade and made provost guard of the Army of Northern Virginia.[43] In any event, it was not until June, 1863, that orders were issued detailing "temporarily" the 1st Virginia Battalion for provost duty with the army. Major Bridgford was ordered to report to the headquarters of the Army of Northern Virginia. The army roster for Gettysburg shows that Bridgford and his men were the provost guard at army headquarters. General Jubal Early, in a post-war article on Confederate strength at Gettysburg, also stated that the battalion was the army provost guard.[44] An official report on Lee's army at the end of 1863 shows that the 1st Virginia under Bridgford was still the army provost guard.[45]

The unit remained on provost duty for the rest of the war. In the spring of 1864 Lieutenant Charles A. Davidson of the battalion complained in a letter that he "was tired and disgusted with being on Provost duty and should greatly

---

SHSP, XI (rpr. 1977), 569; Brock (ed.), *Paroles*, 271–73; *OR*, Vol. XLVI, Pt. 1, p. 1278. The staff and provost guard of the 3d Corps consisted of 28 officers and 119 men.

42. Charles W. Turner (ed.), "Major Charles A. Davidson: Letters of a Virginia Soldier," *Civil War History*, XXII (1976), 20. At the end of the war Davidson was a major commanding the battalion (Lee A. Wallace, *A Guide to Virginia Military Organizations, 1861–1865* [Richmond, 1964], 206).

43. *OR*, XXI, 1074, 641–42; John H. Worsham, *One of Jackson's Foot Cavalry* (1912; rpr. Jackson, Tenn., 1964), 95.

44. Special Order 151, June 4, 1863, *OR*, Vol. LI, Pt. 2, p. 721; Early, "Relative Numbers," 18, 36.

45. *OR*, Vol. XXIX, Pt. 2, p. 899.

Returns for the Provost Guard of the Army of Northern Virginia

	Present for duty	
Date	*Officers*	*Men*
1864		
January 10	21	275
January 31	14	281
February 10	17	228
February 20	20	236
March 10	17	239
March 20	20	237
April 10	22	286
April 20	27	293
October 20	22	194
October 31	24	205
November 10	21	200
November 30	21	219
December 20	22	239
1865		
January 10	22	219
January 31	21	199
February 10	20	188

SOURCES: *OR,* Vol. XXXIII, 1075, 1135, 1157, 1191, 1216, 1234, 1271, 1298, Vol. XLII, Pt. 3, pp. 1156, 1187, 1209, 1236, 1285; Vol. XLVI, Pt. 1, pp. 384, 386–87.

prefer being with the Brigade where there is a chance for promotion and where I could feel I was performing some service."[46] This comment is fairly typical of the attitudes of officers and men who served with provost units. Additional ones in similar vein are quoted in Chapter 14.

The strength of the 1st Virginia is well documented throughout the last year of the war by the official returns of Lee's army (see table). These returns are interesting in that they show little change in the numbers present for duty over the span of a year, which included the battles of the Wilderness and Spotsylvania and the siege of Richmond. This would seem to indicate that the battalion did not participate in combat for that period, or at least did so to a very limited extent. The figures must have included the headquarters staff officers because a battalion of five companies would not reasonably have had more than six or seven officers at most. It is likely that the figures for men included soldiers

46. Turner (ed.), "Major Charles A. Davidson," 36.

from other units in view of the severely reduced strength of all commands at this point in the war. The obvious attempt to keep the battalion up to strength is indicative of the importance placed on the provost's contribution to the army's performance. April, 1865, strength returns show that the provost guard of the Army of Northern Virginia consisted of the 1st Virginia and B Company of the 44th Virginia Battalion. Appomattox parole rosters list both battalions as belonging to General Richard Ewell's Reserve Corps. The rosters indicate that 120 men of the 1st Virginia and 8 men of B Company of the 44th were present at the surrender.[47]

It is indeed unfortunate that none of the officers or men of the 1st Virginia wrote in any detail of their police service, but nevertheless, available information gives a good picture of one unit that spent almost the entire war as provost. The officer we know most about is Major David B. Bridgford, who was associated with the battalion from the date of its entry into Confederate service.

It is also unfortunate that the provost guard of the 1st Corps, Army of Northern Virginia, cannot be identified. There is no doubt that such a unit existed, for in a letter to President Davis in November, 1862, Lieutenant Colonel Robert P. Blount noted that he was "attached to General Longstreet's staff and have command of his provost guard." Blount signed the letter "Provost-Marshal First Corps, Army of Northern Virginia." Blount was also listed as the provost marshal at Hamilton's Crossing, Virginia, in June, 1863.[48]

Like all units, provost units would have required administrative support: clerical, pay, transportation, medical, quartermaster, and ordnance. Some of these functions were the responsibility of staff officers within the provost itself, but for clerical support some personnel were detailed specifically as "provost clerks," as opposed to merely as provost. If this were the general pattern throughout the provost organization it would have imposed an additional and relatively heavy drain on the available manpower. For example, just three references show nine or ten individuals serving as provost clerks.[49]

47. *OR,* Vol. XLVI, Pt. 1, p. 1277; Katcher, *Army of Northern Virginia,* 34; Brock (ed.), *Paroles,* 447–51. A list of officers is also included.

48. *OR,* Ser. II, Vol. IV, pp. 949–50. Blount's service record sheds no light on the matter. His unit, the 9th Alabama Battalion, did not serve in the Army of Northern Virginia (*OR,* Vol. LI, Pt. 2, p. 721). The troops with Blount at Hamilton's Crossing were ordered to rejoin their commands on June 4.

49. John B. Jones, *A Rebel War Clerk's Diary* (1866; rpr. ed. Earl Shenck Miers. New York, 1958), 70. An entry for March 13, 1862, indicates that at least four clerks were busy issuing passports in the Richmond Provost Marshal's Office. John O. Casler, *Four Years in the Stonewall*

Only one reference was found regarding medical officers attached to provost commands. The *Southern Historical Society Papers* list two surgeons belonging to corps provost guards in the Army of Northern Virginia.[50] It is assumed that attachments of medical officers would have been a general practice.

Transportation resources allocated to the provost did not entail detaching any additional manpower from the field armies, at least not after the autumn of 1864, when army teamsters were replaced by Negroes. It appears that the provost in the major field armies and in the departments were getting a fair share of the horses and wagons available for the transport of the army. For once, the Army of Tennessee appears to have been organizationally ahead of Lee's army: allocation of transport to corps provost guards in the Army of Tennessee was made in August, 1863, but in the Army of Northern Virginia not until April, 1864.[51]

Provost pay was a contentious issue and one that Congress seized upon to ensure that fiscal control of the provost remained with the legislative body of the Confederacy, rather than going by default to the executive. In April, 1862, Major General Mansfield Lovell, conducting the defense of New Orleans, queried Secretary of War Randolph on the payment of provost marshal expenses. No immediate answer was made, but a month later a provost marshal in Tennessee was told that the salary for the office had "not as yet been determined." The subject surfaced in Congress on August 27, when the president was asked to inform the Senate whether the secretary of war had authorized provost marshals the pay of a captain to be paid by the Quartermaster's Department and by what authority provost pay and allowances had been set. The reply by Secretary of War Randolph on September 11 advised that provost marshals were paid as captains of infantry (in some cases they received the pay of field

---

Brigade (1893; rpr. Dayton, 1971), 228, reveals that Tom Wilkins, 10th Virginia, was detailed as a provost clerk in 1864. Brock (ed.), *Paroles,* 451–52, lists four privates, all from the 1st Virginia Battalion, who served as clerks in the Provost Marshal's Office. *OR,* Ser. IV, Vol. II, pp. 202–203, an act of Congress on October 9, 1862, decreed that each military court would have a clerk.

50. Brock (ed.), *Paroles,* 185, 449.

51. *OR,* Vol. XXXIX, Pt. 2, pp. 835–36; Vol. XXX, Pt. 4, p. 556. General Order 171, August 26, 1863, allocated one four-horse wagon to the provost marshal and judge advocate of each corps of the Army of Tennessee. General Order 27 of the Army of Northern Virginia, April 5, 1864 (*OR,* XXXIII, 1262–63), made the same allocation to each corps provost guard but also gave each division provost guard one four-horse wagon. The Department of North Carolina issued a general order on February 10, 1865, giving each division provost guard one wagon (*OR,* Vol. XLVII, Pt. 2, p. 1153).

officers) by the Quartermaster's Department. No mention was made of any "authority" for these salaries.[52]

Congress thereupon resolved that it would fix provost pay rates; the secretary of war had no business setting either the rank or the pay of provost marshals without the consent of Congress. During the first month of 1863, Congress considered legislation on the payment of provost marshals appointed from civilian life.[53] Another bill entitled "An act to provide for compensation to certain provost-marshals, commandants of posts and provost guards" limited the pay of a provost marshal to that of a captain of infantry and stipulated that a provost guardsman would receive the same pay as any other soldier. The bill was tabled on April 25, 1863.[54] Amendments to the pay regulations continued until almost the end of the war. Congress did, however, have its way. It controlled the pursestrings of the provost.[55]

For his eleven dollars a month the provost soldier was required to carry out a wide range of often oncrous and virtually always thankless duties. The Confederacy received full value and more for the generous stipend it paid to its overworked watchdogs.

52. *OR*, VI, 877; Ser. II, Vol. II, p. 1423; *Journal of the Confederate Congress*, II, 241; "Proceedings of First Confederate Congress, Second Session in Part," *SHSP*, XLVI (rpr. 1980), 104.

53. *Journal of the Confederate Congress*, II, 325–26, 452. A resolution was offered in the Senate on September 24, 1862. On October 9 as part of approving "An act to organize military courts to attend the Army of the Confederate States in the field and to define the powers of said courts," Congress set the pay of a court provost marshal at that of a captain of cavalry. See "Proceedings of First Confederate Congress, Second Session in Part," *SHSP*, XLVI (rpr. 1980), 226; "Proceedings of First Confederate Congress, End of Second Session, Third Session in Part," *SHSP*, XLVII (rpr. 1980), 32; *Journal of the Confederate Congress*, VI, 57; "Proceedings of the First Confederate Congress, Third Session in Part, January 29–March 19, 1863," *SHSP*, XLVIII (1980), 224.

54. *Journal of the Confederate Congress*, VI, 155, 305, 312, 428.

55. "Proceedings of the Second Confederate Congress, Second Session in Part," *SHSP*, LII (rpr. 1980), 29–30, 35. In December, 1864, pay and allowances were granted for personnel other than officers acting as provost marshals or provost clerks. See also *Journal of the Confederate Congress*, VII, 375, 495; IV, 390, 467, 480, 486.

4

The Duty of the Provost

*Do your duty in all things. You cannot do
more. You should never wish to do less.*

R. E. LEE

Although Confederate States provost performed basically the same duties that contemporary provost do, other responsibilities, some peculiar to the time, devolved on them. Duties were delegated to the provost either because commanders felt that certain tasks were appropriate for them, or, more likely, because in many instances there were no other troops able or available to perform these duties.

The evidence is clear that in the course of time the Rebel watchdog became a vigilant and ubiquitous beast, monitoring, in some areas to a remarkable degree, virtually every aspect of the discipline, movement, and operation of the army. Add to this the thorny issue of overseeing the activities of the general population to meet the demands of war, and it is obvious that the Confederate military policeman faced a multitude of diverse and demanding tasks. These absorbed so much manpower that the provost were never able to do their job to the full. Demand for provost was so constant and widespread that the thin blanket of manpower could not cover the whole bed. The same may be said of the Confederate armies as a whole; both army and provost were severely handicapped by lack of adequate means.

Chapter 2 described the effect of conscription on the ability of the provost to meet its assigned roles in the rear areas. At the front the high quality of the units used as provost was both a blessing and a curse. The increasing use of provost for combat duty to relieve critical situations resulted in severe casualties and a corresponding decline in strength and efficiency. This was particularly detrimental to the provost's efforts to control straggling and desertion, two evils that had disastrous consequences for the nation's ability to continue the war. All too often the diversion of provost guardsmen to combat left none available to prevent the drain on the army's fighting strength.

The extent of documentation on particular provost duties varies greatly. For some, such as shipping control, the information is relatively thin but still sufficient to give a flavor of the duties and to indicate that they were assuredly a matter of provost concern. Other duties—fortunately, the most important ones—are so well documented that they allow a comprehensive picture of the provost's responsibility.

The Union, because it started the war with an established army, led the way in defining the duties of provost guards. General George McClellan, with his talent for organization, was the first to delineate the tasks of the provost. Writing on operations between July, 1861, and November, 1862, he noted that he had assigned the following duties to his provost:

Suppression of marauding and depredations, and of all brawls and disturbances, preservation of good order, and suppression of disturbances beyond the limits of the camps.

Prevention of straggling on the march.

Suppression of gambling houses, drinking houses, or bar-rooms, and brothels.

Regulation of hotels, taverns, markets, and places of public amusement.

Searches, seizures and arrests. Execution of sentences of general courts-martial involving imprisonment or capital punishment. Enforcement of orders prohibiting the sale of intoxicating liquors, whether by tradesmen or sutlers, and of orders respecting passes.

Deserters from the enemy.

Prisoners of war taken from the enemy.

Countersigning safeguards.

Passes to citizens within the lines and for purposes of trade.

Complaints of citizens as to conduct of the soldiers.[1]

The performance of these duties, plus those assumed during the occupation of enemy territory, placed great strain on Union provost. In 1863 a Union provost marshal at Fayetteville, Arkansas, listed his contributions to the war effort as follows:

Exercising the functions of judge, jury and sheriff; empowered to arrest deserters, whether regulars, volunteers or militia, and all disloyal persons; to enquire into and report upon treasonable practices; to seize

1. *OR*, V, 30.

50

stolen or embezzled property belonging to the [United States] Government; to detect spies of the enemy, and put a stop to miscellaneous
pillaging. . . . Added to these labors, bonds are to be taken and safeguards given; a general pass system devised and occasionally re-con-
structed; oaths of allegiance administered and paroles subscribed; proofs
of loyalty made and endorsed . . . in short . . . the general administration of the law during a suspension of civil process.[2]

The duties specified by McClellan and those described by the Union provost
marshal applied equally to the Confederate provost. There were others, such as
the impressment of Negroes, which were unique to the Confederate States
service. It is interesting, too, to compare Civil War provost duties with those of
today. Many are the same. The modern-day military policeman would be
familiar with all of the duties on McClellan's list and might perhaps categorize
them under general headings of disciplinary duties, control of stragglers and
deserters, duties of arrest and detention, control of prisoners of war, and
movement control. To these he would no doubt add various tasks associated
with field operations, including participation in combat.

In the Introduction it was pointed out that the authority for virtually all
provost activity in the Confederate States was the Articles of War, which
provided for military courts and provost marshals. Having enacted the legislative basis of the provost, the Confederate Congress gave its opinion as to
provost duties:

> The duty of a provost-marshal shall be to take charge of prisoners in
> camp or at posts who are committed to his custody by regular legal
> military authority, and to execute such duties in connection with pris-
> oners and other offenders against the articles of war and the rules and
> regulations of the Army, and such other duties connected with the police
> and discipline of the camp or post as may in published orders be given in
> charge to the provost-marshal by the general commanding the army or
> department.[3]

General Leonidas Polk translated this legislative verbiage into a statement
that the duties of the provost were to "check all disorders . . . and arrest and
return to their commands all stragglers and deserters . . . and this is a measure
indispensable to the peace and quiet of my department, the security of the

2. Harold M. Hyman, "Deceit in Dixie," *Civil War History,* III (rpr. 1963), 67.
3. *Journal of the Confederate Congress,* VII, 664.

property and lives of the citizens, as well as the good order and discipline of my army in the field." A soldier of the 1st Missouri, who served as a provost guardsman, wrote, "The duty of the provost marshal was to grant passes coming in or going out of the army's lines, to take charge of all prisoners brought in until sent to their destination, to keep under guard men of our own army arrested for any offence, and turned over to us for confinement." In the capital of the Confederacy, under Provost Marshal General John H. Winder, the provost were responsible not only for the prison camps in the vicinity of Richmond but also "for the arrest and return of deserters, and for the maintenance of order in a city swelled to more than twice its normal size by the war."[4] Another Confederate general, Arthur Manigault of the Army of Tennessee, said:

> The Provost Guard, as its name would imply, was strictly a police force, in no manner charged with the protection of the camp, but responsible for the safe keeping of all culprits, carrying out the sentences of Courts Martial, or the infliction of such punishment as the brigade commander authorized, and correcting all breaches of camp orders, a detachment of them being nearly always on duty, scouting around the neighbourhood, arresting all stragglers, marauders, or men absent from their commands without leave. In battle they are most often used, deployed in the rear of the line, to prevent any skulking or passing to the rear without proper authority, although on several such occasions they were attached to some regiment and took part in the fight, or were used to prolong a line, when the space allotted us was rather greater than we could fill with safety, without making use of them. All prisoners captured were turned over to them for safe keeping. On the march they brought up the rear, allowing no one to drop behind without authority, or to straggle on the flanks of the column, into farm houses, orchards, or fields of corn, sugar-cane, or the like.[5]

In a general sense the provost system was established to provide police protection in a country at war. Briefly, the provost was responsible for the arrest of offenders against Confederate military law, including the drunk and disorderly and the cowards who attempted to desert their units. The guarding of

4. *OR,* Vol. XXXII, Pt. 3, pp. 723–25; Anderson, *Memoirs,* 204; Ezra J. Warner, *Generals in Gray: Lives of the Confederate Commanders* (Baton Rouge, 1959), 340–41.

5. R. L. Tower (ed.), *A Carolinian Goes to War: The Civil War Narrative of Arthur Middleton Manigault Brigadier General C.S.A.* (Columbia, S.C., 1983), 166.

these prisoners and deserters was also a provost concern. In addition, provost controlled the departure of ships from Confederate ports; posted guards on railroads to control initially military and then civilian traffic; controlled the impressment of Negroes, so necessary to sustain the war effort; and provided guards for the protection of military installations throughout the Confederate States. As well, provost administered the passport system, which was designed to check desertion and straggling, detect spies, and prevent communication with the enemy. And finally, in places like Richmond, Charleston, Norfolk, and Portsmouth, where martial law was imposed, the provost were responsible for administration of the law.

In the beginning the provost had no authority over civilians, but the harsh realities of war led to great extension of their power. Provost duties, particularly those associated with movement control and martial law, conferred a high profile, and unfortunately the provost were soon seen as doing no good. For them to err on the side of ensuring the maximum degree of public and military security incurred viperous public wrath, including accusations of interference with liberty and charges of usurpation and harassment. Strict adherence to the limitations of the law, however, would have resulted in the total breakdown of military and civilian order and cries of inefficiency and uselessness. For the provost it was a conundrum.

5

There Will Be Discipline

Men in the army and out of the army thought for a
long time the usual laws of discipline inapplicable
to them. Were they not all gentlemen? And what
gentleman would do a mean thing, steal a horse or
plunder a chicken coop? . . . Were they not all
brave and bold? And what brave man would linger
behind on the march or turn his back to the enemy
in battle? It was thought enough at first to operate
upon the men by appeals to their zeal, their
patriotism, and honor.
Richmond *Enquirer,* November 4, 1864

Robert E. Lee never doubted the requirement for strict discipline. In his opinion too much reliance had been placed on the soldier's innate "merit" and not enough had been done to instill that instinctive obedience which builds good units. As late as 1865 he felt compelled to issue a circular reminding the army of the lost opportunities and the hundreds of lives uselessly sacrificed because of poor discipline.[1] That Lee considered such a circular necessary even as the Confederacy tottered on the edge of extinction says something about the state of discipline in the Army of Northern Virginia. In view of this particular army's unique character and its unmatched record, one can well imagine the state of discipline elsewhere in the Confederate armies.

One of the primary duties of the Confederate provost—perhaps *the* primary duty because everything else stemmed from it—was the maintenance of discipline in the armies. This is not to say that the provost usurped the responsibility of commanding officers to maintain the internal discipline of their commands. Commanding officers were expected to do this in their areas or lines, but beyond that the provost were to assist in the maintenance of discipline. In

1. Bell Irvin Wiley, *The Life of Johnny Reb: The Common Soldier of the Confederacy* (1943; rpr. Baton Rouge, 1978), 242–43; A. L. Long, *Memoirs of Robert E. Lee* (New York, 1887), 685–86.

practice this division of responsibility meant that the soldier away from his unit because of leave, sickness, detachment, or absence without authority was sure to encounter provost who would demand to know the reason, with proof, for his whereabouts. Provost assistance to unit commanders also included a crime prevention program, the investigation of crimes committed by military personnel, the custody and escorting of service offenders, and the apprehension of deserters and absentees. The latter problem occupied so much of the provost's time and energy that it deserves and receives detailed attention in a separate chapter.

Crime prevention and investigation were key elements in provost responsibility for good order and discipline. Looting, irregular requisition (in blunt terms, pillaging), offenses against military security (loose talk), and vice-related offenses were just a few of the crimes the provost dealt with. In the fight against vice the Confederate military policeman encountered liquor-related offenses, gambling, and prostitution. The latter profession carried the potential to create tremendous waste of manpower because of the spread of disease. This fight was complicated by the breakdown of normal life and morals under wartime conditions in a beleaguered Confederacy. Liquor and prostitution were less of a problem at the front, although the soldier's ability to find these comforts was nothing short of remarkable, but in the rear areas and in the cities they were more easily obtainable and a prime attraction for the troops, both on and off duty. Front or rear, however, a highly visible provost was essential to good discipline.

Liquor-related offenses presented the provost with a persistent and ubiquitous problem that went far beyond the soldier in the ranks. A taste for good liquor, or bad for that matter, was a characteristic of all ranks up to and including general officer. Accusations of drunkenness among generals were not uncommon during the Civil War. John Barleycorn often exercised an irresistible appeal to John Reb; what's more, John Reb possessed a unique talent for finding a drink. It was said, for example, that a Missourian could "smell whisky a mile and a half." With this situation in mind, in May, 1862, the Confederate Congress attempted to control liquor consumption by passing legislation entitled "AN ACT to punish drunkenness in the Army."[2] Not surprisingly, such legislation had about the same deterrent effect as King Canute did in his famous encounter with the North Sea.

2. R. S. Bevier, *History of the First and Second Missouri Confederate Brigades, 1861–1865* (1879; rpr. N.p., 1985), 312; *OR*, Ser. IV, Vol. I, p. 1126. On May 22 the legislation was published as a general order.

The injurious effects of liquor on discipline were very evident in Virginia, the state with the largest concentration of Confederate troops, and especially in Richmond, the scene of much mayhem and disorder because of the consumption of drink. The imposition of martial law in March, 1862, put an end to the practice of saloonkeepers filling up the soldiers with cheap whiskey in exchange for their pay and then flinging them out penniless into the streets. All saloons and distilleries in the city and for ten miles around were closed, and the railroads were prohibited from carrying liquor into Richmond. Nevertheless, liquor could still be had, either as bootleg hootch or through druggists on a prescription basis. Members of the city's provost professed no immunity to drink. Their position made it easy for them to forge the prescriptions necessary to obtain a steady supply of brandy. To add insult to injury, the druggists who had sold the brandy to the provost were then promptly arrested. Out West, meantime, some men serving as provost were known not to refuse a drink: one private soldier in the fall of 1861 noted in his diary that "the provo[st] marshal was also drunk." The Richmond papers of the summer of 1862 reported on the "drunken soldiers and quarreling women [who] crowded the mayor's courtroom daily." By autumn the commandant of the city, General John H. Winder, attempted to limit the supply of liquor by prohibiting the importation of more than 150 barrels (6,000 gallons) into Richmond. None could be sold to soldiers.[3]

Many soldiers in transit to the army in Virginia spent much of their time in pursuit of whiskey. A sergeant of the 27th Mississippi Infantry, on provost duty at Atlanta in July, 1863, recalled the crowds of men who broke their journeys to frequent the dives where whiskey was readily available. The guard, according to the sergeant, had "often a tough element to handle, but we had to do our duty, and were not afraid to do it without fear or favor."[4]

Somewhat later in the war one brigade had a wild party at Montgomery, Alabama, while en route to North Carolina. Despite the best efforts of the provost, Hiram Granbury's Texas Brigade virtually took control of the city. An all-night dance at a "beer-jerking" place went fairly quietly until barrel-size

3. Alfred Hoyt Bill, *The Beleaguered City: Richmond, 1861–1865* (New York, 1946), 103–104; Jones, *Rebel War Clerk's Diary,* 70; Emory M. Thomas, *The Confederate State of Richmond: A Biography of the Capital* (Austin, 1971), 83, 67, 107; Robert Augustus Moore, *A Life for the Confederacy,* ed. James W. Silver (Jackson, Tenn., 1959), 77.

4. J. W. Simmons, "Conscripting Atlanta Theater in 1863," *Confederate Veteran,* XI (rpr. 1983), 279.

tots of "bad Georgia pine-top whisky" were added to the fun, and the boys drank like "thirsty chickens around a pan of water on a hot summer day." One Texan theorized that the size of a drinking cup might have some bearing on how drunk a soldier could get—and how quickly. In any event, the boys and the "female women" (?) present all got as "drunk as lords" and many did not return to camp until the next day, most considerably the worse for wear and some with less hair or fewer ears than they took to town. It is entirely understandable that the good citizens of the first Confederate capital had an "earnest" desire to see the last of the Texans.[5]

Closer to the front liquor controls were also imposed. On March 17, 1862, the provost marshal at Orange Court House, Virginia, Colonel Thomas H. Taylor of the 1st Kentucky Infantry, was ordered to close all shops and stores where liquor could be purchased. Liquor consumption was vigorously regulated by the provost throughout northern Virginia. On April 5, for example, several Texans of Hood's brigade ran afoul of the provost during a visit, no doubt protracted, to a saloon in Falmouth.[6] The cold and snow of the winter of 1862–1863 and the temptation of a warming libation were, for many, sufficient reason to risk arrest by the provost.

In the western armies liquor control was complicated by the home-brew fraternity. During Christmas of 1861 the Missouri Brigade camps at Springfield, Missouri, were besieged by purveyors of "double-distilled damnation." No general orders or provost on earth could have entirely stopped the sale of festive grog. General Basil Duke, in 1863 commanding a regiment in John Morgan's command, recalled the numerous stills and that commanders were "compelled to keep a strong detail on duty . . . as provost . . . keeping men away from the stills." Whenever they found a closed distillery the Orphans of the Kentucky Brigade could be relied upon surreptitiously to put it back into operation: "How often the smell of sour mash led the provost to the Kentuckians at a still!" The Army of the Mississippi reacted to the drink problem in 1862 by prohibiting "the sale or supplying in any manner of intoxicating liquors within 5 miles of any station occupied by troops or within 1 mile of any public highway used for military purposes. . . . All grogshops and drinking

---

5. R. M. Collins, *Chapters from the Unwritten History of the War Between the States; or, The Incidents in the Life of a Confederate Soldier in Camp, on the March, in the Great Battles, and in Prison* (1893; rpr. Dayton, 1982), 273–75.

6. *OR*, Vol. LI, Pt. 2, pp. 504–505. See also H. B. Simpson, *Hood's Texas Brigade: Lee's Grenadier Guard* (Waco, 1970), 92.

saloons within such limits will be closed and the supplies packed, subject to military inspection."[7]

In 1864 one senior provost officer, Colonel Martin H. Cofer, fought a losing battle against the Orphan Brigade's Kentuckians, many of whom had a particularly sharp appetite for liquor and an even sharper sense of how to obtain it:

> Indeed, here at Dalton [Georgia] the Orphans and their whisky-drinking ways caused more problems than anywhere else in the war. Poor Lewis, always a bit "straight" though the boys loved him for it, actually issued general orders in attempting to stem the tide of John Barleycorn. He called on all the regimental commanders to stop the evil of drunkenness "lest the cantonment of this Brigade shall ere long, assume the character of a Pot House." He should have known it was useless to try. Cofer had won promotion to provost marshal general of the Army . . . and thus it was one of their own that the Orphans had to deceive in getting whisky into their camps. Cofer tried manfully to enforce the edict against liquor in the bivouacs, but without success. When he posted guards to search all entering camp and confiscate whisky, some of the boys dressed as guards themselves, confiscated the "article," and then smuggled it into camp in hollowed pumpkins. Johnny Green found one such ingenious Orphan whose "entire mess were mellow for several days after that."
>
> Worse yet, since all whisky was reserved for medical uses under Cofer's care, some of the Orphans actually arranged for shipment of the beverage to them, yet marked to Cofer's attention. Gladly he guarded their boxes until called for, entirely unaware of his integral role in the "jug trade."[8]

An earlier provost marshal general of the Army of Tennessee, Colonel Benjamin J. Hill, was less concerned with the evils of drink. Colonel James Nisbet of the 66th Georgia got some idea of Hill's fondness for liquor during the withdrawal from Resaca in May, 1864. Reporting to Hill for temporary duty on the night of May 15, Nisbet was offered a tot of "old Lawson Hill's apple brandy . . . five years old, aged in wood." Suddenly a shell crashed through the roof of the dugout and burst. Neither officer was injured, but Hill's first

7. Bevier, *History of the First and Second Missouri Confederate Brigades,* 312; Basil W. Duke, *Reminiscences of General Basil W. Duke, C.S.A.* (1911; rpr. Freeport, N.Y., 1969), 275; William C. Davis, *The Orphan Brigade: The Kentucky Confederates Who Couldn't Go Home* (New York, 1980), 204; *OR,* Vol. X, Pt. 2, pp. 297–98.

8. Davis, *Orphan Brigade,* 204–205.

thought was the safety of the jug: "Colonel Nisbet, did they break the bottle?" On being assured that it was safe and sound, Hill rejoined, "Thank the Lord for that!" Later, before the fall of Atlanta, it appears that liquor was getting the better of Hill. One witness reported, "Under the stress of the times, Hill had taken to the bottle. Usually drunk, he was generally belligerent." Hill was relieved on August 24 and promoted to brigadier general in November.[9]

Another task for the provost was the suppression of gambling. Poker and other games of chance in themselves may have been harmless; after all, a Confederate private with eleven dollars monthly from a grateful government could spend only a limited time at the table unless he was extraordinarily lucky. The greater danger was that gambling attracted not only the curious and the wishful thinkers but also the hardened criminal element that did pose a threat to public and military order. One Richmond policeman recalled that "the sporting fraternity had friends from the slums to the pulpit." The gambling dens, the "Hells" as they were known, also attracted the wealthy and the influential, thereby making prevention of gambling even more difficult. Frequent raids by the city police, probably in concert with the provost, failed to close the gambling halls. Poker was a favorite pastime throughout the South. General Basil Duke recalled that General John Morgan ordered his provost to arrest every dealer and all men found in gambling establishments. Following the retreat from Jackson, Mississippi, after Vicksburg fell, General John Breckinridge became so concerned about gambling in the Orphan Brigade that he sent in his provost to try to end the pastime. The effort failed, as did similar attempts in 1864: "The gambling could never be stopped no matter how the officers tried."[10]

Prostitution was another widespread vice and one of particular worry to the medical staff because of the inevitable spread of venereal disease. Richmond's numerous prostitutes added many men's names to the casualty lists: "The Tenth Alabama Regiment, which arrived in Richmond in the early summer of 1861 . . . had in July (with a mean strength of 1,063 men), 62 new cases of gonorrhea and 6 of syphilis. . . . The Eighteenth Mississippi (mean strength-975) had 25 new cases of gonorrhea in July, and in August the Sixteenth Mississippi (mean strength-972) reported 32 new cases of gonorrhea and

9. James Cooper Nisbet, *4 Years on the Firing Line* (1914; rpr. ed. Bell Irvin Wiley. Jackson, Tenn., 1963), 186–87; Samuel Carter, *The Siege of Atlanta, 1864* (New York, 1973), 274; Joseph H. Crute, *Confederate Staff Officers, 1861–1865* (Powhatan, Va., 1982), 85.

10. Thomas, *Confederate State of Richmond,* 66; Duke, *Reminiscences,* 282; Davis, *Orphan Brigade,* 178, 204.

11 of syphilis. The Eighth South Carolina (mean strength-828) in the same month reported 25 new cases of gonorrhea." Statistics for units employed as provost are no better. The 55th North Carolina, for example, while on duty at Petersburg in October, 1862, reported 13 new cases of gonorrhea. Another Tar Heel regiment, the 47th, reported 10 new cases for the same period in Petersburg.[11]

As well as being the national capital, Richmond could also lay claim to being the vice capital of the Confederacy. Swollen to twice its normal size by large numbers of transient soldiers and civilians, the city presented serious problems of law and order for Confederate authorities. Often violence spilled over from the gambling halls, the brothels, and the saloons, resulting in fierce brawls in the streets much to the terror of the citizen: "Disorder was everywhere and nowhere was safe at night." Military policemen were hard-pressed to keep some semblance of peace, and the surge in population, accompanied by a wave of crime, all but submerged them. General John H. Winder's police received some credit for their efforts to reduce crimes of violence, but by December, 1862, robberies and murders claimed victims daily. The Richmond *Whig,* having witnessed the cavortings of the drunken soldiery and the inmates of the many brothels, the public disorder, and the rising crime rate, observed, "In the aggregate, no army in the world is composed of more quiet and orderly soldiers, but the exceptions are numerous enough to justify more rigid discipline at the camp."[12]

One challenge to law and order the provost was not involved in was the Richmond "Bread Riot," which broke out on April 2, 1863. Early that Thursday morning a mob of about a thousand "low men & women (the latter mostly Irish)" looted stores of bread and other food items and then, as always in such situations, pillaged shops containing silks and clothing, shoes, and jewelry. Attempts by Mayor Mayo and Governor John Letcher failed to disperse the looters. Finally, the military and President Davis, whose icy calm was impressive in the face of the mob, broke up the riot. The provost were placed on the alert to check any further disturbances, but none occurred. Nor did the provost become involved in the March 18 riots at Salisbury, North Carolina, or those at Petersburg, Virginia, on April 1. In comparison, these were tame affairs.[13]

11. Wiley, *Life of Johnny Reb,* 55–57.

12. Clifford Dowdey, *Experiment in Rebellion* (New York, 1947), 177; Bill, *Beleaguered City,* 205–206; Thomas, *Confederate State of Richmond,* 67.

13. William Kauffman Scarborough (ed.), *The Diary of Edmund Ruffin* (Baton Rouge, 1972),

It was April, 1865, before the city authorities again faced such a situation. Just before the fall of the city, General Richard Ewell, the city commandant, was powerless to enforce order because of the lack of any troops to do so. The provost guard, one understrength battalion of Virginia reserves, could not be spared from preparing the city for evacuation, and the mobs soon got out of hand.[14] Full order was restored only with the arrival of the victorious Union army.

In all the armies throughout the war poor discipline hindered army operations and necessitated the allocation of large numbers of provost guards to preserve order. Many towns in northern Virginia were rigidly policed by the provost to keep order and return stragglers and deserters to their units. That stern disciplinarian Stonewall Jackson never hesitated to enforce army regulations. During the Valley campaign of 1862 his army took on an unauthorized bluish tinge when the men appropriated Federal uniforms to replace their tattered clothing. Stonewall stopped this practice by ordering his provost to hold soldiers in blue as prisoners until they could prove their identity.[15]

Indiscipline also accompanied Lee's army as it moved north into Maryland in September, 1862. Before the offensive Lee cautioned the army against

I, 612; Varina Davis, *Jefferson Davis, Ex-President of the Confederate States: A Memoir by His Wife* (2 vols.; New York, 1890), II, 373–76; Jones, *Rebel War Clerk's Diary*, 183–84; Thomas, *Confederate State of Richmond*, 119–22; Bill, *Beleaguered City*, 165–66; Manarin (ed.), *Richmond at War*, 311–13; W. Buck Yearns and John G. Barrett (eds.), *North Carolina Civil War Documentary* (Chapel Hill, 1980), 219–21; Sallie A. Putnam, *In Richmond During the Confederacy* (1867; rpr. New York, 1961), 208–210; Judith W. McGuire, *Diary of a Southern Refugee During the War* (Richmond, 1889), 202–204; *OR*, XVIII, 977–78; A. A. Hoehling and Mary Hoehling, *The Day Richmond Died* (New York, 1981), 31–32. The references disagree as to exactly what troops put down the riots. One refers only to military, another to state guards and police, one does not say, two refer to the Public Guard, two mention that the City Battalion was present, and two state that a company from the Confederate armory put down the riot. The authors of *The Day Richmond Died* state that the Public Guard, "a city battalion with police duties," was at the scene but also that "Confusion stamped the whole episode," and "how the mob was dispersed [was] also variously described." I would like to agree that it was the Public Guard, but I believe the armory company must get credit for breaking up the mob. I say this for two reasons. First, the company commander was named, a detail that adds veracity to its involvement. Second, and more important, Varina Davis, the wife of the president, says it was the armory company. As her husband was at the scene and in the best position to know, and the affair was no doubt a topic of conversation between them, the armory troops seem the most logical choice.

14. Irvine, "Fall of Richmond," 386.

15. J. William Jones, "Reminiscences of the Army of Northern Virginia. Paper No. 5—How Fremont and Shields 'Caught' Stonewall Jackson," *SHSP*, IX (rpr. 1977), 273.

committing any excesses. Brigadier General Lewis A. Armistead, appointed provost marshal of the army on September 6, was given ample force and authority to deal with indiscipline. He was directed to follow in the rear of the army with his guards and "correct irregularities against good order and military discipline, and prevent depredations upon the community." Lee's order extended protection to Unionist as well as Southern supporters in Maryland. On September 6, when a Southern mob attacked a Unionist newspaper office, the provost intervened to prevent its destruction and dispersed the mob.[16] The following day Lee wrote President Davis: "I find that the discipline of the army, which, from the manner of its organization, the necessity of bringing it into immediate service, its constant occupation and hard duty, was naturally defective, has not been improved by the forced marches and hard service it has lately undergone." After the army's return to Virginia the 1st Corps published a general order designed to tighten up discipline. The order instructed the provost to arrest any soldiers who had committed excesses.[17]

On his next move north in June, 1863, Lee once again insisted that the army behave itself in the enemy's country. Wherever Confederate troops operated in Pennsylvania, provost were present to ensure that military discipline was not relaxed. At Greencastle, for example, as soon as Robert Rodes entered the town his divisional provost guard was patrolling the streets. When his division moved on to Chambersburg, the divisional provost marshal maintained strict order in that town.[18]

Early's campaign in the Shenandoah in 1864 was not as disciplined or as successful as Jackson's in 1862. After the rout at New Market in late October, Major General Bryan Grimes noted that the disciplinary failings were such that the "only salvation for this army and the country [was] to inflict severe punishment on all who fail to discharge their duty." Failure, as he put it, was no fault of Early's, but rather could be attributed to "Simply want of discipline among the troops."[19]

In the western armies discipline was even worse. The surrender of Vicksburg, that other disaster of July, 1863, provides a perfect example of what

16. *OR,* Vol. XIX, Pt. 2, p. 596. See also Richard R. Duncan, "Marylanders and the Invasion of 1862," in John T. Hubbell (ed.), *Battles Lost and Won* (Westport, Conn., 1975), 185, 188.

17. *OR,* Vol. XIX, Pt. 2, p. 597; Vol. LI, Pt. 2, p. 651.

18. Edwin B. Coddington, *The Gettysburg Campaign: A Study in Command* (New York, 1968), 163–64.

19. Gary W. Gallagher (ed.), *Extracts of Letters of Major-General Bryan Grimes . . . Together with Some Personal Recollections of the War* (1883; rpr. Wilmington, 1986), 76.

happened to discipline when the provost were not in a position to enforce it. Almost as George Pickett's charge was in progress far to the east, General John C. Pemberton was seeking terms from Grant for the surrender of Vicksburg. Pemberton had hoped to keep his army together and ready for immediate service as soon as it was exchanged, but with no weapons with which to arm his provost, it proved impossible after the surrender to prevent the men from falling out of ranks and going home. Without armed provost, discipline disappeared and so did Pemberton's army.[20] Grant was delighted. The large Confederate garrison of Vicksburg was scattered, and it would take considerable time before it could be reconstituted in anything even approaching its former strength.

Elsewhere in the West the troops were equally careless of discipline. In the Atlanta campaign of 1864, for instance, the post commandant considered that at least a regiment was required for the "proper preservation of order . . . and for preventing officers and soldiers belonging to the army from remaining here without proper authority."[21] On March 20 two regiments, the 8th and 28th Tennessee from Major General Benjamin Cheatham's division of the Army of Tennessee, were on provost duty in Atlanta. Indiscipline was endemic in the western cavalry, much of which was irregularly raised and maintained. One brigadier, Lawrence Ross, warned his officers and men that any culprits would be immediately transferred to the infantry. Such transfers would presumably make soldiers less inclined to wander and certainly would dramatically shorten their plundering reach. The brigade provost marshal was ordered to arrest all offenders with a view "to the prompt punishment by transfer to infantry."[22] This view of infantry service as a punishment was unfortunately all too common and goes far in explaining the inordinate number of western cavalry units.

There can be no doubt that discipline was extremely difficult to inculcate and then enforce in an army raised in the Confederate manner. Regulation, entreaty, threat, and provost control all too often had little or no effect. As a consequence, a system of punishment for offenders had to be at hand. This system, consisting of a means of trial, as part of military law, and punishment, through the military penal system, for those who overstepped the bounds of good order and discipline, was a provost responsibility. Provost attempts to measure up to this responsibility were to become a contentious issue.

20. Anderson, *Memoirs,* 557.
21. *OR,* Vol. XXXII, Pt. 3, pp. 642, 657.
22. *OR,* Vol. XXXVIII, Pt. 5, pp. 963–64.

6

Provost Judge, Provost Jailer

The laws are silent in the midst of arms.

CICERO

The variety of provost duties described in Chapter 4 makes it clear that a Confederate provost marshal functioned as policeman, magistrate, and jailer. Often the magisterial and custodial sides took precedence, and many of the inmates, soldiers and civilians, of the military prisons were incarcerated by direct courtesy of the provost.

The relationship of the provost to Confederate military law begins with the legislation that established the system of courts-martial. The Articles of War, adopted on March 6, 1861, provided for these tribunals to try military personnel accused of offenses against military law. As originally enacted, the procedures for courts-martial were so inefficient that major amendments were soon required. The deficiencies were corrected by an act of October 9, 1862, which authorized a military court for each army corps in the field.[1] Each court was permitted to appoint a provost marshal with the rank and pay of a captain of cavalry to execute its orders, and provost jurisdiction was extended to include offenses against the articles and customs of war and Confederate and state law.[2] In modern parlance these courts would be described as standing courts-martial.

Occasionally general courts-martial were also established. These, too, had their own provost marshals. As an example, during the sojourn of the 3d

1. Beers, *Guide to the Archives*, 142–43; Winchester Hall, *The Story of the 26th Louisiana Infantry, in the Service of the Confederate States* (1890?; rpr. Gaithersburg, Md., 1984), 115; *OR,* Ser. IV, Vol. II, pp. 202–203, 248. The act, Statute 71 of Congress, was entitled "AN ACT to organize military courts to attend the Army of the Confederate States in the field and to define the powers of said courts." In 1864 A. P. Hill's 3d Corps in the Army of Northern Virginia, Nathan Bedford Forrest's and Stephen D. Lee's cavalry divisions, and the District of Northern Alabama were authorized to establish military courts. Eventually each geographical department and each state within the departments were authorized courts. These courts exercised unrestricted jurisdiction over military personnel and civil jurisdiction in occupied areas.

2. *OR,* Ser. IV, Vol. II, pp. 202–203, 248. See also "Proceedings of First Confederate Congress, End of Second Session," *SHSP,* XLVII (rpr. 1980), 18–19.

Louisiana Infantry as provost guard at Fayetteville, Arkansas, over the winter of 1861–1862, an officer of the regiment was appointed provost marshal of a general court-martial. This officer recorded many journeys on court business to various places in the state. In June, 1862, another soldier, Sergeant Edwin Fay, assumed the duties of provost marshal with the general court-martial of the Army of the Mississippi at Camp Priceville, near Tupelo, Mississippi. Fay likened his duties to that of a sheriff in a civilian court and told his wife in one of his many letters that he was responsible for recording court proceedings and testimony. Provost Marshal Fay is somewhat unusual in that he is the only noncommissioned officer positively identified as a provost marshal. His letters show him to have been an erudite man; his B.A. and M.A. from Harvard no doubt contributed to his appointment as a provost marshal. Another example of an officer who served as a provost marshal of a military court was Lieutenant Edward Neufville, Confederate States Marine Corps. In January, 1864, Neufville was ordered to duty with a naval general court-martial at Savannah, Georgia. As provost assignments to naval courts were a secondary duty for marine officers at Savannah, other marine officers undoubtedly saw provost service with the courts.[3]

Although the intent of the Articles of War was to provide for the trial of military offenders against military law, their imprecise wording could be construed as making civilians answerable to military courts. The wording of two particular articles is a case in point. The first, Article 56, stated: "Whoever shall relieve the enemy with money, victuals, or ammunition, or shall knowingly harbor or protect an enemy, shall suffer death, or such other punishment as shall be ordered by . . . a court-martial." Article 57 continued: "Whoever shall be convicted of holding correspondence with or giving intelligence to the enemy . . . shall suffer death."[4]

The practical application of these articles in the field and in the departments depended greatly upon individual commanders. These men and their subordinate officers established the codes and opinions, the attitudes, the standards of discipline, and the degree to which inhumanity would be tolerated in the imposition of discipline. It follows that their provost marshals assumed powers to a level compatible with the attitudes of their commanders. Some viewed the activities of the provost with irritation and were suspicious of what seemed to be

3. Tunnard, *A Southern Record,* 119; Fay, *"This Infernal War,"* 89, 93; Ralph W. Donnelly, *The History of the Confederate States Marine Corps* (Washington, N.C., 1976), 68–69. Neufville was relieved of provost duty on February 1.

4. *OR,* XV, 806.

the plenary power of the military police. Other commanders took the word *whoever* in the Articles of War to mean exactly that and gave their provost *carte blanche* in determining who was subject to military arrest.

A general order of September 8, 1862, ordered provost marshals in several counties of Mississippi and Louisiana to keep order and prevent contact with the enemy by either "citizens or soldiers." This order further directed that provost marshals would confine their duties to proper military jurisdiction in accordance with Articles 56 and 57. This left no doubt in the provost marshal's mind as to the extent of his jurisdiction. Although some provost officers exercised their wide powers with tact and sound judgment, others were tactless and arbitrary and proved unable to enforce the law without needless friction. The provost's assumption that they could apply Articles 56 and 57 to civilians aroused a strong reaction from Governor Thomas Moore of Louisiana. On October 2 he demanded of General Daniel Ruggles, who, as commander of the District of the Mississippi, had issued the order, whether the two articles applied to civilians. Moore was adamant that they did not, but he requested, if it proved there was a difference of opinion, that General Ruggles hold execution of the order in abeyance until such time as the views of President Davis could be ascertained. Ruggles, meantime, was warned by James Fuqua, his judge advocate and provost marshal general, that a military court had no authority to try civilians charged with spying.[5]

An incensed Governor Moore allowed Ruggles no time to answer. On October 3 he advised President Davis of Ruggles' order and expressed regret for the constant conflict with the military. Ruggles was soon dismissed. As he put it, the whole affair *might* not have prejudiced the president against him, but it was significant that at about the same time it surfaced, he was relieved and shifted to an unimportant command.[6]

Nor was trial of civilians by military tribunal the only question. Earlier in the war a large number of civilians had been arrested under cover of "An Act respecting alien enemies," which was approved by President Davis on August 8, 1861. Provost arrests of citizens and the search and seizure of premises and property had brought the face of military power home to the public as did no other measure during the war. The act was useful in the apprehension of persons holding allegiance to the old government, but its powers of arrest soon were so

5. *OR,* XV, 805–806, 894; Ser. II, Vol. IV, pp. 894–97.
6. *OR,* XV, 891–94.

abused that a special commission was established to review all arrests made under its authority. Many prisoners were subsequently released and the provost cautioned that they would be required to obey the writs of *habeas corpus,* and if judges released prisoners the provost could do nothing but appeal to the Confederate district judge. By November the adverse public reaction to military arrests was so strong that a second commission, consisting of a civilian judge and an army provost marshal, had to be set up in the Department of the West to investigate the many arrests.[7] The decisions of this commission also led to the release of many prisoners.

Contrary to general belief, military arrests of civilians were far less common in the Confederacy than in the United States, primarily because, unlike Abraham Lincoln, President Davis was only sparingly granted the right of suspension of the writ of *habeas corpus.* Davis' authority for suspension, first given him on February 27, 1862, for a very short period, was renewed in October, to extend until February, 1863, but was then withheld until February, 1864. This renewal, which was to expire in August, 1864, was limited in that suspension applied only to prisoners arrested directly by authority of Davis or the secretary of war. The writ was not again suspended in spite of the urgent pleas of the president.

Notwithstanding *habeas corpus,* the military continued to arrest civilians. This is obvious in a letter from Secretary of War Judah Benjamin to General Joseph Johnston, dated January 5, 1862, in which Benjamin berated Johnston for sending to Richmond prisoners arrested on suspicion. Johnston was told that without specific charges such prisoners could not be held. In April new legislation restricted provost powers of arrest of civilians to those committing crimes against the Confederacy. In February, 1863, James Seddon, Benjamin's replacement, advised Congress: "No arrests have been made at any time by any specific order or direction of this Department. The persons arrested have been taken either by officers of the Army commanding in the field or by provost-marshals exercising authority of a similar nature and the ground for arrest is or ought to be founded upon some necessity, or be justified as a proper precaution against an apparent danger." This policy, applied generally throughout the Confederacy, proved particularly helpful in the Department of East Tennessee, where disaffection with the Confederate cause was rampant. But even there the storm of protest provoked by arbitrary arrests was so strong that the provost

7. *OR,* Ser. II, Vol. II, pp. 1368–69, 1398–99.

were told to use the power conferred by Congress sparingly and delicately. Provost officers in some counties were told to "make no arrests [of civilians] unless you are forced to do so."[8]

By the summer of 1862 the authorities realized that one possible method of reducing unjust arrests of civilians was to require provost marshals to submit reports on the identity, number, and condition of prison inmates. In July provost in East Tennessee were instructed that as soon as any arrest was made, full details of the case and the names of any witnesses had to be forwarded to department headquarters. Other commands issued similar instructions. For instance, an order issued in the District of the Mississippi by General Ruggles—the one that had drawn fire from Governor Moore of Louisiana—specified penalties for provost marshals who did not submit reports on prisoners within twenty-four hours.[9]

The provost record in submitting these reports is checkered. Major George Washington Lee, provost marshal of Atlanta, advised the headquarters of the Department of South Carolina, Georgia, and Florida in November, 1862, that "I have the honor to inclose the report of prisoners now confined at this post." By early 1863 the adjutant general of the Confederacy made monthly reports on all civilians under military arrest mandatory in all departments. In April the Department of Alabama, Mississippi, and East Louisiana ordered strict compliance with this order. This was not the case in Florida. The provost marshal at Tallahassee reported in February, 1864, that no records of prisoners were available and some had been in confinement for months with no charges filed against them.[10] In spite of the best intentions, there were still injustices in the system, either because the message had not filtered through to the outer reaches of the nation or because of the arbitrary nature of some local commanders.

In both the Union and the Confederacy some cases of military arrests of civilians were highly conspicuous because of the prominence of the civilian in question or the unique circumstances of the case. In the North the arrest of Clement Vallandigham was well known. A parallel case in the Confederate States was the arrest of John Minor Botts, a prominent Virginia legislator and a determined enemy of secession. Arrested in March, 1862, for his "crimes

---

8. *OR,* Ser. II, Vol. II, pp. 1411, 1423; Thomas, *Confederate State of Richmond,* 83; *OR,* Ser. II, Vol. V, p. 838.

9. *OR,* Ser. II, Vol. IV, p. 826; XV, 805–806. Present-day practice is that custodians of offenders must submit within twenty-four hours a full report of the offense and the particulars of the person committing the offender to custody.

10. *OR,* Vol. X, Pt. 1, p. 639; Ser. IV, Vol. II, p. 459; Vol. XXIV, Pt. 3, p. 743; LIII, 308–309.

against the Confederacy," Botts was lodged temporarily in Castle Godwin, a Richmond provost prison, and then allowed to leave the city. Later he was arrested and freed on the same day and thereafter left strictly alone.

A second and more tragic case in the South was the "Great Gainesville Hanging" in Texas in the fall of 1862. This affair commenced with the discovery of a plot to restore Texas to the Union. Martial law was imposed in the disaffected area of the state and a large force of militia was called out. By October 1, mass arrests, totaling 60 or 70 men, had been made, and eventually the number rose to 150 or so. In short order 7 of the ringleaders were hanged under army arrangements and within a month 36 more went to the gallows.[11]

Notwithstanding efforts to prevent provost abuse of the power of arrest, the provost in many instances rode roughshod over the rights of the citizen. Their often blatantly overbearing manner is exemplified in one case in which a provost marshal arrested a civilian and then confiscated and sold his property at public auction.[12] The arrests of numerous civilians, often in the absence of any evidence, and their detention in military prisons, without knowing the charges against them, became intolerable to politicians. Some state governors saw the issue as yet another example of Confederate government interference with states' rights. The civilian judiciary also registered disapproval by actively working against the provost in the performance of their duties. Provost marshals in Texas in 1863 suffered the indignity of witnessing local magistrates free men who had been in custody for military offenses.[13] The incidence of obstruction of military justice rapidly increased when some judges thwarted the arrest and detention of men evading conscription.

The military in Texas, however, sometimes got its own back. Two cases in the spring of 1864 illustrate the "subversion of due judicial process by the military" and the "impotence of the civilian judiciary when confronted with the might of the army." The first case involved the arrest of five civilians in October, 1863, on charges of treason. General John Magruder, the officer ordering the arrests, admitted that because the writ of *habeas corpus* had not been suspended he had no power to arrest civilians, but he had done so because of "military necessity." Provost guardsmen put the five men in irons and took them to the military stockade at San Antonio, where they languished while their civilian lawyer attempted to obtain their release. In February, 1864, legislation

11. Philip Rutherford, "The Great Gainesville Hanging," *CWTI*, XVII (April, 1978), 12–20.

12. Edward Younger (ed.), *Inside the Confederate Government: The Diary of Robert Garlick Hill Kean* (New York, 1957), 42–43.

13. *OR*, XV, 978–79.

proposing that the commander of the Trans-Mississippi Department be authorized to suspend *habeas corpus* failed to pass Congress. Magruder therefore continued to have no legal authority for any further arrests.

Five months later the Texas Supreme Court, acting on a writ of *habeas corpus,* summoned General Magruder and Lieutenant Thomas E. Sneed, the officer commanding the San Antonio provost guard, to show cause why the five men should be held. The transfer of the five to civilian custody prompted the military to provide proof positive of the prisoners' intent to commit treason and to request that they be returned to military custody. That very night, March 25, a platoon of armed soldiers under the Austin provost marshal, Major J. H. Sparks, forcibly removed the men from the civilian jail and incarcerated them in the Austin military stockade. Magruder was duly summoned for contempt and pronounced guilty, although in the event the Texas Supreme Court, having in mind the ominous war situation, forbade "to punish him by imprisonment." For the five accused a bargain was arranged

> which would permit the sheriff to resume custody of the accused while allowing the military to maintain a guard over them. . . . Sparks . . . offered to return the prisoners if the court would authorize a provost detail to accompany them to the county jail. The court, however, refused to accept the prisoners unless they were surrendered unconditionally—but one of the justices quietly intimated . . . that if the prisoners were surrendered, the court would release them and make no subsequent attempt to interfere should the military again seize them! . . . Sparks surrendered the prisoners to the sheriff; the court discharged them; Sparks at once arrested them; and a military guard carried them off to a military stockade at Anderson.[14]

The second case again shows the power of the military, although this time it backfired. It involved one Andrew McKee, a purchasing agent for the Cotton Bureau, who, though paid by the military and wearing the uniform of a major, did not in fact hold a commission. In the spring of 1864 McKee was arrested by the army on charges of treason, espionage, and aiding the enemy and was sentenced to be shot. An application for *habeas corpus* to the Confederate District Court for West Louisiana on the grounds that McKee was a civilian and therefore not subject to military arrest was granted, but Brigadier General John

14. Robert L. Kerby, *Kirby Smith's Confederacy: The Trans-Mississippi South, 1863–1865* (New York, 1972), 270–75.

Walker, commanding the District of West Louisiana, adamantly refused to release McKee. Argument and counterargument led to a compromise whereby the army would surrender McKee to the court, which would prefer charges against him. To Walker's chagrin, as soon as McKee was turned over, the court promptly granted bail and McKee fled.[15]

Officers in the army also criticized the military legal and penal system. Robert E. Lee himself raised the matter with Jefferson Davis just before the Battle of Sharpsburg: "We require more promptness and certainty of punishment."[16] The subject of the punishment of offenders leads naturally into provost involvement with the Confederate States military prisons.

Provost responsibility in this area can be stated simply as the operation and administration of detention facilities and service prisons for the confinement of service offenders. The man responsible was General John H. Winder. Initially appointed inspector general of all camps, including the prisons, in the Richmond area, he later became the commander of the Department of Henrico and provost marshal general of Richmond. The unpopular Winder left Richmond in June, 1864, to become the commandant of Andersonville Prison. On July 26 he was placed in charge of all prisons in Alabama and Georgia and then in November became commissary general of all prisons east of the Mississippi, presumably including both Confederate States military prisons and prisoner of war camps. The Confederate roster in the *Southern Historical Society Papers* refers to Winder as "Commanding Prison Camps and Provost Marshal General."[17] When Winder died in February, 1865, he was replaced by Brigadier General Daniel Ruggles.

Winder's first command, the post of Richmond, had five departments: the Provost Marshal's Department, commanded by Major Isaac H. Carrington and consisting of a passport office and a police organization; the prisons for captured Federal soldiers; prisons for Confederate offenders and deserters from the army; a forwarding barracks for transient soldiers; and a staff department.[18]

The prisons used to hold Confederate offenders were Castle Lightning and Castle Thunder. The latter, the chief provost prison in the South, opened for business in August, 1862. It soon achieved notoriety in the army and was a

15. *Ibid.*, 274–75.

16. *OR*, Vol. XIX, Pt. 2, p. 597.

17. Warner, *Generals in Gray*, 340–41; Charles C. Jones, "A Roster of General Officers, Heads of Departments, Senators, Representatives, Military Organizations, &c., &c., in Confederate Service During the War Between the States," *SHSP*, I (rpr. 1977), 7.

18. *OR*, Ser. II, Vol. VII, p. 205. This organization was current as of May 31, 1864.

place best avoided by the wise soldier. A former tobacco warehouse, located on Cary Street near the Mayo Bridge, it held political prisoners, captured Union citizens, foreigners, deserters, Confederate soldiers undergoing punishment, court-martial prisoners, suspected spies, and captured Negroes. Only very rarely were Union soldiers held there. The initial population, about 250 men, was transferred from Castle Godwin, another provost prison. The prison commandant, Captain G. W. Alexander, and the prison enjoyed such a black reputation that soon soldier bards were proclaiming:

> I'd ruther be on the Grandfather Mountain
> A-taking the snow and rain
> Than to be in Castle Thunder
> A-wearin' the ball and chain.[19]

Stories were legion of prisoners suffering cruel and inhuman punishments: "bucking and gagging," wearing "barrel-shirts," beatings, and suspension by the thumbs. These stories, magnified by rumor, no doubt helped to ensure an orderly prison population and may have had some effect on discipline in the army as a whole, but by the spring of 1863 Alexander's vigorous discipline led to an investigation by Congress. Captain Alexander was acquitted of any wrongdoing, although the decision was not unanimous.[20] The population of Castle Thunder, reported to be several hundred in the summer of 1864, was mostly men from the Army of Northern Virginia. Presumably the prison population did not decrease measurably, for General Ewell, the city commandant during the evacuation, reported that "all the guard forces were required to take the prisoners from the Libby and Castle Thunder."[21]

Provost responsibilities in regard to courts-martial were not particularly onerous because the requirement was confined to the provision of some officers and clerks to the corps and district courts. But the drain on provost manpower was heavy in the operation of military prisons, which became increasingly expensive to maintain as the prison population expanded. This was inevitable as the war situation and home-front life deteriorated, leading to demoralization and a wave of crime, disloyalty, and desertion, which the provost had somehow to check. Often, imprisonment was the only recourse.

19. Thomas, *Confederate State of Richmond,* 106.
20. Beers, *Guide to the Archives,* 27; *OR,* Ser. II, Vol. V, pp. 871–924.
21. *OR,* Vol. XL, Pt. 3, p. 765. A complete list of the Castle Thunder prisoners was sent to Major D. B. Bridgford, provost marshal of Lee's army, in July, 1864 (*OR,* Vol. XLVI, Pt. 1, p. 1293).

If the war against disloyalty and desertion was to have even a fighting chance there had to be a means whereby the provost could first identify and then control those traveling within the Confederate States. This system, and how the provost ran it, had dramatic implications for life in the war-torn Confederacy.

7

Passports
Ubiquitous and Effective

*I am a man under authority, having soldiers under
me: and I say to this man, Go, and he goeth; and to
another, Come, and he cometh.*

MATTHEW, 8:9

The Confederacy, with a total white male population of perhaps 2.8 million in the states that seceded, and able to draw on about half a million more sympathizers in the border states, put into the field between 600,000 and 1.4 million men. The best estimate of Confederate army strength at its apex, 750,000 soldiers, or roughly one man in every four in uniform, represents a remarkable achievement. These figures lend credence to Grant's assertion that the Confederacy had robbed the cradle and the grave. Jefferson Davis served notice in 1864 that the war would go on "till the last man of this generation falls in his tracks and his children seize his musket and fight his battle."[1]

Mobilization of so many men over such a vast geographical area as the Confederacy created a gigantic movement control problem for the provost. This task was further complicated by one new aspect of the war: the use of railroads to convey troops and supplies rapidly from one battle front to another. To control troop movements effectively a widespread and pervasive apparatus of provost checkpoints, stations and units, and procedures had to be established. One of the devices hit upon to assist in controlling movement was the passport system, which was designed to "restrain stragglers and deserters, prevent communicating with the enemy, and detect spies."[2] Implementation of

---

1. These figures are from Long, *Civil War Day by Day,* 704–705. Interested readers would also do well to consult Thomas Leonard Livermore, *Numbers and Losses in the Civil War in America* (1901; rpr. Bloomington, 1957), and Randolph Harrison McKim, *The Numerical Strength of the Confederate Army* (New York, 1912). McKim believes Livermore's figures for the Confederate army are far too high. Davis' sentiments are in Foote, *Civil War,* III, 468.

2. Beers, *Guide to the Archives,* 260; "Proceedings of First Confederate Congress, End of Second Session, Third Session in Part," *SHSP,* XLVII (rpr. 1980), 47.

the system by the provost was perceived as yet more interference with the liberties of the citizen—in this case the assumed right to unhindered travel—and it brought additional odium down upon the provost. Such a system was very manpower-intensive and resulted in substantial numbers of able-bodied men being held back from the battles raging at the various fronts.

At first, passes were required only in the immediate vicinity of the armies. In the West, for example, Private Ephraim Anderson of the 1st Missouri Brigade recalled that following the evacuation of Corinth, Mississippi, on May 30, 1862, passes were necessary only when going into or coming out of the army's lines. Similarly, orders of the Army of Northern Virginia in early 1863 show that passports were required only in the army's lines. One such order illustrates both the reason for passes and the operation of the system: "I. The presence of citizens in the camps or within the lines . . . unless authorized is forbidden. Persons coming into the lines . . . must make it known to the provost-marshal. Citizens properly vouched for will be allowed to visit . . . with passports signed by division commanders. II. Corps commanders. . . . will cause the immediate arrest of all unauthorized persons. . . . to prevent spies and improper persons from remaining in the lines of the army."[3]

It proved impossible to confine the use of passports to the vicinity of the armies. Soon the provost were "requiring the civil population to carry passes miles away from the military lines." In the end, the passport system blanketed the Confederacy and her citizens. One writer categorizes the provost's management of pass controls throughout the nation and assumption of authority over the citizen as galling in the extreme. Their presence certainly became oppressively obvious. They took up position wherever travelers congregated at stage depots and train stations; they took seats on the trains and stages; they were everywhere they "could intercept travelers—to catch spies and traitors. Anyone not able to show a passport was . . . held until his identity could be established."[4] Because the apprehension of spies and disloyal persons was one of the main purposes of the passport system, the military police became the judges not only of the legitimacy of the passes that were grudgingly, often fearfully, tendered by the citizens, but they also decided who was known enough, loyal enough, and responsible enough to receive the coveted paper.

The authority under which the provost assumed the right to issue passports to soldiers and citizens was the general orders of the adjutant general of the

3. Anderson, *Memoirs,* 204; *OR,* Vol. XXV, Pt. 2, p. 629.
4. Owsley, *State Rights,* 52; Coulter, *Confederate States,* 395–96.

Confederacy. These orders show that in March, 1862, the provost marshal of Richmond had taken over from the secretary of war the responsibility for the issuance of passports. That prodigious diarist John B. Jones, the "Rebel war clerk," noted that by March 13 he was temporarily signing passports "issued by the authority of the Secretary of War. They are filled up and issued by three or four of the Provost Marshal's clerks."[5]

Meantime, farther west, the provost marshal general of the Department of East Tennessee, Colonel William M. Churchwell, dispatched blank passports to the deputy provost marshals of at least two counties, telling them to issue passports on their own responsibility. Churchwell cautioned his deputies that only he could approve applications for passports to visit other states, and under no circumstances would passports be issued to anyone wishing to cross the lines toward the enemy. Further, he warned that the passes of persons from other districts were to be carefully scrutinized, and the bearers of those found wanting were to be arrested. About a year later Churchwell's successor, Colonel John E. Toole, was directed to ensure that all applications for passports be made through the deputy provost marshals to him.[6] The reason for this change is not precisely known, but in view of East Tennessee's decided coolness for the Confederate cause, the department commander probably wanted the tightest possible control of passports. It may be, too, that he doubted the efficiency of the provost deputies.

Farther south, although somewhat later, the Department of Alabama, Mississippi, and East Louisiana took a similar step. On July 1, 1864, a department order revoked the authority of the provost marshal general to issue passports for the purpose of passing through the lines. Under the new policy such passes could be issued only directly by the headquarters. As the provost marshal general was an officer on the staff of the department commander, at that time Major General Stephen D. Lee, one wonders who, short of Lee himself, authorized the issuance of these passes. No explanation was given for the revocation of the authority. Department correspondence also furnishes a good example of the passport procedure as it functioned at the unit level. Early in 1865 Brigadier General Lawrence Ross, commanding a cavalry brigade in the department, directed that all passes for movement beyond the lines of his brigade would be authorized by his provost marshal, Lieutenant J. P. Alex-

---

5. Beers, *Guide to the Archives,* 268; Jones, *Rebel War Clerk's Diary,* 70.
6. *OR,* Ser. II, Vol. II, p. 1423; Vol. XXIII, Pt. 2, p. 731.

ander. This officer was required to maintain a record of all passes issued and note the time of their return.[7]

Richmond is a good place to start in examining the operation of the passport system. The dramatic increase in population, the large numbers of transient soldiers and civilians, and the city's proximity to the front made passports essential for the control of movement. At first, only soldiers were required to produce some recognizable authority for their visits to the city, but the system soon broadened to include civilians who had business with or wished to visit the army. Eventually passports became mandatory for anyone leaving the city, even those who wished simply to go to their homes.[8] This policy gave the provost the power to decide who should be classed as fit to receive passports; military exigency had provided a ready, convenient, and viable justification for the exercise of power over the citizens.

The requirement for passports in Richmond had originally been a feature of the martial law imposed on the capital on March 1, 1862, but they proved so useful that they were *de rigeur* for the rest of the war. General John H. Winder established a passport office soon after taking up his appointment in June, 1861. This office, complete with guards and clerks, was reestablished in the Winder Building at the corner of 9th and Broad streets in the western part of the city on March 12, 1862. Reportedly, the office was "filthy" and the clerks were "rowdy."[9] The larger office was necessary to accommodate the swarms of people who required passes; the guards were present, with bayonets fixed, to control the crowds, which grew larger because of the requirement that all persons leaving or entering the city have a military pass. Those who journeyed to Richmond by rail found that along the way their names had been passed to the provost marshal. Once in the city, the hotels in which they put up would, the morning after their arrival, provide the free and unsolicited service of ensuring that the Provost Marshal's Office knew of their whereabouts.[10] Those leaving the city received similar attention.

7. *OR,* Vol. XXXIX, Pt. 2, p. 680; Vol. XLIX, Pt. 1, p. 998.

8. Bill, *Beleaguered City,* 104.

9. *OR,* Vol. LI, Pt. 2, p. 482; Thomas, *Confederate State of Richmond,* key to city map following p. 22. *Ibid.,* note 39, indicates that the building also housed the provost marshal, medical director, and headquarters of the Department of Henrico. The original location of the passport office is not given. Jones, *Rebel War Clerk's Diary,* 69–70; Bill, *Beleaguered City,* 104, also refers to the filthy state of the offices and the rowdy clerks who bullied applicants.

10. Thomas, *Confederate State of Richmond,* 82.

The experiences of two soldiers who had occasion to visit the passport office are revealing of the *modus operandi* of the Richmond military police. The first, Edmund Patterson of the 9th Alabama Infantry, visited the passport office in November, 1862, to obtain papers for travel from Richmond. He was directed to the office of Sergeant B. M. Crow, presumably a well-known location, for Patterson commented, "What soldier in the army of Northern Virginia does not know where that is?" Mingling with a large crowd outside the worthy Crow's door, Patterson became suspicious when he observed that those who entered did not reemerge. Patterson assumed that they were forced to remain in the building at least overnight. Averse to being cooped up until his train left the next day, Patterson made a hasty departure. The other soldier, John Worsham of the 21st Virginia Infantry, Stonewall Brigade, had a similar experience in early December, when he attempted to get a pass permitting him to leave Richmond by the next available train. Worsham, too, was ordered to report to Sergeant Crow, who it appears customarily conducted such applicants under guard to their units. "I did not intend to submit to this indignity," said the young Virginian, who forthwith decamped from the vicinity of Crow's office.[11]

Other personal accounts testify to the efficiency of the provost in enforcing the passport regulations. Alexander Hunter of the 17th Virginia Infantry recalled that illicit visits to Richmond to relieve the boredom of camp life were a hazardous business because all access routes were picketed by provost to prevent any soldier without a pass from entering the city. Once in Richmond the soldier on "French leave" had to exercise great caution to avoid the provost patrols that roamed the streets: "Woe to any poor soul who fell into their clutches; he was ignominiously hurled into Castle Thunder for the day." The intuitive cunning of the ordinary Johnny Reb sometimes came to his rescue, though. An example is Hunter's description of a "dodge" worked on the provost: "We got muskets and equipments and walked boldly out on the

11. John G. Barrett (ed.), *Yankee Rebel: The Civil War Journal of Edmund DeWitt Patterson* (Chapel Hill, 1966), 80–81. The editor states in a footnote that "Patterson very wisely did not attempt to travel without a passport. The ubiquitous and efficient provost guards could arrest anyone traveling without proper papers." Patterson visited the passport office on November 18. See Worsham, *One of Jackson's Foot Cavalry*, 92–93; E. Leslie Spence, "Reports of the First, Seventh and Seventeenth Virginia Regiments in 1862," *SHSP*, XXXVIII (rpr. 1977), 262–63. In a brief description of the burning of Richmond (H. H. Sturgis, "About the Burning of Richmond," *Confederate Veteran*, XVII [rpr. 1983], 474), one Confederate soldier recalled being on duty during the evacuation "at the Soldier's Home, more generally known as Crow's Nest, in charge of Sgt. Crow. The Home was a stopping point for soldiers going on furlough or returning to their commands, and also a place to keep any soldiers who were in Richmond without leave."

streets, demanding the passports of every man we met, and playing the part of Winder's pets to perfection. . . . whenever we saw the bona fide creature of the provost marshal's coming we dived down the first alley or into the first store we came to."

As these escapades were carried out in broad daylight it may have been that provost guardsmen wore no badge or device identifying them as such. Unfortunately, Hunter does not say how he could recognize the real provost. Surely he did not know every one of Richmond's provost by sight. Was it that provost squads were remarkable for their smart bearing and marching when on duty? Or could it be that Confederate provost, like their Union counterparts, wore a metal star that would have been difficult to obtain and copy? Or is it possible that provost "insignia" was as simple and as easily recognizable as fixed bayonets when on duty? This was the case, according to Joseph B. Polley of the Texas Brigade. From a police point of view it makes sense; better to threaten with a bayonet first, saving shooting as the last resort. To take it one step further, did Confederate provost carry one other form of insignia—a baton to persuade the unruly to behave? In Stonewall Jackson's corps men detailed to take care of the wounded wore a "prescribed badge." Therefore, it seems logical that another group of men who had specific tasks to perform, the provost, would have had their own insignia. There is no definitive answer.[12]

It was obvious, too, that the passes, mostly handwritten on crude brown paper, were highly susceptible to forgery. Johnny Reb was not above such tinkering if it would smooth his way. One North Carolina soldier, stationed at Wilmington in January, 1863, complained that his regiment was bothered by the provost because so few could imitate the commanding general's signature. When a soldier could not forge a simple pass, dealers in illegally obtained travel documents could provide the necessary paper. Business was brisk. Many of these surreptitious transactions used as their stock in trade passes sold by provost guardsmen for a little ready cash with which to enjoy the big city. A Louisiana gunner, Lieutenant Napier Bartlett of the renowned Washington Artillery of New Orleans, noted that the provost were quick to find fault with the passes tendered to them. During a trip to Richmond in January, 1863, a

12. Hunter, *Johnny Reb and Billy Yank*, 124, 607; Francis A. Lord, *Civil War Collector's Encyclopedia* (Harrisburg, 1963), 137. A photo shows a Union eight-pointed star enscribed "Provost Guard Birney's Brigade." J. B. Polley, "Concernin' of a Hog," *Confederate Veteran*, V (rpr. 1983), 56, states that bayonets were customary provost insignia. Colonel G. F. R. Henderson, *Stonewall Jackson and the American Civil War* (1898; rpr. New York, 1943), 643, refers to badges for ambulance attendants in the Confederate army.

suspicious provost marshal first lectured Bartlett on the propriety of reporting for duty and then scrutinized his pass askance.[13]

On the other side of the fence, Lieutenant LeGrand Wilson, a member of the 42d Mississippi Infantry, recalled his experiences as a provost officer in Richmond in June, 1862. An officer and twenty men from the regiment were on duty each day until 6 P.M. stopping every man to determine if each had a valid pass signed by "General Lee." Wilson was horrified to see two guardsmen, thirteen-year-old boys, halt President Davis and request his pass. Wilson's apology for their actions was presumably accepted because Davis subsequently invited the two lads to dinner. Trouble erupted later on, when the provost marshal of Richmond decided that only passes signed by himself would be acceptable.[14] This step was no doubt taken to reduce the opportunity for soldiers to take advantage of forged travel documents; presumably the provost marshal's signature was well known to all members of the provost.

As the war situation worsened and desperate days faced the Confederacy, often even valid passes were not security against arrest. Late in September, 1864, the panic in the city caused by the loss of Fort Harrison led to the call-out of every available local defense organization. As well, the provost arrested every able-bodied man they could find, even those with legitimate passes. By November, with Grant thundering at Richmond's door, "grim" provost sentinels were busily engaged in seizing all men from fifteen to fifty-five, regardless of the papers they carried, and sending them directly to the front.[15] These were desperate days indeed! In four short months blue-coated provost would be checking passes in Richmond.

In the rest of Virginia and elsewhere in the Confederate States, pass controls were firmly in place. Because of its front-line geographical position, Virginia is a good place to get a feel for how the passport system operated throughout the Confederacy. Before the first Christmas of the war it appears that no passport regulations were in effect. Early in December, 1861, Major R. L. T. Beale, a

13. James Reese, "Private Soldier Life—Humorous Features," *Confederate Veteran,* XVI (rpr. 1983), 164; Napier Bartlett, *Military Record of Louisiana Including Biographical and Historical Papers Relating to the Military Operations of the State* (1874; rpr. Baton Rouge, 1964), 172.

14. LeGrand James Wilson, *The Confederate Soldier* (Memphis, 1973), 88–89. The 42d Mississippi was also required to furnish guards for the Federal prisoners on Belle Isle. See the illustration of a Provost Marshal's Office in *ibid.* Hunter, *Johnny Reb and Billy Yank,* 599; Bill, *Beleaguered City,* 205–206.

15. Thomas, *Confederate State of Richmond,* 183; Richard J. Sommers, *Richmond Redeemed: The Siege at Petersburg* (New York, 1981), 159; Bevier, *History of the First and Second Missouri Confederate Brigades,* 452.

provost marshal in northern Virginia, confused and unsure of his authority, queried the secretary of war regarding his power to govern movement between Virginia and Maryland. Beale felt that unless he could control such movement his duties as provost marshal could not be effectively carried out, and for all he knew deserters and any military information they possessed could cross the lines at will. Secretary of War Judah Benjamin, already anticipating military requirements, replied that authority for such movement was at the discretion of the military. He would not interfere with any precautions that the army considered prudent.[16]

Information on provost activity elsewhere in Virginia reveals that pass controls had become a permanent part of provost duties in some commands. Stonewall Jackson's strict approach to military discipline became apparent early in the war. In November, 1861, he prohibited any officer from leaving camp without a written pass specifying whether the officer was on public or private business. His regimental commanders, considering this an unwarranted slight on the officers, complained to Jackson. Stonewall's reply left no doubt as to who was in command and reminded them that incompetency or slackness had resulted in officers and men visiting Winchester without authority, thus disorganizing their commands. The order stood.

John Casler, a private in the 27th Virginia Infantry of the Stonewall Brigade, recalled that some soldiers of his regiment who had decided to visit Winchester were fearful of arrest by the provost stationed in that Shenandoah Valley town. Regulations published by Jackson in May, 1862, prohibited visits to the town except by those who had a pass signed by their brigade commander. The provost were directed to check that every soldier in Winchester had a valid pass. Those who did not were to be immediately returned under guard to their units.[17] The order was dated the same day as the Battle of Winchester so it must have been published almost as that luckless Federal, General Nathaniel P. "Commissary" Banks, was bounced out of the town.[18] Ever anxious to pursue a beaten foe, Jackson would have strictly enforced the order to ensure that every man

16. *OR,* V, 990–91, 996–97.

17. E. S. Riley, *"Stonewall Jackson" : A Thesaurus of Anecdotes of And Incidents in the Life of Lieut.-Gen. Thomas Jonathan Jackson, CSA* (Annapolis, Md., 1920), 58–59; Casler, *Four Years in the Stonewall Brigade,* 60; *OR,* Vol. XII, Pt. 3, p. 900.

18. Banks received the sobriquet "Mr. Commissary" after one retreat during the Valley campaign when he was forced to abandon his wagon train and supplies to Jackson. See G. B. Philpot, "A Maryland Boy in the Confederate Army," *Confederate Veteran,* XXIV (rpr. 1983), 314; John C. Stiles, "Mr. Commissary Banks," *Confederate Veteran,* XXIV (rpr. 1983), 496.

was with his command. In Joseph E. Johnston's army, too, stringent regulations concerning passes had been promulgated in March, 1862. Before the move to the Peninsula a special order announced that unauthorized personnel either in or attempting to enter the town of Orange Court House would be arrested by the provost.[19]

The change in command brought about by Johnston's wound at Fair Oaks reinforced the passport system. In the autumn, as Robert E. Lee moved north into Maryland, instructions were issued to prevent unauthorized visits to Maryland towns. A special order of the Army of Northern Virginia in September, 1862, strictly forbade visits of officers and men to Frederick City unless they were on official business and had a pass signed by their division commanders. The provost marshal in the town was ordered to clear it of all unauthorized soldiers.[20]

Following the return to Virginia after the repulse at Sharpsburg, the army continued to enforce the pass regulations. A general order published by General Longstreet in late November decreed that every road leading to Fredericksburg would be picketed by provost to keep soldiers out of the town. Any absentee found in Fredericksburg was to be arrested and the firmest measures were to be taken to prevent "excesses" by the troops. The relatively long stay at Fredericksburg and the attractions it held for the troops, who sought relief from the harsh winter and the drudgery of the camps, strengthened the requirement for a guard in the town. Provost efficiency is testified to by one Texas private on sick leave in Fredericksburg, who was routed out of a hotel bed in the middle of the night so the provost could check his pass. Nor were officers immune to the power of the provost. Captain James Nisbet of the 66th Georgia recalled that while he was in ill health in December, 1862, he was fortunate that "the physician's signature prepared me for the certain inspection of the provost guard who paraded the streets with orders to arrest all officers and men who could not show in writing a good reason for being away from their command."[21]

For the remainder of the war pass regulations were a feature of the Army of Northern Virginia wherever it moved. During the Gettysburg campaign, as the army successively occupied a number of Pennsylvania towns, provost were

19. Special Order 30, March 17, 1862, *OR*, Vol. LI, Pt. 2, pp. 504–505.

20. Duncan, "Marylanders and the Invasion of 1862," 186; Taylor, *General Lee His Campaigns in Virginia*, 123.

21. *OR*, Vol. LI, Pt. 2, p. 651; William Andrew Fletcher, *Rebel Private Front and Rear* (Austin, 1954), 13; Nisbet, *4 Years on the Firing Line*, 80.

quickly inserted to prevent unauthorized entry to the towns. Lee was determined to end any excesses by his ill-dressed and ill-equipped but magnificent fighting men. He was equally determined to keep his army together and in perfect fighting order to meet any eventuality. At Gettysburg, for example, a bandsman of the terribly decimated 26th North Carolina of Henry Heth's division, when told to go to the rear, expressed his concern that to do so without written authority would not be safe.[22] The following year, in the face of Grant's relentless advance, pass controls were vital to keep every man in the thinning Confederate battle line. The stream of stragglers and the flood of deserters, seemingly impervious to entreaty and the desperate state of the cause, had to be checked or utter ruin would result. In the Shenandoah following Jubal Early's 1865 disaster at Cedar Creek and the virtual disintegration of his army, the provost guard scoured the countryside picking up any men who were out of camp without passes.[23] Meantime, Lee's army clung grimly to its trenches in front of Richmond, the city that had become the Confederacy and the cause.

The largest department of the Confederacy, with the exception of the Trans-Mississippi, was the Department of Alabama, Mississippi, and East Louisiana. Here, too, it had been necessary to impose passport regulations, initially only in the vicinity of the armies, but then, like everywhere else, the system had rapidly expanded throughout the department. A good illustration is the establishment of the passport apparatus in New Orleans, the South's largest city. In the ominous atmosphere engendered by the approach of Admiral David Farragut and his fleet it had been considered essential that Major General Mansfield Lovell, commanding the defense of the city, receive every power and authority that could possibly assist him in turning back the Federals. He certainly had authority to control movement; a case in point was his order that every person in the city must carry a pass signed by the provost marshal.[24] It was unfortunate for the Confederacy that his powers of command of the military and naval forces in the city were not so all-encompassing.

In Mississippi, a district within the department, orders were issued in March, 1862, that anyone who attempted to evade guard posts would be regarded as suitable for target practice. Those who survived the fusillade or any others suspected of trying to evade the posts would be arrested and turned over

22. Coddington, *Gettysburg Campaign*, 163–64; Julius Leinbach, "Regiment Band of the 26th North Carolina," ed. Donald McCorkle, *Civil War History*, IV (rpr. 1963), 230.

23. G. W. Nichols, *A Soldier's Story of His Regiment (61st Georgia) and Incidentally of the Lawton-Gordon-Evans Brigade Army Northern Virginia* (1898; rpr. Kennesaw, Ga., 1961), 202.

24. Owsley, *State Rights*, 154–55; *OR*, VI, 857–58; XV, 740.

to the provost marshal. Infraction of the passport regulations was viewed as a serious matter indeed. In Memphis Private James Henry Fauntleroy of the 1st Missouri Cavalry described how one hundred men of his regiment had spent a week in the city as provost arresting all men without passes. Another Missouri regiment, the 2d Infantry, performed similar duties at Tupelo, Mississippi, in June probably helping to ensure that the Tupelo end of Bragg's rail move to Chattanooga in July, 1862, worked smoothly. A Tennessee soldier recalled the generous nature of a provost marshal in another town in Mississippi who furnished him with travel documents supposedly good from Florence, Alabama, to Grenada, Mississippi. The soldier was astonished: "This was a wide territory for the authority of a petty provost to cover."[25]

In Alabama, too, the provost and their notorious passports were in full sway. That unique and effective instrument of Confederate propaganda in Europe, the *Index,* had in its columns for August 27, 1863, a six-month-old order issued by the Mobile, Alabama, provost marshal directing that hotel and boardinghouse proprietors forward to the provost the names of all persons resident in their establishments for longer than twenty-four hours.[26]

In every situation in which the Confederacy faced special peril tight controls were placed on movement. This was the case in the summer of 1863 at Jackson, Mississippi, where Johnston was trying to concentrate enough men to pry open the Federal vise on Vicksburg. Johnston's very first general order at Jackson warned that only those with passes from the provost marshal or the headquarters of the army would be allowed to leave the lines.[27] Johnston's precautions and his presence forty miles east of Vicksburg could do nothing to relieve the Confederate garrison. Pemberton surrendered on July 4.

To the north, the Department of East Tennessee was particularly interested in any means that would help control the largely hostile population. As early as November, 1861, Colonel S. A. M. Wood of the 7th Alabama, provost marshal at Chattanooga, told Braxton Bragg, commanding at Pensacola, Florida, that under martial law regulations he had forbidden anyone from leaving the city, by any means, without an exit permit. Provost guards were also deployed along the Kentucky-Tennessee border to stop anyone leaving Tennessee without a valid passport. It was hoped that this would end the crossing of the lines by those who

25. *OR,* Vol. X, Pt. 2, p. 337; Calkin, "Elk Horn to Vicksburg," 14; Anderson, *Memoirs,* 203, 212, 500. The 2d Missouri was on provost duty at Tupelo from June 9 to July 29, 1862 (Hubbard, *Notes of a Private,* 68).

26. *Index,* III (August 27, 1863), 278.

27. General Order 1, June 5, 1863, *OR,* Vol. XXIV, Pt. 3, p. 950.

were passing information on Confederate strength and dispositions to the enemy. Passports were not considered necessary for Confederate citizens or persons sympathetic to the Confederate cause who remained within the Confederate States.[28] Here, too, the provost decided who was loyal enough to receive a pass.

At a time when many Union supporters opted to leave the new Confederacy or when they were expelled, the provost were required to arrange the departure of these hostile elements. The provost marshal general of the department, Colonel William M. Churchwell, was instrumental in the expulsion of, among others, the family of the notorious Unionist Parson William G. Brownlow. On April 21, 1862, Churchwell advised Brownlow's wife that she and her children had thirty-six hours in which to leave the Confederacy. She was told that passports for the journey would be issued by his office. Churchwell handled the Brownlow affair himself but then on May 1 issued instructions to his deputies regarding the authorization of passports to such persons in the future.[29]

Nepotism hindered or enhanced, depending on one's interest and involvement, equitable application of passport regulations. Private William W. Heartsill found no difficulty in obtaining a pass because his cousin was a staff officer with department headquarters. His travel permit, dated May 13, 1863, and personally signed by Colonel John E. Toole, Churchwell's replacement as provost marshal general, allowed him to visit Tullahoma, Tennessee, as long as he did not reveal any information that might be damaging to the Confederacy.[30] Braxton Bragg's army was at Tullahoma on May 22 and withdrew south of the Tennessee River late in June. Those with no provost connections were not as fortunate as Heartsill, as Private J. B. Polley of the Texas Brigade discovered in January, 1864, in Tennessee, when he and some companions were arrested as stragglers while on a foraging expedition.[31]

The most southerly command, the Department of South Carolina, Georgia, and Florida, was slow to recognize the value of passports and movement control, at least in Atlanta in July, 1862. The system had not been imposed in one of the largest cities in the Confederacy so it seems logical that it would not have been in effect elsewhere in the department. Captain G. J. Foreacre, the provost marshal of Atlanta, complained bitterly of the hundreds of men roam-

28. *OR*, IV, 249, 397.

29. *OR*, Ser. II, Vol. I, p. 929; Ser. II, Vol. II, p. 1423.

30. W. W. Heartsill, *Fourteen Hundred and 91 Days in the Confederate Army* (1876; rpr. ed. Bell I. Wiley, Jackson, Tenn., 1954), 128.

31. J. B. Polley, "Texans Foraging for Christmas," *Confederate Veteran*, III (rpr. 1983), 362.

ing the city without papers or with forged ones. Many of these miscreants, he noted, were officers.[32] Foreacre warned his superiors that because he had no authority he was powerless to correct the situation.

Department provost must soon have received the required authority for Samuel R. Watkins of the 1st Tennessee described in detail his arrest by the Montgomery, Alabama, provost for being without a pass.[33] Isaac Hermann, a gunner with the Army of Tennessee, related his troubles with the Macon and Atlanta provost. Before the Battle of Chickamauga, Hermann was granted a thirty-day furlough to recuperate from illness. His battery commander, unaware of the furlough, listed Hermann as a deserter, and he was arrested by the Macon provost. The local provost marshal, a Major Roland, declared Hermann's papers to be forgeries. The colonel of the 46th Georgia, who happened to be present, interceded on Hermann's behalf after a gunpoint confrontation between Hermann and Roland and convinced the provost marshal to allow Hermann to report back to his hospital. Obviously, the colonel was a smooth talker—shoving a gun in the face of a provost marshal was not recommended procedure. Eventually Hermann was discharged from active duty because of ill health and returned to Atlanta, where he served as a hospital steward. He was soon sent on a foraging expedition to secure food for the hospital. In a hurry to be on his way, he neglected to carry his travel papers and as a result was arrested at Griffin, Alabama, in December, 1863. Some of the staff of Captain Willis, the Griffin provost marshal, attempted to "buck and gag" Hermann, provoking him into physically resisting. The lucky Hermann was rescued from this wrangle by another colonel who berated the provost marshal as "not fit for a hog herder much less to be in command of human beings."[34] Hermann was free again, and although he was returned to Atlanta under guard, he was able to convince an Atlanta provost officer, Captain Beebee, of his innocence. Hermann wasted no time in returning to the hospital to recover his papers.

Sherman's advance on Atlanta highlighted the pressing need for strict pass regulations in the Army of Tennessee. At Dalton a regiment was posted to ensure that every officer and man in the town possessed a valid pass. A private

32. *OR,* Ser. IV, Vol. II, pp. 9–10; Escott, *After Secession,* 131.

33. Samuel R. Watkins, *"Co. Aytch" Maury Grays First Tennessee Regiment or A Sideshow of the Big Show* (1900; rpr. Jackson, Tenn., 1952), 184–85. Arrest may have been a unique experience for Watkins. His regiment, the 1st Tennessee, and presumably Watkins himself, had been on provost duty at Chattanooga in April and at Shelbyville in May, 1862.

34. Hermann, *Memoirs,* 133, 135, 137–39, 159–65.

soldier of the regiment related how he and a companion took advantage of their position to demand a pass from Joseph E. Johnston. In the Army of Tennessee many men who left their commands without authority had only one thought in mind: to desert and get away from the fighting. Deserters who were apprehended suffered prompt and fatal justice, as fifteen of the breed found out when they were shot at Dalton in the spring of 1864.[35] In areas that were menaced by an advancing enemy, stern, even draconic measures were implemented to deter troops from leaving their commands.

Such was the case in South Carolina in the spring of 1862, when the excitement caused by the fall of New Orleans led to the imposition of martial law in Charleston. General John C. Pemberton, then commanding the Department of South Carolina, Georgia, and Florida, appointed Colonel Johnson Hagood of the 1st South Carolina provost marshal and ordered him to establish a system so thorough that "a *dog* could not enter the town without the knowledge of the provost marshal and his ability to lay hands upon said dog at any moment . . . was required." Hagood delegated responsibility for pass control for military personnel and civilians to Captain W. J. Gayer and Mr. W. E. Dingle respectively. Federal spies and informants were presumed to be present in large numbers, and therefore the strictest controls were deemed necessary. Provost regulations stipulated that no one could leave the city without a written permit from the provost marshal, and anyone entering the city had to report to the provost. So all would be aware of the regulations, extracts appeared in the city's newspapers. Not surprisingly, the movements of soldiers to the city or within it were tightly regulated, and even officers were subject to strict controls. Those from camps outside the city had to report their presence to the provost on entering the city, and those stationed in Charleston were required to obtain special permission to leave their camps.[36]

These regulations remained in force as long as the city was under martial law. As time passed and it became obvious that the Federal navy could not immediately batter its way into Charleston, pass controls were relaxed and eventually fell into disuse. The chief of staff at Charleston was informed of this laxity in October, 1863, by a senior officer complaining that men were in the city without passes or with forged ones. According to the complainant, many of these men were committing offenses such as plundering, and many were proba-

35. P. F. Lewis, Letter to Editor, *Confederate Veteran*, II (rpr. 1983), 332; Bromfield Lewis Ridley, *Battles and Sketches of the Army of Tennessee* (1906; rpr. Dayton, 1978), 283–86.
36. Hagood, *Memoirs*, 71, 74–76, 79.

bly deserters. He suggested that pass controls be reinstituted and the provost be ordered to arrest offenders.[37]

The far West of the Confederacy, the Trans-Mississippi Department, was also subject to passports and movement control. An unidentified provost marshal in eastern Texas was ordered to establish the strictest military discipline and arrest all suspicious characters, most of whom were either spies or marauders. Private William W. Heartsill had occasion to recall his earlier quest for a pass at Shreveport, Louisiana, just before Christmas of 1863. Heartsill and some comrades must have been traveling without passes, for he noted that "the first 'Provo Guard' we met, we enquired for the Provost Marshal's office, before they had time to ask us for our papers." The provost marshal, Colonel W. R. Shivers, issued a pass ordering Heartsill and his friends to report to their command.[38]

Even in the most remote parts of the Trans-Mississippi passport controls were in effect. In March, 1864, the District of the Indian Territory imposed passport regulations. Brigadier General D. H. Cooper, the district commander, noted that among the many shady characters roaming the district were spies, deserters, conscript evaders, traitors, renegades, and other marauders, including the horse-stealing "gentry." He directed enrolling officers to act as provost marshals responsible for the apprehension and detention of all such riffraff. The newly appointed provost officials were especially cautioned that anyone attempting to cross the lines without proper authority was to be arrested and the details reported to the district chief provost marshal, Lieutenant Samuel R. Mebane.[39]

There is no doubt that passport controls were helpful and indeed essential to the war effort, but they had drawbacks. One of the unfortunate side effects was the inevitable but regrettable extension of controls to furloughed men. Orders and other published instructions on passports refer specifically to men on furlough, as do numerous reminiscences by veterans. A fairly common recollection was how men gathered at railway stations to catch leave transport blanched at hearing the cry, "All furloughed officers and men to report to the provost marshal."[40] All too often this call meant a hurried return to the front. Certainly furloughed men in Richmond in 1864 and 1865 knew that furloughs would not prevent their being swept up by the provost. At a time of emergency,

37. *OR,,* Vol. XXVIII, Pt. 2, pp. 386–87.
38. *OR,* Vol. XXVI, Pt. 2, pp. 125–26; Heartsill, *Fourteen Hundred and 91 Days,* 187.
39. *OR,* Vol. XXXIV, Pt. 2, pp. 1045–46.
40. Hunter, *Johnny Reb and Billy Yank,* 598.

personnel proceeding on leave were very vulnerable; to get home they had to congregate where transportation was available or pass through cities and towns en route. Unfortunately for them, these very places were generally the abode of the provost. One wonders how many men, gathered at central points, anxiously listening for the whistle of the leave train, suddenly found themselves hustled back to the front. German troops on the eastern front in World War II, awaiting leave transport in centers behind the front, could easily identify with Johnny Reb; "Jerry," too, would have known the despair caused by the abrupt cancellation of hard-earned leave.

Men returning from leave were also at the whim of movement control authorities. Generally these men were held at rail or other depots behind the front until sufficiently large groups had been gathered to justify the dispatch of the necessary transportation. Short of wagons and rolling stock and hard-pressed to maintain the flow of essential supplies to the armies, the Confederacy could not afford to waste precious transportation resources. Nor could manpower be wasted; if the men were to march to their units, as they usually did as the transportation network progressively deteriorated, it was better to send large groups and thus economize on the number of escorts required to ensure that the men proceeded directly to their commands. As an example of this policy, in March, 1862, officers or men returning to the Army of Northern Virginia from leave were not allowed to pass forward of Orange Court House. Orange was an ideal location at which to hold the men: it was on the railroad from Richmond and Gordonsville yet far enough to the rear to make it secure. From Orange troops could be sent west to Stonewall Jackson in the Shenandoah, or they could reinforce Johnston as necessary. A similar policy was in effect in the western armies. In January 1865, General Joseph Wheeler forbade officers and men on leave from entering the operational area of his command without his express approval.[41]

Another inevitable side effect of the passport system, and one with strong political repercussions, was its impact on civilians, who felt that martial law and conscription had already amply infringed on their liberties. Civilians found the imposition of military authority over their right of free travel intolerable. Loyal citizens could perhaps see the necessity for controls at or near the fronts, but the provost's demands for passes in areas of the Confederacy far removed from the military lines left them unsympathetic and outraged. One recurring complaint was that obtaining passports meant great inconvenience because

41. *OR,* Vol. LI, Pt. 2, pp. 504–505; Vol. XLVII, Pt. 2, p. 998.

passport offices were only open at certain times of the day. In Charleston, for example, the offices were open from 8 A.M. to 1 P.M. and from 4 P.M. to 7 P.M., but time and effort still had to be expended in getting a passport even though the Charleston office was better organized than most, with separate desks for civilians, Negroes, and the military.[42]

Some remarks made by Major Isaac H. Carrington, provost marshal, on an April 5, 1864, listing of provost employees indicate that the Richmond passport office was open from 6 to 7 A.M. and from 8 A.M. to 2:30 P.M. On August 8 Carrington ordered that office hours on Sundays would be from 6 to 10 A.M. and from 4 to 6 P.M. For military purposes a clerk would be on duty all day Sunday. The press of applicants for passports was so great that a guard with fixed bayonets was needed to keep order. Human nature being what it is, some provost were tactless and tyrannical in the extreme in dealing with the public. A Mississippi senator complained bitterly that one provost guard had threatened to run him through with his bayonet.[43]

Reaction to such conduct was so strong that even the president received complaints: "It seems that instead of these disgraceful, lawless, unfeeling and impolite *men,* not Confederate soldiers in the strict sense, being at the front . . . they . . . are running around over town and country insulting even weak unprotected women." Virtually every complaint echoed this sentiment: the provost should be put into the fighting, where every able-bodied man was desperately needed. Even congressmen could not travel without passports. A Georgia legislator and a Texas senator expressed indignation that they had to obtain passes on the same basis as did Negroes. To appease its members, in 1864 Congress had special passports issued "for the gaze of the 10,000 provost marshals who line all the highways and byways."[44] Presumably, these were "open" passports—good anywhere, anytime—and absolutely provost-proof.

Even the military were disillusioned and disgusted with the system. Furloughed men often missed the infrequent trains because of the need to obtain passports. In view of the crumbling railroads, any delay could cost days in

42. Owsley, *State Rights,* 52; Hagood, *Memoirs,* 79.

43. War Department, Collection of Confederate Records, Record Group 109, Chap. IX, Vol. 250; List of Officers and Employees in Provost Marshal Office, Richmond, April 5, 1864, Department of Archives and Manuscripts, Louisiana State University; Bill, *Beleaguered City,* 104; Barrett, *Yankee Rebel,* 80–81; "Proceedings of First Confederate Congress, First Session Completed, Second Session in Part," *SHSP,* XLV (rpr. 1980), 224–26.

44. Coulter, *Confederate States,* 395–96; "Proceedings of First Confederate Congress First Session Completed," *SHSP,* XLV (rpr. 1980), 226.

reaching home, thus shortening, for no good reason, their brief and all too infrequent leaves. In Richmond missing a train meant staying at least another day and night in the city, often in the custody of the provost: "Many a poor soldier with a few days leave spent it in Winder's lockup."[45]

The army also became increasingly angry about arbitrary provost pronouncements. Alexander Hunter's encounter with the "Melish" provost of Richmond is a case in point. The refusal of the provost to accept passes authorized by General Lee did not sit well with "Lee's Miserables," who revered him above all else.[46] This decision may well have been in retaliation against the field commanders who were refusing to honor the provost passes on the grounds of military security. There was no doubt some justification for their attitude; the absence of visitors to the army—and their wagging tongues— meant that "no information was to be had now." Cases of money exchanging hands for passports were not uncommon. The assistant secretary of war, Judge John Campbell, openly stated that provost marshal passes could be readily obtained for a hundred dollars. The army simply did not trust the provost or his passes, and open contempt was directed at the "elegant young assistant provost marshals," who slouched with their polished boots on their desks.[47] Everyone, soldier and citizen, was unhappy with the passport system.

The railroads greatly complicated movement control. The ability to move large numbers of men rapidly over long distances to meet strategic requirements was an advantage to commanders, but it presented new and difficult challenges for the transportation staffs and the provost. It is remarkable how well these new responsibilities were met.

Joseph E. Johnston used the railroad to good advantage when he moved more than two brigades to Manassas in July, 1861. The following spring more than twenty thousand troops were moved between Richmond and the Shenandoah Valley. Just a few weeks later, in July, Braxton Bragg shifted the greater part of what was to become the Army of Tennessee over an unprecedented distance. To forestall the Union General Don Carlos Buell, moving south from Corinth, Bragg had to get his army from Tupelo, Mississippi, to Chattanooga, Tennessee, before Buell could reach that city. In the absence of a rail line— recommended but not built before the outbreak of war—from Meridian, Mississippi, to Selma, Alabama, the projected move would involve a lengthy run

45. Bill, *Beleaguered City,* 205–206.
46. Hunter, *Johnny Reb and Billy Yank,* 599.
47. Bill, *Beleaguered City,* 132, 205–206.

south to Mobile, across Mobile Bay by ferry, and then north to Chattanooga, a total of 776 miles. The management, the locomotives, and the rolling stock of six different railroads would have to be so well coordinated that more than thirty thousand Confederate soldiers could arrive in time to deny Buell access to Chattanooga. Based on the amount of rolling stock available, a plan was worked out to dispatch one division every two days starting on July 23. Everything was taken into account: sufficient rations were issued to the men as they boarded the trains so they would not have to forage en route, and commanders were warned to be extra vigilant at rail junctions to prevent "the more adventurous from disrupting the schedule by stealing away for a visit to the fleshpots."[48] The thorough and precise planning, so typical of Bragg, and the strict discipline for which he was already famous won him the race. Buell would not get Chattanooga in 1862.

Another large-scale rail movement occurred in September, 1863, when Longstreet's 1st Corps reinforced Bragg at Chickamauga. Once the decision for the deployment was taken, it was quickly implemented. On September 6 Lee ordered his transportation staff to arrange the move of two divisions. Two days later they were on their way. This move, too, was highly complex and a supreme test of the railroads' ability to move troops. Knoxville, Tennessee, had fallen the week before— "Gone to Hell" was the apt phrase—and with it the direct route from Gordonsville, Virginia, to Dalton, Georgia. The only alternative was a thousand-mile journey through southern Virginia and the Carolinas and then west across Georgia on a dozen different rail lines with no chance of through trains because of the different gauges of track. South through Richmond and on to Weldon, North Carolina, the trains chugged, taking alternate routes at Weldon to ease the pressure on the creaking rails, meeting again at Kingsville, South Carolina, south again to Branchville, west to Atlanta, and finally north to Bragg. Five of Longstreet's brigades arrived in time to help Bragg win the barren victory at Chickamauga. Like Bragg on his move in 1862, Longstreet had taken steps to ensure no "French leave" for the troops en route: his guards and the local provost at every major junction along the way would have seen to that.[49]

These organized moves of troops on definitive timetables with set routes and stops, all under the immediate supervision of brigade officers, were only part of the provost's responsibility for railroad movement. They were perhaps the easy

48. Foote, *Civil War,* I, 574–75.
49. *Ibid.,* II, 709–711.

part. The other portion, controlling the mostly individual movement of civilians and soldiers on leave, deserting, or otherwise traveling without authority, was the *real* challenge. Provost presence along the routes of the railroads and on the cars themselves also helped to ensure that the many soldiers on the trains behaved themselves, causing no injury or damage to the citizen or his property. These tasks, which had to be carried out along the almost eight thousand miles of track the South possessed at the outbreak of war, caused a heavy and increasing drain on the always slender slate of manpower available to the provost.

It was also essential that the enemy be prevented from damaging or otherwise sabotaging the trains and the track. Although prevention of sabotage was not a primary provost task—they were far too few in number to have taken on a job of such magnitude—the physical security of the railroads often consumed provost time and strength simply because in many cases they were the only troops available. As John Singleton Mosby put it, this new mode of moving men and material was both vital and vulnerable. Grant learned just how precarious reliance on the railroad could be. The destruction by "That Devil Forrest" of a lengthy section of the Mobile and Ohio, Grant's main supply line, between Jackson, Tennessee, and Columbus, Kentucky, and Earl Van Dorn's devastation of the main Union supply base at Holly Springs, Mississippi, ended Grant's December, 1862, try for Vicksburg.

The Confederacy, too, learned how vulnerable the railroads were. The "Great Locomotive Chase" of April, 1862, highlighted the serious threat that even a few men could pose to an army's lines of communication. Twenty-one Union soldiers disguised as civilians stole a locomotive and some cars at Big Shanty, Georgia, and headed for Chattanooga, intending to destroy the line, including bridges and tunnels, as they went. Their plan was frustrated by the dogged pursuit of W. A. Fuller, a train conductor. The entire Federal party was captured, and seven were later executed.[50] This raid, which nearly achieved its object, caused the Confederates to station permanent guards on the railroad's main bridges. Some of these guards may have been provided by the provost.

The provost's involvement in duties associated with the railroads was probably greatest in Virginia, which had almost two thousand miles, or about one-quarter of the total track in the Confederacy. One of the earliest references to the policing of the Virginia railroads is in a letter from J. S. Barbour, president of the Orange and Alexandria Railroad, to the secretary of war in January, 1862.

50. *OR*, Vol. X, Pt. 1, pp. 635–39.

From the letter it is apparent that as early as April, 1861, immediately after secession, the governor of Virginia had agreed to maintain night guards on the bridges along the rails between Lynchburg and Manassas. The company provided bridge guards by day. Virginia maintained the guards at her expense until November, 1861, when she decided that because the main user of the railroad was the Confederate government, it should pay the costs of security. Barbour then requested that the secretary of war recognize the guard as a "proper military expense."[51] He also advised that General Johnston was already providing guards for some bridges on the line. Even at this early stage of the war it was clear that the railways were too important militarily to risk leaving them unprotected.

By May, 1862, straggling had become a serious problem in Johnston's army. Some means had to be found to check it. Early that month Johnston told General Lee that the country was full of stragglers, many of whom were in Richmond. D. H. Hill echoed the thought to Secretary of War Randolph, requesting that the Richmond provost marshal, Brigadier General Winder, take immediate steps to arrest any soldiers without passes. Men were simply leaving their units and going to Richmond: "The sick and stragglers, without passes and with their arms, come in large numbers daily to the city by the railroad trains. No guard at either end and no officer on the trains." Lee replied that guards would be stationed at the Richmond rail depot to arrest stragglers from the army.[52]

Shortly thereafter, in an initial and makeshift attempt to prevent stragglers and deserters from riding the rails, railway employees were asked to check the papers of soldier passengers. This expedient proved futile. In November the obvious remedy was applied: provost detachments of one officer and three men were ordered to make return trips daily on the trains from Culpeper Court House to Gordonsville, from Gordonsville to Lynchburg, and from Richmond to Staunton. Their responsibilities were to prevent disorder on the trains and to check that each soldier had valid authority to travel. Those without passes were to be arrested and turned over to the nearest provost marshal. At the end of each trip a full report on the arrests was to be submitted to army headquarters. From these reports it would have been easy to identify units in which discipline needed to be improved.[53]

These train guards, to be provided by the commanding officers at Culpeper Court House, Gordonsville, and Richmond, were cautioned not to "interfere

51. *OR*, Vol. LI, Pt. 2, p. 451.
52. *OR*, Vol. XI, Pt. 3, pp. 503, 506, 514, 516.
53. Ella Lonn, *Desertion During the Civil War* (New York, 1928), 43–44.

with the management of trains, being desired only for duties indicated, and when called upon, to afford assistance to the conductor."[54] Already there had been complaints that the provost's well-meaning but misguided efforts to improve efficiency were endangering passengers and trainmen alike. This could not be tolerated, nor could provost tampering with the fragile schedules be permitted because delay or other disruption entailed frantic reshuffling of the inadequate rolling stock to meet conflicting and urgent demands for transportation.

The initial allocation of provost guards was obviously inadequate for the task. Two weeks later, Lee ordered General James Longstreet to detail train guards from the 1st Corps. By December, 1862, a train without provost aboard would have been unusual. George Greer of Jubal Early's staff recorded that during a trip to Richmond from Guiney's Station on December 21 he had been asked to assist two elderly ladies onto the train. He subsequently turned them over to the care of the provost marshal, who promised to watch over them until the train reached Richmond. John West of the Texas Brigade also noted that every train seemed to have its provost; he watched the Richmond military police eject a number of Texans from the trains because they had no passes.[55]

Jeb Stuart's cavalry corps was also using precious manpower to prevent soldiers stealing away on the trains. In July, 1863, after the return from Pennsylvania, Stuart put detachments of his provost aboard the trains. Any man found on the trains was to be returned under guard to his command, and officers of less than brigade commander status who authorized the absence of a soldier would be arrested and tried. Stuart's guards were told to preserve order, prevent damage to public or private property, and prevent outrage or injury to civilian passengers. Additional manpower was allocated to the railroads in November, when General Wade Hampton stationed provost detachments of one noncommissioned officer and six men, of which two were to be mounted, at Spotsylvania Court House, Guiney's Station, and Bowling Green, the last two being stations on the Richmond, Fredericksburg, and Potomac Railroad. The guards were ordered to pay close attention to any trains passing through; the mounted men were presumably detailed to escort soldiers removed from the trains.[56]

The relative quiet of the second half of 1863 allowed Stuart the extravagance of detaching large guards. With the resumption of active campaigning in the

54. *OR*, Vol. XIX, Pt. 2, p. 722.

55. *OR*, XXI, 1037–38; George H. T. Greer, "All Thoughts Are Absorbed in the War," *CWTI*, XVII (December, 1978), 35; John C. West, *A Texan in Search of a Fight* (1901; rpr. Waco, 1969), 52.

56. *OR*, Vol. XXVII, Pt. 3, p. 1050; Vol. LI, Pt. 2, pp. 785–86.

spring of 1864, he was forced to withdraw the guards to beat off the increasingly effective Union horse. Lee, too, had to recall many of the "train" provost to the army to face the third "On to Richmond." Fortunately, the resumption of military operations would fully employ the troops and give them less time and opportunity to straggle aboard the trains. On major lines like the Richmond and Danville, provost from Richmond replaced the detachments from the Army of Northern Virginia.[57]

Troop movements were also tightly controlled on the railroads in other states. Braxton Bragg, commanding the Army of the Mississippi in March, 1862, placed the main east-west railroad, the Memphis and Charleston, and one of the north-south routes, the Mobile and Ohio, under military control (his quartermaster was given responsibility for the railroads) and ordered that a detachment of one noncommissioned officer and five men ride each passenger train. Before this, guards had been stationed only at railway stations, an inadequate precaution and one relatively easy to circumvent. Lieutenant LeGrand Wilson of the 42d Mississippi related that he avoided the Memphis depot provost simply by jumping from the train as it slowed to approach the station.[58] The new train guards were to suppress disorder, arrest those traveling without passes, and prevent crime. In the same order Bragg wisely closed all drinking establishments within five miles of any station.[59] In view of the bone-shaking effects of riding the cars, the troops would have far preferred to ride well "oiled," but drunken soldiers, added to all the other miseries of the railroads, would have been intolerable. Similar controls were imposed in Georgia, Alabama, and Florida to ensure that the overburdened trains would carry only authorized travelers.

Captain Isaac Hermann also had hard luck with rail travel. In December, 1863, while traveling without a pass from Atlanta, he was removed from a train at Griffin and detained by the provost marshal there. That worthy subsequently returned the errant traveler to Atlanta under guard of an officer and four men. Hermann eventually got to Macon by train, noting as he passed Griffin the same provost who had initially arrested him. The redoubtable Sam Watkins of the 1st Tennessee also had bad luck on the trains running into Atlanta. How he boarded a coach of the Alabama and Florida Railroad at Montgomery, Alabama, with-

57. War Department, Collection of Confederate Records, Record Group 109, Chap. IX, Vol. 250.

58. Wilson, *Confederate Soldier*, 80–81.

59. *OR*, Vol. X, Pt. 2, pp. 297–98.

out a pass and succeeded in reaching Atlanta is indicative of the "old soldier's" guile:

> I, you remember, was without a pass, and did not wish to be carried. . . before that good, brave, and just provost marshal. . . . I got on the cars, but was hustled off mighty quick, because I had no pass. A train of box-cars was about leaving for West Point, and I took a seat on top of one of them, and was again hustled off; but I had determined to go, and . . . slipped in between two box-cars . . . and rode this way until I got to West Point. . . . When I got to West Point, a train of cars started off . . . and I arrived safe and sound at Atlanta.[60]

In 1864 and 1865 the provost in Alabama and Georgia appear to have done more than merely control troops on the trains. No rigid government transportation regulations were imposed until February 19, 1865, when Congress authorized the last secretary of war, General John Breckinridge, to take charge of any railroad required for military purposes. In the interim, provost were increasingly involved in the actual operation of the lines. The provost marshal of the First District of Alabama, Lieutenant Colonel John W. Estes, suggested to Major Jules C. Denis, provost marshal general of the Department of Alabama, Mississippi, and East Louisiana, in April, 1864, that it was necessary to repair the Memphis and Ohio and the Memphis and Charleston railroads. In February, 1865, the provost marshal at Augusta, Georgia, was ordered to ensure that cars would be available for the evacuation of government stores from the city, even if private freight had to be thrown off.[61] It is clear that in many areas directly and immediately threatened by the enemy, the military, through the provost, was in full control of the railroads. Regrettably, these controls came far too late to be of any real help to the Confederacy.

From the beginning many viewed the provost and their passports as an unnecessary interference with the right of free travel. One exchange in October,

---

60. Hermann, *Memoirs*, 159, 162, 165; Watkins, *"Co. Aytch,"* 187.

61. Robert C. Black, *The Railroads of the Confederacy* (Chapel Hill, 1952), 280. The bill regarding transportation was entitled "An Act to provide for the more efficient transportation of troops, supplies and munitions of war upon the railroads, steamboats and canals in the Confederate States, and to control telegraph lines employed by the Government." Section 4 authorized the secretary of war to take over any railroad, and all employees were to be considered part of the Confederate army. For Estes to Denis, see *OR*, Vol. XXXII, Pt. 3, pp. 804–807; Vol. XLVII, Pt. 2, p. 1094.

1862, in the Confederate Senate between William S. Oldham of Texas and Gustavus A. Henry of Tennessee illustrates this commonly held opinion:

> Mr. Oldham: Whilst every able-bodied citizen was . . . put into the army, there were at least ten thousand men and five thousand Provost Marshals along the railroads . . . who should be in the field. . . . It was time this public evil should be put down.

> Mr. Henry: [I] had traveled on the railroads, and had never been asked for a pass. The gentleman from Texas who had been so much annoyed by the Provost Marshals must have something suspicious in his appearance.

> Mr. Oldham: If the gentleman from Tennessee had never been asked for a pass, it was because he had evaded the provost guard and slipped into the cars just as they were starting.

Another senator was visibly indignant with the efficiency of the provost on the railroads:

> When Congress shall adjourn I wish to go home, but before I can be permitted to do so I must get some one who can identify me to go along with me to the Provost Marshal's Office to enable me to get a pass. At the Provost's I shall be met at the door by a soldier with a bayonet. After getting the pass, I shall be again met at the cars by other soldiers with bayonets, who will demand to see my pass. The conductor must then see my pass. At other towns along my route I must be confronted by other armed men, and be obliged to obtain other passes and undergo other examinations. This system will be kept up until I arrive at home with a pocket full of Provost Marshal's passes.[62]

There were also complaints about inefficiency, mostly from the army. These allegations posed a dilemma for the provost: where they were not, they were demanded; where they were, they were bludgeoned as ineffective and wasteful. An early report on the provost's efficiency on some of the railroads in Mississippi was produced by Lieutenant John Otey, a staff officer of the Army of the Mississippi, in March, 1862. He reported that on the Mississippi Central, the most westerly north-south route, no military police were available. They were urgently required to prevent stragglers from passing south of Grand Junction, Tennessee, into the rear of the army. On the other north-south route, the Mobile

---

62. "Proceedings of First Confederate Congress End of Second Session," *SHSP*, XLVII (rpr. 1980), 72–73, 46–47.

and Ohio, he found that men without passes were not arrested but merely put off the trains. Officers riding the Mobile and Ohio were not even subject to pass inspection; their word was accepted at face value by the provost.

Otey reserved his worst criticism for the Memphis and Charleston Railroad, which ran roughly parallel with the Tennessee border. He reported that in not one instance had he seen a provost officer demand a written pass, their inquiries being confined simply to "Who are you?" "Where from?" "Where going?" Otey characterized the provost's performance as "palpable dereliction of duty," particularly on the section of line between Huntsville and Decatur, Alabama, where he personally saw "seven coaches filled with stragglers and sick . . . subject to no other inspection than that above indicated." Lieutenant Otey was also disturbed to find that on none of the lines were there any guards at the depots, so that men could step on and off trains with no fear of pass inspection. He recommended that a guard be placed at the door of each car to check the passes of those entering, then as the train departed, each guard could swing aboard and ride the train to its destination, thereby ensuring good order and discipline among the passengers. At the time of his inspection, when no guards were present, he had witnessed the "grossest misconduct" by some troops. Otey concluded by pointing out that the provost's delinquencies in the performance of their duties "seem to be owing to a want of proper instructions . . . than to a disposition to shirk them, they being in most cases men of inferior intelligence."[63]

Other officers were of a different opinion on the matter of stationing guards aboard the trains. In August, 1863, Colonel M. H. Wright, the post commandant of Atlanta, asked the chief of staff of the Army of Tennessee, Brigadier General W. W. Mackall, whether guards should ride the trains. Wright believed that little or no good was accomplished by such guards because they would only annoy soldiers and civilians, yet unauthorized travelers would continue to get through. In any event, the whole matter was doubtful because of the "class" of men available to do the duty. He hastened to add that this comment did not apply to the men provided by the Army of Tennessee.[64]

Otey's report did lead to some changes. The provost marshal general of the Department of Alabama, Mississippi, and East Louisiana, Major Jules C. Denis, in a general order in May, 1864, directed that henceforth officers would be employed on the trains to control passes. These officers were ordered to

63. *OR*, Vol. X, Pt. 2, pp. 304–305; Wiley Sword, *Shiloh: Bloody April* (New York, 1974), 72.
64. *OR*, Vol. XXX, Pt. 4, p. 520.

examine *all* passes, regardless of the rank of travelers. Otey's recommendation that additional provost be allocated to the railroads was also implemented. Before long the augmented police presence drew complaints from both the army and the civilian population. Civilians were particularly vociferous; they were annoyed at being endlessly accosted by guards demanding to see their passports. In the aftermath of the 1864 Conscription Act, the governors of the states east of the Mississippi met to discuss an appropriate response to the Confederate government. The furor over harassment by provosts on the trains boiled over at about the same time. Both matters were included in a resolution in October, 1864, in which the governors pledged to do all they could to help the war effort, but in return they wanted the central government to send every able-bodied man to the field, without exception. They were especially incensed that the provost, that "unnecessary annoyance . . . of no possible benefit to the country," should remain out of the fighting.[65]

Nor was the military happy with the continued presence of able-bodied provost in virtually every town and city and on every train at a time when the last soldier was needed to stem the Yankee tide. Throughout the autumn of 1864 and over the winter, complaints from officers of all ranks filtered through the levels of command to the desks of the War Department in Richmond. As late as February 24, a staff officer of the Department of Alabama, Mississippi, and East Louisiana complained of the large numbers of able-bodied men visible throughout the department. Richmond was too busy to listen. In any event, those men who were not in the field could not now reach there soon enough to stave off the approaching *Gotterdammerung*.

It is obvious that the control of movement, made even more complicated by the railroads, kept a good many able-bodied men out of the fighting for good, or at least for extended periods. Had these men been present at, say, Chancellorsville, where Lee fought without Longstreet's corps, they would have improved the fortunes of the Confederate States of America.

It is also apparent that the original purpose of the passports, to prevent desertion, had become perverted. The extension of the system to every area of the nation became another divisive issue, creating additional discord and a lack of unity that harmed the war effort. Nevertheless, the system had to be maintained, regardless of the human or political cost; there was no better means of

65. War Department, Collection of Confederate Records, Record Group 109, Chap. II, Vol. 196; *OR,* Vol. XLII, Pt. 3, p. 1150.

preventing a mass ingestion of Federal spies, saboteurs, and *agents provocateurs,* while at the same time ensuring that Confederate soldiers stayed with the colors.

This latter aspect was the most crucial task facing the provost. Because Lee's army and the others "carried the Confederacy on its bayonets," it was essential that the soldier be purged of his tendency to straggle. Internal discipline of the commands was helpful, as was individual and unit pride and confidence, but in the final analysis, and particularly as the South's fortunes waned, the major commitment of the provost was to prevent straggling.

This evil, so highly destructive of army discipline and efficiency, rapidly became an abomination in the eyes of commanders and provost alike. Eventually, countering it consumed a major part of provost manpower and effort.

8

Stragglers
The Artful Dodgers

My army is ruined by straggling.

R. E. LEE

Lee's words were no exaggeration. One of the most notable characteristics of the highly individualistic Southern soldier was his tendency to wander from his command when the whim struck him; according to General D. H. Hill: "His disregard of discipline and independence of character made him often a straggler, and the fruit of many a victory was lost by straggling."[1] The predilection for rather freer movement than the army could allow was often a severe limitation on its strength and performance, but in spite of the strictest and most diligent measures straggling was never entirely checked. It was as much of a problem at Appomattox and Bentonville as it had been at First Manassas and Shiloh.

Modern military police usage defines the straggler as a soldier who has become separated from his unit without authority, the separation occurring either in battle or on the line of march. Probably the best wartime thumbnail sketch of the straggler was provided by D. H. Hill, who, during the Sharpsburg campaign, categorized the straggler as "generally a thief and always a coward, lost to all sense of shame; he can only be kept in ranks by a strict and sanguinary discipline."[2]

Civil War history, which abounds in material on straggling, clearly indicates that Confederate leaders were cognizant of its various causes. Lee described one cause just before Sharpsburg when he advised President Davis that the sick and feeble straggled from "necessity." Hard marching, the battles the troops had engaged in, and the lack of proper food and rest had caused many men to become so exhausted that they could not keep up with the army. Lack of shoes, a chronic deficiency in the army, also had deleterious effects on the men's

---

1. D. H. Hill, "Address," *SHSP*, XIII (rpr. 1978), 261. Henderson, *Stonewall Jackson*, 612.
2. *OR*, Vol. XIX, Pt. 1, p. 1026.

marching performance. In Lee's opinion, however, by far the largest number of men straggled by "design," either because of simple cowardice or because they wished to take advantage of opportunities to plunder, drink, or indulge in other vice.[3] A third cause, not mentioned by Lee and still rare at a time of bright Confederate prospects, was that the straggler, always a potential deserter, sometimes hoped to be captured by the enemy. In 1862, while the war was still in the "gentleman" stage, capture generally meant parole and a ticket home, not to serve again until properly exchanged.

A contributory cause of straggling during the first year or so was poor march discipline. This necessary refinement to the movement of an army had not been part of the education of amateur officers and soldiers who had no experience of the military or war. Stonewall Jackson's repulse at Kernstown in the Shenandoah Valley in March, 1862, although primarily resulting from the lack of proper reconnaissance and briefing, poor intelligence, and an ill-prepared attack (Jackson was still learning, too), had also been caused by bad marching. Covering forty miles of road over March 22 and 23 cost Jackson fifteen hundred stragglers, almost one-third of his strength, and gave the Union General James Shields a three-to-one advantage.

Following Kernstown, march discipline in Jackson's army improved somewhat, but not enough, and on May 13, just after the Battle of McDowell, he issued specific orders as to how the army would march in the future. This order prescribed that the men would fall into ranks, presumably in the habitual column of fours of the Confederate army, and set intervals were to be maintained between units to prevent bunching. For fifty minutes of each hour the men would march, with the other ten minutes for rest. These regulations, which may have been written by Jackson himself, aimed at limiting the opportunities for straggling. Company officers, for example, were directed to march in the rear of their commands, and brigade commanders and such staff officers as they wished were to rove up and down the columns to ensure that the ranks remained full and closed up. Any soldier who pronounced himself unfit to march was required to have his regimental medical officer's concurrence with that diagnosis before he could get a seat in an ambulance. Men who had to leave the columns for "necessity" were not permitted to take their muskets with them. Roll calls were to be more frequent to "verify" the presence of the men.[4] In time the men grew accustomed to the system; the initial grumbling over Jack-

3. *OR*, Vol. XIX, Pt. 2, p. 597.
4. Lenoir Chambers, *The Legend and the Man to Valley V*, Vol. I of *Stonewall Jackson* (2 vols.; New York, 1959), 519–20.

son's precise standards gave way to pride of membership in Jackson's foot cavalry. To Jackson, the straggler was anathema: "He classed all who were weak and weary, who fainted by the wayside, as men wanting in patriotism. If a man's face was as white as cotton and his pulse so low you could scarcely feel it, he looked upon him merely as an inefficient soldier and rode off impatiently."[5]

About a week after the Battle of McDowell, Jackson received three thousand reinforcements in the form of General Richard Taylor's Louisiana Brigade. Taylor's men were as impeccable in their marching as they were in their dress, "neat in fresh clothing of grey with white gaiters, bands playing . . . not a straggler, but every man in his place, stepping jauntily as if in parade, though it had marched twenty miles or more." From a subsequent conversation between the two generals we learn that Jackson was still unhappy with the straggling in his army. When Taylor reported to Jackson, the latter, having witnessed the arrival of the Louisiana Brigade, inquired how far the brigade had come that day: "Keezleton road, six and twenty miles." "You seem to have no stragglers." "Never allow stragglers." "You must teach my people; they straggle badly."[6]

On occasion Jackson changed marching procedure so that instead of fifty minutes of marching, twenty minutes became the norm. All ranks were expected to adhere to the timings, as A. P. Hill discovered to his cost when he kept his division moving during a rest halt. Jackson ordered one of Hill's brigade commanders to halt the Light Division, then promptly put the angry Hill under arrest.[7]

Meticulous march discipline may have made Jackson's command unique. Johnson Hagood, a South Carolina brigade commander, relates in his *Memoirs* how poor march discipline caused unnecessary fatigue, unacceptable lengthening of the columns, and a decrease in marching speed. According to Hagood, Lee's army on the march did not adhere to regular halts of set duration; it was common for the head of a column to resume marching with no word of warning to those behind. This meant that the men in succeeding regiments often had to jump up from positions of rest and quickly double forward to close up the column. The resulting extra fatigue negated the benefit of the rest halt. Those who have experienced a good deal of marching know well how this can adversely affect temper and stamina. Often, too, in areas where the route bends and turns it is possible to miss the departure of those ahead, thereby causing elonga-

---

5. Foote, *Civil War,* I, 426.

6. Riley, *"Stonewall Jackson,"* 44–45; Henderson, *Stonewall Jackson,* 238–39.

7. Riley, *"Stonewall Jackson,"* 19–20.

tion and even separation of the column. The subsequent "concertina" effect makes rapid marching all the more tiring.

Hagood, in contrast, in 1864 stated that in marches under his authority he "always ten minutes after the march commenced halted for ten minutes to allow the men to adjust their packs and attend to the calls of nature. Afterwards he halted ten minutes in every hour. He always, too, after one of these halts, gave a preliminary signal to march." Hagood also insisted that the column of fours be adhered to even when encountering obstacles; though it took a battalion only ten minutes to break into file, it took a brigade almost an hour and a division five hours, during which time a battle could be lost or won.[8] Although he does not mention it, his careful regard for the best marching methods suggests that Hagood may also have followed the practice of rotating his units between the head and tail of the brigade column. The benefits thereby gained would be familiar to any infantryman; it can be almost restful occasionally to march at the head of a column, where, psychologically, the march seems much easier.

Although good march discipline helped to decrease straggling, it could not entirely cure the disease. The most serious side effect of straggling was that it reduced the fighting strength of the army. Other side effects such as the depredations stragglers engaged in gave rise to hard feelings between soldiers and civilians. Such bad conduct by the army, which after all was the government's creature, weakened the determination of the citizen to support his national government in the pursuit of independence. General John Breckinridge, a division commander in the Army of Tennessee in 1863, clearly recognized this problem. He published a circular in July of that year calling attention to the prevalence of straggling in the division and the many complaints that had reached him regarding the depredations these stragglers were committing. Breckinridge warned that unless these ceased "the presence of the army will be regarded as a curse."[9]

As early as April, 1862, the pernicious cancer of straggling was attacking the vitals of Albert Sidney Johnston's army at Shiloh. Major F. H. Clack, commanding a battalion during the battle, observed that stragglers falling to the rear continued to fire to their front, endangering those who remained steadfast in the battle line, and that bad discipline was evident in the alacrity with which the men seized the chance to pillage and plunder. One of the strongest inducements to straggling, and increasingly so as the defective Confederate subsis-

---

8. Hagood, *Memoirs*, 211, 213.
9. *OR*, Vol. XXIV, Pt. 3, p. 988.

tence system floundered, was the desire for a full, or at least fuller, belly. Private Ephraim Anderson of the 1st Missouri recalled that the provost guard had arrested a number of men for killing hogs, an unwarranted charge in view of the vicious and aggressive nature of these predatory animals.[10]

Another private, Joseph Polley of the 4th Texas, Hood's Texas Brigade, in one of his letters to "Charming Nellie," recollected the pursuit by two of his messmates of a "quadruped of the porcine persuasion." While en route to camp with their freshly skinned and illegally impressed porker, the two foragers inadvertently stumbled upon a squad of provost under command of an acquaintance from the 1st Texas. Though the Texan was personally inclined to let them go, in the presence of the Georgians of his squad he found it necessary to arrest them rather than chance the loss of his "soft berth" as a member of the provost. As they approached camp, the Texans overheard one of the provost brag of the "grease an' good eatin' " that would be the provost's that night. In the end, the provost were foiled in their attempt to confiscate and masticate the evidence. A sympathetic officer allowed the Texans to keep the hog and host their company to a good feed of fresh meat.[11] Nor was "mobile bacon" the only wild beast at large in the Confederacy. Even chickens became so fierce that they launched unprovoked attacks on the defenseless men of the army, forcing these innocents to defend themselves to the last extremity.

Crops, too, were a target for the hungry troops. Brigadier General Humphrey Marshall, commanding the Abingdon District of Virginia in November, 1862, advised Judge John Campbell, the assistant secretary of war, that the danger posed to the crops was so great that he had established mounted patrols to arrest soldiers found in the gardens and cornfields of the citizens. Crops in the eastern part of the state were also at risk. For three summers the Union and Confederate armies had lived off the fat of the land between the Potomac and Rapidan rivers, stripping the area of all it could furnish. This pillaging, coupled with the heavy rains of 1863 and the plundering of the many Confederate stragglers, created a severe supply problem for Richmond. It was a toss-up as to whether Reb or Yank had perpetrated the most damage on the farmers of Virginia. The situation was equally bad in the Army of Tennessee. In mid-1863 Major General A. P. Stewart, a division commander in D. H. Hill's corps, strengthened his provost guard so it could better protect farm crops.[12]

Private property, too, was a target for the straggler; money, silver, jewelry,

10. *OR,* Vol. X, Pt. 1, p. 512; Anderson, *Memoirs,* 91.

11. Polley, "Concernin' of a Hog," 56–58.

12. *OR,* Vol. XX, Pt. 2, pp. 400–401; Vol. XXIII, Pt. 2, p. 954.

clothing, anything that could be turned to profit was stolen. Lee admitted that the destruction and theft of private property by stragglers from his army during the Sharpsburg campaign had weighed heavily on his mind. Stragglers had done considerable damage even though his provost marshal, Brigadier General Lewis A. Armistead, had diligently enforced measures to protect citizens from stragglers.[13]

In the Army of Tennessee the situation was as bad, if not worse. By August, 1864, Hood was forced to admit that "the lawless seizure and destruction of private property by straggling soldiers . . . has become intolerable." In desperation he published a general order requesting soldiers and citizens to arrest anyone destroying or illegally seizing property. Little if any good came of this order. A month later, another went out advising corps and division commanders of the necessity to prevent straggling. Hood was "pained," to use his expression, that most of the straggling stemmed not from exhaustion but from the desire to leave the ranks to plunder.[14] In Hood's command and in others in the West, the innumerable orders and instructions and the understrength provost proved unable to prevent the damage wreaked by the straggler.

Once the army was in the field, one of the most important, if not the most vital, of the provost's many duties was to bring desertion and straggling under control. The latter had to be the initial aim because the straggler was always a potential deserter. Provost responsibility here was threefold: collection, custody, and the speedy return of the maximum number of stragglers to their units so that maximum combat effectiveness could be maintained.

Many stragglers were men who had become separated from their commands through confusion or exhaustion. If it was apparent that they were genuinely trying to rejoin their units, the solution was sometimes only a matter of providing directions. The difficulty arose with men who straggled because of fear of facing the enemy. The provost had to return these men to their units under guard. More often than not, inability positively to determine a man's reason for straggling meant that all stragglers had to be escorted to their commands, a not inconsiderable burden in view of the small number of provost available. Provision also had to be made for a third category of straggler, the recognizably sick or wounded man who could not keep pace with his unit and had to be evacuated for medical reasons. The thousands of men in one or the other of these categories posed an exceedingly tough problem for the provost.

13. *OR,* Vol. XIX, Pt. 2, p. 596.
14. *OR,* Vol. XXXVIII, Pt. 5, p. 960; Vol. XXXIX, Pt. 2, p. 833.

Straggling was a pervasive weakness of every army the Confederate States fielded, not excepting that body of "incomparable infantry," the Army of Northern Virginia.[15] From the very first, the Confederate soldier had served notice that he would indulge his God-given right to go where he pleased, when he pleased, but it was not until early 1862 that commanders began to appreciate just how damaging straggling was to Southern military prospects. As earlier noted, Stonewall Jackson had been one of the first to recognize the menacing nature of the disease, and as an initial step he had instituted measures to improve the march discipline of his Shenandoah Valley army. Although some reduction in the incidence of straggling was achieved, march discipline alone did not deter the wandering soldier. Nor could the officers of a unit, no matter how firm their discipline, entirely prevent men from leaving their commands. Something more had to be added to tip the balance against the mania for straggling. This something was the provost of the army.

By the late spring of 1862, straggling was identified as a very serious matter demanding urgent attention. The ever-growing number of offenders convinced a good many officers of all ranks that they had to stop the rot. The period immediately before and during the Seven Days' Battle is indicative of the extent of straggling in the field army in Virginia. Before the army was moved to the Peninsula, General Joseph E. Johnston found it necessary to station provost guards in the towns of northern Virginia to deny stragglers who were bored with camp life and looking for diversion access to the brothels and barrooms. At Orange Court House, for example, he appointed Colonel Thomas H. Taylor, the commanding officer of a Kentucky regiment, as provost marshal and authorized an "efficient" guard of two hundred men under Captain Joseph Desha of the same regiment to arrest all stragglers without passes who were in the town or trying to enter it.[16] How "efficient" this guard was is not recorded, but the inclusion of the word in Johnston's order reveals that he knew how important the task was and that only the best available men could adequately perform it.

After the move to the Yorktown line on the Peninsula, there was no diminution in the straggling. General D. H. Hill observed during the subsequent withdrawal, which started with the evacuation of Yorktown on May 3 and continued through and beyond Williamsburg on May 5, that straggling "was and still is the curse of our army. This monstrous evil can only be corrected by a

---

15. Robert Debs Heinl, *Dictionary of Military and Naval Quotations* (Annapolis, Md., 1966), 18.

16. *OR*, Vol. LI, Pt. 2, pp. 504–505.

more rigid government and a sterner system of punishment than have yet been introduced."[17] By May 9 Johnston was so concerned about straggling that he took time from an otherwise busy program—fending off McClellan—to advise Lee in Richmond that stragglers were everywhere, including the capital, which was no doubt crawling with absentees from the army. On May 10 D. H. Hill urged that the Richmond provost marshal, General John H. Winder, devote his efforts to the arrest and return to their commands of these "miserable wretches," although on their return, Hill, for one, did not intend to retain them. He would shave their heads and drum them out of the service. Lee replied to Johnston on May 14, telling him that Winder would do his best to arrest stragglers from the army the minute they showed their faces in Richmond.[18]

On May 31 Johnston attacked McClellan, striking at the two corps that had become isolated south of the Chickahominy River near Fair Oaks, east of Richmond. Poor coordination resulted in the piecemeal commitment of many commands, while others did not get into action at all, and by the end of the day the Confederate impetus was gone. So, too, was Johnston; seriously wounded he gave way, first to General G. W. Smith, and then on June 1 to Robert E. Lee, who would make the Army of Northern Virginia one of the most celebrated commands in the history of warfare. But first the new commander had to take steps to prevent straggling. On June 5, his fifth day in command, in the first of what proved to be a series of general orders relating to straggling, Lee directed the establishment of a provost guard in each division to consist of one lieutenant, one noncommissioned officer, and ten privates from each regiment. These men were to be of the highest caliber; they were to be selected from those most "efficient and reliable." Had this order been fully complied with by the eleven divisions of the army, which at the time had 166 infantry regiments and several battalions on its rolls, the total provost strength of the infantry component of the army would have been 166 officers, a like number of noncommissioned officers, and 1,660 men.[19]

In the same general order Lee ordered Brigadier General J. E. B. Stuart to station one cavalry company in Richmond to arrest military personnel absent without authority. When on duty in the city, the guard commanders were instructed to report to General Winder, for as provost marshal it was prudent and necessary that he know what other provost commands were present. Other-

17. *OR*, Vol. XI, Pt. 1, p. 606.
18. *OR*, Vol. XI, Pt. 3, pp. 503, 506, 516.
19. *Ibid.*, 576–77; Katcher, *Army of Northern Virginia*, 32–34.

Colonel (Brigadier General) Benjamin Jefferson Hill
Courtesy Library of Congress

Colonel Charles G. Livenskiold
Courtesy Norman C. Delaney, Department of History, Del Mar College, Corpus Christi, Texas

Brigadier General John H. Winder
From the White-Wellford-Taliaferro-Marshall Family Papers, courtesy Southern Historical
Collection, University of North Carolina, Chapel Hill

Castle Thunder, Richmond, Virginia
Courtesy Massachusetts Commandery Military Order of the Loyal Legion and the U.S. Army
Military History Institute

Libby Prison, Richmond, Virginia
Courtesy Massachusetts Commandery Military Order of the Loyal Legion and the U.S. Army
Military History Institute

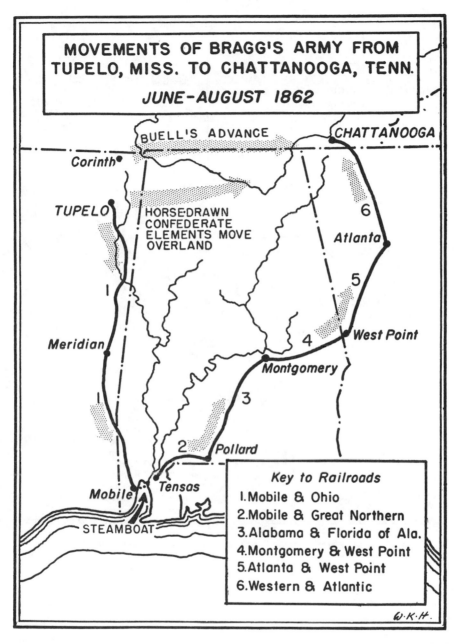

Movements of Bragg's Army from Tupelo, Mississippi, to Chattanooga, Tennessee,
June–August, 1862

From Robert C. Black III, *Railroads of the Confederacy,* © 1952, University of North Carolina
Press. Reprinted by permission of the publisher.

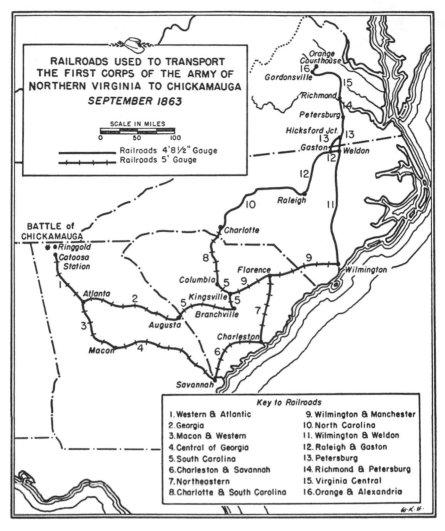

RAILROADS USED TO TRANSPORT
THE FIRST CORPS OF THE ARMY OF
NORTHERN VIRGINIA TO CHICKAMAUGA
SEPTEMBER 1863

SCALE IN MILES
0   50   100

—————— Railroads 4'8½" Gauge
—+—+—+— Railroads 5' Gauge

Orange Courthouse
Gordonsville
Richmond
Petersburg
Hicksford Jct.
Gaston Weldon

Raleigh

Charlotte

BATTLE of
CHICKAMAUGA
Ringgold
Catoosa
Station

Atlanta

Florence
Columbia
Kingsville
Branchville
Augusta
Charleston
Macon

Wilmington

Savannah

Key to Railroads

1. Western & Atlantic
2. Georgia
3. Macon & Western
4. Central of Georgia
5. South Carolina
6. Charleston & Savannah
7. Northeastern
8. Charlotte & South Carolina

9. Wilmington & Manchester
10. North Carolina
11. Wilmington & Weldon
12. Raleigh & Gaston
13. Petersburg
14. Richmond & Petersburg
15. Virginia Central
16. Orange & Alexandria

Railroads Used to Transport the First Corps of the Army of Northern Virginia to
Chickamauga, September, 1863

From Robert C. Black III, *Railroads of the Confederacy,* © 1952, University of North Carolina
Press. Reprinted by permission of the publisher.

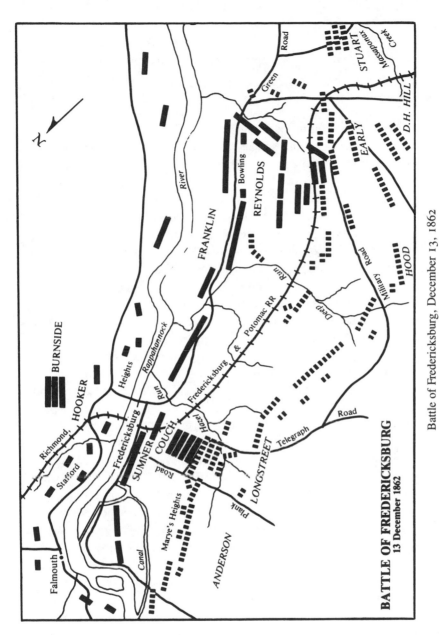

Battle of Fredericksburg, December 13, 1862

wise, confusion, jurisdictional disputes, and duplication of effort would result. As it was, there was soon a head-on clash: "When Jeb Stuart came into the city to round up his own men, Winder threatened him with arrest, and Stuart, at the head of 30 of his troopers, scoured the streets, daring Winder to do his worst."[20] The reason for the collision is not known; perhaps mutual animosity overrode good sense, or perhaps Stuart, as a brigadier general, was not about to report to an officer of equal rank, and therefore Winder reacted in the only way he felt open to him. He may well have overreacted. Many in and out of the army thought him a grim martinet, extremely jealous of his authority, although others such as President Davis, Secretary of War Seddon, and Adjutant General Cooper felt that he was much maligned. For his part, the ebullient Stuart, with his "if you want a good time, join the cavalry" philosophy, would most assuredly have not been above twisting the provost marshal's tail.

It is obvious that not all of his division commanders complied with Lee's order. Alexander Hunter of the 17th Virginia, which, together with the 1st, 7th, and 11th Virginia, formed James Kemper's brigade of Longstreet's division, recalled that at the Battle of Frayser's Farm on June 30 "stragglers were beginning to drop into line . . . this was optional with them, for then we had no provost guard to hurry the men up from the rear." Lee must have been aware of such shortcomings for on July 11 a second general order directed that division commanders station provost guards around their camps to prevent straggling and conduct frequent roll calls during the day to ensure that the men remained in camp.[21]

Following the Peninsula campaign both armies were exhausted, and the quiet allowed the Confederates to go into camp near Richmond. The proximity of the city once again made it a mecca for those who could not resist its many barrooms, brothels, and gambling dens. For this reason, and perhaps because of the continued inaction by some senior officers, Lee felt it necessary to issue on July 15 what may have been a letter meant for all division and brigade commanders. Although the copy of the letter in the *Official Records* is addressed to one brigade commander, P. J. Semmes, its tenor suggests that it was meant for all. Had it been for Semmes alone, it seems reasonable to assume that Lee would have forwarded it through James Longstreet, Semmes's corps commander. Or perhaps Semmes's brigade figured so prominently in the statistics of arrested stragglers that Lee decided to instruct Semmes directly to improve his

20. *OR*, Vol. XI, Pt. 3, p. 577; Bill, *Beleaguered City*, 205–206.
21. Hunter, *Johnny Reb and Billy Yank*, 187; *OR*, Vol. XI, Pt. 3, p. 639.

brigade's record. Whatever the case, Lee made it clear that unless commanders at all levels displayed "proper energy" in keeping their commands together, there was no means of correcting the "evil" and any orders would be useless. Lee reminded his officers of his "grave" concern for the "numerous desertions and stragglings from the army" that had prompted him to order General Winder to arrest all absentees. Lee expected all commanders to hold these men "to a strict account for their delinquencies."[22]

It is interesting to speculate whether Jackson's corps received the circular letter. Kemper's brigade, which, according to Alexander Hunter, lacked a provost guard and Semmes's brigade were both part of Magruder's division, which was under Longstreet. Jackson's well-known intolerance of straggling may have made it less of a problem in his divisions. After one tiring march the following message went to Jubal Early, one of his division commanders: "Gen. Jackson's compliments . . . and he would like to be informed why he saw so many stragglers in rear of your division to-day." Early's reply made even Jackson laugh: "General Early's compliments to General Jackson, and he takes pleasure in informing him that he saw so many stragglers in rear of my division today, probably because he rode in rear of my division."[23]

By July 13 Jackson's corps was advancing on Gordonsville, and other elements of Lee's army began moving north from Richmond. Simultaneously, John Pope and his newly formed Union Army of Virginia were moving south from Washington to take some of the pressure off McClellan, who was still on the Peninsula. On July 17 the Federals took Gordonsville. These preliminary operations by both armies, very soon to culminate in Federal humiliation at Second Manassas, indicated to Lee, now that the army was again in motion, that some refinements were necessary to his orders against straggling. Two days after Cedar Mountain, which foretold of Pope's intention to launch a major offensive, Lee increased the earlier established division provost guards by 166 men. These guards were directed to march at the rear of their divisions, and each guard would be accompanied by a medical officer, who would issue chits for a place in the ambulances to any straggler sick enough to deserve a ride. Those sick only of marching or hanging back for other reasons were to be escorted to the camps by the guards.[24]

These and other precautions were implemented to reduce to the minimum

---

22. *OR*, Vol. XI, Pt. 3, p. 643.

23. Robert Stiles, *Four Years Under Marse Robert* (New York, 1903), 190.

24. General Order 94, August 11, 1862, *OR*, Vol. XII, Pt. 3, p. 928.

any opportunity for stragglers to desert the camps or the line of march. It was hoped that the division provost guards would discourage the men from falling out of the ranks on the march and that the regimental officers, checking on their columns frequently, would ensure that the ranks remained closed up and in perfect order. When the army went into camp, it was thought that the frequent roll calls and the provost surrounding the camps would greatly reduce straggling. These measures were a good start, but much remained to be done.

The Sharpsburg campaign vividly illustrates the disastrous effects of straggling on the army's combat capability and performance. The extent of the problem, the efforts made to check it, and the results of these efforts are well documented. The number of stragglers is staggering; they were described variously as "enormous," "of the greatest concern," and "evil."

On September 2 McClellan was restored to full command of the disheartened Federals. The Confederates, meanwhile, massed near Chantilly, Virginia. On September 4, the day Lee's army, bayonets glistening, bands playing "Dixie" and "Maryland, My Maryland," crossed the Potomac into Maryland, Lee issued another general order on the subject of straggling. The division provost guards were now joined by army and brigade guards. Brigadier General Lewis A. Armistead, a brigade commander in Benjamin Huger's division during the Seven Days' Battle, was given command of the army provost guard, which was to follow the army to arrest stragglers, keep the men with their commands, and summarily punish looters. Armistead later received the personal thanks of General Lee for his discharge of his provost duties. Armistead's *modus operandi* in regard to stragglers was not so much to punish the men who had straggled as to hold the officer who had permitted the offense responsible: "The private must answer to the officer, but the officer to him."[25] Brigade commanders were also ordered to establish rear guards to prevent the men from leaving the ranks to the front or rear or to either flank. This latter measure was designed to prevent lateral movement of stragglers, which the division guards could not see because of the length of the columns.

In Lee's opinion the cowardly straggler, who deserted his comrades in peril, was especially deserving of odium and the provost's attention. Although there was no denying the usefulness of the provost guards, one element of straggler control was still missing: there was no means of punishing offenders. Lee

---

25. James E. Poindexter, "General Armistead's Portrait Presented: An Address Delivered Before R. E. Lee Camp No. 1, C.V., Richmond, Va., January 29, 1909," *SHSP*, XXXVII (rpr. 1979), 145.

moved to correct this situation by suggesting that a military commission accompany the army to back up the provost with drumhead courts-martial. The earlier military tribunals, which were more suited to garrison or camp life, had not been able to punish offenders with the required alacrity. In Lee's mind, if the men could be brought to see that straggling did not pay, the army "would be able successfully to resist any force that could be brought against it."[26] It is almost inconceivable that with Sharpsburg in the offing the general officer commanding the army was forced to become so deeply engrossed in a military police matter.

Sharpsburg was proof that antistraggling measures had largely failed. Official Confederate reports at all levels show graphically the pernicious effects of straggling on Confederate strength in the battle. One source estimates that Lee lost about twenty-five thousand men by straggling, and though this figure is probably too high, it does justify Lee's exclamation that the army was ruined by straggling. Another writer estimated almost fifteen thousand stragglers, mostly "laggards broken down in body or skulkers broken down in spirit." Lee himself noted that many men never crossed the river into Maryland and many who did either recrossed into Virginia at the first opportunity or hid to avoid fighting. Cavalry had attempted to check this straggling but to no avail, and with the army's efficiency "greatly paralyzed" by the losses from the ranks, Lee expressed to President Davis the "greatest concern" for its future. The thousands of absentees had left him to face McClellan with fewer than forty thousand men.

In view of this situation and the disaster that could unfold if it did not improve, Lee reiterated the pressing need for legislation to allow the most summary and drastic punishment for offenders. He reckoned that the only solution was to equate straggling with the offense of desertion in the face of the enemy, thereby bringing the offense under the Articles of War. To give the president some feeling for the "woeful" state of the army, Lee provided some telling figures: "General Evans reported . . . but 120 of his brigade present, and that the next brigade . . . consisted of but 100 men . . . the brigades of Generals Lawton and Armistead . . . contained about 600 men."[27] Overall, strength returns show that Longstreet's and Jackson's corps totaled 36,407 on September 22, rising to 48,689 by October 1. The difference, about 12,000

26. *OR*, Vol. XIX, Pt. 2, pp. 592, 597.

27. Alexander, "Sketch of Longstreet's Division," 514; Foote, *Civil War*, I, 663; *OR*, Vol. XIX, Pt. 1, p. 143; Gilbert Moxley Sorrel, *Recollections of a Confederate Staff Officer* (1905; rpr. ed. Bell Irvin Wiley; Jackson, Tenn., 1958), 103. Sorrel believed the principal reason for straggling at Sharpsburg was the want of food.

men, represents those who had straggled and then rejoined the army eight days later.[28]

The reports of other senior officers of the Army of Northern Virginia further illustrate the disastrous effects of straggling. D. H. Hill, commanding a division under Jackson, reported that three days before the battle his division was down to five thousand men as a result of "heavy marches, deficient commissariat, want of shoes, and inefficient officers." Additional straggling reduced Hill to three thousand on the morning of the battle, a loss of two thousand in three days. Later, Hill concluded that Sharpsburg would have been a "glorious victory" but for three reasons: separation of Confederate forces, bad handling of artillery, and the enormous straggling. Although Hill recognized that many men had not been able to keep up with the army because they were totally exhausted, he condemned the thousands of thieving cowards who could be kept in ranks only by the strictest discipline. Better discipline was instituted in Hill's division; it soon reached a strength of nine thousand, primarily because of his promise to arrest any officer who permitted men to leave the ranks without good cause. He also insisted that every unit in his command be followed up by a provost guard to pick up stragglers.[29]

Regimental and brigade commanders added to the catalog of disheartening reports on the abysmal straggling. Captain E. J. Willis, commanding the 15th Virginia of Semmes's brigade, noted a regimental strength of 14 officers and 114 men on the morning of the battle. Brigadier General James Archer, commanding a brigade in A. P. Hill's Light Division, reported after his arrival at Sharpsburg on September 17 that the four regiments of his brigade were down to 350 men but not because of faintheartedness. At 6:30 that morning, having received the order to rejoin the hard-pressed Lee, Hill and his Light Division hastily left Harpers Ferry. They marched seventeen miles with only three brief halts, pounding down the road, the panting troops still on their feet being prodded to Push On! Close Up! Others, cotton wool in their mouths, staggered exhausted into the ditches, ignored in the frantic urgency to reach the fighting. And reach it they did, less than three thousand out of a division of five thousand, but enough to save Lee.[30]

Once the army crossed into Maryland, the many stragglers had to be collected together at some convenient point south of the Potomac because it was

28. *OR,* Vol. XIX, Pt. 2, pp. 621, 639.

29. *OR,* Vol. XIX, Pt. 1, pp. 1021–22; Hal Bridges, *Lee's Maverick General: Daniel Harvey Hill* (New York, 1961), 154.

30. *OR,* Vol. XIX, Pt. 1, pp. 880, 1000.

too dangerous for individuals or small groups to rejoin their commands in motion in Maryland. Winchester, at the northern end of the Shenandoah Valley, was chosen as the straggler collecting point for the army. In a letter on September 21, Lee advised the president that he had ordered Brigadier General J. R. Jones to the Valley town to arrest stragglers. His choice of a general officer from Jackson's corps indicates how seriously Lee viewed the situation.[31] On the same day, Brigadier General George H. Steuart was also sent to Winchester to arrange the escort of all fit officers and men to the army.[32]

As he passed through Winchester en route to the army just before Sharpsburg, Colonel Walter Taylor of Lee's staff noted the large number of fit officers and men in the town, awaiting word from General Lee as to the route they should take to rejoin the army. Even larger numbers of "sick, footsore and broken down" men were present; the worst of these were probably held at Winchester until the army had returned to Virginia. Both categories of straggler were under rigid charge of the provost to ensure that none would leave the town.[33]

Brigadier General Jones's report of September 27 on chasing stragglers helps to explain why two general officers were in Winchester performing what appeared to be the same duties. Jones stated that following Steuart's arrival, his cavalry had been relieved in Winchester, leaving him free to operate in the area surrounding the town. From this it is clear that Steuart was responsible only for Winchester. Jones reported that on September 26 alone he had arrested 150 stragglers, and he intended to sweep the countryside for more west toward Romney and south toward Front Royal. According to Jones, the country was full of stragglers, and he had already returned over 5,000 to the army, no thanks to the provost guard, which was of "little" assistance. He professed astonishment at the number of officers skulking in the area and advised that after giving public notice of his intentions he had ordered the cavalry to arrest all officers and men found in the area without proper passes. Jones, who must have been a man of some humor, noted that this order created "quite a stampede" in the direction of the army. He also mentioned that there were about 1,200 barefooted men in Winchester, many of whom had probably thrown away their shoes so they would not be forced forward to the army. George Wise remem-

31. *Ibid.*, 143.

32. *OR*, Vol. XIX, Pt. 2, pp. 614–15.

33. Walter H. Taylor, "The Battle of Sharpsburg," *SHSP*, XXIV (rpr. 1977), 273; Taylor, *General Lee His Campaigns in Virginia*, 121.

bered that in his regiment, the 17th Virginia, many of the men were ordered to remain in Virginia for want of shoes.[34]

General Steuart remained at Winchester for some time after the army returned to Virginia. On October 13 he advised Secretary of War Randolph that Winchester was quiet and in good order, and he would ensure that provost marshals took the greatest care "to prevent soldiers from passing through who have not proper authority to leave their regiments."[35]

In the camps of the army, officers at all levels no longer looked charitably on stragglers. Sharpsburg had been a severe shock to the army, and it had made evident the damaging effect of straggling to hopes for a clear-cut victory. Stonewall Jackson's adjutant general estimated that there had been twenty-five thousand stragglers during the campaign, and Jackson had no patience left for the breed. He ordered his provost marshal, Major David B. Bridgford, "to shoot all stragglers who refused to go forward, or, if caught a second time, upon the evidence of two witnesses to shoot them." One of Jackson's other "cures," a remedy he started at Second Manassas, was to bundle stragglers together into closely supervised companies and commit them to the heaviest fighting "as much for punishment as for the real benefit they might be." Others encouraged stragglers to keep up by means of "sharp play" with the flats of their swords. A. P. Hill was even more direct: during the forced march to Sharpsburg on the morning of September 17 he had used the point of his sword to prod stragglers forward.[36]

On Monday, September 22, Lee ordered his two corps commanders, Longstreet and Jackson, to establish corps provost guards under the command of "efficient, energetic and firm officers." Both corps commanders were asked to make the most determined efforts to improve discipline, which along with greater mobility and higher inspiration would have to counterbalance the superior numbers and equipment of the Federals.[37]

It would seem that Lee had done just about all he could in an organizational

34. *OR*, Vol. XIX, Pt. 2, p. 629; John Gallatin Paxton (ed.), *The Civil War Letters of General Frank "Bull" Paxton, C.S.A., a Lieutenant of Lee and Jackson* (1905; rpr. Hillsboro, Texas, 1978), 91–92; George Wise, *History of the Seventeenth Virginia Infantry C.S.A.* (1870; rpr. Arlington, Va., 1969), 108.

35. *OR*, Vol. XIX, Pt. 2, pp. 664–65.

36. Henderson, *Stonewall Jackson*, 551, n. 35; Schenck, *Up Came Hill*, 229; *OR*, XXI, 641; William C. Oates, *The War Between the Union and the Confederacy and Its Lost Opportunities* (1905; rpr. Dayton, 1974), 144; Sorrel, *Recollections*, 101–102; Foote, *Civil War*, I, 699.

37. *OR*, Vol. XIX, Pt. 2, pp. 618–19.

sense. The general order of June 5, which established division provost guards, had been followed by the order of September 4, which organized both army and brigade provost guards. And now corps guards had been established, providing provost at all levels of the Army of Northern Virginia.

No one can say that Sharpsburg would have been conclusively a Confederate victory if the enormous straggling could have been reduced before the battle, but the presence of the fifteen thousand or more stragglers might have resulted in another triumph. Such an outcome could have decisively influenced the chance of foreign intervention in the war. Before the campaign, Southern prospects were so bright that the British foreign minister said that the time had come for "offering mediation to the United States Government, with a view to recognition of the independence of the Confederates . . . in case of failure, we ought ourselves to recognize the Southern States." Lord Palmerston, the British prime minister, replied that such an initiative must await the outcome of the battle.[38] The Confederate repulse dashed hopes of early foreign intervention. Never again would the South be so close to foreign recognition.

Lee's organizational measures and a renewed commitment by the high command to check straggling resulted in a dramatic improvement in discipline during the winter of 1862–1863. The feeling of invincibility that had crept into an army flushed with constant success, save Sharpsburg, which was viewed as a fluke or aberration, may well have lessened the desire to straggle. There was also the feeling that one more push would topple the Union monolith, and no soldier wanted to miss seeing that. With morale sky high, confident and contemptuous of the Yankee, Johnny Reb was perhaps finally recognizing the benefit of good discipline; maybe Lee's reminders that safety lay in discipline and duty were having some affect. Or perhaps straggling was down not through lessened desire but because of fear of punishment such as Jackson's dire threat to shoot offenders. Possibly, too, it may have been harder to straggle because the numerous, experienced, and increasingly effective provost guards would have served as a powerful deterrent.

There are a number of indications that straggling was on the downturn. Even before the resounding success at Fredericksburg, which resulted in twelve thousand Federal casualties, there was evidence of a new spirit in the army. Late in November Lieutenant Colonel Robert P. Blount, provost marshal of Longstreet's corps, notified President Davis that he had "nearly broken up the straggling from the army."[39]

38. Foote, *Civil War*, I, 666.
39. *OR*, Ser. II, Vol. IV, pp. 949–50.

His counterpart in Jackson's corps reported similar success. At Fredericksburg the 2d Corps provost consisted of the 1st Virginia Battalion, supplemented by a squadron of cavalry, both under the command of Major David Bridgford. His report on provost operations during December is very instructive of the methods of the provost and the success they were enjoying at the time. The report described how on December 12 at Hamilton's Crossing, about three miles southeast of Fredericksburg, Bridgford placed his guard, infantry and cavalry, in a line approximately one-half mile to the rear of Jackson's two-mile front along the railroad. The guard was ordered to arrest any men absent from their commands without proper passes and escort them to the provost surgeon, who would examine all those claiming to be sick. Those incapable of further service would be retained behind the lines, but malingerers would be escorted to the "first major general whose command was going into the fight, to place them in front and most exposed portion of his command." Bridgford recorded that arrests on December 12 were "comparatively few"; the same held true on December 13 and 14, when only 526 men were sent forward under guard. "Numbers" were returned to their commands because they did not have proper passes allowing them to the rear to "cook, and etc." He was obviously relieved that he had not had to comply with Jackson's instructions to shoot stragglers, but had there been a need, he said "it certainly should have been executed to the very letter." On December 17 Bridgford moved his guard to the rear of D. H. Hill's division on the Port Royal road and remained there through the eighteenth. The conclusion of Bridgford's report was good news for Jackson's corps: "I am happy to inform you that there was little or no straggling; the number did not exceed 30. . . . It is my belief . . . that there was less disposition on the part of the men to shirk from duty. . . . The present system of provost guard, if carried into effect, will prevent all future straggling."[40] This was Bridgford's last report to Stonewall Jackson; around Christmas he and the 1st Virginia Battalion became provost marshal and provost guard respectively of the Army of Northern Virginia.[41]

Close reading of Bridgford's report reveals three specific methods of control that seem to have worked for the provost. These could be referred to as the "straggler line," the "straggler post," and the "straggler patrol." The first is evident in Major Bridgford's placement of the provost in a line parallel with and behind the line of battle to prevent unauthorized rearward movement of troops.

40. *OR*, XXI, 641–42.
41. Worsham, *One of Jackson's Foot Cavalry,* 95.

It can be safely assumed that Bridgford would have carefully sited this straggler line so as to control natural exits which stragglers would have used to get out of the immediate battle area. In addition to monitoring these routes, the straggler line would have been sited to exercise surveillance of the rear area of the corps. Second, Bridgford chose an easily identifiable checkpoint or straggler post behind the railway embankment, which stragglers had to cross when leaving their commands. Here he could quickly gather stragglers and, on the advice of the medical officer, retain them or return them to their units. Because he had to cover two miles of frontage, Bridgford probably had more than one straggler post. The attached squadron of cavalry functioned as the third control method by patrolling along the straggler line, acting in support of the straggler posts, and conducting sweeps of areas where stragglers were likely to gather. It can be assumed that very careful records of the names and units of the stragglers were maintained by Jackson's provost guard.

The 5th Alabama Battalion, provost guard of A. P. Hill's 3d Corps, performed similar duties in similar manner in April and May, 1864. Lieutenant William Fulton recalled how during the action at the Wilderness the battalion deployed as a "straggler line" to the rear of Hill's corps to catch stragglers and return them to the fighting, an "important work . . . fraught with much danger." At Spotsylvania the battalion was again busy catching strays and returning them under guard as quickly as possible to their regimental officers in the trenches. This "Provost Guard duty," according to Fulton, required constant "vigilance and diligence" since there were always those who sought safety in the rear, using "every artifice" to slip away from the front.[42]

Some, of course, always evaded the provost. How this could happen is clear from the recollections of Sergeant B. F. Brown of the 1st South Carolina. During the time the army was entrenched along the Virginia Central Railroad near Hanover Junction in May, 1864, the provost guard of Samuel McGowan's brigade was extended in a line some two hundred or so yards behind the brigade lines. One dark, rainswept night while in charge of a detail taking cooked rations forward, Brown and his party passed through the provost line without seeing one of them. Continuing on through a gap in the breastworks, he eventually noticed some men that he believed were provost but who were in fact part of the Confederate picket line. Fortunately for Brown and his party, the

<hr>

42. William Frierson Fulton II, *The War Reminiscences of William Frierson Fulton II 5th Alabama Battalion Archer's Brigade A. P. Hill's Light Division A.N.V.* (N.d.; rpr. Gaithersburg, Md., 1986), 96–97, 101.

pickets challenged and then guided the party back to the Confederate lines. The story illustrates that the provost line could be inadvertently or deliberately bypassed.[43]

Stonewall Jackson was pleased indeed with the performance and the results obtained by Bridgford and his provost. Jackson's year-end report on Fredericksburg noted that the small number of stragglers afforded strong evidence of the "improving" discipline of the army. Nor were provost reports the only good news; regimental and brigade commanders as well were delighted with the dramatic decrease in straggling. The commanding officer of the 1st Virginia Regiment, describing the regiment's activities in the Fredericksburg area before the battle, noted that not one man had been absent during the movements of December 13 and 14. Brigadier General Frank Paxton, who had assumed command of the Stonewall Brigade on November 6, described the dramatic improvement in his new command: "We made a long march from Winchester—the longest the brigade has ever made without stopping. . . . Out of the last five days of the march, on three of them every man was present when we reached the camp in the evening; on the other two days but one was missing each day." A few days later Paxton commended the brigade for its gallantry at Fredericksburg but also directed regimental commanders to review the conduct of officers and men closely. Any who had remained in the camps or straggled or had fled from the enemy were to be arrested and punished; the latter in particular would merit "the just sentence of military law—to die under the colors he disgraced and by the muskets of the gallant comrades he deserted."[44]

After Fredericksburg the Army of Northern Virginia enjoyed a period of relative quiet, the boredom being relieved only by the comedy of General Ambrose E. Burnside's "Mud March" in late January and, for the soldiers, by an occasional furtive visit to the towns near the camps. With the army static for a change it was easy for the provost to establish guards in the small towns of northern Virginia and on the roads and railroads to intercept those who sought relief from the camps. Some of Hood's brigade, for example, who tarried in the barrooms of Fredericksburg were quickly arrested by the provost and returned to their camps.[45] All in all, the provost and the army did not have a bad winter. The men were relatively comfortable and at rest in winter quarters, the supply

43. B. F. Brown, "A Unique Experience," *Confederate Veteran*, XXXI (rpr. 1983), 100–101.

44. *OR*, XXI, 635; Spence, "Reports on the First, Seventh and Seventeenth Virginia Regiments in 1862," 267; Paxton (ed.), *Civil War Letters of Frank Paxton*, 67, 93.

45. Simpson, *Hood's Texas Brigade: Lee's Grenadier Guard*, 92.

of food was better than it had been, morale and confidence were high, and the army had time to heal its wounds and strengthen itself for the 1863 campaign.

By April 1 Longstreet's corps was gone from the camps of the Army of Northern Virginia, and on the eleventh he was besieging Suffolk in southern Virginia. Meantime, with hard marching ahead, Jackson made it clear to his corps that he expected a very high standard of march discipline. He served warning, for example, that divisions would march "precisely" at the given times, ten-minute rest periods each hour would be adhered to, and the rate of march would not exceed one mile in twenty-five minutes. As well, officers at all levels were to see that orders were strictly enforced and the opportunities for straggling curtailed. To put a stop to the practice of men leaving the ranks to care for the wounded, Jackson directed that men detailed for this task would wear the "prescribed" badge.[46]

Longstreet's corps was not at Chancellorsville, but Federal ineptitude and the brilliance of Lee and Jackson administered yet another thrashing to the Army of the Potomac, inflicting over seventeen thousand casualties, but at terrible cost. Stonewall Jackson, wounded in the flank attack that shattered Howard's 11th Corps, "crossed over the river" on May 10. There was no replacing him. On June 3 the Army of Northern Virginia, now in three corps under Richard Ewell, A. P. Hill, and James Longstreet, was on the move, the lead elements of the army's seventy-five thousand men marching rapidly westward from the deserted camps in the Fredericksburg area. The Gettysburg campaign was under way. By the eighth Longstreet and Ewell were at Culpeper Court House, and four days later Ewell was in the Shenandoah, en route to Winchester, where he defeated Robert Milroy on the fifteenth, paused briefly to tidy up, and then pushed on into Maryland on the sixteenth. Meanwhile, Hill and Longstreet were moving to join him, crossing the Potomac on the twenty-fourth bound for Pennsylvania.

Just before Longstreet crossed into Maryland he issued a general order calling on his officers and men to do their duty, particularly in preventing straggling, reminding them that "negligence in this respect has . . . already brought on us incalculable harm." The implication to the incredible straggling at Sharpsburg is clear. Longstreet also directed that a field officer and a surgeon were to march at the rear of each regiment to examine and give written permits to men who were not fit to march. Likewise, at the rear of each brigade a

---

46. Henderson, *Stonewall Jackson*, 643.

surgeon and a staff officer were to examine the permits and countersign them if they considered them legitimate.[47]

The other two corps of the army had their share of stragglers. John Worsham of the 21st Virginia remembered that on arriving at Staunton at the southern end of the Shenandoah on June 22, his company had been ordered to escort about a hundred stragglers to their units with the Army of Northern Virginia. Another company of the 21st was at Harpers Ferry engaged in the same task. These stragglers were probably from Ewell's 2d Corps. In the 3d Corps General Dorsey Pender, commanding a division under Hill, wrote his wife that "Lee was in a relaxed mood and had joshingly said that he was going to shoot us if we did not keep our men from straggling."[48] Still, the problem was nowhere as severe as it had been at Sharpsburg; action taken during the year had worked wonders on the army's discipline, and the military police had become a highly efficient organization. Colonel Walter Harrison, Pickett's inspector general, testified to the dramatic improvement, noting that during the Gettysburg campaign "there was no straggling, no desertion, nor disorder; and comparatively no plundering nor destruction of private property." Jacob Hoke, a resident of Chambersburg, Pennsylvania, was not as complimentary as Harrison: "The Confederate infantry, as they marched through Chambersburg, presented a solid front. They came in close marching order . . . all well armed and under perfect discipline. . . . Straggling was scarcely seen, but when some of them did wander . . . they did not hesitate to appropriate to themselves hats, boots, watches and pocketbooks. This proves that their good behavior when under the eyes of their officers was due to discipline rather than innate honesty and good breeding."[49] Julius Leinbach, a musician in the band of the 26th North Carolina, also provided a testimonial for the provost. He recalled that although he and some companions were told to accompany the wounded to the rear, they were loath to do so because "we were not quite sure that it would be safe . . . without some written authority from our officers."[50]

Stuart's cavalry had not been immune to the curse of the straggling either, although it was not until the return to Virginia that Stuart formally established

47. General Order 16, June 22, 1863, *OR,* Vol. LI, Pt. 2, p. 725.

48. Worsham, *One of Jackson's Foot Cavalry,* xxi, 103; Coddington, *Gettysburg Campaign,* 105.

49. Walter Harrison, *Pickett's Men: A Fragment of War History* (1870; rpr. Gaithersburg, Md., 1984), 82; Jacob Hoke, *The Great Invasion* (1887; rpr. New York, 1959), 208.

50. Leinbach, "Regiment Band," 230. Leinbach got away from Gettysburg with the rest of the army on July 4.

provost guards in his command. This is somewhat surprising as the mobility which a horse gave to the cavalry trooper made it much easier for him to straggle and harder for infantry provost to catch him. Stuart may earlier have considered and rejected the idea of forming provost guards. Unlike the infantry, which tended to remain together as regiments, cavalry units were often detached in squadron size or less to perform such duties as reconnaissance and outpost patrols, and therefore he may have felt that the establishment of cavalry provost was impractical.

Stuart's decision to organize guards after Gettysburg could well have stemmed from a feeling that he had not pleased Lee in Pennsylvania. The painful memory of July 2, when Lee had greeted him with icy reserve and an exasperated "General Stuart, where have you been?" no doubt caused him to resolve that never again would General Lee have reason to rebuke him. In any event, on July 29 a provost guard was established for each brigade and detachment of his cavalry, and guards were ordered aboard the railroad trains to prevent stragglers from taking the trains to the rear. Stuart expressed his conviction that without prompt and certain punishment of stragglers "all discipline is gone, and with it the efficiency of the cavalry division." A favorite punishment for troopers caught straggling was transfer to the infantry, where they could be put under more "rigid" discipline. No punishment was more feared by the trooper.[51]

With Lee once again in Virginia it was a time for introspection and assessment of what had gone wrong in Pennsylvania for both armies. In spite of the setback in the North and the loss of Vicksburg, the Confederacy could yet inflict vicious injury. This was proven by the Southern riposte at Chickamauga ("River of Death" in the Cherokee language), which brought the Federal momentum to a shuddering halt, and the successful containment of the Union thrusts at Charleston, South Carolina, and in Texas. It was soon conceded, however, that Chickamauga was a barren victory for the South. Everywhere the Confederacy stood on the defensive, yet the war was far from over, and with Lee anything was possible. The Confederacy could still win!

As 1863 turned to 1864, many Confederate commands continued to perfect their antistraggling measures. Johnson Hagood, commanding a brigade at Charleston, South Carolina, before Christmas of 1863, had taken just about every measure possible to prevent straggling. In his command no man could fall out of a march without obtaining the permission of his officers, and those

---

51. Foote, *Civil War,* II, 461; *OR,* Vol. XXVII, Pt. 3, p. 1050; Lonn, *Desertion During the Civil War,* 46.

officers were prepared to employ any means, regardless of severity, to check straggling. Once his brigade arrived in Virginia, the second in command of each regiment, accompanied by the regimental surgeon or his assistant and a noncommissioned officer and a "file of men," were ordered to march in the rear of their regiments to prevent straggling. The brigade rear guard, accompanied by the brigade surgeon, would march in the rear of the last regiment in the column. On the order of the brigade surgeon, any genuinely sick men would ride in the brigade ambulances, but men who straggled without authority would receive "severe and summary discipline; it is the highest military offense, next to desertion."[52]

Before the new year the provost were still demonstrating commendable efficiency as the Texas Brigade discovered while in winter quarters with Longstreet at Greeneville, Tennessee, in December. One of J. B. Polley's letters to "Charming Nellie" shows that the provost were still very much on the *qui vive*. Polley and two companions were apprehended by the provost, those "despised but lordly individuals," near Bean's Station on the Virginia and Tennessee Railroad on December 22. Despite their protests of innocence, the Texans were arrested as stragglers, the provost guard proclaiming their orders to stop anyone that "hain't a pass." It seems almost a tall tale, but according to Polley a bout of fiddle playing so bedazzled the provost that they released the Texans and gave them directions to camp. Polley ended his account of this narrow escape by confiding that they had avoided punishment for an offense that had put a number of their comrades in the guardhouse.[53]

The last spring and summer of the war broke upon the Confederacy in full fury with Grant striking for Richmond, determined to crush the only obstacle in his path, the legendary Army of Northern Virginia, and Sherman relentlessly forcing Johnston back to the gates of Atlanta. By May 4 Grant's juggernaut was over the Rapidan and Lee deployed to meet him. The waiting was over; the fighting would be nonstop until the Confederacy slumped exhausted in defeat.

Many in the South perceived that only hope was left, and maybe not much of that. Those in the army saw the signs—fewer soldiers, less food and equipment—in short, less chance to win, and these signs of despair were mirrored on the home front. From this time on, as the numbers of fainthearted grew, straggling and desertion would swell to epidemic proportions and could not be stopped. On May 5 the first great battle between Lee and Grant erupted in the

52. Hagood, *Memoirs,* 211–12.
53. Polley, "Texans Foraging for Christmas," 362.

Wilderness, where Lee hoped to negate the advantage of the Union's superior strength. Through the long summer of 1864 the fighting ground on, Grant sidestepping right but always finding Lee in front of him until finally both armies were dug in east of Richmond. It had taken Grant forty days and almost fifty-five thousand casualties—a figure larger than the combined infantry and artillery strength of the Army of Northern Virginia—to achieve a little better than the line McClellan held in 1862. But the end was in sight; Petersburg and Richmond were under siege, which as far back as June Lee had said would make defeat only a matter of time.

By late September straggling had once again become a major problem in Lee's army. An adjutant general's report blamed a loosening of discipline for the significant increase in straggling, that "greatest evil." The increase was such that the subject was raised, along with other matters pertaining to manpower, at a conference of the state governors at Augusta, Georgia, on October 17. They presently framed a resolution, directed to President Davis, asking for "the arrest and return to their commands of all deserters and stragglers."[54] By mid-November there was "continual complaint" of men straggling to the rear of the Richmond lines and committing depredations. So serious was the problem that Pickett's inspector general urged him to reinforce his provost guard of one officer and eighty-five men. Sometimes, as at Fisher's Hill in the Shenandoah in the autumn of 1864, it was not merely an urge to straggle that seized the troops, but mad panic. So demoralized were some Confederates on the field that the provost guards were ordered to check the precipitous rout by firing on the runaways.[55] Unfortunately, little time or opportunity remained to the army to correct its shortcomings. During the Appomattox campaign, the last of the war, straggling in the Army of Northern Virginia was not so much straggling as the disintegration of the army and the nation.

In the Army of Tennessee the fight against straggling was made even more difficult by the serious flaws in the army's structure: pronounced personality conflicts, lack of rapport, and unending leadership changes. During its short existence the army had suffered nine commanding generals of varying caliber and an unceasing shuffle in and out of corps and division commanders. This sorry record detracted greatly from the army's organizational sophistication, and many innovations, including disciplinary controls, were slower to appear,

---

54. *OR*, Vol. XLII, Pt. 2, p. 1276, Pt. 3, p. 1150.

55. Harrison, *Pickett's Men*, xxiii; George Wilson Booth, *Personal Reminiscences of a Maryland Soldier in the War Between the States, 1861–1865* (1898; rpr. Gaithersburg, Md., 1986), 148.

often by as much as a year or more, than in Lee's army. This not only hurt the consistency of the army's combat record but also greatly increased the difficulty of building *esprit de corps*. The army recognized early on that it had a discipline problem. A battalion commander at Shiloh, Major F. H. Clack, was among the first to voice his dismay at the effects of straggling on the army.[56] Between Shiloh and Perryville it got worse, much worse.

Late in July, 1862, Bragg shifted his army by rail from Tupelo, Mississippi, to Chattanooga, Tennessee, and then crossed the Tennessee River in late August on a new campaign designed to recover eastern Tennessee and Kentucky. By September 14 Bragg was moving to surround Munfordville, Kentucky, having bypassed Don Carlos Buell at Murfreesboro and Nashville. The day before, Major General Sam Jones, in command at Chattanooga in Bragg's rear, wrote to advise Bragg that fourteen hundred stragglers under the charge of an officer of the 1st Louisiana were en route to the army. Presumably these men reached the army in time for the Battle of Perryville, which was fought on October 8. Jones could have spared them the march forward and then back for by October 10 the Confederates were recoiling southward with a bloody nose suffered at Perryville. Edmund Kirby Smith, for one, pointed to the "unusually great" straggling after Perryville, noting that by October 22 he was reduced to fewer than six thousand men. Bragg was in a similarly weakened state by early November with some of his regiments down to one hundred men. The entire army mustered only thirty thousand men even though some stragglers had returned to their units.[57] As 1862 ended, Confederate prospects were anything but bright: Lee had not won in Maryland, Bragg had lost in Kentucky, and everywhere Southern hopes were dimming.

The first half of 1863 was relatively quiet for Bragg's Army of Tennessee, but in late June William Rosecrans' Army of the Cumberland lurched forward toward Tullahoma, the movement culminating on July 3 with the expulsion of the Confederate army from Tennessee. For the Confederates the period following June 23 was not a happy one; the unending retreat was hard on equipment and men, but most of all it was hard on morale. Demoralization was revealed by, among other things, a sharp increase in straggling, a development that drew strong response from the senior officers of the army. On the twenty-sixth Lieutenant General William Hardee, commanding the 2d Corps, had a staff

56. *OR*, Vol. X, Pt. 1, p. 512.

57. *OR*, Vol. XVI, Pt. 2, p. 819; Foote, *Civil War*, I, 739–40, 742; Thomas Lawrence Connelly, *Autumn of Glory: The Army of Tennessee, 1862–1865* (Baton Rouge, 1971), 17–18.

officer write to A. P. Stewart, one of his division commanders, "I learn that numbers of your men have straggled," to remind him that brigade provost guards had been organized to prevent straggling, rather a stinging remark in its presumption of ignorance or neglect on the part of Stewart. John Breckinridge, a division commander under Bishop Leonidas Polk, had also been chastised for the straggling in his division, and he passed the complaint on to his brigade commanders, calling their attention to the "hundreds of men wandering through the country . . . and complaints . . . of serious depredations." They were told to strengthen their brigade provost and put a stop to the irregularities.[58]

Stewart, meantime, had not reacted to Hardee's letter, probably because the latter was replaced on July 19 by D. H. Hill, an officer who had not shown any sympathy to stragglers at Sharpsburg and was not about to now. On August 6, however, Stewart ordered frequent provost patrols to arrest any stragglers, and the officers of his division were told to make every effort to prevent the troops from plundering the gardens and cornfields of local farmers. Such efforts were to little avail. Texans in Deshler's brigade of Patrick Cleburne's division "found plenty of ripe sweet potatoes, green corn, and garden truck, and while the orders forbidding foraging were strict, and the provost guard on the watch, yet we managed to beat them all and lived fine."[59]

Not surprisingly, D. H. Hill moved quickly to establish strict discipline in his new command, and not without reason, for Rosecrans was over the Tennessee River near Bridgeport, Alabama, on September 1. That same day Hill warned his officers that any who permitted straggling would be arrested. Bragg was now seriously threatened from the south and west with Rosecrans moving toward his rear, and it was becoming clear that the evacuation of Chattanooga was imminent. The city was abandoned on the ninth. On the seventh Lieutenant General Polk had taken the precaution of advising his division commanders of the order of march of his corps: "The brigade provost guards will bring up the rear of each brigade. Division provost guards will follow each division, arresting stragglers and keeping the column well up."[60] These orders assisted in keeping straggling down during the move to La Fayette, Georgia. Longstreet's two divisions of the Army of Northern Virginia were meantime en route to Bragg.

---

58. *OR,* Vol. XXIII, Pt. 2, p. 886; Vol. XXIV, Pt. 3, p. 988.
59. *OR,* Vol XXIII, Pt. 2, p. 954; Collins, *Chapters from the Unwritten History,* 143.
60. *OR,* Vol. XXX, Pt. 4, pp. 580, 621.

Longstreet must have wondered what he was getting into. Arriving at Catoosa Station about 4 P.M. on September 19, he found no guide waiting nor any word from Bragg, and all he could do was saddle up and ride toward the sound of the guns. On the way he encountered a stream of traffic: ambulances, ammunition wagons, walking wounded, and stragglers, none of whom knew where the army or its commander was.[61] Night fell and Longstreet, together with three staff officers, had a second encounter, this time with Federal pickets. Narrowly avoiding capture or worse, the party finally reached Bragg's headquarters a little short of midnight. The next day's hard-won victory meant nothing because of Bragg's decision to starve out rather than destroy what remained of Rosecrans' army. By October 2, twenty thousand fresh men were en route to Rosecrans, with five more divisions under Sherman to follow. Bragg would soon be in the novel position of besieging superior numbers, made worse by his decision to send Longstreet and his corps against Burnside in East Tennessee.

The hiatus after Chickamauga did not do much for the men of the Army of Tennessee; disillusionment and bitterness gripped the army over Bragg's failure to exploit victory—Forrest fumed, "What does he fight battles for?"—and the army was starving, subsisting mostly on parched corn. These conditions encouraged straggling and marauding to obtain food, and soon many reports spoke of "an alarming number of stragglers . . . officers and soldiers, visiting, loitering and marauding."[62]

Then on November 25 came the debacle at Missionary Ridge, the center of the army streaming to the rear in headlong flight, the Yankees in hot pursuit, overrunning Bragg's headquarters, causing him to remark on the "panic" he had not seen before. Arthur Manigault, a brigade commander during the battle, observed individuals attempting to sneak to the rear and ordered his provost marshal to shoot any unwounded men leaving their positions. The numbers abandoning the field soon swamped the provost (the brigade provost was thirty-two strong—twenty-six privates, two corporals, two sergeants, and two officers), and all efforts to check the stampede were futile. According to Manigault, it was numerical disparity of forces and Bragg's bad defensive dispositions that created the panic. Hard-fighting Patrick Cleburne, who covered the retreat over Chickamauga Creek, noted with disgust the stragglers who lin-

---

61. Glen Tucker, *Chickamauga* (New York, 1961), 212; Sorrel, *Recollections*, 182–84.
62. Lonn, *Desertion During the Civil War*, 42–43; *OR*, Vol. XX, Pt. 2, p. 446.

gered so they could be captured: "fainthearted" men giving in to hardship and "imagined" hopelessness.[63] Cleburne's rear-guard action was about all there was to praise. Bragg lost almost seven thousand men, and the straggling as the army retreated to Dalton, Georgia, was heavy.

On November 28 Bragg resigned, leaving behind gloom and the Army of Tennessee sadly depleted, physically and morally. At year's end Secretary of War James Seddon's annual report admitted the serious setbacks of 1863 and highlighted the reduction of military effectiveness caused by the increased straggling, desertion, and absenteeism. The Army of Tennessee went into camp at Dalton under its new commander, Joseph E. Johnston.

Over the winter Johnston worked miracles on both the moral and physical condition of the army. The food and clothing shortages were solved, and the system of furloughs which he initiated rejuvenated the spirit of the men. His proclamation of amnesty for all who would return to the ranks added "several thousand" absentees—deserters and quasi-deserters—to the colors.[64] In addition, Johnston improved the discipline of the army, adopting every measure he could to prepare for the spring campaign, which Sherman and his hundred thousand men would launch on May 7.

Johnston's long retreat from Dalton to Peachtree Creek, just six miles short of Atlanta, illustrates what happens to morale and discipline when an army is constantly falling back. Not surprisingly, there were many who evaded Johnston's provost as the army moved down through Resaca, Cassville, and Marietta. After Kennesaw Mountain, for example, the Atlanta *Intelligencer,* in an article on the breakdown of law and order in the city, reported that the thousands of deserters and stragglers from Johnston's army had become an "unmitigated" annoyance. An officer of the army recalled stragglers "plundering and pilfering" all over Atlanta. These comments are undoubtedly true because the few provost in the city at the time could have done little to control the offenders. The Atlanta Provost Battalion had present for duty 9 officers and 79 men in early July, increasing to 13 officers and 155 men ten days later.[65] Still, in spite of the long retreat and the shirkers in the rear, Johnston, when relieved on July 17, turned over to Hood an army in generally good fighting trim.

63. Stanley F. Horn, *The Army of Tennessee* (New York, 1941), 301; Tower (ed.), *A Carolinian Goes to War,* 140, 142, 166.

64. Horn, *Army of Tennessee,* 312.

65. Carter, *Siege of Atlanta,* 169, 240; *OR,* Vol. XXIII, Pt. 1, p. 586, Pt. 2, p. 920; Vol. XXX, Pt. 4, p. 519.

And it was to get fighting—battles at Peachtree Creek and Atlanta—two fiascos at a cost of over seven thousand casualties and more to come. Both failures were laid at Hardee's door. According to Hood, Hardee's corps had been late getting into action on the twentieth and twenty-second, prompting him to tighten up march discipline by establishing a sixty-man provost guard in each division of the army.[66] The good they did was problematical. Twelve days after the evacuation of Atlanta, Hood revealed that he was "pained to see that . . . two-thirds of the straggling was caused not from the fatigue . . . but by want of discipline . . . and the great desire of the men for leaving their commands and plundering the citizens."[67] Corps and division commanders were directed to make every effort to prevent straggling. Every man would be needed in Hood's subsequent Tennessee campaign, a somewhat unique event in that two hostile armies, each supposedly dedicated to the destruction of the other, set out in opposite directions. Disaster awaited in Tennessee: the battles of Franklin and Nashville virtually destroyed Hood's army.

Straggling in the western cavalry under Joseph Wheeler and Nathan Bedford Forrest was, if anything, even worse than in Stuart's cavalry in the East. Wheeler realized from the start that discipline was not one of the best features of his command, but the extent of the deficiency became manifest after Chickamauga, when a torrent of complaints reached his headquarters on the depredations his straggling cavalrymen were committing. He reacted by issuing comprehensive instructions designed to put an end to the indiscretions of his troopers. As a first step, division commanders were ordered to organize provost guards of "efficient and trustworthy" men, who were to sweep the areas within five miles of any camps, arresting any cavalrymen absent from the bivouacs without written authority. Those caught were to be sent under guard to the provost marshal, who would arrange their transfer to the infantry. Every ten days division provost marshals were required to submit lists of the names and units of any men who had been arrested, along with a certificate confirming that no exceptions had been permitted. Division commanders were told to dispatch provost to any locality, regardless of the distance involved, at which stragglers

66. Richard M. McMurray, *John Bell Hood and the War for Southern Independence* (Lexington, Ky., 1982), 141; *OR*, Vol. XXXVIII, Pt. 5, p. 909. The ten infantry divisions of Hood's army would therefore have had a provost strength of six hundred men. The estimated strength of the army, including the Georgia militia, was sixty-four thousand, according to Carter, *Siege of Atlanta*, 413. This figure agrees with the official army returns of July 31 (*OR*, Vol. XXXVIII, Pt. 3, p. 680).

67. *OR*, Vol. XXXIX, Pt. 2, p. 833.

were known to have congregated. They were also warned that passes must be issued to officers and men who left the camps for any reason. This was to apply even to detachments proceeding on duty.

According to Wheeler's apologist, William Carey Dodson, these orders and Wheeler's disciplinary measures were "so exacting and efficient . . . that no complaints whatever were made of bad conduct of the troops . . . during the winter and spring of 1864."[68] This statement is not entirely borne out by subsequent events. During 1864 Wheeler had to issue further orders on the subject of straggling. In December he directed that each division form a reg-imental-size provost guard; the basis of selection was to be good conduct. The guards were to function as advance guards while the cavalry was on the march, picketing every house along the way to prevent any outrages on civilians or their property. While in camp the guards would station a detachment at each house within the division's area.

Wheeler seems to have finished the war with a fairly good record in regard to straggling, according to an inspection report on his command in April, 1865, prepared by Colonel E. E. Portlock of the Adjutant General's Office. The section of the report devoted to straggling is interesting for two reasons: first, it points out the unique problems associated with the control of straggling in the cavalry; and, second, it illustrates that Wheeler, in taking every possible mea-sure to control it, had achieved considerable success:

> To a casual observer, there is much straggling among the soldiers of this corps; but an investigation will satisfy anyone that the causes which produce this are in many instances induced by the necessities of the service. Being the only cavalry to watch the enemy's movements, and to impede his progress . . . this corps had to picket all the roads, remove stock and harass him as much as possible . . . and as its movements were compelled to conform to those of the enemy, which could not be known until developed by him, pickets and other bodies of observa-tion—sometimes composed of a regiment but generally small parties— would be cut off and compelled to find their way to the main body by circuitous routes as best they could . . . .
>
> These causes considered . . . my own observation has satisfied me that there is no unusual amount of straggling in this corps. The system to

68. William Carey Dodson (ed.), *Campaigns of Wheeler and His Cavalry, 1862–1865* (Atlanta, 1899), 373–85. These instructions were published as General Order 11 on October 30, 1863.

prevent straggling is good and effective, as it is immediate in punishment . . . . All men absent from their commands without permission are arrested, "bucked and gagged," and sent under guard to their proper officer. This system of prompt punishment has produced a wholesome fear of the Provost-Guard. That some straggling does exist is matter beyond dispute, and much of it is due to the leniency of the officers in charge of details.[69]

Nathan Bedford Forrest had been careful throughout the war to ensure that his command was aware of his desire to control straggling. His division commanders were instructed to use brigade provost guards as rear guards to prevent soldiers from slipping away from the columns. Those that were apprehended without passes were returned under guard to their units. This procedure was put into effect by Forrest's chief provost marshal, Captain John Goodwin, in late 1864. By the following March, these instructions were extended down to company level: "There must be a field officer, with a suitable rear guard, to march in the rear of each regiment; a company officer from each company in the rear of their respective companies; and the brigade provost guard . . . in rear of each brigade."[70] Private John Hubbard of the 7th Tennessee, one of Forrest's regiments, recalling his service with a brigade provost guard, stated that the primary duty was to follow in the rear and prevent straggling. In commenting on the provost's efficiency in preventing straggling after Nashville in 1864, one Confederate trooper stated that Forrest himself was more effective in this role than the provost.[71]

It would be fair to say that Johnston's army, like Lee's, was plagued to the end by straggling. On March 25, 1865, Johnston published a general order, one of his last, reminding his officers that the army's recent marches—presumably the withdrawal from Sherman's overwhelming force at Bentonville—had disclosed "several irregularities which seriously impair its efficiency. Among these the most flagrant and mischievous are: The enormous straggling . . . marching without arms; disregard of regular formation . . . and the common habit of permitting slightly sick men to march without order or officers."[72] It no longer mattered. Johnston surrendered on April 26.

69. *Ibid.*, 393–94, 426.

70. *OR*, Vol. XLV, Pt. 2, p. 682; Vol. XLIX, Pt. 1, pp. 1025–26.

71. Hubbard, *Notes of a Private*, 183; James H. M'Neilly, "With the Rear Guard," *Confederate Veteran*, XXVI (rpr. 1983), 339.

72. *OR*, Vol. XLVII, Pt. 3, p. 688.

Other armies and department commands of the Confederate States had also faced the threat posed by the straggler. The various commanders of the Army of the Mississippi, for example, had on numerous occasions published orders and instructions on the subject of straggling. Major General William Hardee, commanding the army for about a month in mid-1862, issued the first, a call on all officers to enforce discipline and prevent straggling. In August the new commander, Braxton Bragg, ordered the establishment of rear guards for the purpose of arresting and returning stragglers to their units. According to Bragg, straggling, which was always "injurious" to discipline and efficiency, had now become "dangerous." In November additional orders were published "prohibiting" straggling. It would be naive to assume that any of these orders had the desired effect. During roughly the same period, Brigadier General Earl Van Dorn, commanding the District of Mississippi, directed the attention of his officers to the army's straggling and pillaging. He had "repeatedly" done so, presumably with no effect, and therefore commanders were ordered to organize provost guards to end the "irregularities," a euphemism for the marauding that was in progress. Van Dorn continued to urge his officers to employ the most "stringent" measures to prevent straggling.[73]

To the east, in the Department of North Carolina and Southern Virginia, Major General G. W. Smith issued a directive in January, 1863, ordering the formation of one-hundred-man-strong brigade provost guards. These guards would follow the army on the march, and in battle they would be stationed in the rear of the battle line to stop stragglers and return them to the front. This procedure parallels in time and method the system in use in the Army of Northern Virginia.

Across the Mississippi, Edmund Kirby Smith had an immense straggling problem on his hands, one greatly complicated by the vast extent—six hundred thousand square miles—of a department consisting of Missouri, Arkansas, four-fifths of Louisiana, Texas, the Indian Territory, and the short-lived Confederate Territory of Arizona. When he took command of the Trans-Mississippi Department in early 1863, straggling and desertion had shown such an increase that both the Arkansas and Texas legislatures passed draconic measures for the punishment of deserters. Major General John Magruder, commanding the District of Texas, New Mexico, and Arizona, found straggling so menacing that he appealed to the governor of Texas for state aid in the arrest of stragglers.[74] A

---

73. *OR,* Vol. XVI, Pt. 2, p. 788; Vol. XX, Pt. 2, p. 396; Vol. XVII, Pt. 2, pp. 729–30, 745.
74. *OR,* XV, 975.

number of Texas newspaper articles testify to the severity of the problem. A May 16 issue of the Dallas *Herald* listed forty-three absentees from one regiment. An item in another paper carried a plaintive appeal asking that men absent from the 29th Texas Cavalry report immediately or be declared deserters.

To the east, in Louisiana, the Confederate retreat before Nathaniel P. Banks in April led to such heavy straggling that General Richard Taylor, goaded beyond all patience, relieved the commander of a cavalry brigade. His replacement failed to control stragglers any better, and finally Taylor pulled the brigade out of the fighting to give it an opportunity to collect its stragglers. During the summer Taylor's Texas troops became so demoralized that many headed west for home, and he requested that crossings on the Sabine River be picketed to stop their flow.

In the northern part of the department, the abortive Confederate attack on Helena, Arkansas, resulted in sixteen hundred casualties and a lengthy retreat to Little Rock, during which the army literally melted away: "Stragglers dropped out by squads; desertions dissolved whole companies; Jo Shelby recommended that his entire brigade be furloughed to prevent wholesale mutiny." Even the provost, when and if they were available, could do little to check the tide. During July, Brigadier General W. L. Cabell's command was so shattered near Fort Smith, Arkansas, that the men, in a panic to get to the rear, ran through the provost guard, which was busy guarding deserters.[75]

Confederate operations in Arkansas were dogged with bad luck and worse management from the beginning. Earl Van Dorn's relentless pursuit of Samuel Curtis in the early spring of 1862 exhausted his ill-disciplined and poorly armed army even before the action at Elkhorn Tavern started on March 7. The ensuing defeat caused a stampede to the rear and just about every other direction. Fortunately, Curtis made no effort to interfere with the departing Confederates, and the clean break from the battle allowed Van Dorn gradually to piece his army together.[76]

General Sterling Price had no better luck with straggling in his Army of Missouri despite the orders to organize brigade provost guards of fifty "picked" men and four officers and the appointment of division provost marshals.[77] During the October, 1864, retreat from Missouri, Price reportedly lost "thou-

75. Kerby, *Kirby Smith's Confederacy*, 60, 104–105, 120, 133; *OR*, Vol. XXII, Pt. 1, p. 606.

76. Robert G. Hartje, *Van Dorn: The Life and Times of a Confederate General* (Nashville, 1967), 127–57.

77. *OR*, Vol. XLI, Pt. 1, p. 648.

sands" to straggling as his army fled from Westport, and by the time safety was reached in southwest Arkansas the army was down to thirty-five hundred totally demoralized men. Price's conduct of the campaign resulted in so much bitterness and recrimination, including charges of ill discipline and plundering, that he requested a court of inquiry to clear his name. The court convened and proceeded to amass evidence proving the charges against Price, but before he could rebut, the court, and the Confederate States of America, had ceased to exist.

It is evident that every army the South put in the field was weakened by straggling. Always prone to wandering, the Southern soldier became more so as hopes of victory waned, particularly in the last year of the war, when it was obvious that the Confederacy could not win. There were many reasons why men opted to leave their units. Some left the ranks because they could not keep up; they were sick and feeble, broken down by bad food and exhaustion, or they lacked shoes, without which many were soon physically incapable of marching. Destitution forced many to forage, while others, destitute of spirit or of criminal bent, left their comrades to pillage and plunder. Others, disgruntled with conditions in the army, slipped from the ranks to cater to their appetites for drink and other comforts. Then there were the cowards, who deserted to avoid the dangers of the front, some of them so base as deliberately to seek capture by the enemy.

The effects of straggling were debilitating. The most pernicious was the decrease in strength, capability, and performance of the army in battle, the prime example being bloody Sharpsburg, which destroyed hopes of early foreign intervention. Had the thousands of stragglers been present, fit and ready to do their share, who is to say that Lee might not have decisively beaten McClellan and "conquered peace for Dixie." But straggling had other side effects that sapped the Confederate war effort. The spirit of indiscipline engendered an atmosphere of lawlessness and disorder, which, because of the pillage and plunder of the citizen, loosened the cohesion of the cause and damaged the support and loyalty given to the national government.

Control of straggling once the army was in the field was a primary duty of the military police and one that occupied a very large percentage of their time and manpower. The provost had very little use for stragglers or for commands that habitually straggled; a party of soldiers from the 3d Texas Cavalry encountered a provost marshal who "cursed them as damned stragglers belonging to a straggling brigade."[78]

78. S. B. Barron, *The Lone Star Defenders: A Chronicle of the Third Texas Cavalry, Ross' Brigade* (1908; rpr. Waco, 1964), 192–93. The confrontation occurred at Talladega, Alabama.

The "monstrous evil" of straggling was never eradicated in spite of appeals issued by officers at every level from Lee down or the threats of dire punishment, including execution, which emanated from virtually every command in the Confederacy. Nor did the establishment of provost guards in the armies, corps, divisions, and brigades and in the departments, cities, and towns of the South entirely cure the disease. There were the happy times like the autumn and winter of 1862 and the spring of 1863, when straggling was almost nonexistent, but in the main, straggling was a chronic sickness throughout the war. The provost's "cure" was varied and uneven, and although at times the malignancy seemed to be in remission, it always came back with renewed force. As the Union war machine gathered momentum and the Confederacy shriveled, the strength and availability of the provost correspondingly decreased. References to efforts by the provost to control straggling during the last year of the war are markedly sparse because by then the provost with the armies could not be spared from combat, even for the shortest periods. Every bayonet was required on the line; noncombatants could not be afforded.

The second reason for the provost's failure was the commonly held belief, which proved true in practice, that the straggler would not be punished as he deserved. There were exceptions (the unpopular Braxton Bragg was notoriously hard on wrongdoers), but generally punishment was, in Lee's terms, neither prompt nor certain. As this became common knowledge, contempt for the provost increased, and the ground was cut from beneath their feet.

Earlier in this chapter it was remarked that the straggler was always a potential deserter. It was difficult for the provost to differentiate between the two offenses. The methods used to control the straggler applied equally to the deserter, the similarity between the two causing this natural extension of controls. The struggle to check desertion was to prove exceedingly difficult and exhausting.

9

Let Me Lament the Exodus

An adversary is more hurt by
desertion than by slaughter.

VEGETIUS

It was remarked in the Preface that the loser in any war is never as well documented as the victor. Those who would study the loser and try to assess why he lost must decide how best to penetrate and interpret the myth and legend that over the years envelops the defeated. There are many instances of how the passage of time can color and change our perceptions of men and events. Nowhere in history is this more true than of the Confederate States of America. An aura of mysticism and tales of valiant deeds of valiant men blur the successes and failures of the "Lost Cause," the issues that led to the war, and the men who fought and died under the "Star Crossed Banner."

For a time after the surrender any attack on the Confederate mystique, even when fully supported by fact, was regarded as heresy and treason. Longstreet discovered to his great cost just how dangerous any assault on Confederate memory could be; his statement in 1878 that Robert E. Lee had lost the battle of Gettysburg made Longstreet a pariah in the South. It was not until the unveiling of the Lee statue in Richmond in 1890 that there was any reconciliation between Longstreet and other former Confederate leaders. With the cooling of passions and the demise of many of the participants in the struggle for a separate national life, historians began to relate more impartially those factors that had contributed to the defeat of the South.

The casual reader on the war and the Confederacy could be excused for assuming that Southerners went to war totally united and indivisibly committed to the cause of Southern independence and that they fought heroically and gallantly to the last man and the last ditch, nearly every man a paragon of patriotic and military virtue and all determined to do or die. Although the most ardent pro-Confederate reader would not be surprised to learn that some and, in fact, many Southerners did not possess or display such devotion to the cause, he would probably be amazed and even shocked to learn that desertion must rank as a major factor in Confederate defeat. In the end, the rate of desertion became so appalling that the Confederate armies literally melted away.

The connection between straggling and desertion has already been noted. It is difficult to determine exactly where straggling leaves off and desertion begins; the precise moment when the temporary absentee hardens his resolve to leave the army and the fighting for good is perhaps not definable, but it is certain that in most cases one leads directly and naturally to the other. Regardless of the reason why a soldier left his unit in the forward area, it was imperative that he be apprehended and returned as soon as possible. This was necessary for two reasons: first, it salvaged a soldier for continued duty at the front, the only place where his bayonet counted for anything; and, second, it prevented the shirker from making his way to the rear, where he could hide and take advantage of the dislocation of normal life in a society and a country under siege to indulge his tastes for pillage and plunder. In short, the deserter could not be allowed to feed off the countryside and its inhabitants, thereby weakening not only the nation's fighting power but also civilian loyalty to the central government.

The chronic sickness of desertion spread at epidemic speed; by the end of 1864 approximately one hundred thousand Confederate soldiers had "seceded" from the war. This figure is immensely significant when one considers the great and ever-growing disparity between the Union and Confederate armies. Always desperate for men, the South could not afford such profligate waste of manpower. Without armies she could not achieve independence, and as General Lee wrote Secretary of War Breckinridge in February, 1865, unless the increase in desertion was checked it "will bring us calamity."[1]

Unceasing attempts to control desertion occupied more and more troops, and as the war situation deteriorated, large areas of the Confederate States—in particular western North Carolina and parts of Georgia, Alabama, and Mississippi—became sanctuaries for such large numbers of deserters that state troops were unable to cope with them. This situation led several states to beg the Confederate government for assistance, which that government could not always provide. When aid could be extended, it was at the expense of front-line strength, and conversely, when aid could not be proffered, the local population was quick to perceive that the national government was incapable of protecting its citizens. The resulting decline in confidence and morale significantly decreased the chances of Southern victory.

Well-meaning but misguided leniency to deserters further exacerbated the

---

1. Long, *Civil War Day by Day,* 706, 714; *OR,* Vol. XLVI, Pt. 2, p. 1265.

problem and proved no more effective than the many appeals to deserters to rejoin the colors. In the autumn of 1863, when Secretary of War James Seddon held in abeyance the executions of two deserters from the 41st Virginia Infantry, Lee advised that he had issued the necessary orders, but he had "serious apprehension of a relapse into that lenient policy" which had been "ruinous" to the army:

> Early in the war it was found that stringent measures alone would keep the army together. After a few executions a number of men were pardoned, and the consequence was a recurrence of desertion to a most alarming extent. A return to a sterner discipline was found to be absolutely necessary, and by the executions that have taken place since the proclamation of the President, and by them only, has a stop been put to a spirit that was rapidly growing . . . and that seriously threatened the existence of the army. . . . I am convinced that the only way to prevent them is to visit the offence when committed with the sternest punishment, and leave the offender without hope of escape by making the penalty inevitable.[2]

Unfortunately, a policy of consistent severity of punishment, which had been applied for a time in 1864, was not continued, and in any event it came too late to check the rot in the army.

Many of the causes of desertion were identical to those that precipitated straggling: the boredom and tedium of camp life, failure to receive pay and equipment, lack of adequate food and clothing, poor sanitation and medical care, resentment of discipline, cowardice, and the desire to pillage and plunder. One other major reason for desertion was homesickness and anxiety regarding the condition of families. In view of the ruinous inflation, men wondered if their wives and children were getting enough to eat and whether they were safe from harm, particularly if they were living in enemy-occupied areas. An added complication was the lack of communication between the soldiers and their families. Many a soldier, concerned and depressed by the rumors and the actual cases of marauders and deserters pillaging the home front, felt compelled to desert to protect and provide for his family. Letters from hungry, suffering, and frightened wives were a powerful and often irresistible inducement to desertion. That redoubtable diarist Mary Chesnut told of a "cracker" woman who, at the Charlotte, North Carolina, train station in March, 1865, urged her hus-

2. Long, *Memoirs of Lee,* 630.

band as the provost dragged him away, "You desert again, quick as you kin. Come back to your wife and children. Desert, Jake! Desert agin, Jake!" Possibly the most heart-rending example of the effect of home-front suffering on the combat soldier concerned the trial for desertion of one Edward Cooper, a private in the Army of Northern Virginia. When asked to produce evidence on his behalf, Cooper proffered only the following letter from his wife: "My Dear Edward:—I have always been proud of you, and since your connection with the Confederate army, I have been prouder of you than ever before. I would not have you do anything wrong for the world, but before God, Edward, unless you come home, we must die. Last night I was aroused by little Eddie's crying. I called and said 'What is the matter, Eddie?' And he said, 'O Mamma! I am so hungry.' And Lucy, Edward, your darling Lucy; she never complains, but she is growing thinner and thinner every day. And before God, Edward, unless you come home, we must die. Your Mary." Although much moved by this poignant letter, the court felt duty bound to sentence Cooper to death. Only the personal intervention of General Lee saved him.[3]

Letters such as this refuted Voltaire's theory that it was best to let the soldier marry so he would be bound to his country and family and therefore would not desert. The opposite was often the case in the Confederacy: faced with a choice between country and family, many soldiers put family first and left the army for home and hearth. Numerous letters between Johnny Reb and the home front lead one to conclude that pleas from families induced thousands to desert. One soldier told his sister: "You know not how . . . Depressing it is to get letters that breathe a spirit of Discontent . . . one half of the Desertions from the southern army is caused by the letters they receive." Lee was of the same opinion. He was convinced that a great deal of the desertion was caused by such "discouraging sentiments."[4] Nor did it help when troops were told in letters that absentees from the armies seemed immune to arrest or punishment.

Another major cause of desertion, certainly from 1863 on, was war weariness compounded by a general feeling of despair that no sacrifice or effort would prevail in face of the overwhelming might of the North. The twin disasters of Gettysburg and Vicksburg unleashed a paroxysm of hopelessness, which in turn created a stream of desertion. By late 1864 the stream became a

3. Escott, *After Secession,* 125; Mary Boykin Chesnut, *A Diary from Dixie* (1905; rpr. ed. Ben Ames Williams; Boston, 1949), 512; Lonn, *Desertion During the Civil War,* 13.
4. Wiley, *Life of Johnny Reb,* 135, 210; *OR,* Vol. XLVI, Pt. 2, p. 1265.

flood as many realized that with the end approaching nothing else remained but to "skedaddle" or die uselessly for a lost cause. One Confederate captured in April, 1865, summed up how loss of hope had destroyed the army: "For six or eight months back, our men have deserted by thousands. Those who remain have been held by a sentiment of honor only. They did not wish to disgrace themselves by deserting their flag. They have done their duty to the best of their ability. As to the Southern Confederacy, although they would have liked to have seen it triumph, they lost all hope of it long since."[5]

The home front, too, had suffered a catastrophic shattering of morale, which had weakened devotion to the idea of an independent Confederacy. Discontent, faintheartedness, and the insidious and cancerous "peace at any price" movement made desertion in the eyes of many no longer a crime or disgrace. Once this attitude gained credibility the Confederacy was irretrievably doomed.

There were several subsidiary factors that contributed to desertion: the impossibility of getting the furloughs that had been promised and which the men felt were long overdue; the lack of discipline in the armies; the consolidation of decimated units, which often put strange officers in command of strange troops and resulted in loss of pride and identity; the government's failure to provide adequate or indeed any pay (the Confederate private was theoretically entitled to the munificent sum of eleven dollars a month); and the belief that the government had no right to transfer men away from the areas in which they had been enlisted. Also, desertion fed upon itself as it became apparent that the authorities were incapable of checking it. Impunity became immunity and with it came contempt for the all too often weak and vacillating attempts to reverse the drain on the armies.

All of these factors had contributed to the trickle of deserters that began leaving the armies from the first day of the war, but it was not until the summer of 1862 that the Confederate government began to show real concern. It had been difficult for the government or the people to believe that desertion would become a source of worry—"The idea of men deserting from the Southern Army!"—but as early as October, 1861, the provost were out hunting deserters.[6] Although several commanders had been aware of the problem early in

---

5. Lonn, *Desertion During the Civil War*, 18.

6. John Q. Anderson (ed.), *Brokenburn: The Journal of Kate Stone, 1861–1868* (Baton Rouge, 1972), 60. Kate Stone noted that her brother William R. Stone was an assistant provost marshal in Virginia.

1862, there was no official government reaction until July, when Secretary of War Randolph admitted to the state governors that desertion was preventing the South from exploiting victories.[7]

Randolph's concern was not misplaced: statistics showed an alarming increase in desertion during the six months between January and July. January returns revealed that out of 327,000 enrolled, 259,000 were present for duty. By July, in spite of, or perhaps as some suggested, because of the commencement of conscription in April, the total had dipped to 224,000 present out of a virtually unchanged total enrollment.[8] Even though the figures of those absent would have included a reasonable percentage of sick and furloughed men, they were still worrisome enough for Randolph to urge the governors to make every effort to reverse the trend and to provide assistance in returning absentees to their commands.

The military reacted to the declining strength of the field armies by adding responsibility for the arrest and return of deserters to the ever growing list of provost duties. In May, Brigadier General John H. Winder was directed to arrest any absentees found in the Richmond area and return them forthwith to their units.[9] Other provost marshals throughout the Confederacy received similar orders.

By the autumn of 1862 Robert E. Lee was so concerned about the drop in manpower caused by desertion that immediately after Sharpsburg he appealed to President Davis for legal aid: "Some immediate legislation . . . and the most summary punishment should be authorized. It ought to be construed into desertion in the face of the enemy, and thus brought under the Rules and Articles of War."[10] Although Lee referred specifically to stragglers, it can be assumed that many of the absentees had departed the Confederate columns with no intention of returning.

The active assistance of the state governors and the employment of provost to stem straggling and desertion had some salutary effect because by April, 1863, army strength returns revealed an encouraging upward trend in the numbers present for duty. For that month 360,000 were present out of a total enrollment of 498,000. One writer considers these figures as the apogee of Confederate military strength. After that, the numbers of men present fell rapidly and the rate of desertion rose steeply. A new and even more sinister

7. *OR*, Ser. IV, Vol. II, p. 7.

8. Escott, *After Secession*, 125–26.

9. Special Order 107, May 9, 1862, *OR*, Ser. IV, Vol. I, p. 1120.

10. *OR*, Vol. XIX, Pt. 1, p. 143.

development was reported by the Bureau of Conscription in June, 1863; not only was desertion on the upswing, but those who left the army were displaying a disturbing determination to resist any attempt to return them to duty. This was evident in the activities of armed bands of deserters in every state on both sides of the Mississippi. In some areas, where geography and the lack of effective troops favored the deserters, fairly substantial areas—western North Carolina was especially infested—fell increasingly under the control of these lawless bands. Toward the end of July, Assistant Secretary of War Campbell estimated that some 50,000 to 100,000 men were absent without leave. The despair this figure caused can be guessed at by his resigned query as to whether "so general a habit" as desertion ought to be treated as a criminal offense. Campbell's subsequent recommendation of an amnesty for those who would return to their units was implemented by President Davis on August 1.[11]

This offer of amnesty and later ones appear to have had little impact. It seemed that no amount of hectoring, badgering, or pleading could entice the deserter to return to duty. By November the secretary of war was admitting that "the effective force of the army is generally a little more than a half, never two-thirds of the numbers in the ranks."[12] Even allowing a generous proportion for those absent with permission, Seddon was forced to the realization that illegal absence was sapping up to one-third of the total strength of the army.

Although the harsh measures against desertion instituted during the winter of 1863–64 decreased the rate somewhat, by the end of 1864 only 278,000, or 58 percent of a total enrollment of 465,000, were present for duty. Under Grant's ceaseless hammering, this figure plunged to less than 200,000, and it was painfully obvious that the men were leaving the ranks by the hundreds daily. By April, 1865, with the Confederacy bordering on extinction, it was estimated that only 160,000 men remained out of a total enrollment of 359,000, and of these but 120,000 were actually present for duty. This fatal arithmetic was not altered by Lee's February 14 "final" offer of pardon for all who would rejoin the colors.[13]

Eight days later, on February 22, the anniversary of the birth of the Confed-

11. Escott, *After Secession,* 126; *OR,* Ser. IV, Vol. II, pp. 607–608, 674; Jefferson Davis, "Address of the President to the Soldiers of the Confederate States," *SHSP,* XIV (rpr. 1978), 466–68.

12. *OR,* Ser. IV, Vol. II, p. 995.

13. Escott, *After Secession,* 127; Wiley, *Life of Johnny Reb,* 145. In February, 1865, the Bureau of Conscription estimated that one hundred thousand deserters were on the loose in the Confederacy. See Foote, *Civil War,* III, 786; Long, *Memoirs of Lee,* 680–81; *OR,* Vol. XLVI, Pt. 2, pp. 1229–30.

erate States of America, the Senate passed a bill designed "to provide more effectually for the prevention and punishment of absenteeism and desertion from the armies." It was a pathetic case of far too little, far, far too late. There can be no argument with Ella Lonn's conclusion that desertion played a vital part in the "ultimate failure of the South to achieve independence."[14]

One striking feature of the documentation on provost responsibility for checking desertion is the infrequency of indications of their involvement in that activity in the rear areas of the South. Reports that exist are often fragmentary and ambiguous as to the actual tasks of the provost and lead one to conclude that in areas removed from the fighting, provost efforts against desertion were spotty and marginal. Nonetheless, it is clear that provost were heavily committed to stemming desertion in the immediate operational areas of the armies and that in these areas they had at least a fighting chance to cope with the problem. This is not surprising for a number of reasons. At the front, troops deployed or, when not engaged in operations, camped in specific, ordered, and definable areas under the immediate supervision of their officers. This gave the front-line provost two significant advantages: first, the provost marshals and their guards were able to use the command structure of the army to assist in limiting desertion; and second, the geographical limits of the army's dispositions meant that the provost had a relatively smaller area in which to search for deserters. One other factor eased the burden of coping with desertion at the front: the presence of a sizable, permanent, and stable provost organization, with men trained and motivated to carry out police duties, and one that was, at least for the first two years of the war, adequate in strength to conduct antideserter operations.

Except for some towns and cities, no such provost organization was available in the rear areas. What provost existed were scattered and inadequate to sweep the vast hinterland of the South, where desertion knew no boundaries. It was obvious early on that it would be impossible for the provost alone to cope with the increasing number of deserters lurking in the more rough and inhospitable regions of the Confederate States. Such a task had to be relegated to what other troops were available, either state or Confederate.

One conclusion to be drawn is that desertion was primarily a concern of the provost at or near the fighting fronts, although in certain urban centers they were also required and able to prevent desertion. How the provost marshals and their

14. "Proceedings of Second Confederate Congress, Second Session in Part," *SHSP*, LII (rpr. 1980), 383; Lonn, *Desertion During the Civil War*, v.

guards functioned in relation to desertion in the field is well illustrated in the operations of the two major armies, the Army of Northern Virginia and the Army of Tennessee.

As early as May, 1862, Richmond ordered all officers and men illegally absent from the Army of Northern Virginia to return to their commands. To put teeth in this policy, the commanding general of the Department of Henrico, which included Richmond, was directed to arrest such persons and return them to their units. The provost marshal of the city, Brigadier General Winder, received similar orders through the chain of command. Field commanders were duly advised of the "numerous desertions and stragglings" and reminded that they could best assist the provost in correcting the evil by "keeping their commands together," seeing that orders were faithfully executed, and holding transgressors to a "strict account" for their delinquencies.[15] In other words, brigade and regimental commanders were expected to do their share in preventing and punishing skulking.

By the late summer and autumn of 1862, provost were firmly in place in Lee's army and in position to monitor virtually all road and rail traffic with the aim of detaining personnel unable to produce authority to travel. In addition, mounted and unmounted provost were stationed along the lines of the army, front and rear, to cover any possible escape routes. These efforts and dispositions met with considerable success, although at this point in the war the number of deserters was still at more or less manageable proportions. An artillery unit of the army, for example, reported that the provost marshal had delivered one deserter from the battery on December 12. As the tide of desertion swelled, the provost's successes were less common. By Christmas of 1863 the problem was no longer single deserters but the squads and even whole companies of men who broke away from the army, vastly increasing the pressure on the provost. One report mentions an entire company of deserters caught crossing the James River near Richmond in December, 1863, but electing to fight and in the end killing several of their pursuers. The leaders of this band were subsequently shot.[16]

Worse was to come. In the autumn of 1864 a tide of desertion engulfed the Confederate armies, ending only with the surrender in April, 1865. Pickett's

15. *OR*, Ser. IV, Vol. I, p. 1120; Warner, *Generals in Gray,* 340–41; *OR*, Vol. XI, Pt. 3, p. 643.

16. Robert K. Krick, *Parker's Virginia Battery, C.S.A.* (Berryville, Va., 1975), 320; Charles M. Cummings, *Yankee Quaker Confederate General: The Curious Career of Bushrod Rust Johnson* (Cranbury, N.J., 1971), 313; Sorrel, *Recollections,* 212.

inspector general, for example, reported the desertion within a ten-day period of over five hundred men. This cancer that ate so rapidly at the continuously decaying army afflicted even its command structure; a sergeant, admonished for counseling men to desert, attempted to shoot the officer who had reproached him and was himself subsequently arrested and executed. Even such stalwart units as the 15th Alabama reported frequent desertions, often of squads of men who crossed the lines to the enemy. W. W. Goldsborough, a private in the 1st Maryland Battalion, noted in February, 1865, that the battalion had lost only one man by desertion (a unique achievement), but within the brigade and the division desertions were so numerous that the battalion was entrusted with the task of constant picketing to prevent further desertion. When other units were given this task, the pickets invariably disappeared along with those they were picketing. The 6th South Carolina reported in 1865 that more and more of the fainthearted were leaving for home or, worse, were crossing the lines to the enemy.[17]

The War Department, in receipt of these reports and many others like them, estimated that in the four months between October 1, 1864, and February 4, 1865, nearly seventy-two thousand men had deserted from the armies east of the Mississippi. The course of desertion and the despair it created are evident in Lee's dispatches as he watched his army and the Confederacy disintegrate:

> November 18, 1864, Desertion is increasing . . . not withstanding all my efforts to stop it.

> January 27, 1865. I have the honor to call your attention to the alarming frequency of desertions.

> February 25, 1865. Hundreds of men are deserting nightly and I cannot keep the army together unless examples are made of such cases.

> March 27, 1865. The number of desertions from the 9th to the 18th . . . 1,061. . . . I do not know what can be done to put a stop to it.[18]

---

17. Harrison, *Pickett's Men*, xxiii; Foote, *Civil War*, III, 822; W. A. McClendon, *Recollections of War Times By an Old Veteran While Under Stonewall Jackson and Lieutenant General James Longstreet* (1909; rpr. San Bernardino, 1973), 224–25; W. W. Goldsborough, "Grant's Change of Base: The Horrors of the Battle of Cold Harbor, from a Soldier's Note Book," *SHSP*, XXIX (rpr. 1978), 289–90; James Lide Coker, *History of Company G, Ninth S.C. Regiment, Infantry, S.C. Army and of Company E, Sixth S.C. Regiment, Infantry, S.C. Army* (Greenwood, S.C., 1979), 170, 172.

18. Lonn, *Desertion During the Civil War*, 27; *OR*, Vol. XLII, Pt. 3, p. 1213; Vol. XLVI, Pt. 2, pp. 1143, 1258, 1265; Pt. 3, p. 1353.

No one else, including the provost, knew what to do either. In any event, it was too late to experiment with fresh ideas to reverse the drain from the army. One final reference linking desertion and the provost of the Army of Northern Virginia is the report of a South Carolina regiment that during the evacuation of Richmond it caught several deserters in the city and decided to carry them along for "delivery to the first provost guard we could find on the march."[19] In all probability the first such guard was found surrendered with the rest of the army at Appomattox.

Many of the deserters from Lee's army headed for the mountains of western North Carolina, where it was relatively easy to evade and resist any troops that could be spared to chase them. In these areas, their capture was no longer a provost responsibility because there were not enough guards. Instead, it was necessary to use whatever force was available, which meant local militia, who unfortunately were not often up to the task. By January, 1863, Governor Zebulon Vance advised Secretary of War Seddon that the formidable combination of conscript evaders from East Tennessee and deserters from the army had put the situation beyond the ability of the militia to control it. In lieu he proposed to organize a police force within the state to arrest evaders and deserters. Presumably this force could not be organized (where would the men have come from?) because repeatedly during the first half of 1863 Vance continued to express his deep anxiety over desertion and the lawless situation in the western part of the state. The War Department echoed his concern, feeling that the situation "menaces the existence of the Confederacy as fatally as either of the armies of the United States." The Bureau of Conscription pointed out that if the deserters in the Atlantic states could not be returned to the armies the cause could well be lost.[20]

Vance asked General Lee to return a brigade, or at least a strong regiment, to the state to smash the deserter bands, estimated to number in excess of twelve hundred men in western North Carolina alone. Lee complied by dispatching Brigadier General Robert F. Hoke with two regiments of infantry and a squadron of cavalry. Throughout the autumn of 1863, Hoke conducted antideserter operations in western and central North Carolina but with limited success because of the difficulty in pinning down the deserters, who all too often received assistance from the local population. Unfortunately, Hoke was soon

19. Natalie Jenkins Bond and Osmun Latrobe Coward (eds.), *The South Carolinians: Colonel Asbury Coward's Memoirs* (New York, 1968), 170.

20. *OR*, XVIII, 821–22; Ser. IV, Vol. II, pp. 786, 607.

recalled by Lee. Almost before he departed the situation was much the same if not worse than before his arrival. In spite of every effort by the state and Confederate governments, deserters were so rife in North Carolina that many civilians and soldiers no longer felt that any stigma should be attached to desertion. Desperate appeals to the men to return to the colors and offers of amnesty proved unsuccessful.

There was another blot on North Carolina's participation in the war effort. Although she furnished "one-sixth or one-seventh of all Confederate soldiers," it is estimated that over the four years of the war some twenty-three thousand, or about 20 percent of Tar Heel soldiers, deserted.[21] Only eight thousand of these later returned to their duties. According to General Lee, there was an especially large flood of deserters from the North Carolina regiments in his army, at one point better than fifty men a week opting out of the war but later whole squads and even companies. In one instance the 58th North Carolina lost over a hundred men to the Federal lines. In another case in May, 1863, one of Lee's staff officers, Lieutenant Colonel Walter Taylor, requested that Major General Arnold Elzey, commanding the Department of Richmond, put his guards on the alert to intercept a "party of deserters from the North Carolina regiments" who had left the camps and were headed south to cross the James River. On April 18 Lee had informed the secretary of war of the frequent desertion from the North Carolina units of his army, and in May he wrote again stating that unless Tar Heel desertion was checked the number of North Carolinians in the army would be greatly reduced. Pursuit of North Carolina deserters continued to the very end; as late as February 26, 1865, the 7th North Carolina, some two hundred strong, left the trenches at Petersburg for the Old North State to arrest deserters. According to regimental records, the trip was "quite" successful but short-lived because the regiment had to redeploy to stop a Federal force threatening the vital railway from Salisbury to Danville.[22]

General Lee's correspondence in 1865 indicates his continuing deep concern about the desertion of North Carolina troops. In February he advised Secretary of War Breckinridge of the "alarming" rate of desertion, its bad effect on the troops remaining, and his "painful apprehension" for the future. A letter in similar vein went to Governor Vance of North Carolina.[23]

21. John G. Barrett, *The Civil War in North Carolina* (Chapel Hill, 1963), 192–94, 28.

22. *OR,* XVIII, 998, 1066; Barrett, *Civil War in North Carolina,* 190; J. H. Lane, "Extracts from Letters," *SHSP,* XVIII (rpr. 1977), 421.

23. Clifford Dowdey and Louis H. Manarin (eds.), *The Wartime Papers of R. E. Lee* (Boston, 1961), 910; Long, *Memoirs of Lee,* 686–88.

In the Army of Tennessee and in its rear, desertion was also wreaking havoc as early as 1862. In December of that year the returns of the army revealed "several thousand" officers and men absent. According to Union sources, five thousand men of the Army of Tennessee, left behind during the retreat from Kentucky, remained in Kentucky and Tennessee, making no attempt to rejoin the army. Braxton Bragg, for one, was not prepared to countenance the upsurge in desertion and came down hard on offenders; he thought the sole way to prevent the men from running off was to shoot them. Shoot them he did, whenever possible in front of their comrades, which had the effect of ramming the lesson home but did little to improve Bragg's popularity. Not that this was, or should have been, a prime consideration for Braxton Bragg. One soldier, having viewed a number of the executions, recalled that "almost every day we would hear a discharge of musketry, and knew that some poor trembling wretch had bid farewell to mortal things here below."[24] In the long run, though, even executions could not check the rate of desertion, and men streamed to the rear, intent on reaching sanctuary in Georgia and Alabama.

In those states which the Army of Tennessee was expected to protect, responsibility for deserters consumed a good deal of provost time. In July, 1863, Lieutenant General Leonidas Polk, cognizant of the effect of desertion and conscript evasion on the army, suggested the establishment of a "bureau of reserves" under a general officer who would be charged with enforcing conscription and arresting deserters and personnel absent without leave. This suggestion was not acted upon. In March, 1864, Polk established a military police system throughout the districts of his command, the Department of Alabama, Mississippi, and East Louisiana. Each district had its own provost marshal, all reporting to the provost marshal general of the department. Polk subsequently requested authority to raise companies of exempts to enforce his orders regarding the apprehension of deserters. The correspondence makes it clear that a major task of Polk's provost was to arrest absentees and deserters and to smash the marauder bands that infested the department.[25]

There are indications that within this department provost officers were providing active assistance to commanders. This assistance was primarily advisory, although on occasion provost officers were used in a supervisory or command role in the conduct of antideserter operations. In at least one instance a provost marshal accompanied an expedition against deserters in an area some

24. Lonn, *Desertion During the Civil War*, 25; Foote, *Civil War*, I, 568.

25. *OR*, Vol. XXIII, Pt. 2, pp. 921–22; Vol. XXXII, Pt. 3, pp. 611, 723–25, 817; Vol. XXXIX, Pt. 2, pp. 570, 579–80.

distance from his post. This latter case involved Major, later Lieutenant Colonel, George Washington Lee, the provost marshal of Atlanta, who in October, 1863, was reported to have just returned from an expedition in northeast Georgia "against deserters." There is good evidence that Lee might have commanded this sortie, for the Confederate government had ordered "Colonel Lee to proceed to North Georgia in order to operate against the deserters." Governor Brown of Georgia probably suggested Lee as the most appropriate officer for the task because of a telegram he had sent to the governor: "There is considerable trouble in North Eastern Georgia . . . loyal citizens arrested a number of deserters, who were rescued by other deserters and tories. . . . If you can spare one company . . . send it there." In May, 1863, Governor Brown had issued orders to the officers of his state troops to forward any captured deserters to Colonel Lee, "commanding a Confederate post at Atlanta."[26]

Throughout late 1863 and 1864 other provost marshals became involved in combating the mounting desertion. Major Jules C. Denis, the department provost marshal general, received a plan in March, 1864, from a spy acting for the Confederacy calling for the employment of cavalry in northern Mississippi as a permanent roving provost guard on the theory that the cavalry's mobility would help in maintaining law and order. It was recommended that this mobile provost guard be placed under the command of a provost officer. In April Denis received a letter from one of his provost marshals requesting that cavalry be used for this purpose in Alabama. Such requests dogged Denis during 1864: in July a provost marshal in a Mississippi district requested troops to break up the deserter bands in that state. Denis referred the request, once again for cavalry, to department headquarters.[27]

Often provost channels of communication were used for the transmission of orders and instructions regarding deserters between the Army of Tennessee and the Department of Alabama, Mississippi, and East Louisiana and between the several districts of the department. In April, 1864, for example, provost channels distributed Lieutenant General Polk's proclamation to absentees and deserters within the department. The provost net was also active in passing intelligence on deserters to the various commands. Colonel Benjamin J. Hill, provost marshal general of the Army of Tennessee, in March, 1864, reported

26. *OR,* Vol. XXX, Pt. 4, p. 748; Thomas Conn Bryan, *Confederate Georgia* (Athens, Ga., 1953), 146.

27. *OR,* Vol. XXXII, Pt. 3, pp. 633–36, 745–48; Vol. XXXIX, Pt. 2, pp. 736–37.

that a secret society was operating in northern Alabama, which had as its object the depletion of Confederate strength by actively encouraging desertion. In response to this information, Joseph E. Johnston ordered the temporary deployment of a cavalry division to the area.[28]

Provost were also involved in the conduct of the tragic but all too necessary executions of deserters. In the autumn of 1863, after having had a deserter shot, Stephen Ramseur marched his entire brigade past the body, hoping it would furnish a salutary lesson and a warning. Some failed to heed it, for in the spring of 1864 several more men were shot for deserting, causing Ramseur much sorrow but no loss of resolve: "Why will these poor miserable men commit this crime and folly." George Pickett was no less severe. Following the attack on Newbern, North Carolina, in February, 1864, several Confederate deserters, caught bearing arms and wearing Union uniforms, were hanged for having betrayed their former comrades. At Dalton, Georgia, sixteen deserters were executed in the spring of 1864. A number of witnesses vividly described how the condemned were tied to stakes and how, after their guns were loaded by staff officers, a provost firing squad carried out the prescribed punishment. In yet another instance, Captain Charles W. Peden, the provost marshal at Shelbyville, Tennessee, was called upon to make arrangements for the execution of a soldier from the 8th Tennessee. Such executions continued to the end of the war, a late instance occurring near Selma, Alabama, in March, 1865, when General Forrest had two deserters shot.[29]

At the end of the last chapter I remarked that the methods used to control straggling applied equally to desertion. It was realized in early 1862 that the first step must be to curtail unauthorized movement. To achieve this, the military authorities tried to place provost guards in positions where they could cover every likely avenue of escape of those who might attempt to leave their commands. In practice, this meant that bridges, fords, highway crossings, railroad stations, towns, and the roads leading into them had to be picketed. As well, each train had to have its provost to examine the papers of traveling soldiers. Strategic points had to be guarded to intercept deserters before they could reach

28. *OR,* Vol. XXXII, Pt. 3, pp. 824–25, 681–82.

29. Gary W. Gallagher, *Stephen Dodson Ramseur: Lee's Gallant General* (Chapel Hill, 1985), 84, 91; Harrison, *Pickett's Men,* 116–19; Ridley, *Battles and Sketches,* 283–86; John Anderson, Letter to Editor, *Confederate Veteran,* II (rpr. 1983), 72; Thomas Owens, "Penalties for Desertion," *Confederate Veteran,* II (rpr. 1983), 235; B. L. Ridley, "Camp Scenes Around Dalton," *Confederate Veteran,* X (rpr. 1983), 67–68; John Allan Wyeth, *Life of General Nathan Bedford Forrest* (New York, 1899), 589.

safe haven in the rear. Units in the field and in the camps were subjected to the close scrutiny of their officers to ensure that they stayed together. This was accomplished by organizing rear guards to prevent men from leaving the columns of march and by frequent roll calls to ensure that the soldiers were present. In one brigade it became the custom for noncommissioned officers to patrol the lines constantly, reporting every fifteen minutes to the picket officers.[30]

Although responsibility for stemming desertion rested on commanders at all levels, the provost were readily available to assist. On the march they followed well to the rear of the army, vigilant for any stragglers, and behind units in the line the provost deployed their straggler posts and patrols to prevent men from leaving the firing line without valid reason. The strict system of passes, which irritated soldier and civilian alike, was another tool used by the provost to control movement. So pervasive did this system become that it seemed to many to blanket the entire Confederacy.

In spite of these measures and the commitment of large numbers of provost and other troops to enforce them, there was no way the system could be 100 percent effective. The quick-witted or determined straggler or deserter could always surmount the obstacles placed in his path by the provost. Thousands and thousands of men beat the system.

As difficult as it was, the arrest of deserters may have been easier than ensuring that they were adequately punished. Attempts by the provost to arrest offenders and make them pay for their crime were all too easily frustrated, first, by sympathetic civilians who furnished aid to or harbored deserters; second, by the military courts, which unwisely tended to deal leniently with offenders; and, third, by some members of the civilian judiciary, who held that conscription was unconstitutional, and therefore it was not a crime to resist arrest for desertion.

One of the first reported instances of civilians encouraging desertion occurred early in 1862 in East Tennessee, a not surprising locale in view of the unpopularity of the Confederacy in that region. The Knoxville provost marshal, Colonel William M. Churchwell, reacted by ordering the arrest of any citizen trying to persuade soldiers to desert. According to Churchwell, it was the aim of the provost marshal "to make the masses . . . understand that the Government has powers to enforce its laws."[31] Fortunately for Churchwell, *habeas corpus*

---

30. *OR,* Vol. XIX, Pt. 2, pp. 592, 618–19; Vol. XLVI, Pt. 2, p. 1261.
31. *OR,* Ser. II, Vol. II, p. 1423; Ser. II, Vol. I, p. 888.

had been suspended by President Davis in February, but nevertheless his "arbitrary" arrests were viewed with alarm by those who feared military usurpation of civil liberty.

An officer whom General Lee had assigned in January, 1864, to arrest culpable civilians in several Virginia counties was not so fortunate. During that month the writ of *habeas corpus* was in effect, and as a result, the officer, Colonel Edward Willis, discovered to his chagrin that those he had arrested for harboring deserters could not be held by the provost marshals.[32] Even so august a personage as Lee found his hands tied in the face of such a constitutional obstacle.

Various states had or were about to promulgate legislation designed to punish disloyalty to the Confederacy. Georgia had passed an act in December, 1863, to punish by fine or imprisonment any person who concealed or assisted a deserter in that state. In February, 1864, Louisiana passed similar legislation.[33] It is unlikely that these well-intentioned measures had any dramatic or long-lasting effect.

The civilian judiciary was a continual hindrance in the provost's efforts to hold deserters for punishment. Although the president had asked for and received the right to suspend *habeas corpus* to allow the army to meet the threat of civil disobedience, draft evasion, and desertion, in Texas the courts, supported by the governor, freely granted writs of *habeas corpus* to evaders and deserters. One report in February, 1863, clearly shows how the Texas judiciary emasculated provost efforts to bring deserters to trial: "I sent the prisoners . . . to the provost marshals . . . with directions . . . to turn them over to the civil authorities. . . . The prisoners were turned over to a magistrate, who immediately discharged them all and permitted them to return to their homes." Clearly the military and the judiciary were working at cross purposes. On the very same day that these prisoners were released, Major General John Magruder, commanding the District of Texas, New Mexico, and Arizona, advised Governor Francis Lubbock of Texas that he had ordered the provost to arrest deserters.[34]

In North Carolina, too, constant judicial interference thwarted provost efforts to punish desertion. The record of Governor Vance's bitter opposition to

32. *OR*, XXXIII, 1063.

33. Bryan, *Confederate Georgia,* 147; Jefferson Davis Bragg, *Louisiana in the Confederacy* (Baton Rouge, 1941), 258–59.

34. *OR*, XV, 975, 978.

conscription and other measures of the Davis administration needs no ampli-
fication, but even Vance realized that desertion was severely hampering the war
effort, and he took every "imaginable step" to return deserters to their units. He
received no support from the chief justice of the state supreme court, R. M.
Pearson, who believed that the Conscription Act was unconstitutional and that
an individual had the right to resist arrest for desertion. In spite of President
Davis' suspension of the writ of *habeas corpus,* Pearson never once denied the
writ for the release of conscripts, deserters, or traitors. Shortly after his inaugu-
ration in August, 1864, Vance began using the state militia to arrest deserters
but was again stymied by Pearson, who ruled that the governor had no such
authority. Vance then sought and obtained state legislation permitting use of the
militia for that purpose, and when the militia was abolished, he used its replacement, the Home Guard. He did so in spite of Judge Pearson's rulings against the
practice.[35] Similar judicial prejudice against provost arrests was common in
other states.

Nor were the provost helped or encouraged by the military courts-martial
and special courts that exhibited a frustrating tendency to deal lightly with
deserters. Repeatedly during the war trivial punishments were all too often
handed down, and on the infrequent occasions when the supreme penalty was
prescribed, it was often commuted by the generals, the politicians, or proclamations of general amnesty. In the face of such weakness and vacillation, it was
not long before the soldier held the courts and discipline itself in contempt.
There are abundant data to prove the deep and lasting impression that executions had on the troops. Had desertion, that most heinous of military crimes,
been severely and consistently punished, it well might have ceased or at least
been greatly curtailed.

It is clear, then, that provost responsibility for the control of desertion was
largely restricted to the immediate operational areas of the armies. Beyond that
the provost lacked the manpower to cope with the problem, and it had to be
countered by other troops. Throughout the Confederacy, though, where manpower and circumstances permitted, provost officers and guards were often
active in guarding deserters; in providing advice to commanders and participating in antidesertion operations; and in carrying out executions.

Notwithstanding the best efforts of the provost, the army, and the government, the "calamity" long foretold by Lee was not to be denied. Desertion
could not be stopped, and by late 1864 it was out of control. There is no

---

35. Barrett, *Civil War in North Carolina,* 242.

question that it seriously degraded the South's ability to sustain her armies in the field and that desertion contributed significantly to Southern defeat. As one Alabama private put it at Appomattox: "Who was the cause of it? Skulkers Cowards extortioners and Deserters not the Yankees that makes it woss."[36]

36. Wiley, *Life of Johnny Reb,* 150.

10

Take Charge of All Prisoners

I never had any control over the prisoners except
those that were captured on the field. Then it was
my business to send them to Richmond to the proper
officer who was then the Provost Marshal General.

R. E. LEE

The control, guarding, and disposition of prisoners of war was an extremely important provost responsibility. It was a purely military police function, and unlike most other provost tasks it did not involve provost officers and men in acrimonious dispute with civilians, except perhaps when arguments arose over the siting of prisons. A task without controversy was a pleasant change for the provost, who suffered much abuse in the enforcement of such features of Confederate life as martial law and the passport system. Even the most vociferous antiprovost civilian could see that prisoners of war were one segment of the population that had to be under the strictest control.

In modern practice the provost are responsible for prisoners of war from the moment they are handed over by the capturing troops until they are transferred to base or rear area prisoner of war camps. Lee's comment, which introduces this chapter, clearly implies that Confederate provost operated under the same general terms. This is also evident from the recollections of individual Confederates: Ephraim Anderson of the 1st Missouri Brigade recalled that "the duty of the provost marshal was . . . to take charge of all prisoners brought in until sent to their destination."[1] Another similarity to modern practice is demonstrated by the Confederate provost's use of the existing chain of command to evacuate prisoners of war from the zone of army operations. Correspondence illustrates that prisoners were passed back from brigade provost to division and corps provost and thence to the army provost, who in turn forwarded them to the camps in the rear. Escorts for prisoners as they filtered back along the chain were only infrequently provided by the provost because of their severely limited strength; that duty had to be performed by whatever other troops were

1. Anderson, *Memoirs,* 204.

164

available. The use of this chain of evacuation often allowed the provost to gain intelligence on enemy units and pass it to commanders at all levels.

An estimated 210,000 Union soldiers were captured during the war, and of these a very large percentage would have passed through provost hands.[2] In addition to performing escort duties, the provost assumed custodial responsibility in some of the prisoner of war camps in the rear areas. A number of these establishments included a provost detachment, although in most cases the sole provost representative was the officer in command of the prison or prison guard. Several of these officers spent virtually the entire war on either provost or custodial duties. Captain, later Major George C. Gibbs, for example, spent the first six months of 1862 in command of the Salisbury, North Carolina, prison; he assumed a similar appointment at Castle Thunder in Richmond late in 1863. In late May, 1864, he was assigned to command of the Macon, Georgia, prison. Captain Archibald Godwin, later a brigadier general of infantry, was appointed provost marshal of the eastern district of Richmond on March 1, 1862, when martial law was imposed on the city. In June he replaced Gibbs at Salisbury. Captain G. W. Alexander, assistant provost marshal of Richmond in October, 1863, later commanded Castle Thunder and then Salisbury in May and June of 1864.[3]

Responsibility for the administration and operation of the prisoner of war system was, according to General Lee, the duty of the provost marshal general. A special order of the adjutant general appointed General Winder as inspector general of the camps in the vicinity of Richmond in June, 1861. Among these camps were those earmarked for the custody of prisoners of war. Later, the movement of many of the prisoners to Georgia meant that Winder no longer had direct control over the captives. In June, 1864, he was ordered to the Andersonville camp, and Brigadier General William M. Gardner assumed control of the Richmond prisons. In July Winder was assigned to the command of all military prisons in Georgia and Alabama, and Gardner assumed the same responsibility for the remainder of the states east of the Mississippi River.[4] Soon after his

2. Long, *Civil War Day by Day,* 715. The estimate is that of the U.S. Record and Prison Office.

3. William B. Hesseltine, *Civil War Prisons: A Study in War Psychology* (New York, 1964), 65, 247; J. L. Burrows, "Recollections of Libby Prison," *SHSP,* XI (rep. 1977), 89; *OR,* Vol. XXXIX, Pt. 2, p. 625; LIII, 308–309; Ser. II, Vol. III, p. 770; Ser. II, Vol. VI, p. 440; Thomas, *Confederate State of Richmond,* 81; Louis A. Brown, *The Salisbury Prison: A Case Study of Confederate Military Prisons, 1861–1865* (Wendell, N.C., 1980), 168, lists the Salisbury commandants. See Appendix I for information on personnel who served in the prison system.

4. Douglas Southall Freeman, *R. E. Lee: A Biography* (1934–35; rpr. 4 vols.; New York,

arrival in Georgia, Winder sent some of the prisoners at Macon to Charleston, South Carolina, to preclude their rescue by Federal cavalry raiding in Georgia. Gardner was not apprised of Winder's action, and he remained in ignorance when the prisoners subsequently left Charleston. The muddle was exacerbated by complaints from General Sam Jones, commanding at Charleston, Governor Milledge Bonham of South Carolina, and Gardner himself.

To sort out the tangle, the prison system was reorganized in the autumn of 1864. Winder was appointed commissary general of prisoners, with responsibility for all prisons east of the Mississippi. Department and army commanders were ordered not to interfere with Winder's administration, and prison commandants were made directly responsible to him. From his new headquarters at Augusta, Georgia, Winder assumed command, ordering that reports from all prisons be forwarded to him. Only a few months were left before his death in February, 1865. General Gideon Pillow then assumed the appointment temporarily but was replaced by General Daniel Ruggles late in March.[5]

Numerous reports and letters of the Army of Northern Virginia and the Army of Tennessee describe how the provost and other troops controlled prisoners of war. In the eastern theater of operations, the Confederate victory at First Manassas inundated the army with prisoners of war. The thousand or so Federals who reached Richmond by rail within a few days of the battle proved to be both a curiosity and a nuisance because such numbers had not been expected or prepared for, and, according to J. L. Burrows, a Richmond clergyman, "there was not a Confederate official . . . who had any experience in taking care of prisoners of war."[6] Burrows recalled that inexperience and lack of planning led to considerable improvisation of the accommodation, guard forces, and sustenance required to meet the needs of these first Yankees to reach Richmond. The initial confusion is reflected in the composition of the *ad hoc* guard force that watched over the prisoners. A series of orders throughout August assigned several companies as guards, ordering them to report to General Winder. Almost a full regiment was so detailed. More guards were required because within three months 2,685 Federal prisoners were sent to Richmond.[7]

1959), IV, 254; *OR,* Ser. II, Vol. III, p. 683; Ser. II, Vol. VII, pp. 213–14, 400, 501–502; Hesseltine, *Civil War Prisons,* 163, notes that Camp Ford near Tyler, Texas, the main prison west of the Mississippi, apparently was not under control of the Richmond authorities.

5. *OR,* Ser. II, Vol. VII, pp. 1086–87, 1150, 1193; Hesseltine, *Civil War Prisons,* 171.

6. Burrows, "Recollections of Libby Prison," 83.

7. *OR,* Ser. II, Vol. III, pp. 700, 703–705.

In the field, the system for delivering prisoners to the provost was functioning smoothly. During the winter of 1861–1862 Jeb Stuart's cavalry, deployed near Centerville, was sending prisoners captured on the picket lines or by patrols to the provost marshal of that northern Virginia town. During Jackson's Valley campaign the capture of Winchester resulted in a large number of Federal prisoners, some reaching the provost by unusual means. One Virginia officer, approached by a lady asking him to take charge of "my prisoners," found she had nine Federals locked up in her parlor. The colonel of another regiment, the 5th Virginia, actually put two prisoners in charge of a lady, providing her with a pistol to guard them. She happily took on the task, turning them over to the provost marshal as soon as he had established a headquarters. The 1st Maryland Regiment also noted that it had delivered prisoners once the provost were "thoroughly" in charge of the town. Because of the shortage of provost, other units had to provide guards for prisoners even before Winchester. The Rockbridge Artillery, for example, had a number of supernumerary men detailed to guard prisoners under the command of a provost marshal. These details were not permanent; the men involved were later transferred to other commands. Reports during the remainder of 1862 reflect that the provost continued to meet its responsibilities for the receipt and custody of prisoners of war. Edmund Patterson recalled that at Gaines Mill in June his unit, the 9th Alabama, had picked up four Yankee stragglers and turned them over to the provost. Another Alabama regiment, the 15th, reported handing over a number of prisoners to the provost. Many regiments in several brigades took numerous prisoners; Richard H. Anderson's brigade alone transferred five thousand Yankees to Lee's provost guard.[8]

Similarly, all along the Atlantic seaboard, regimental and brigade commanders were delivering prisoners to the provost; Brigadier General States Rights Gist, for one, reported the transfer of prisoners to provost jurisdiction on June 12, 1862. In turn, Richmond was directing local provost marshals to forward their captives to the capital. The secretary of war himself took time to write to the provost marshal of Petersburg, Captain William Pannill, on July 4,

---

8. *OR,* V, 440; J. William Jones, "Reminiscences of the Army of Northern Virginia. Paper No. 4—Capture of Winchester and Rout of Banks's Army," *SHSP,* IX (rpr. 1977), 235; B. T. Johnson, "Memoir of the First Maryland Regiment. Paper No. 4: The Battle of Winchester," *SHSP,* X (rpr. 1977), 100; "Historical Sketch of the Rockbridge Artillery, C.S. Army, by a Member of the Famous Battery," *SHSP,* XXIII (rpr. 1977), 134–35; Barrett (ed.), *Yankee Rebel,* 34; Oates, *War Between the Union and the Confederacy,* 279; Joseph Cantey Elliott, *Lieutenant General Richard Heron Anderson: Lee's Noble Soldier* (Dayton, 1985), 49.

ordering him to send all Federal prisoners to Richmond and to have the officer commanding the escort report directly to General Winder.[9]

The Confederate triumph at Fredericksburg in December, 1862, gave the Confederacy additional large numbers of uninvited guests, the majority of whom passed through provost hands. Reports submitted by Major David B. Bridgford, the provost marshal of Jackson's corps and later of the Army of Northern Virginia, show that close attention was paid to army regulations, which specified that prisoner returns must include the number, rank, name, and corps of those captured. Bridgford reported that on December 13 and 14 he had sent 324 prisoners of war to Richmond on the order of General Lee. Of these he paroled 11 officers, presumably on the instructions of Lee, who had such authority under army regulations. The names, regiments, and corps of the prisoners were carefully noted because such information was invaluable in determining the enemy order of battle. On December 16 Bridgford loaded a further 109 prisoners on the trains running to the capital. That same day he toured the hospitals of the 2d Corps, paroling 23 Federals—probably men too seriously wounded to be moved—and collecting a "considerable" number of wounded prisoners for transport to Richmond. According to Bridgford, he could not give the exact number because someone had neglected to keep count. General Jackson noted in his report on Fredericksburg that the 2d Corps had captured 521 prisoners, of whom 11 were officers.[10]

Operations in 1863, particularly the Chancellorsville and Gettysburg campaigns, added to the inventory of Federals in Confederate hands. Edmund Patterson reported that his regiment, the 9th Alabama, had delivered prisoners to the provost marshal following the Battle of Chancellorsville so that they could be sent on to Richmond. Gettysburg provided a rich harvest of prisoners. About 4,000 were turned over to George Pickett's decimated division, which, because it was in no condition for further combat following the abortive charge on July 3, was a good choice for temporary duty as provost. The division subsequently escorted the lengthy column of prisoners to the rear. Elsewhere in the East, and certainly in the Department of South Carolina, Georgia, and Florida, the provost continued to run some prisoner of war camps and also took on the task of interrogating them to obtain information of military value.[11]

Provost involvement in the control of prisoners in 1864 is well documented

9. *OR*, XIV, 28; Ser. II, Vol. IV, p. 801.

10. *OR*, XXI, 641–42, 635.

11. Barrett, *Yankee Rebel*, 102; Charles T. Loehr, *War History of the Old First Virginia Infantry Regiment, Army of Northern Virginia* (1884; rpr. Dayton, 1970), 39; *OR*, XIV, 969.

by the reports of provost officers with the Army of Northern Virginia and in Richmond. Early in February, Major G. M. Ryals, the provost marshal of Stuart's cavalry corps, estimated that the cavalry had captured some 1,600 Federals, including those that had been turned over to the infantry and others that had been sent back without passing through provost hands. The inference is clear that the normal procedure was for prisoners to be sent to the rear under provost escort, but often many were taken back by other troops. Infantry brigade provost marshals during the Wilderness campaign reported that substantial numbers of prisoners continued to pass through provost hands. The provost marshal of B. R. Johnson's brigade, for example, took charge of 21 Federals, and the 61st Virginia of William Mahone's brigade got a receipt from the provost for about 40 officers and 474 men of the 7th Pennsylvania Regiment.[12]

During the period from September 29 to October 1, 1864, Major Bridgford noted that he had taken custody of and then forwarded 1,663 prisoners to Richmond. His records show that 688 of these were captured by Major General Wade Hampton, 478 by Major General C. M. Wilcox, and 497 by Major General Henry Heth. All were from the Federal 9th Corps, except for 175 from the 5th Corps.[13]

Procedures for handling prisoners in the western theater of operations were similar but not initially as effective. At Shiloh, where large numbers of Federals were captured, the commanding officer of the 16th Alabama noted that his regiment had escorted Federal prisoners five miles to the rear, turned them over to the provost, and then returned to the battlefield.[14] This ten-mile round trip shepherding prisoners, including wounded, would have kept the Alabamians out of the fighting for a considerable time. One questions the wisdom of stationing the provost so far to the rear in this case; a position closer to the front would have permitted a rapid turnover of prisoners, obviating the protracted absence of combat units from action. Clearly the system of receiving prisoners at Shiloh was inadequate, yet another indication of the less sophisticated command and control structure of the Army of Tennessee.

Reports on the major battles of 1863 reveal considerable improvements in procedures for the receipt of prisoners, including compliance with army regula-

---

12. *OR*, Vol. XXIX, Pt. 1, pp. 453–54; B. R. Johnson, "Operations from the 6th to the 11th of May, 1864," *SHSP*, XII (rpr. 1977), 277; *OR*, Vol. XXXVI, Pt. 2, p. 241; Nichols, *Soldier's Story*, 144.

13. *OR*, Vol. XLII, Pt. 1, p. 870.

14. *OR*, Vol. X, Pt. 1, p. 597.

tions requiring the submission of full particulars on prisoners. At Chickamauga, for example, a brigade commander in Benjamin Cheatham's division, appending his provost marshal's report to his own, noted that the brigade had taken 74 prisoners. Thomas C. Hindman's division alone turned approximately 700 prisoners over to the provost. The Department of Alabama, Mississippi, and East Louisiana also followed regulations by insisting that all provost marshals submit monthly reports on the number of political, Federal, and Confederate prisoners in their charge. Other reports note that on occasion prisoners of war turned themselves over to the provost. After the Battle of Chickamauga the commanding officer of the 19th Alabama reported that "scores of prisoners passed to the rear, whom I ordered to report to our provost guard."[15] The reason for this somewhat cavalier attitude was no doubt that every Confederate was needed on the firing line and on the estimation that the Union soldiers, demoralized by defeat and wanting no more fighting for the moment, would move directly to the rear and obligingly surrender to the gray provost.

Forrest's cavalry operations are particularly instructive on the provost's handling of prisoners. On April 24, 1864, about a week after the capture of Fort Pillow, Captain John Goodwin, Forrest's provost marshal, telegraphed the headquarters of the Department of Alabama, Mississippi, and East Louisiana from Okolona, Mississippi: "I arrived at this place this evening with 250 prisoners from Fort Pillow. Please send guard after them. Let me know when they will get here." Goodwin was obviously anxious to return with his provost to Forrest and hoped that General Polk's department provost would respond quickly. Goodwin took advantage of his short stay at Okolona to compile and forward his report together with an addendum listing the prisoners. Meantime, Forrest's 2d Tennessee Cavalry had been assigned to escort another group of Fort Pillow prisoners to Demopolis, where they were to be turned over to Major Jules C. Denis, provost marshal general of the department. The regiment was four days en route to the Mobile and Ohio Railroad at Verona, where a detachment took the prisoners on to Demopolis by train while the remainder of the regiment rested for five days before moving to Tupelo to take up new duties.[16]

15. *OR,* Vol. XXX, Pt. 2, p. 85; Colonel Douglass West, "'I am Dying, Egypt, Dying!' and Its Author: Touching Account of the Death of Its Gallant Author, Gen. W. H. Lytle," *SHSP,* XXIII (rpr. 1977), 85; War Department, Collection of Confederate Records, Record Group 109, Chap. II, Vol. 196; *OR,* Vol. XXX, Pt. 2, p. 334.

16. *OR,* Vol. XXXII, Pt. 3, p. 797; Vol. XXXII, Pt. 1, p. 619; Edwin C. Bearss, *Forrest at Brice's Cross Roads and in North Mississippi in 1864* (Dayton, 1979), 11.

Perhaps the reason for the seemingly extravagant use of an entire regiment on escort duty is that, because it was leaving Forrest anyway, the assignment gave the regiment a chance to rest en route to its new operational area.

Subsequent captures of prisoners by Forrest included 1,600 taken at Brice's Cross Roads in June. On June 30 Forrest's provost guard consisted of 14 officers and 96 men. From mid-September to October, Forrest operated against Sherman's lines of communication in northern Alabama and middle Tennessee and, according to provost records, captured over 1,300 officers and men and almost 1,000 Negroes.[17]

Other provost marshals in the rear of the Army of Tennessee were similarly receiving large numbers of Federal prisoners. Colonel R. H. Moore of the 65th Georgia was ordered to guard a convoy of prisoners to the rear, where he was to report to Lieutenant Colonel John E. Toole, provost marshal of the District of East Tennessee. Toole subsequently directed Moore to escort the prisoners to Atlanta. Presumably Toole had no provost available or he would not have ordered a regiment from the army to move so far from the front. Another commanding officer, Colonel S. S. Ives of the 35th Alabama, forwarded large numbers of prisoners to Tuscaloosa, Alabama, where they were turned over to the provost marshal of the Second District of Alabama, Lieutenant Colonel T. H. Baker.[18]

In addition to receiving and escorting prisoners, at times the provost had to guard or assist in guarding the prisoner of war camps in the rear. There is abundant evidence that provost augmented the regular prison guards for extended periods in at least four camps: Augusta and Andersonville, Georgia; Salisbury, North Carolina; and Belle Isle in Richmond, Virginia. It can be assumed that they performed similar duties at some of the other military prisons. Richmond alone had sixteen prisons, and sixty-five more operated within the Confederate States.[19]

17. *OR,* Vol. XXXIX, Pt. 1, p. 227, 548. Bearss, *Forrest at Brice's Cross Roads,* 133; *OR,* Vol. XXXIX, Pt. 2, p. 675.

18. *OR,* Vol. XXX, Pt. 2, p. 443; Hesseltine, *Civil War Prisons,* 63–64, 237; *OR,* Vol. XXXII, Pt. 1, p. 662, Pt. 3, p. 611.

19. A list of principal Confederate military prisons is in *OR,* Ser. II, Vol. VIII, p. 1004. The primary prisons were Libby and Belle Isle in Richmond; Danville, Lynchburg, and Petersburg elsewhere in Virginia; Salisbury in North Carolina; Charleston, Florence, and Columbia in South Carolina; Millen, Macon (Camp Oglethorpe), Atlanta, Savannah, and Andersonville in Georgia; Cahaba (Castle Morgan), Tuscaloosa, and Mobile in Alabama; New Orleans in Louisiana; and Camps Groce and Ford in Texas. Still other prisons were at Castle Thunder, Crew's, Grant's Factory, Pemberton's, Scott's, and Smith's Factory in Richmond; Charlotte and Raleigh in North

Richmond became virtually a prison city, housing thousands of Federals. One of the best-known Richmond prisons was Libby, a large three-story brick tobacco factory, which within a week after First Manassas was bulging with Federals. The initial thousand or so were crowded in haphazardly, but soon officers and men were separated, the latter occupying a tent city on Belle Isle in the James River.

Brigadier General John H. Winder, appointed inspector general of the Richmond camps before the battle, viewed Richmond as a collecting point from which prisoners could be sent to locations farther from the battle zone. Although many were moved, approximately two thousand remained throughout 1861, necessitating substantial numbers of guards. A member of one of the seven companies ordered to that duty in August was Private Henry Wirz, who reported to General Winder for special duties. Movement of prisoners in and out of Richmond continued during the winter of 1861–1862, many going to Charleston and New Orleans in September and others to Tuscaloosa, Alabama, in November under the charge of the newly promoted Sergeant Wirz. Other prisoners reached Tuscaloosa from Confederate commands in the West. A large group, presumably of fair size because fifty guards were required for the escort, was moved to Tuscaloosa via Memphis and Mobile in March, 1862. It is interesting in view of later events that Wirz was popular with the inmates of the Tuscaloosa prison, and apparently conditions there were much better than in the Richmond prisons. Other prisoners were dispatched to the newly completed Salisbury, North Carolina, stockade, where they were received by the provost.[20]

These movements reduced the Richmond prison population only temporarily for following the Seven Days' Battle in June, 1862, many Federals found themselves inmates of the prisons in the capital. Their presence, always a burden to a city struggling to secure and transport adequate supplies to feed

---

Carolina; Camp Lawton, Augusta, Marietta, and Blackshear in Georgia; Shreveport in Louisiana; and Montgomery in Alabama. For additional information, consult Hesseltine, *Civil War Prisons*. There is also much useful information in Earl Antrim, *Civil War Prisons and Their Covers* (New York, 1961), 120–60. A map showing the Richmond prisons is in *ibid.*, 145. William C. Davis (ed.), *Fighting for Time* (New York, 1983), 396–449, Vol. IV of Davis, *The Image of War, 1861–1865*, 6 vols., describes Confederate prisons and includes many excellent photographs of Libby, Castle Thunder, and Andersonville. See also Beers, *Guide to the Archives*, 250–59.

20. *OR*, Ser. II, Vol. III, pp. 700, 703–705, 711; Vol. X, Pt. 2, pp. 297–98; Hesseltine, *Civil War Prisons*, 62–65; *OR*, Vol. XVI, Pt. 2, pp. 881, 940.

its swollen population, also imposed additional tasks on the military authorities. Commissary General Lucius Northrop was not alone in wishing the prisoners out of Richmond. Often unable to feed even the Confederate army properly, he foresaw no way to provide for useless Federal mouths and pointed out the danger posed to the city by the mob of hungry men under inadequate guard. Other soldiers became involved in the problem when they drew the highly unpopular assignment of guarding the prisoners, a task many found distasteful and even degrading. Certainly LeGrand Wilson, a lieutenant in the 42d Mississippi, found these duties "very disagreeable" during a tour of duty on Belle Isle.[21]

Conditions at both Belle Isle and Libby became extremely bad in 1863. Brigadier General Neal Dow, one of the few Union generals to experience captivity, testified that during the winter of 1863–1864 some thousand Federal officers incarcerated in Libby were contending with starvation rations, lack of warm clothing, overcrowding, and brutal guards. Life on Belle Isle was even worse; according to Dow, many of the soldiers had no shelter, and men actually froze to death. Overcrowding in both prisons reached a desperate state about this time. In December, 1863, the Richmond provost marshal, Major Isaac H. Carrington, responding to a request for information from the Confederacy's agent of exchange, Robert Ould, reported that 11,650 prisoners, including 1,044 officers, were confined in the Richmond prisons.[22] It had become progressively more difficult to feed and guard such numbers, a situation that General Lee recognized when he recommended that prisoners no longer be held in Richmond. He proposed that Danville, Virginia, become a main prison center, although in the event, accommodation there was inadequate for any additional prisoners of war.

Eventually, in November, 1863, General Winder ordered a reconnaissance party to select a site for a new prison near Americus, Georgia. Andersonville was chosen as the best possible location to hold captured Federals, and although the new prison was in no way ready to receive them, the first convoy of prisoners from Belle Isle reached Andersonville on February 27, 1864. By March, four hundred a day were en route to Georgia, a stream of men that resulted in fifteen thousand residents in May, climbing to twenty-two thousand in June, and finally by the end of July almost thirty-two thousand were

21. Wilson, *Confederate Soldier*, 93.
22. Frank L. Byrne (ed.), "A General Behind Bars: Neal Dow in Libby Prison," *Civil War History*, VIII (June, 1962; rpr. 1972), 164–83; Hesseltine, *Civil War Prisons*, 121.

crammed into Andersonville's twenty-six acres. This figure included twenty-three hundred Belle Isle prisoners who had been the subject of correspondence in June between Major Carrington and the War Department. On the twenty-eighth of that month Carrington advised that twenty-three hundred men were fit to be moved, although he had not previously been notified that Lynchburg was their destination, and he was unable to determine who had issued the order to move the men. This confusion is another instance of the muddle that existed between Generals Winder and Gardner before the prison reorganization in the autumn. Carrington's letter passed rapidly through the War Department to Secretary of War Seddon, who instructed the adjutant general to issue the necessary orders. According to a notation by Seddon on the letter, "Notice has been sent orally to Major Carrington to prepare, and the instructions can be at once carried out." That same day Adjutant General Cooper ordered the movement of these prisoners to Lynchburg, where reserves would relieve the provost guards and then take the prisoners on to Andersonville.[23]

Andersonville was also receiving sick and wounded prisoners from other locations. The provost marshal at Charleston, South Carolina, was ordered to clear the city's hospitals of any inmates designated by the medical officers as fit to stand the journey to Andersonville. Few of those selected would likely have retained sufficient strength to withstand the rigorous hardships of that infamous camp. Although the Charleston authorities gave notice that future Federal prisoners would not be admitted to Charleston hospitals, unwounded prisoners continued to arrive in the city, some reaching the main prison, Castle Pinkney, by the most circuitous routes.[24] One former Union army provost marshal, Lieutenant Edmund Ryan of the 17th Illinois, recalled his tour of the Southern prisons after his capture near Meridian, Mississippi, in February, 1864. Ryan was six days en route to the Cahaba, Alabama, prison, which he described as an old warehouse crawling with vermin, a species that he conjectured had more to eat than the men. In late May Ryan was sent on to the officers' prison at Camp Oglethorpe in Macon, Georgia, where he joined twelve hundred other officers. From there he was moved again, reaching Savannah on July 29, and yet again to Charleston on September 13. Ryan remembered that the Charleston prison, a stuccoed masonry structure crowned by a forty-foot tower, housed several hundred convicts, Negro prisoners, military offenders, and deserters from both

23. *OR*, Ser. II, Vol. VI, pp. 925–26; Hesseltine, *Civil War Prisons*, 131, 135, 146; *OR*, Ser. II, Vol. VII, pp. 422–23, 215.
24. *OR*, Ser. II, Vol. VII, p. 215.

sides. The Union prisoners occupied the prison yard, a fate Ryan was to endure for only two weeks because on September 28 he was exchanged at Atlanta.[25]

Those Federals who did enter Andersonville's gates after June, 1864, would no doubt have encountered the camp provost marshal, Captain W. Shelby Reed, who had been assigned by the War Department to that position on June 11. His duties were soon extended to include command of the post provost guard, an appointment published in camp orders on the twenty-second, presumably by authority of General Winder, who had arrived on June 8. As of August 5, the provost consisted of four officers and eighty-five men. This force was probably not adequate for policing a prison guard composed primarily of ill-disciplined and ill-trained Georgia militia.[26]

The officer population of Libby Prison in Richmond was also drastically reduced in May, 1864, when the occupants were moved to a new prison for officers at Macon, Georgia, but by autumn an influx of new prisoners and the overcrowding at Macon and Andersonville necessitated use of the Richmond prisons. By the end of September, 1864, Belle Isle once again held more than 6,000 Federals. The manpower bill to control these prisoners was high; Brigadier General William M. Gardner, who had been made responsible for the Richmond prisons in July, estimated that 150 privates were required daily as a guard force, and the system of relief every third day meant that 450 guards were required. The battalion providing the guards was not strong enough to furnish these numbers, and therefore from time to time reserve troops had to serve, as did 200 men from the heavy artillery battalions of Richmond's defenses.[27]

More prisoners arrived daily. William McClendon of the 15th Alabama added one to the total in early October. The Alabamian, while on picket near Petersburg, grabbed one Yankee and had the unfortunate captive escorted to the rear, where he was turned over to the provost. In all likelihood, this Federal ended up on Belle Isle, and he may have been included in a convoy of 7,500 prisoners that left Richmond for the Salisbury, North Carolina, prison in October. This shipment much reduced the prison population of the capital, leaving "only a few hundred prisoners from recent captures and those awaiting special exchanges."[28]

25. William M. Armstrong, "Cahaba to Charleston: The Prison Odyssey of Lt. Edmund E. Ryan," *Civil War History,* VIII (June, 1962; rpr. 1972), 218–27.

26. *OR,* Ser. II, Vol. VII, pp. 397, 518, 553; Hesseltine, *Civil War Prisons,* 143.

27. *OR,* Vol. XLII, Pt. 2, pp. 1237–40.

28. McClendon, *Recollections,* 219–20; Hesseltine, *Civil War Prisons,* 169.

It would appear that even these few hundred kept the Richmond provost busy. Escapes were of course inevitable, but perhaps none was so inventive as that of one Federal who escaped from Castle Thunder by playing dead. As soon as the escape was noticed, the alarm was sounded and the errant Federal was picked up within a day by the provost and returned to the Castle. The continued presence of Federal prisoners of war in the city consumed Confederate manpower to the end of the war. Efforts to maintain law and order during the last chaotic days before the fall of the city were hampered by the need to evacuate the inmates of the military prisons. Lieutenant General Richard Ewell, commanding the city at the last, was hard-pressed to keep order because the provost guard, the 2d Battalion of Virginia Reserves, had to be used to shepherd the prisoners. This left only a few men of the Local Defense Brigade—by this late stage little better than a corporal's guard—and an equally small provost guard to keep order.[29] It was a hopeless task, and only the entry of Federal troops brought quiet to the city.

Elsewhere, as late as mid-February, 1865, prisoners continued to flow into the military prison system. The district commander of northeast Georgia reported that according to his provost marshal there had "hardly been a week for months past that from 20 to 50, and frequently as high as 200 prisoners, have not been forwarded . . . to Augusta." One company of troops had been constantly engaged in guarding these prisoners.[30]

From the mass of data available it is obvious that control of prisoners was a major task of the Confederate provost. Of the approximately two hundred thousand Federals who passed into Confederate hands, it can be assumed that the majority at one time or another found themselves under provost jurisdiction. Such a large number in itself indicates the degree of provost time and manpower required to control, move, and guard these visitors. Some economy in provost officers was achieved in areas where prison camps were located with the headquarters of district provost marshals. In Atlanta, Tuscaloosa, and Charleston officers could act as both provost marshal and prison guard commander. Other economies were made possible by prison commandants doubling as commanders of the post provost guards, when and if these were available. Such savings did not apply to the provost guards themselves, because those that existed could not often be spared for such tasks as guarding prisoners. Other bodies of men—junior and senior reserves, militia, and state troops—had to fill the gap.

29. Burrows, "Recollections of Libby Prison," 91–92; Irvine, "Fall of Richmond," 386.
30. *OR*, Vol. XLIX, Pt. 1, pp. 974–76.

At the fighting fronts, however, it was a different story. There the provost took on virtually total responsibility for prisoners once the capturing unit had turned them over. From that point on they guarded, accounted for, and moved the prisoners out of the way of the army, thus performing a vital service for the fighting troops and the country as a whole. Even the most rabid antiprovost soldier or citizen could not argue with the convincing evidence that the provost met this responsibility in a most commendable and efficient manner throughout the war.

The overall manner in which the provost carried out their duties under martial law received more mixed reviews. There is a good case for saying that the provost's efficiency made martial law in the Confederate States of America a significant cause of excitement and controversy. Sometimes the provost were *too* efficient, extending their hand into matters not intended for their jurisdiction. And efficiency was too often accompanied by arrogance. As the enforcing agency of martial law the provost was once again to find itself caught between the millstones·of the public and the government.

11

The Provost Marshal's Law

In its proper manifestation the jealousy between
civil and military spirits is a healthy symptom.

A. T. MAHAN

Martial law and its restrictions on normal civil liberties were most unpopular in the Confederate States. Staunch advocates—and there were many—of the philosophy of states' rights, perhaps the major cause of secession and the guiding political credo of the Confederacy, could not tolerate martial law. Most civilians and even some senior army officers simply could not see the necessity, whatever the circumstances, for interfering with civilian legal jurisdiction, the writ of *habeas corpus,* and other civil rights. Martial law was, in their opinion, a tyrannical device of a central government determined to substitute "despotism" for constitutional government.[1]

Their enforcement of martial law regulations did not endear the provost to civilians; with normal legal proceedings suspended, provost could arrest at will with no danger of civil suit or criminal prosecution to deter precipitate action. Such periods of absolute provost power were, however, infrequent and relatively brief in duration. Unlike Lincoln, who could and did impose martial law on his own volition—thereby giving the Union provost a free hand—President Davis could not impose martial law without congressional authority. Contrary to popular belief, the Confederate Congress was extremely loath to give the chief executive such powers, conferring them only sparingly after acrimonious and protracted debate. Authority to suspend the writ of *habeas corpus* was given but three time to Davis: in February, 1862, for a very short period; from October, 1862, to February, 1863; and from February to August, 1864. During this last period the president's power was restricted in that suspension of the writ applied only to those prisoners whose arrest was authorized directly by Davis or the secretary of war.

The jealousy with which Congress guarded its prerogatives is evident in its

1. Brigadier General Albert Pike, commanding the Indian Territory, July, 1862, to the Secretary of War, *OR,* Vol. XIII, p. 856.

resolution on September 24, 1862, that the War Department could not appoint or employ provost marshals and give them authority over civilians or responsibility for law and order in towns and cities, nor could the secretary of war limit or restrict jurisdiction of the civil courts. Davis himself had initially been reluctant—at least so he professed in a speech on November 18, 1861—to act like Lincoln: "a President making war without the assent of Congress . . . judges threatened because they maintain the writ of *habeas corpus* . . . justice and law trampled under the iron heel of military authority, and upright men and innocent women dragged to distant dungeons upon the mere edict of a despot."[2]

Davis probably regretted these comments. Two days later, on November 20, 1861, the general insurrection that erupted in East Tennessee, an area festering with Unionist sentiment, forced him to react strongly in imitation of his northern counterpart. In short order troops were dispatched to the troubled area, and the local authorities, released from the obligations of *habeas corpus,* were able to arrest a large number of Unionist ringleaders, including William Brownlow, who had sworn to fight secession "on the ice in hell." Davis ordered that any apprehended insurrectionists be held as prisoners of war except those known to have burned bridges along the vital Confederate supply routes. These latter were "to be tried summarily by drumhead court martial, and, if found guilty, executed on the spot by hanging." Five hangings provided a chilling testimony to the efficiency of the military courts established on December 11 by Brigadier General William Carroll, commanding at Knoxville, when he declared civil tribunals suspended and proclaimed martial law in the city of Knoxville.[3] The insurrection was swiftly smashed.

A subsequent request by Davis for authority to suspend *habeas corpus* in February, 1864, reveals how suspiciously Congress regarded such requests, even at a time when the sternest measures were desperately required to counter defeatism and disloyalty. Hostility to many government policies had ballooned to such proportions that conscription could not be enforced or evaders prosecuted, and disloyal gatherings and activities were widespread. Recognizing that without suspension any countermeasures would be ineffective, on February 3 Davis advised Congress that "discontent, disaffection, and disloyalty" and worse, outright "hostility" to the cause, forced him to request suspension of the writ of *habeas corpus.*

2. *Journal of the Confederate Congress,* II, 325–26; Foote, *Civil War,* I, 132–33.
3. *OR,* VII, 760.

To allay any apprehension of misuse of the powers he was seeking, the president assured Congress that only the disloyal need fear martial law; the loyal and true citizen would in no way be threatened. Twelve days of bitter debate ensued before Congress agreed to a six-month suspension of the writ. Vice-President Alexander Stephens, his supporters in Congress, and the vociferous anti-Davis press unleashed a tirade of recrimination and accusation against the president and his "unlimited military authority," which aimed at nothing less than the "consolidation" of the rights of the states.[4] Not again would the chief executive receive the power to impose martial law.

In each case for which the president sought extraordinary powers there was sound reason why the normal constitutional devices would not suffice. The first legislation granting extraordinary powers, enacted February 27, 1862, gave the president power to suspend the writ of *habeas corpus* in cities, towns, or areas in such danger of attack that martial law was required for their effective defense. That very day he suspended civil jurisdiction and the privilege of *habeas corpus* in the cities of Norfolk and Portsmouth and the immediate area surrounding them.[5] Both cities, the eastern part of the Peninsula, and perhaps even Richmond were threatened by the Union buildup at Fort Monroe.

Davis took special care not to shock civilian sensitivities too much with his new powers. Foreseeing that martial law would be better accepted if it were administered by local men, on March 5 Davis instructed Secretary of War Benjamin to inform Major General Benjamin Huger, commanding at Norfolk, that "some leading and reliable citizen [is] to be appointed provost-marshal in Norfolk and another in Portsmouth." For Norfolk the president suggested the mayor for the position. Benjamin also directed Huger to implement a number of measures which the president felt necessary for the safety of the threatened area. These measures, some of which later stirred discontent, authorized, among other things, the seizure of all weapons and cotton and the strict control of liquor. In addition, restrictions placed on movement made it mandatory that any person wishing to leave the area give twenty-four hours' notice so that written passes could be issued. Those without passes from the provost would be arrested. Physicians, however, would retain their freedom of movement, a relaxation of the rules doubtless designed to show how reasonable the regulations were. These instructions were issued on March 6 by Lieutenant W. A. Parham of the 41st Virginia Infantry, possibly on the authority of the mayor of

4. Foote, *Civil War*, II, 950–51.
5. *OR*, Ser. IV, Vol. I, p. 954; IX, 46; Foote, *Civil War*, I, 231.

Norfolk, but it is interesting that Parham signed the instructions as "provost marshal," and no reference was made to the mayor. Subsequent correspondence indicates that the president's nominee for provost marshal had not been Huger's choice. He no doubt was more comfortable with a military provost marshal.

It is obvious, too, that President Davis was not prepared to condone over-zealousness by the military, as was soon made clear to General Huger, who, it appears, had considerably overstepped his authority. On March 22 General Lee advised Huger that both the governor of Virginia and the attorney general of the Confederacy were less than happy with his conduct of affairs. In particular, his appointment of a "civil and military governor of the district composed of the cities of Norfolk and Portsmouth" was abhorrent and illegal. "Especially has the officer appointed by you," Lee pointed out, "no power or control over the militia . . . it gives that officer no power to decide upon the right of any person to exemption from military duty." The letter went on to admonish the errant Huger that martial law did not in any way suspend the laws of the state, nor did it invest the military with any general or arbitrary control of civilian matters. Lee cautioned that only the writ of *habeas corpus* and the action of the courts in civil cases were in suspension. Huger was *not* to make any appointments other than a provost marshal. Huger took no immediate notice of Lee's letter. A week later Lee specifically ordered Huger to abolish the office of military and civil governor and to appoint provost marshals as necessary to preserve order. Huger was also told to bear in mind that the criminal jurisdiction of the state remained in effect and that offenders arrested by the provost marshal were to be turned over to the ordinary criminal courts.[6] Huger's "military governor" was anathema to almost everyone, but others, including a number of senior generals, could not even accept that provost marshals had any power whatsoever outside the strictly military environment.

Norfolk and Portsmouth were only the first of several cities to experience the iron hand of martial law. Two days after they passed under military control, Richmond joined them. The city woke on March 1 to discover that martial law had been declared and Brigadier General Winder was busy establishing "efficient military police" to enforce it. Some thought the pronouncement was "not too soon" and that firm controls were required for a city "full of soldiers on leave or on their way back from hospitals to their organizations." As a first step, Colonel John Potter was appointed provost marshal of the capital. Two assistants, Captains Archibald C. Godwin and J. C. Maynard, assumed responsibility for the administration of the eastern and western districts respectively. With the provost firmly in place, the first of a stream of orders regulating life in the city flowed from Winder's headquarters.[7]

On March 2 the precaution was taken of prohibiting the sale and distillation of liquor by closing all saloons and distilleries in Richmond. And it was not a moment too soon, according to Edmund Ruffin, a longtime advocate of secession: "For some time back the great assemblage of soldiers, generally without command, and their drinking, have made Richmond a sink-hole of drunkenness, rowdeyism, and crime." Within a few days, having learned through experience, Winder considerably refined his initial attempt to ban liquor. To prevent it from reaching the city, he prohibited its transport by rail. Those unfortunates who had not had the foresight to lay in a private stock now had only one source of supply: the city apothecaries. But not for long. Winder effectively cut that pipeline by ensuring that apothecaries could purchase liquor only with the permission of his headquarters and could sell only to those who presented a physician's prescription. The provost, or "plug uglies" as they came to be known, took full advantage of their position: "It was not long before Winder's detectives were forging prescriptions for brandy, drinking the brandy, and then arresting the unfortunate apothecaries who had sold it to them." Even patent medicines did not escape General Winder: Elijah Baker's "Baker's Bitters" was declared contraband and seized.[8]

Winder's next step was to impose tight controls on movement within Richmond. No one was allowed to enter or leave the city without a military pass. Railroads had to supply the provost with lists of all passengers carried, and hotels were forced to provide lists of new guests each morning. This system, with refinements added from time to time, was to continue in Richmond to the fall of the Confederacy.[9]

The economy, too, was subject to Winder's direction. Alarmed at the serious inflation and extortion that ravaged the city, he used martial law to combat

7. Foote, *Civil War,* I, 231; *OR,* Vol. LI, Pt. 2, p. 482; Bill, *Beleaguered City,* 103; Thomas, *Confederate State of Richmond,* 81–83.

8. Richardson (ed.), *Messages,* I, 220–21; Scarborough (ed.), *Diary of Edmund Ruffin,* II, 246; Bill, *Beleaguered City,* 103–104; Thomas, *Confederate State of Richmond,* 83. At least four apothecaries suffered such indignity.

9. Thomas, *Confederate State of Richmond,* 82.

the ruinous price rises in food. On March 31 he set maximum prices on domestic produce such as fish, butter, eggs, and potatoes but made no attempt to set tariffs on imported articles. To enforce the new prices the provost confiscated any item offered for sale above the maximum. The system failed. Within a month farmers avoided the Richmond markets, preferring not to sell at a loss, and supplies dried up. Pressure from the local citizens' committee forced Winder to revoke the fixed prices. A second try in July, this time setting maximums for corn and livestock fodder, also failed. Harried by numerous complaints, the War Department finally stepped in, declaring in August that martial law granted no power to set prices.[10]

In other ways, life in Richmond continued much as it had been. Civilian courts, for example, carried on throughout the period of martial law. The Mayor's Court never closed, and on March 8 the president opened the Hustings Court, probably on the good advice of the Confederate attorney general, who felt that civil jurisdiction of the courts should continue as usual, with exceptions being made only in absolute necessity. Early in May the secretary of war informed local judges that courts should continue to grant injunctions when necessary. This would prevent martial law from interfering with normal routine. If cases arose in which the courts could not execute the judgments, they could be turned over to the provost marshal, who would receive orders through military channels to carry out court decisions. Provost marshals were informed of these guidelines in June and given strict orders not to take cognizance of civil cases. The civil police also carried on, although, as always under martial law, they were subject to the overall control of the provost marshals. The president's restraint may well have influenced Winder in his decision to employ his provost primarily for the execution of military orders, leaving the civilian police to carry out the usual police functions. Some civilians, of course, ran afoul of the military regulations, but the military tribunals could award only a month's hard labor to civilian offenders. By April Congress further limited provost power by restricting military arrests of civilians to those apprehended committing crimes against the government.[11]

Shady dealings in liquor were not the only abuses perpetrated by the provost that came to light during Richmond's time under martial law. The confiscation

10. Warner, *Generals in Gray,* 340–41; Putnam, *In Richmond During the Confederacy,* 113; Bill, *Beleaguered City,* 105; Thomas, *Confederate State of Richmond,* 87, 105–106.

11. Thomas, *Confederate State of Richmond,* 83; *OR,* Vol. LI, Pt. 2, p. 551; Ser. IV, Vol. I, p. 1149; Beers, *Guide to the Archives,* 260. During periods of martial law, provost marshals assumed control of police departments, detectives, and other civilians who could assist the military police.

of private weapons by the military police had not gone down well with the public, nor had Winder's threats to close newspapers that took a hostile line to him been considered part of his mandate. These matters, however, were overshadowed by the complaints stemming from the provost's arrests of civilians and their incarceration in the city prisons. By the middle of March, thirty civilians, including two women, were locked up in Castle Godwin on charges of suspected disloyalty. It is impossible to say whether these charges were valid, but many felt they were not. One irate citizen, furious at the arrogance of the "plug uglies," complained of Winder's "lords of the ascendant. . . . One word of remonstrance, and the poor victim is sent to Castle Godwin." Other citizens questioned the integrity and efficiency of the provost during their "reign of terror." Nevertheless, the majority of Richmond's inhabitants clearly felt that the provost had performed commendably. An article in the Richmond *Dispatch* in April reflects this attitude: "Men, women and children now sleep the sleep of security; their dreams are not disturbed . . . by the vile rows of drunken soldiery. Our streets are quiet. Brawls are rare. . . . The streets are morning, noon and night being patrolled by guards, who arrest all loiterers, vagabonds. . . . And the consequences are peace, serenity, security, respect for life and property and a thorough revival of patriotism and enthusiasm."[12]

During the first half of 1862, other areas in Virginia experienced martial law. On March 8 the president imposed military rule in Petersburg, the "Cockade City," ordering the provost marshal, Captain William Pannill, to establish the necessary military police. One of Pannill's first acts was to prohibit the sale of liquor: difficulty in getting a drink was becoming a common feature of life under martial law. A week later the military took control of most of the Peninsula. Major General John Magruder, appointed provost marshal on March 14, soon forbade the sale and distillation of liquor and at every post and camp appointed provost marshals to enforce martial law rigidly and arrest all offenders. Early in May all five counties of the District of Abingdon in southwest Virginia were placed under martial law, and the district commander, Brigadier General Humphrey Marshall, was ordered to establish strict control.[13]

Events in South Carolina also illustrate how martial law involved a unique blend of civil and military sovereignty. Colonel, later Brigadier General Johnson Hagood, the provost marshal who administered martial law in the city of Charleston from May 5 to June 9, 1862, fortunately left a detailed record of his

12. Jones, *Rebel War Clerk's Diary,* 73, 75–76; *Confederate State of Richmond,* 84.

13. *OR,* Vol. LI, Pt. 2, p. 493; Vol. XI, Pt. 3, p. 386; Vol. X, Pt. 2, pp. 484–85. Martial law was proclaimed in the Virginia counties of Lee, Wise, Buchanan, McDowell, and Wyoming.

and the city's experiences under military rule. His account is most revealing of the regulations and standing orders entailed in martial law, of the passport control measures and the other duties performed by the provost, and of the men who enforced the system.

The fall of Fort Donelson and then New Orleans and military reverses in South Carolina in early 1862 had caused great anxiety in Charleston. State authorities were also concerned about the extent of the Confederate commitment to the defense of Charleston should a siege be undertaken by the Federals. These doubts and a clamor for urgent improvements to the city's defenses convinced Governor Bonham that martial law was necessary in Charleston. Consequently, on May 1 he ordered noncombatants to leave and proclaimed martial law, avowing that the city would be defended regardless of the cost in lives and property; in the final extremity a city in ruins would be far preferable to evacuation or capitulation. The governor's fears regarding Confederate intentions were unfounded, for on May 1 Jefferson Davis placed not only Charleston but all of South Carolina from the Santee River to the South Edisto River under martial law. The commander of this area, Major General John C. Pemberton, was directed to organize an efficient military police as quickly as possible.

Four days later Pemberton issued his own proclamation of martial law in Charleston and appointed Colonel Hagood of the 1st South Carolina Volunteers provost marshal of the city. Hagood was told to form the necessary guard force and then, of course, to prevent the sale of liquor.[14] *Habeas corpus* was also suspended, as was civil jurisdiction except for such mundane matters as probate of wills, appointment of guardians, matters dealing with property, and assessment and collection of taxes.

Hagood soon found himself in the position of playing the game without knowing the rules. Pemberton was no wiser. Hagood's request for additional guidance drew no response other than reference to Richmond's general order and an admonition that Pemberton expected the strictest system of military police. The state attorney general was similarly unable to enlighten Hagood as to what martial law entailed in a jurisdictional sense, and therefore Hagood set his own rules. His basic assumption that martial law meant the "execution of such existing law as it was deemed necessary to retain, with the making of such additional law as the military exigency required" induced a curious reaction from the mayor. In a fit of pique he declared the city municipal government

14. Hagood, *Memoirs*, 69; *OR*, XIV, 489, 492.

deposed. In effect, the mayor's precipitous action also disbanded the city's police force, which was hardly to Hagood's liking, and he attempted to rectify it by publishing the following notice: "His Honor Charles McBeth, Mayor of Charleston, is respectfully invited and expected to continue in the exercise of his municipal functions, as far as they shall not infringe upon any requirements of martial law. . . . It is the earnest desire of the major general commanding that the provost marshal and the mayor will act in entire unison and render such mutual aid as may be necessary to the efficient discharge of their respective duties."[15]

Other jurisdictional disputes quickly arose to make life awkward for the military. On May 5 the justice of the state Court of Common Pleas and General Sessions followed the mayor's lead with a little deposing of his own. His adjournment of his court on the grounds that his jurisdiction was suspended by martial law put the military in the position of having to amend the martial law proclamation or take responsibility for hearing civil cases and trying criminal ones. The latter option was impossible. That very day a general order announced that it was not intended that martial law should interfere with the business of this court. Hardly had the general order been distributed when a fresh complication surfaced: the presidential suspension of civil jurisdiction, which affected both the courts and the police. Pemberton was therefore forced to yet another *volte-face,* this time resuspending the function of the state court and the municipal government and declaring their prerogatives to be his under presidential authority. The requirement to hear civil cases was circumvented by simply placing such cases in abeyance, and though the mayor's council remained suspended the civilian police force continued to operate under provost supervision. The effectiveness of the police was degraded by the bad relations that had grown up between Mayor McBeth and Colonel Alexander H. Brown, the assistant provost marshal.[16] Further controversy was close at hand.

In view of the protracted confusion over what martial law entailed and the lack of direction from higher authority, it is to Colonel Hagood's credit that martial law regulations were published as early as May 12. The regulations came none too soon, for already the city's papers were denouncing the badly

15. Hagood, *Memoirs,* 70–72.

16. *Ibid.,* 72–73; Alexander Haskell Brown, M-91 Record Book, 1862, Southern Historical Collection, University of North Carolina, Chapel Hill (hereinafter cited as AHB Book). Brown's book contains a good deal of correspondence to and from Mayor McBeth on a wide variety of issues relating to civilian-military cooperation during the time Charleston was under martial law. Mutual irritation and dislike are often evident in the correspondence.

disciplined troops for "outrages . . . committed with impunity by those of lower grade." Tight controls over the movement of soldiers and citizens in and out of the city were also urgently required; it was common knowledge that Charleston was "infested with spies and the enemy in daily receipt of information." It was widely recognized that the mayor's almost farcical passport system had done nothing to correct the situation. Determined to impose order, Hagood opened his headquarters in the city courthouse, set specific office hours, and published martial law regulations in all the city newspapers. These orders included establishment of a guard force and a provost marshal court to try offenses formerly within civilian jurisdiction and offenses against martial law, stipulation that anyone entering or leaving the city must have a pass from the provost, and prohibition of the sale and distillation of liquor. [17]

More detailed instructions for the guidance of the guard force were also published in the city's press. These were concerned primarily with the maintenance of strict control on the movement of troops. As an example of the severity of the regulations, officers resident in camps in the city were prohibited from leaving the camps without the express permission of the camp commandant; those stationed outside the city were required first to provide written leaves of absence to the officer of the guard and then to confirm their documents personally with the provost marshal. Other ranks were subject to similar restrictions. Civilians were treated a little more leniently in that they were required only to register with the guards on arrival in Charleston. The guards were cautioned to maintain good order and set the example. Offenses against martial law by those entrusted to enforce it were considered "aggravated," and offenders would be subject to the sternest punishment. [18]

The press appeared relatively happy with the regulations, one paper going so far as to say that the provost appointments were all "good and acceptable as conferred upon able, worthy and patriotic men." Colonel Brown, it was noted, was particularly well chosen because "everyone remembers what an energetic and efficient captain of the city guard or chief of police he made in bygone days." Hagood later recalled his amusement at this comment, characterizing Brown as an "arbitrary and overbearing man . . . with very decided affinities

17. Hagood, *Memoirs*, 73–75; AHB Book. The ban on liquor sales resulted in many complaints by members of the medical profession. On August 1 sale of liquor for medical use was permitted. Brown's book also contains many letters to unit commanders advising of punishment (confinement and corporal) awarded to soldiers for various offenses, including counterfeiting, larceny, and just about every crime one can name.

18. Hagood, *Memoirs*, 75–76.

and repulsions, and . . . some were disposed to think . . . that his little finger was heavier than other folk's hands." Another paper adopted a wait-and-see attitude: "If the officers . . . exercise their functions with wisdom, firmness and impartiality, this . . . martial law will prove to be a welcome—as well as beneficial measure."[19]

By May 14 some of the happiness was wearing off, mainly because of the passport controls. Unlike the mayor's old system under which passports could be obtained day or night, the new limited office hours—11 A.M. to 1 P.M.— were creating great inconvenience. These hours had been set at the insistence of Colonel Brown, the assistant provost marshal, because of his belief that only his personal presence at the passport office would ensure proper supervision of the issuance of passports. Unfortunately, his other duties prevented his attendance for more than two hours a day and often not even that. As a result, the crush of citizens at the passport office at the courthouse was soon so great that many failed to obtain passports to leave the city before the office closed.[20] The *Courier,* hitherto content with Colonel Brown and company, was incensed, calling the short office hours a "grievous and intolerable oppression—an unreasonable and tyrannical measure." Hagood agreed. On May 21 he extended the office hours from 9 A.M. to 2 P.M. and from 4 to 6 P.M. and appointed six civilians to issue civilian passports. Passports for soldiers were issued at City Hall under the direction of Captain W. J. Gayer. Eventually both passport offices became models of efficiency: "two offices in different departments, one for citizens with separate desks of application for males and females (whites), and for negroes bond and free; another for the military with a separate desk for invalid soldiers from which all other applicants were excluded." The *Courier* promptly did an about-face, asserting its pleasure that Colonel Hagood had so magnificently satisfied the needs of the community.[21]

Colonel Brown, meantime, was able to get on with wearing his other hat, that of chief of the general police department. Brown's daily routine included investigations and trials of the many offenders brought before him, referring more serious matters to the provost marshal, Colonel Hagood, when necessary.

19. *Ibid.,* 43, 76–77.

20. AHB Book. Hagood instituted various measures to ease the burden of obtaining passports. On May 15 he decreed that white women and children could leave Charleston without papers. After a trial period of seven days, as of May 22 women and children no longer needed to have papers. On May 19 he authorized the president of the South Carolina Railroad to sign passports and later renewed this authority for an indefinite period.

21. Hagood, *Memoirs,* 78–79; AHB Book.

Brown also spent a good part of his time supervising his detectives and the regular city police.

As might be imagined, a large provost force was required for duties in the city. The chain of sentinels and guard posts surrounding Charleston and within it, the requirements of the passport office, and general police duties all consumed their share of manpower. Hagood was fortunate in having immediately available to him his own regiment, the 1st South Carolina, and a battalion of cavalry. This force was often and easily supplemented by the regiments passing through the city on the way north. Each rested in Charleston for a few days, and each during its stay performed provost duties. At times six or seven thousand troops were in the city, and on such occasions a brigade structure was created for these temporary provost.[22]

Sometimes, however, this proliferation of riches was interrupted. On June 2 the Federal landing on James Island forced the deployment of all regular forces to the threatened area. All male citizens up to fifty years of age were called for duty as provost. When only one man turned up, with no prospect of more appearing, the Charleston Reserves were mobilized to take over the city, though only 150 paraded out of a paper strength of 1,250. According to Hagood, who was to rejoin his regiment on James Island on June 9, the reserves performed admirably as provost. Colonel Alexander H. Brown replaced him as provost marshal of Charleston.[23]

It should not be surprising to learn that once the immediate danger to the city was past, some people decried the need for provost and wished them abolished. One Charlestonian, possessed of a short memory and an ungrateful nature, complained to Adjutant General Cooper in late June of the "unwise" military assumption of power over matters having nothing to do with the military: "The old laws . . . have been suspended. . . . New ones are to be supplied, or there are to be none save the *sit justitia* [state of justice] of the general commanding or his provost."[24] Martial law was suspended in Charleston on August 19, 1862.

February, 1862, closed badly for the Confederacy. On the sixth Fort Henry on the Tennessee River fell, and on the sixteenth catastrophe struck when Fort

---

22. AHB Book. Some tasks were very manpower-intensive. To guard two of the three railroads out of Charleston required seventy-two men. The requirement to search all vehicles entering Charleston consumed much provost manpower and time. In an order on June 12 Major General Pemberton, commanding the Department of South Carolina and Georgia, placed all troops in Charleston under control of the provost marshal.

23. Hagood, *Memoirs*, 80–83.

24. *OR*, XIV, 570–71, 599; AHB Book.

Donelson on the Cumberland surrendered unconditionally to Grant. The twelve thousand or so men lost were only a hint of the magnitude of the disaster. On this single day Albert Sidney Johnston's long western line was pierced at its center, Kentucky was lost, and the door to Tennessee was kicked wide open. The news alarmed the entire Confederacy, including the city of New Orleans, which was preoccupied with the ominous massing of Federal naval forces just below the city.[25] It was clear that an attack on the city would not be long delayed.

Major General Mansfield Lovell, charged with defending New Orleans, had frighteningly little with which to resist the coming blow. Forts Jackson and St. Phillip at the mouth of the Mississippi had only fifteen hundred men, and in New Orleans itself there were barely three thousand defenders. Other worries plagued him: the motley naval fleet assembled to face Farragut existed separately from his command, and much time and effort were expended in ensuring coordination and cooperation; he also faced increasing pressure to protect the city from acts of subversion perpetrated by the rumored Yankee spies and sympathizers.

Bowing to public pressure, Lovell and Louisiana Governor Thomas Moore jointly requested on March 12 that President Davis declare martial law in New Orleans. The following day Davis authorized martial law in several parishes around the city. All adult males, with the exception of unnaturalized foreigners, were required to take the oath of allegiance to the Confederate States, and anyone unfriendly to the cause was warned to leave without delay. Due, and by now customary, attention was also paid to passports and liquor. The proclamation announced a system of registry and passports, stipulating that no one would be allowed to remain without satisfying the provost marshals of his or her loyalty. Good citizens were asked to assist the provost by reporting any persons suspected of hostility. Liquor outlets were ordered to close by 8 P.M. daily. The men responsible for carrying out these orders, the provost marshals, were a mix of military officers and locally prominent citizens, including one judge.[26]

Another general order, published on March 18, announced that provost offices, properly manned by clerks and assistants, would be established in each district of the parishes. The newspapers would publish the locations of the offices. This order specified that every white male over age sixteen, whether citizen or alien, should appear within six days before a provost marshal to be

25. Anderson, *Brokenburn*, 100.
26. *OR*, VI, 856–58; LIII, 793.

registered and to provide the authorities with any information desired. For aliens there were special requirements, including promising to abide by Confederate law and not to pass any information to the enemy. Those who had entered the state or the city after May 21, 1861, from any of the states at war with the South were required to obtain permits to remain, signed by either the commanding general or the provost marshal of their district. Without such permits these persons would be arrested.

The order also warned that disobedience of provost orders would be summarily dealt with, no doubt by military tribunal. All officers were directed to comply promptly with any requisitions made on them and to furnish whatever aid the provost marshals required. The city police, as in Charleston and Richmond, were expected to "render every assistance in their power when called on." "Martial law," said Lovell, "has not been declared for the purpose of annoying unnecessarily the true and loyal citizens. No greater restrictions will be imposed . . . than are deemed absolutely necessary . . . to attain the objects in view, which are mainly to ascertain and remove . . . those who . . . are endeavoring . . . to impede our onward progress towards independence." It is difficult to think of further restrictions that could have been imposed. To some of the inhabitants of the city the regulations came as a shock. Certainly between March 18, when they were published, and March 22, Lovell must have received considerable numbers of complaints. On the latter date, doubtless to forestall these complaints, Lovell penned a lengthy letter to Secretary of War Benjamin, portraying the rapture with which the population had received his provost marshals: "The universal approval of my appointments . . . and the satisfaction and quiet so apparent all lead me to infer that the difficulty has been entirely solved."[27]

In mid-April Lovell followed up by advising that the "good" citizens were petitioning to have martial law extended. It is hard to reconcile this statement with other evidence of what was actually going on. By April Lovell had gone far beyond his mandate under martial law: the banks, for example, were told that they were permitted to issue notes only in accordance with the views of the provost marshals. Various other state institutions suffered continual interference from the provost. These arbitrary actions and reports of blatant arrogance on the part of the provost soon reached Richmond and a Confederate government still sensitive at this early stage of the war to charges of military despotism. On April 23, two days before the fall of New Orleans, President

27. *OR*, VI, 860–61, 865.

Davis ordered Lovell to "confine the functions of your provost-marshals to subjects proper to military police." The city had not had a happy time under martial law; as Governor Moore wrote to Davis on May 21: "It was not to be expected that I would ever again consent to the proclamation of martial law by General Lovell after the urgent and persistent complaints I made to you of the action of his provost-marshals."[28]

Upriver from New Orleans the situation in February and March, 1862, was causing considerable trepidation in the Confederate high command. "We have suffered great anxiety because of recent events in Kentucky and Tennessee," said Davis to Albert Sidney Johnston. "I suppose the Tenn. or Mississippi river will be the object of the enemy's next campaign, and I trust you will be able to concentrate a force which will defeat either attempt."[29] His anxiety was somewhat relieved by the junction of Beauregard and Johnston at Corinth, Mississippi, in late March. At least now the troops were in a position to resist the Federals moving on the Tennessee River. A major clash was unavoidable, and it soon came; two bitter April days at Shiloh resulted in the Confederate army recoiling southward to Corinth. Fortunately, no attempt to pursue was made until early May, when General Henry W. Halleck began a ponderous lurch toward Corinth. Minor skirmishing between the two armies continued until Beauregard's withdrawal to Tupelo at the end of May.

Meantime, the Federal advance along the upper Mississippi continued, and by early June Memphis had fallen, opening the river to the Federals except in the state of Mississippi. Vicksburg was to be the next Union objective. Below the city Farragut assembled his fleet and prepared to move north, while Major General Earl Van Dorn, newly charged with defense of the Mississippi, ordered Vicksburg's garrison to hasten work on the city's bastions. To Governor John Pettus of Mississippi President Davis confessed his inability to meet the military needs of the state, but to Van Dorn at Vicksburg he said, "The people will sustain you in your heroic determination."[30]

Independence Day at Vicksburg found the city under mortar bombardment by the Federal fleet. Before the close of the day Vicksburg was also under martial law. A proclamation issued by Van Dorn as commander of the Department of Southern Mississippi and East Louisiana declared martial law in nine counties in Mississippi and in all Louisiana parishes east of the river. The

28. *Ibid.*, 877, 883; XV, 740.
29. Long, *Civil War Day by Day,* 184.
30. *Ibid.*, 230.

regulations included penalties for those who attempted to trade or communicate with the enemy and appointed provost marshals in each county. The provost marshal of the department, Colonel Fred Tate, enforced the martial law regulations to the letter, meting out swift disciplinary punishment to any who violated them. According to James Morgan, a celebrated blockade runner, many civilians were arrested by the provost, mostly on charges of actual or suspected disloyalty and all too often without any substantive evidence.[31]

Some of Van Dorn's regulations went far beyond martial law as it existed in other areas. Like Lovell in New Orleans, Van Dorn was brought up short by the president for meddling with the economy. The controversy his regulations caused reverberated throughout the Confederacy, especially in Congress, where there was heated debate over the need for legislation to restrain the authority of the military and prevent the usurpation of power by field commanders. Other generals and the newspapers soon got into the act, bitterly condemning Van Dorn's actions. The debate raged on until September, when the secretary of war announced that martial law could henceforth be declared only by the president, and as he had not done so in Mississippi, martial law in that state was revoked. On September 5, Brigadier General Daniel Ruggles, temporarily replacing Van Dorn, revoked martial law and ordered all civilian prisoners to be turned over to the civil authorities. Provost marshals were also abolished. This shortsighted move was hastily corrected on September 8 by a general order announcing the appointment of "temporary" provost marshals "to preserve order among military persons and to prevent improper intercourse with the enemy, by either citizens or soldiers." Ten counties in Mississippi and eight parishes in Louisiana received "temporary" provost marshals, most of whom were prominent citizens, including judges and physicians.

With martial law no longer in effect, and hence with their powers much reduced, the provost marshals were cautioned to confine themselves to "proper military jurisdiction" in accordance with the Articles of War, which prescribed courts-martial for those who assisted, harbored, or communicated with the enemy.

The presumption that civilians were subject to court-martial drew a hostile response from some quarters, especially from Governor Moore of Louisiana. Even some provost marshals felt that civilians were not subject to court-mar-

---

31. *OR*, XV, 771–72; Amann (ed.), *Confederate Armies*, 197; James Morris Morgan, *Recollections of a Rebel Reefer* (London, 1918), 75. The department was redesignated the District of the Mississippi on August 17.

tial.[32] Before the fall of New Orleans Governor Moore had experienced quite enough of the provost and martial law and the assumptions the provost made under martial law. He was not prepared to accept more of the same.

On Tennessee's northern border the evacuation of the Confederate stronghold at New Madrid on the Mississippi in mid-March was followed by Union capture of nearby Island Number 10 on April 17. These successes, which opened the river to Union forces as far south as Memphis, gave rise to apprehension for the safety of the city. On March 5 the headquarters of the Army of the Mississippi declared martial law at Memphis and ordered Brigadier General Daniel Ruggles to appoint a "firm and discreet officer" as provost marshal. The officer selected was to publish the appropriate orders and request the commandant of Memphis to supply the guards to enforce them.[33]

Confederate prospects elsewhere in Tennessee were gloomy indeed, particularly in East Tennessee, which was threatened without by Union troops and within by ardently pro-Union civilians. The latter were playing the same havoc with the army's lines of communication as they had in November, 1861, and open insurrection was again a distinct possibility. President Davis reacted much as he had before, proclaiming martial law over the Department of East Tennessee on April 8. Civil jurisdiction and the writ of *habeas corpus* were suspended, and Major General E. Kirby Smith, commanding the department, was ordered to establish an efficient military police and enforce martial law regulations, which, as always, included a ban on the sale and distillation of liquor and strict passport controls.[34] From his headquarters at Knoxville the provost marshal general, Colonel William M. Churchwell, ordered his provost marshals to use the powers granted by martial law "with delicacy yet firmness," making no arrests unless they were forced to do so. Provost officers were also told that they were not to issue passports to anyone going toward enemy lines or out of the state.

Civilians persuading soldiers to desert would be arrested. Many citizens were arrested on these charges or on suspicion of disloyalty. Some confusion ensued as to what should be done with such prisoners. "Please inform me," wrote Captain Charles W. Peden, provost marshal at Chattanooga, "what disposition should be made of Union men arrested and brought to this post." Some of the "political prisoners" were subsequently released on the condition that they give a "bond," but many others, among them hard cases like Parson

32. *OR,* Vol. XVII, Pt. 2, p. 694; XV, 805–806, 894; Ser. II, Vol. IV, p. 894.
33. *OR,* Vol. X, Pt. 2, pp. 297–98.
34. *Ibid.,* 402.

Brownlow, were expelled from the Confederate States. In most cases, the families of those expelled quickly followed them into the Union lines.[35]

Churchwell's reports on the arrests of civilians for disloyalty make it clear that he intended to make the population realize that the government had the grit and the means to enforce obedience to the laws of the land. He did not, however, attempt to impose any regulations on the currency and was able to reply in that vein when asked if he had done so. "The operation of the law in this department," he claimed on May 21, "seems to be working as well as could be expected when the deep-rooted disaffection is considered." The validity of this statement is debatable considering that the Conscription Act, declared throughout the nation on April 16, had to be suspended in East Tennessee on May 11 because of the violent opposition to it.[36]

Atlanta, Georgia, was another Southern city that was under martial law for a time in 1862. It is clear that there were sound reasons for imposing it. In July, G. J. Foreacre, the provost marshal of the city, reported that "hundreds" of men were loitering in the city, many without papers and some with forged ones. He requested instructions on what to do with these men. His replacement as provost marshal, Major George W. Lee, was likewise confused about his powers and sought advice. A letter dated October 27 from Acting Secretary of War Campbell to Major General Sam Jones, commanding at Knoxville, Tennessee, testifies to Lee's predicament. The letter also provides a succinct statement as to why martial law was considered essential: "Your memorandum, referring the letter of G. W. Lee . . . in which he requests instructions . . . has been received. The proclamation of martial law . . . implies . . . a more vigorous police has become necessary to preserve the efficiency of the army and to maintain its discipline. . . . The object of the proclamation there was to secure the safety of the hospitals, public stores, railroad communication, the discipline of the troops *in transitu,* and to collect deserters and absentees along the railroads and guard against espionage on the part of the enemy."[37]

Martial law was not unknown in the Trans-Mississippi Department. Texas was the first state west of the Mississippi to feel the powerful hand of military authority. In mid-May, 1862, the Federal naval demonstration against Galveston excited great concern for the safety of that city and for Houston and the Texas coast, including Brownsville, which up until its capture in November,

35. *OR,* Ser. II, Vol. II, p. 1423; Ser. II, Vol. IV, p. 910; Ser. II, Vol. I, pp. 883–85, 929.

36. *OR,* Ser. II, Vol. I, p. 888; Ser. II, Vol. IV, pp. 834–35; Ser. II, Vol. III, p. 876; Ser. II, Vol. II, p. 1424.

37. *OR,* Ser. IV, Vol. II, pp. 9–10; Vol. XVI, Pt. 2, pp. 979–80.

1863, was the South's major cotton export center. Brigadier General P. O. Hebert, then commanding the Department of Texas, was sufficiently concerned to issue on May 30 a proclamation of martial law over Texas. It was almost identical to the one earlier issued by General Lovell in New Orleans but contained two additional provisos. The first empowered provost marshals to "order out and remove . . . all disloyal persons." The second warned that "any attempt to depreciate the currency . . . is an act of hostility." There was one other major difference in the two proclamations. Lovell's had intimated that the city police were required to assist the provost. Hebert's was much more specific: the "civil authorities, while they were to continue their function, were placed under supervision of the military authorities."[38]

In June another region of the Trans-Mississippi experienced martial law. The Trans-Mississippi District, which in May, 1862, consisted of Louisiana north of the Red River, the Indian Territory, Arkansas, and most of Missouri, was placed under military rule by its commander, Major General Thomas C. Hindman, on May 30. He appointed provost marshals in each county and district and organized independent companies of troops into regiments and brigades to enforce the law. According to Hindman, martial law "put an end to the anarchy . . . exorcised the devil of extortion that was torturing soldiers into desertion by starving their wives and children; . . . restored the credit of Confederate currency . . . broke up trading with the enemy and destroyed or removed . . . cotton . . . insured the exclusion of spies, the arrest of traitors, stragglers and deserters, and the enforcement of the conscription."[39]

Hindman's regulations drew considerable criticism even from other general officers in his command. Albert Pike, commanding the Indian Territory, was particularly incensed by Hindman's arbitrary rules. He made his opposition clear to Secretary of War Randolph: "There is no power on earth . . . that could take me within the sphere of his martial law and the jurisdiction of his cloud of provost-marshals."[40]

Major General T. H. Holmes, first commander of the Trans-Mississippi Department, which was formed by merging the Texas and the Trans-Mississippi districts, also found that martial law won few friends and much abuse. In October, 1862, Secretary of War Randolph expressed the president's concern over the many adverse reports on the continued excessive enforcement of martial law in Arkansas and the arbitrary arrests of civilians by the provost. The

38. *OR*, IX, 715–16; Owsley, *State Rights*, 157–58.
39. *OR*, XIII, 39.
40. *Ibid.*, 856.

overzealous Holmes was ordered to restrict the provost to military duties and desist from undue interference with civilian affairs. His proposal to enforce a system of fixed prices by using his police was also vetoed. Such matters were to be left to the state authorities. Later Davis wrote directly to Holmes: "Many complaints were made against the attempt to subject the people of Arkansas to a military police. The effort was certainly unwise."[41]

General Pike, meantime, elaborated on his view of martial law and the provost. He would not appoint provost marshals within the Indian Territory because such appointments were "null and void" and a usurpation of state authority. As to martial law, it did not exist. The only laws available were the normal civil and criminal laws and the Articles of War, War Department regulations, and acts of Congress, which governed military affairs. There was not even an equivalent to the British mutiny act, nor could there be without new legislation. Any general who attempted to impose his will as law or transferred the civilian judicial function to provost marshals was, in Pike's opinion, guilty of the "highest degree of treason—the subverting of the constitution." Likewise, any newspaper editor who defended martial law was an "advocate of high treason, an apologist for usurpation, and the parasite of an odious tyranny." To back up this position Pike cited Vice-President Stephens, who had publicly stated that even Congress could not declare martial law. In sum, Pike was adamant that "neither generals nor their provost-marshals have any power to make, alter or modify laws . . . nor can they declare what shall be crimes . . . or establish any tribunal to punish what they may declare."[42]

Regarding provost marshals Pike was just as dogmatic. To him a provost marshal was merely "an officer of the camp of an army," and according to the Articles of War, which, he noted, were based on the British Kings Regulations and Orders for the Army, that was all they could be. Regulations provided for no such officers as "chief provost-marshals" and "provost-marshal-general" but only one provost marshal in the rank of captain and assistants for each brigade or division. The duties of such officers, again according to the regulations, were purely military: the custody of convicted offenders and their summary punishment; the preservation of good order and discipline; and the prevention of crime. According to Pike, the "powers of a provost marshal cannot extend beyond the army."[43]

Senator Oldham of Texas was of similar opinion. He believed that the War

41. *Ibid.*, 886–87; Escott, *After Secession*, 147; *OR*, LIII, 846.
42. *OR*, XIII, 900–902; Hartje, *Van Dorn*, 194.
43. *OR*, XIII, 900–902.

Department had no authority to "vest provost marshals with any authority whatsoever over citizens not belonging to the army, or to police towns and cities in any of the Confederate States, and that all such attempts . . . were unauthorized and illegal." His opinion was reflected in a resolution of Congress in late September, 1862, but in practice neither would stand up to the exigencies of a war in which every tool at hand had to be thrown into the fray. Provost marshals carried on much as before, perhaps a little more circumspectly, but nevertheless they carried on. And so did martial law. In theory, after September, 1862, only the president could declare martial law and, also in theory, only during periods when Congress had given him the right to suspend the writ of *habeas corpus*. The situation in practice was quite different. The local authorities at Corpus Christi, Texas, for example, chose to ignore theory in May, 1863, when it appeared that the Federals had serious designs on the city. At this time no authority existed for Davis or anyone else to impose martial law. Notwithstanding, on May 21 martial law was locally imposed in four counties around the city, and provost marshals were appointed to administer it.[44] So much for the resolutions of Congress.

The inevitable use of the provost to enforce martial law further tarnished their image. Even more serious was the effect on the army as a whole; President Davis, for one, rightly feared that the provost, and the army by association, aroused only opposition and dissension when it dealt with civilians. Military interference with civil liberties, viewed by so many as intolerable oppression, also raised doubts about the value of a separate national existence. Was Confederate tyranny, after all, any better than Union tyranny?

There is considerable evidence of overzealousness on the part of provost marshals and their guards in carrying out duties associated with martial law. This, coupled with the arrogance and lack of tact displayed by some generals, led very quickly to a deluge of complaints from state and local officials, from the press, and from some Confederate officers. There could be no reconciling those who championed states' rights and those who were prepared to accept any action, even the abrogation of states' rights, to win independence. Between the two camps no compromise was possible. The controversy extended even to the two leading politicians in the land, Vice-President Stephens, "champion" of liberty, and President Davis, the "tyrant." Behind these two men stood powerful spokesmen who used Congress and the state legislatures, the press, and

44. Owsley, *State Rights*, 167; Hartje, *Van Dorn*, 195; *OR*, Vol. XXVI, Pt. 2, p. 16.

every other available forum to espouse their views regarding the place of the military in Confederate national life. The question was repeatedly asked: What is the proper balance between military power and civil liberty? An answer satisfactory to all proved impossible.

12

Do Your Duty in All Things

In doing what we ought, we deserve no praise,
because it is our duty.

ST. AUGUSTINE

In addition to their primary duties, the provost had numerous other ones, which, although secondary, were important to the national war effort. Some of these became a provost responsibility simply because it was felt that they were properly a military police task, while others went to the provost by default because in many areas they were the sole military organization available to carry them out. Most of these secondary tasks were performed in the normal course of events by the provost and entailed no additional manpower or they were so infrequent and so minor that no extra effort was required. Others necessitated a major diversion of manpower and consumed much time and effort.

The provost's secondary duties can be grouped functionally into three distinct categories: security of personnel, which might be described as tasks relating specifically to the control of people; security of material, which involved the protection or the destruction of public and private property; and security of information, which aimed at preventing the passage of intelligence to the enemy. There were, in addition, a large number of miscellaneous tasks that defy categorization. Circumstances often allocated these to the provost.

One task relating to security of personnel that involved the provost was control of Negroes. They were responsible for ensuring that Negroes, who were a valuable labor resource, were not captured by the enemy or allowed to run to the Union lines. They were also responsible for the custody of soldier or civilian Negroes captured by Confederate forces. And finally, the provost occasionally rounded up slaves needed to construct fortifications or do other work for the army in the field. Such black laborers eventually became essential to the war effort.

Union threats to the South Carolina coast in early 1862, particularly in the Charleston area, resulted in one of the first provost efforts to ensure that slaves were not seized by the Federals. To prevent the Yankees from achieving a deeper penetration inland, Confederate troops moved forward to positions near Secessionville. One of the units deployed was the 25th South Carolina Battalion under Major John G. Pressley. In mid-May he was appointed provost marshal and with his unit was assigned to superintend the removal of the planters and their Negroes from the threatened area.[1] On completion of this chore the unit returned to its normal duties on the line.

Similar precautions were taken by Major General Lovell after the fall of New Orleans. Having withdrawn his troops and what military stores he could from the abandoned city, Lovell took the first step at his new headquarters near Tangipahoa, Louisiana, to prevent Negroes from reaching sanctuary within the new Union lodgment. On July 4 orders were issued prohibiting the movement of Negroes, slave or free, toward the enemy lines without passes from the provost. In addition, Negroes coming from the enemy lines were to be escorted to the nearest provost marshal.[2] It was hoped that interrogation by the provost would identify any Negroes who, at the behest of their Union "liberators," had entered Confederate lines for the purpose of subversion or other troublemaking.

Provost were also frequently responsible for the custody of runaway slaves and those who had donned blue uniforms to fight their former masters. Less frequently the provost participated in operations aimed at the capture of those classes of Negroes. Those taken in arms were hated and despised, receiving little tolerance or compassion from the enraged Confederate soldiers. During the Gettysburg campaign, Major General A. P. Hill, provost marshal at Carlisle, Pennsylvania, ordered that any Negroes taken were to be turned over to him and he would ensure that they were taken to the provost guard. James Nisbet of the 21st Georgia recalled the capture of about a hundred "runaways from Virginia," some of whom may well have never been south of the Mason-Dixon line. How these Negroes were identified as runaways was not noted. From 1864 on, with numerous Negro regiments in the Union army, the number of Negro captives steadily increased. In March, 1864, the provost marshal of Charleston, Captain W. J. Gayer, was directed by the headquarters of the Department of South Carolina, Georgia, and Florida to provide a "descriptive" list of the black prisoners that had been turned over to state authorities since the beginning of the year. When possible, descriptions were to include the time and mode of capture and the names and residences of the Negroes. From this list it may have been possible to identify and return runaway slaves to their legal

1. Major John G. Pressley, "The Wee Nee Volunteers of Williamsburg District, South Carolina, in the First (Hagood's) Regiment," *SHSP*, XVI (rpr. 1978), 148.

2. *OR*, Vol. XVII, Pt. 2, p. 638.

owners. Negro soldiers captured during the Battle of the Crater at Petersburg in the summer of 1864 were similarly listed by the provost marshals.[3]

The state of South Carolina, as might be expected, intended stern measures against Negro captives. Governor Bonham reminded the secretary of war in August, 1864, of his decision a year earlier to have South Carolina provost marshal courts try black prisoners found in arms against the lawful authority of the state.[4] Bonham's intention was not implemented and for good reason because it would have affected Confederate prisoners in the North, where the authorities had threatened retaliation if Negro prisoners were not treated in the same way as whites.

Provost in the western part of the Confederacy also became responsible for large numbers of blacks captured while under arms. In at least one case the provost were assigned to plan and execute an operation designed to capture armed Negroes. Brigadier General W. R. Scurry, commanding the eastern subdistrict of Texas, issued such orders to the provost marshal of Niblett's Bluff late in July, 1863. "If an opportunity offers," reads the order, "penetrate the dens of thieves, jayhawkers and runaway negro harborers . . . and shoot them down unless they surrender." Captain John Goodwin, the provost marshal of Forrest's cavalry, also encountered black soldiers. Following the alleged "massacre" at Fort Pillow in April, 1864, Goodwin advised the headquarters of the Department of Alabama, Mississippi, and East Louisiana, then under Leonidas Polk, that the Negroes taken at Fort Pillow would be kept at Okolona, Mississippi, where they would be used as railway laborers. Goodwin assumed responsibility for yet more blacks in June, when he took charge of some that had been picked up during Forrest's pursuit of Federal cavalry under Samuel Sturgis.[5]

The last aspect of provost responsibility for Negroes concerned the task of mobilizing and guarding the gangs of black laborers required for military purposes. The mobilization phase of the task soon involved the provost and the army as a whole in yet more disputes between the government and the citizens. Early enthusiasm to lend Negroes or whatever else was required to advance the cause soon waned. In late 1861, for example, notice that five thousand Negroes were needed to build defensive works near Fort Donelson

3. Nisbet, *4 Years on the Firing Line*, 121; *OR*, Vol. XXXV, Pt. 2, p. 330; Spencer Glasgow Welch, *A Confederate Surgeon's Letters to His Wife* (1911; rpr. Marietta, Ga., 1954), 104.

4. *OR*, Ser. II, Vol. VII, p. 673.

5. *OR*, Vol. XXVI, Pt. 2, pp. 125–26; Vol. XXXII, Pt. 3, p. 797; Bearss, *Forrest at Brice's Cross Roads*, 132.

on the Tennessee resulted in only one-tenth of that number coming forward. This case and others left impressment as the only option, and often it was provost that did the impressing. That it was done without basis in law— Congress did not authorize Negro impressment until 1864—and founded only on claims of military exigency made impressment odious to the slaveowner. Nevertheless, when and where it was necessary the provost got on with it. An example occurred just before the Seven Days' Battle in May, 1862, when an additional bridge was urgently needed to span the James River above Drewry's Bluff to permit the rapid deployment of troops against McClellan. Captain W. W. Blackford, an engineer on the staff of Major W. H. Stevens, who was charged with preparing Richmond's defenses, suggested that a pontoon bridge consisting of river craft linked by timber spans could be quickly put in place. Given the chance to implement his idea, Blackford gathered the stores and timber, obtained the necessary labor force, courtesy of the provost marshal, who had impressed more than five hundred Negro laborers, and finished the bridge within three days.[6]

In the Army of Tennessee the provost also gathered up Negro labor, although this practice was deviated from during the fortification of Atlanta in 1864. In an article in the *Confederate Veteran,* Brigadier General F. A. Shoup, the army's chief of artillery and sometimes chief engineer, recalled a reconnaissance he made of the city's defenses after the withdrawal of the army from the Chattahoochee River line on July 9. Shoup subsequently reported the inadequacies of the existing fortifications, promising to rectify the shortfalls within a week providing he could be supplied with one vital commodity: "I said that the most important matter would be to get the negroes." Unfortunately, the Negro laborers collected earlier had been allowed to disperse. Joseph E. Johnston suggested that others could be obtained from the provost marshal, but Shoup demurred, thinking it "better to do it direct from headquarters . . . that General G. W. Smith, who was in command of the Georgia Militia should be directed . . . to gather gangs of negroes." In the event, nothing was done, and according to Shoup, Atlanta fell because of the "extraordinary failure to seize a few thousand negroes for ten days."[7]

To the west, in the Trans-Mississippi, by 1863 the authorities were facing other problems related to Negroes. The large-scale impressment of blacks was one reason for a dramatic fall in demand for slaves at the auction markets,

6. James L. Nichols, *Confederate Engineers* (Tuscaloosa, 1957), 98.

7. Brigadier General F. A. Shoup, "Dalton Campaign—Works at Chattahoochee River— Interesting History," *Confederate Veteran,* III (rpr. 1983), 263–65.

weakening confidence in the economy and embittering those whose property included significant numbers of slaves. It also appeared that the authorities, including the police, were increasingly unable to control the slave population of the Trans-Mississippi. By the fall of 1863 the need for fortifications at Shreveport, Louisiana, led to an influx of Negro laborers into the area. Department headquarters, located in Shreveport, was inundated with requests from alarmed citizens for a regiment or at least a battalion to be stationed near the city to keep the large numbers of unruly Negroes under control. Kirby Smith took no immediate action, probably because no troops were available. Local citizens then suffered, according to them, two months of Negro thievery and depredations—"Our police is so limited that they cannot properly patrol the town at nights"—before a temporary provost guard of four hundred conscripts, parolees, and convalescents imposed an "ironclad" passport system on the city. A request to Major General Richard Taylor, commanding the District of Louisiana, for a regiment of regulars to relieve the ad hoc provost guard went unfulfilled.[8]

Another major task concerned with personnel was the enforcement of conscription from 1864 on. General Leonidas Polk, commanding a corps in the Army of Tennessee in mid-1863, was the first to suggest such a role for the provost on the grounds that it would achieve savings in manpower. "One set of troops," he wrote, "then could do the work of conscription, arrest deserters and paroled prisoners, and maintain a proper military police." In Polk's opinion, the establishment of an adequate provost guard would ensure that "every man liable to military duty" would be put into the field.[9]

In July, 1863, Polk sent Edward Walthall's Mississippi Brigade from his corps back to Atlanta for a rest. While there the brigade provost guard conducted normal law-and-order duties but was also assigned to assist the conscript officer in "conscripting a theater." On the evening chosen, the guard infiltrated the crowd in the theater and at the end of the play sealed all the exits. According to one provost sergeant, more than three hundred men without papers, including many junior officers and even some majors, were caught in the net. All were shipped under guard to Virginia the next morning. The conscript officer duly complimented the brigade guard for a good night's work. As the sergeant put it, the guard was also delighted with the evening: "We knew the city was full of able-bodied men who ought to be in the army as well as us."[10]

---

8. Kerby, *Kirby Smith's Confederacy,* 256–57.
9. *OR,* Vol. XXXII, Pt. 3, pp. 580–81; Vol. XXIII, Pt. 2, pp. 921–22.
10. Simmons, "Conscripting Atlanta Theater," 279.

By May, 1864, Polk, now commanding the Department of Alabama, Mississippi, and East Louisiana and tired of the continuing embarrassment of poor administration of the conscription laws and the "failure" of the Bureau of Conscription, announced to Richmond that he had reorganized his department to exercise "proper military authority." His new-look department featured provost at all levels up to the department provost marshal general, Major Jules C. Denis. The system was designed to ensure that all men subject to military service reported to the enrolling officers.[11]

In the field the provost of the Army of Tennessee were also assigned to gather up those who attempted to evade conscription. During the advance into Tennessee, Stephen D. Lee published a corps general order in late November, 1864, charging "every officer and man . . . with enforcing the conscript act, and every man subject to military duty found in our line of march will be arrested and turned over to the provost-marshal of the corps." Identical instructions were issued to the division provost marshals of Forrest's cavalry corps by Forrest's chief provost marshal, Captain John Goodwin, in December: "The orders are to arrest and forward all men liable to military duty from seventeen to fifty."[12]

Less than a month before the collapse of the Confederacy, the provost were still enforcing conscription. In mid-March, 1865, officers at Mobile, Alabama, which was to fall on April 10, requested that the department commander return all Missouri soldiers who were not on active service and all others subject to conscription to their units.[13]

Even before the first winter of the war was over, it was apparent that the provost were going to be heavily involved in a third personnel security task: pursuing the spies that would soon infest the Confederacy. It was relatively easy for spies to enter the Southern lines, and once in, they enjoyed virtually unrestricted freedom of movement. This situation continued until the authorities instituted the passport system, which had as one of its aims the detection and arrest of spies. The enforcing agency of the system was the military police. Before the implementation of passports, the perilous situation in East Tennessee in November, 1861, led to the first suggestion that the provost would be the most appropriate agency to take on responsibility for capturing spies. An entry for November 11 in the diary of John B. Jones, a War Department clerk, pointed out that "a military police . . . might do much good, or prevent much

11. *OR*, Vol. XXXIX, Pt. 2, p. 570. For details of Polk's reorganization measures see Chapter 3.
12. *OR*, Vol. XLV, Pt. 1, p. 1245, Pt. 2, p. 682.
13. *OR*, Vol. XLIX, Pt. 2, pp. 1117–18.

evil." He referred specifically to the Unionists of East Tennessee, who had destroyed several railroad bridges, sorely damaging the lines of supply, and were otherwise in almost open rebellion against the Confederate government. Jones attributed most of the trouble to the release of spies captured earlier in West Virginia and Tennessee. Martial law and the strong measures taken by the provost, including the hanging of five Union arsonists, enabled the authorities to reassert control over the rebellious region.[14]

Provost antiespionage measures in Richmond, characterized primarily by the passport system, which was rigidly enforced from the summer of 1861 on, have been fully described in Chapter 7. Suffice it to say that the threat of spies was very real in the capital and in the field. The vigilance that the provost exercised in the Army of Northern Virginia is clearly illustrated in Longstreet's report on the Gettysburg campaign. On the night of June 27, when his corps and A. P. Hill's were bivouacked near Chambersburg, Pennsylvania, Longstreet's chief of staff, Colonel Moxley Sorrel, advised Longstreet that the corps provost marshal had arrested a "suspicious person," who, as it turned out, was one James Harrison, a noted Rebel scout. Even before the invasion of the North, Lee took steps to make access to his army considerably more difficult for Union agents. A general order of February 16 prohibited the presence of civilians in the camps or within the lines of the army except for those who had cleared their visit with the provost marshal. The decision, necessary to keep spies and "improper" persons out of the lines of the army, was strictly enforced.[15]

Beyond the Mississippi, the military adopted similar security precautions. In July, 1863, provost in the District of Texas, New Mexico, and Arizona were directed to arrest "suspicious characters so as to keep the place free from marauders and spies." The commander of the Indian Territory followed suit, although not until the following spring. He ordered enrolling officers to perform the duties of provost marshals. It was assumed that these officers would be so efficient that spies and deserters would soon seek "a more congenial clime among their northern brethren." The provost guards were ordered to keep a constant watch for spies.[16]

Throughout the Confederacy the provost also acted as executioners for spies that were apprehended. One of the first such instances occurred during the

14. Jones, *Rebel War Clerk's Diary,* 54.
15. James Longstreet, "Causes of Lee's Defeat at Gettysburg," *SHSP,* V (rpr. 1977), 59; Sorrel, *Recollections,* 155; *OR,* Vol. XXV, Pt. 2, p. 629.
16. *OR,* Vol. XXVI, Pt. 2, pp. 125–26; Vol. XXXIV, Pt. 2, pp. 1045–46.

Valley campaign in 1862, when a provost officer of Stonewall Jackson's command arranged the execution of a spy by soldiers of the 37th Virginia. Sam Watkins of the 1st Tennessee recalled a similar execution at Chattanooga just before the city fell to the Federals. "The ropes were promptly adjusted around their necks by the provost marshal," he declared. Other hangings under provost auspices occurred in Texas in 1864. Deserters and others who had committed offenses serious enough to warrant the death penalty were shoved directly into eternity by provost executioners. One of the first executions—the first, according to Lieutenant General Richard Taylor—in the Army of Northern Virginia took place shortly after First Manassas when two men from Major Roberdeau Wheat's notorious Louisiana "Tigers" Battalion were shot for being the ringleaders of a gang that beat up an officer who tried to prevent the gang from freeing some friends from the guardhouse. A ten-man firing party, which Taylor insisted come from Wheat's battalion, carried out the executions under command of a provost marshal.[17]

Another provost duty related to personnel was responsibility for Union deserters. Until December, 1862, Confederate policy was to treat them as prisoners of war. They were accorded no privileges beyond those extended to captured Union soldiers, and in some ways they were worse off: put to work under guard, they sweated prodigiously to earn what bits of food they received, and as turncoats they suffered contempt and discrimination at the hands of their warders.[18] This harsh treatment was discontinued in the winter of 1862–1863, when it was belatedly realized that Union prisoners who would swear allegiance could be useful. Those who did so were released and permitted to seek work, which a number found at the Tredegar Works in Richmond and at factories elsewhere in Virginia and North Carolina. Union deserters in the western theater of operations were allowed employment in the niter mines in Tennessee or were sent to Richmond to find employment. This system proved unworkable, partly because of the enmity of Southerners for them but mostly because of their unreliability.

Nevertheless, the Confederate authorities were actively encouraging desertion from the Union army at the fronts and among the prisoners in the various

17. F. T. Mindler, "Levi Strauss, the Spy," *Confederate Veteran,* XVI (rpr. 1983), 17–18; Watkins, *"Co. Aytch,"* 108; Rutherford, "Great Gainesville Hanging," 12–20; Richard Taylor, *Destruction and Reconstruction* (New York, 1879), 25; Terry L. Jones, *Lee's Tigers: The Louisiana Infantry in the Army of Northern Virginia* (Baton Rouge, 1987), 40–41.

18. *OR,* XV, 825; XXI, 824.

military prisons. Only a few accepted the inducements, and these galvanized rebels made poor soldiers with which to fight the South's battles. In particular, they usually could not be trusted.

A new attempt to encourage desertion, one that avoided the pitfalls of using such men as workers or soldiers, was made in August, 1864. After consultation with President Davis and Secretary of War Seddon, on August 15 General Lee published an order guaranteeing protection and sustenance to deserters until they could be "forwarded to the most convenient points on the border, where all facilities will be afforded them to return to their homes."[19]

At this point the provost again entered the picture. On August 26 the adjutant general made Major Isaac H. Carrington, provost marshal of Richmond, responsible for "receiving and sending off deserters who may come in under the invitation of the War Department." Five days later, Carrington was told to forward deserters "without delay to Abingdon, Virginia, thence to be sent to Kentucky and Ohio." Early in September, Carrington's orders were further amended, this time directing him to send to Abingdon only those who wished to leave the Confederacy. General Grant, meantime, admitted that men were taking advantage of the new Confederate policy. According to the Richmond papers of September 5, hundreds of Union soldiers were deserting. Overall, the new policy may have affected several thousand men. There is no doubt that many were crossing the lines, for on September 8 Adjutant General Cooper received requests for guards to escort Yankee deserters. Those deserters who chose to remain in the Confederacy were allowed to do so but only if they secured work from persons known to the provost marshal of the area they were in.[20]

Another duty performed by the provost under the general heading of security of personnel was that of guarding hospitals. There is evidence to suggest that, at least during the first two years of the war, the task was highly expensive in manpower, indeed prohibitively so. General Order 20, published by the Army of Tennessee in December, 1862, committed a minimum of 525 guards to some ten hospitals in the rear of the army. Other provost troops were frequently assigned to escort men discharged from the hospitals back to their units.[21] This was necessary to ensure that these men actually rejoined their units.

The surgeon general of the Confederacy, Brigadier General Samuel Moore,

19. *OR*, Vol. XLII, Pt. 2, p. 529.

20. *Ibid.*, 1204, 1210; Vol. XLIII, Pt. 2, p. 29; Vol. XLII, Pt. 2, pp. 1237–40; Ser. IV, Vol. III, p. 865.

21. *OR*, Vol. XX, Pt. 2, p. 455; AHB Book.

estimated before the Seven Days' Battle in 1862 that there were thirty thousand sick and wounded men in Richmond's many hospitals. With no central agency to keep track of inmates, immense confusion and anxiety arose as to the condition and location of these men. It became almost impossible for units or provost, or anyone else for that matter, to obtain data on men absent from their units. One proposal, the organization of an Army Intelligence Office that would be responsible for the collection of information on casualties, was quickly approved by Secretary of War Randolph. This bureau, which functioned as a personnel office for the army, soon became the repository of detailed information regarding Confederate dead and wounded. So efficient did it become that the provost routinely advised the office of army inquiries on the location of absent men.[22]

Finally, the provost were responsible in several regions for preventing unauthorized departure from the Confederacy through the various ports. This would have required less and less effort as the Union blockade tightened and fewer ships left from fewer Southern ports. Nevertheless, considerable data indicate that the Charleston provost, for example, were heavily involved in such duties while the city was under martial law in the summer of 1862. Other information shows that along the Texas and Florida coasts the provost were also engaged in port control duty. The reports of Colonel Charles Livenskiold and R. H. Chinn, respectively provost marshals of Corpus Christi and Matagorda, Texas, show that following the sighting of Federal warships in Aransas Bay in July, 1862, Chinn was ordered to prevent any vessels from leaving the harbor. Similarly, the authorities in the District of East Florida, part of Beauregard's Department of South Carolina, Georgia, and Florida in 1864, issued orders in January aimed at preventing unauthorized departure from the Confederate States. The commanding officer of Camp Finegan, who was also responsible for the port of Jacksonville, received special instructions for his provost to arrest all strangers without proper passes.[23]

Security of public and private property was another provost duty. In the case of public property, precautions were necessary to ensure that captured material

22. W. A. Crocker, "The Army Intelligence Office," *Confederate Veteran*, VIII (rpr. 1983), 118–19.

23. AHB Book contains considerable correspondence relating to shipping in and out of Charleston. Most of the documents refer to crew lists and passports, fishing licenses and vessels, and other maritime matters. See also *OR*, IX, 610–13, 724–27; Vol. XXXV, Pt. 1, p. 516; Norman C. Delaney, "Corpus Christi—The Vicksburg of Texas," *CWTI*, XVI (July, 1977), 6. *CWTI* spells the name "Livenskiold," but Delaney spells it "Lovenskiold."

would be put to the use of the Confederacy and not be looted. Likewise, it was vital that public and private property did not find its way to the Union lines, where it would enrich Lincoln's war coffers. Initially this was not a problem as in the first flush of war patriotic Southerners preferred patriotism to profit.

As enthusiasm for the war waned and the opportunities for individual profit became too tempting to resist, illegal trade rapidly expanded. Nowhere was this more true than in the cotton belt, where the Confederacy's "white gold," or "King Cotton," was subject to fevered speculation. One of the first instances of provost involvement in preventing cotton trade with the enemy occurred in Texas in mid-1862. William Heartsill recalled that Major William Bradfield, provost marshal of Marshall County, had requisitioned thirty men from Heartsill's unit, the W. P. Lane Rangers, for the purpose of intercepting steamboats carrying contraband cargoes down the Red River. Across the Mississippi, Polk's decision to reorganize the provost in the Department of Alabama, Mississippi, and East Louisiana in late 1863 was based partly on his desire to check the "large and increasing" trade with the enemy. That this trade was extensive, condoned, and even participated in at the highest level is evident from the provost reports. Captain Blayney T. Walshe, the provost marshal of the Lake Shore District of Louisiana, with headquarters at Covington just north of Lake Pontchartrain, reported to Secretary of War Seddon on December 29 just how serious the situation was: "Most of the leading men . . . have been engaged in shipping cotton to New Orleans, and in many instances, under the orders of general officers. . . . I have been approached for permission to ship cotton . . . under an order from General Maury, commanding the Department of the Gulf."[24]

Walshe then reported that he had destroyed four vessels positively identified as being involved in the illicit trade. "I would respectfully," his letter concluded, "ask instructions in regard to parties having or claiming permission . . . to ship cotton through the lines, and also how far the order of a superior officer giving such permission is to be obeyed."[25] Only the news of the destroyed vessels went forward through the chain of command. The contents of the rest of the letter make it clear why the conscientious Walshe chose to bypass his superiors and write directly to Seddon. One wonders just how highly placed these "superior" officers were and how many were involved.

Throughout 1864 Confederate cotton continued to flow into New Orleans.

24. Heartsill, *Fourteen Hundred and 91 Days*, 81; *OR*, Vol. XXVI, Pt. 2, pp. 558–59.
25. *OR*, Vol. XXVI, Pt. 2, pp. 558–59.

Provost and other staff reports reflect the official concern over the trade. The provost marshal at Clinton, Louisiana, Colonel Frank Powers, notified his superiors of the large amounts of cotton shipped to the enemy by civilians in his district. By May, Colonel George B. Hodge of Polk's staff wrote to Adjutant General Cooper that "the whole tier of counties in Mississippi and East Louisiana on the Mississippi River swarmed with . . . persons engaged in illicit trade with the enemy."[26]

Some of this trade was going downriver to New Orleans, but a substantial amount was also going north to Memphis. The provost marshal general of Polk's department, Major Jules C. Denis, was so informed by another staff officer on March 15, 1864. According to this officer, the excuse for those engaged in trading with the enemy was the need to obtain food and clothing. Lieutenant Colonel Joseph Hanlon, chief provost marshal of the Third District of Mississippi, also passed on to Denis reports he had received from Grenada, Mississippi, on cotton smuggling. According to an infantry regimental commander at Grenada: "Blockade running of cotton . . . is carried on extensively and openly, no one, officer or citizen, interfering with it."[27]

There were also times when provost were required to assist in removing property, both private and public, from the enemy's path, or failing that, in the final extremity they were called upon to destroy it. The Trans-Mississippi in 1862 affords a number of examples of the provost commitment to ensuring that the enemy did not capture valuable property. In July of that year the sight of Union warships off Matagorda, Texas, and the fear of enemy landings caused the local commander to institute measures designed to minimize the gains of the Federals should they attack the area. One of these concerned the disposal of property. On July 15, R. H. Chinn, the provost marshal, was told of the "absolute necessity that the inhabitants of Matagorda and vicinity shall place all their property . . . out of reach of the enemy." He was ordered to destroy "such cotton as cannot be removed." In September similar precautions were taken at Galveston when a Union attack appeared imminent. During that month the city's provost marshal was ordered to remove "all the machinery" he could, and the officer commanding the city was directed to assist in the operation. Meantime, the provost marshal was told to ensure that the local population removed their stock, grain, and other produce from the area.[28]

26. *OR,* Vol. LII, Pt. 2, p. 703; Vol. XXXIX, Pt. 2, p. 570.
27. *OR,* Vol. XXXII, Pt. 3, pp. 633–34, 710.
28. *OR,* IX, 726; XV, 148, 150, 846–47.

The Confederate capital was another place where the provost were responsible for the removal or destruction of property. During April and May of 1862, Richmond's chances of avoiding Federal occupation appeared so slim that on April 22 Congress adjourned, and on May 10 the president's family fled the city. Meantime, Secretary of War Randolph put in motion several contingency plans to prepare the city in the event that the unthinkable should happen and the army be forced to evacuate. These plans, which included the removal and destruction of property, were also to apply to Petersburg. The provost marshal there, Captain William Pannill, received orders on May 6 to prepare to destroy cotton and tobacco to prevent the enemy from seizing it. Three days later, when President Davis received warning that Union gunboats were coming up the James River toward the capital, Randolph instructed Pannill to "move 10,000 pounds (cotton or tobacco) to Raleigh and 5,000 to the nearest safe place. . . . Get all out of reach from the river at once."[29] John B. Jones, a war clerk in Richmond, recalled that on May 12, the day after the ironclad *Virginia* was blown up to prevent her capture, he had reminded the provost marshal of the act of Congress that required the destruction of tobacco and cotton should it be in danger of capture. The Richmond City Council, which in the emergency met almost daily, was also in contact with the provost on this subject. On May 19, in response to a request for assistance from the provost marshal, Major Elias Griswold, the City Council ordered the city engineer and the fire department to "assist the Provost Marshal in any measures relating to the tobacco in the warehouses which may prevent the burning of the tobacco from endangering contiguous property."[30]

Several sources testify that privately owned tobacco was not exempt from destruction. Although the army prepared to burn "enormous" piles of tobacco, foreign-owned tobacco was another matter. According to one writer on wartime Richmond, "Until the foreign consuls protested regarding tobacco held for foreign account the Provost Marshal's men went about with wagons and a hundred Negroes impressing tobacco for burning in case the city should fall."[31]

The city did not panic, however, and neither did the army. Biding his time and waiting for McClellan to blunder, Joseph E. Johnston soon had his chance. On May 31 he pounced on the two isolated Union corps at Seven Pines and drove them back but failed to turn the repulse into a rout because of the serious

---

29. *OR*, Vol. XI, Pt. 3, pp. 495–96, 502.

30. Jones, *Rebel War Clerk's Diary*, 76; Manarin (ed.), *Richmond at War*, 177–78.

31. Robert G. Tanner, *Stonewall in the Valley* (New York, 1976), 236; Bill, *Beleaguered City*, 127.

wound he suffered. It would be left to the new commander, R. E. Lee, to banish the Federals from the immediate area of Richmond. And he did just that. Seven bloody days at Cold Harbor, at Savage Station, at Glendale and White Oak Swamp, and finally at Malvern Hill, pushed the Yankees back to Harrison's Landing on the James, some twenty-five miles away. Richmond was saved.

Not for almost three years would the capital again be so menaced. Besieged and at bay from the fall of 1864 on, in February, 1865, the city and the cause faced great peril, and no one, from Lee down, could see a way out. Once again the possibility of evacuation had to be considered. Once again measures were taken to ensure that the enemy would not get Confederate cotton, tobacco, or other valuables. In late February, Major Isaac H. Carrington, provost marshal of the city, advised the members of the City Council that whatever cotton and tobacco could not be removed would be destroyed.[32] Carrington was probably acting on the order of the city commandant, Richard Ewell, who had been warned by Lee to prepare to destroy the cotton and tobacco. Following discussions with Mayor Mayo and a visit to all the city warehouses, which Ewell concluded "could be burned without danger of a general conflagration," the general ordered Carrington to make the necessary arrangements for destruction. These arrangements included distribution of a circular by the provost to the merchants and owners of the cotton and tobacco. Some apparently thought the order was to be immediately carried out, a misapprehension which Ewell corrected in a memo advising that the "necessity had not yet arisen."[33]

According to Ewell, the necessity arose at 10 A.M. on April 2, when he received word to evacuate Richmond, destroying any stores that could not be removed. "All that time allowed was done," he later informed Lee. Lieutenant Colonel Richard T. W. Duke of the 1st Battalion Virginia Reserves, which served as a provost guard, testified to the receipt of a written order "to fire the warehouses at a given signal." One soldier, in an article in the *Confederate Veteran*, recalled that his unit, the 2d Virginia Battalion, entered Richmond on April 2 and reported to the Provost Marshal's Office on Broad Street. Here large quantities of government papers were burned, after which the unit burned warehouses filled with tobacco. Other witnesses swore that they saw the provost set the warehouses alight.[34] These fires, added to those set by rampag-

32. Manarin (ed.), *Richmond at War*, 571–72.

33. *OR*, Vol. XLVI, Pt. 1, p. 1293.

34. R. S. Ewell, "Evacuation of Richmond," *SHSP*, XIII (rpr. 1978), 247–48; W. L. Timberlake, "Last Days in Front of Richmond, 1864–65," *Confederate Veteran*, XX (rpr. 1983), 119;

ing mobs in the streets, caused a great conflagration. Setting the city afire later became a highly controversial matter, with many blaming Ewell and his provost for the damage.

Custody and safeguarding of captured enemy material and equipment was another important provost responsibility. During the war the Confederates evolved a system for salvaging arms and munitions from the battlefields to supplement home-produced and imported equipment. So vital was this salvage that it was the subject of Article 58 of the Articles of War: "All public stores taken in the enemy's camp . . . shall be secured for the service of the Confederate States." In practice, this meant that all captured property had to be guarded, and provost marshals were to use the most "stringent" measures to prevent individuals from looting.[35] Certainly these controls were necessary. There are examples of whole regiments reequipping, on the orders of superiors, with the spoils of war, but there were also cases when troops were able to pillage captured materials because no provost were available to prevent it. One such instance occurred after Second Manassas, when the ravenous soldiers of A. P. Hill's Light Division plundered Pope's supply depots.

One of the first provost units to be made responsible for guarding captured property was the 5th Alabama Battalion, later the provost guard of A. P. Hill's 3d Corps. The battalion's initial experience with the task was at Harpers Ferry in the autumn of 1862, when it remained behind to guard property while the rest of the Light Division marched to aid Lee at Sharpsburg. It is evident that provost marshals were taking possession of captured stores even earlier. Colonel Bradley Johnson, commanding the 1st Maryland at Winchester during Jackson's Valley campaign, recalled turning over prisoners and captured property to the provost marshal of the town once that officer had established control. Other materials, according to Johnson, were retained by the regiment: "The amount of plunder accumulated . . . was indescribable." One provost marshal had the unique distinction at Madison Court House, Virginia, in February, 1864, of receiving from Major G. M. Ryals, provost marshal of the cavalry corps of the Army of Northern Virginia, a total of 107 "long range guns," probably a mix of captured guns and Confederate guns surplus to establishment. In Georgia, too, in 1864, the provost were caring for captured stores. At

---

Timberlake, "The Last Days in Front of Richmond," *Confederate Veteran*, XXII (rpr. 1983), 303; Irvine, "Fall of Richmond," 387, n. 32.

35. *OR*, XV, 806; Vol. XXVII, Pt. 3, p. 895.

Columbus, Georgia, Major T. B. Howard, with his 27th Georgia Battalion, was guarding public property and performing general provost duties.[36]

The need to ensure that the enemy did not obtain information of intelligence value also became a provost task, at least in some regions of the Confederacy. As might be expected, Richmond provides an illustration of provost involvement in this task. During May, 1862, when it seemed the Federals might seize Richmond, in addition to the instructions he issued for the removal of property, Secretary of War Randolph prepared a plan to ensure that government archives would not fall into enemy hands. On May 10 he told the bureaus of the War Department to prepare their records for removal. On May 28 he ordered the boxes taken to the railroad depot, telling the bureau chiefs that wagons would be at the War Department at nine o'clock that night "to commence the removal, which should be conducted quietly and from the rear of the building to avoid panic or excitement. . . . The provost marshal will conduct the trans-shipment." The archives did not in fact leave the city. They remained at the depot until June, when the provost returned them to the War Department.[37]

Censorship was another device used by the military police to prevent information from reaching the enemy. It was most often enforced in places where martial law had been imposed, and Richmond, Charleston, New Orleans, and Vicksburg are examples of cities where censorship prevailed. The regulations invariably forbade the "publication of any article . . . in reference to movement of troops," but at Vicksburg Van Dorn went so far as to order editors of newspapers to print no items "calculated to impair confidence in any of the commanding officers." Certainly, all too often editors ignored the demands of military security and printed detailed and accurate accounts of military dispositions and plans. This infuriated the army, causing officers to complain that "worst of all was the leakage of military information."[38] Lest it be thought that only Confederate editors were guilty of such stupidity, many high-ranking Confederates, including Lee, customarily read the northern papers as sources of valuable intelligence.

Sometimes, too, the provost ordered editors to print false or exaggerated military information to mislead the enemy. A case of such "disinformation"

---

36. Johnson, "Memoir of the First Maryland Regiment," 100, 102; *OR,* Vol. XXIX, Pt. 1, p. 454; Ser. IV, Vol. III, p. 460.

37. *OR,* Vol. XI, Pt. 3, pp. 504, 557; Jones, *Rebel War Clerk's Diary,* 84.

38. *OR,* XV, 771–72; Hartje, *Van Dorn,* 192; Bill, *Beleaguered City,* 125. The comment was made during the Seven Days' Battle.

occurred in June, 1863, when Colonel Alex McKinstrey, provost marshal of the Army of Tennessee, telegraphed the editor of the Chattanooga *Rebel:* "Publish an article to this effect: 'We are happy to see that re-enforcements continue to arrive for Bragg's army. Our trains are loaded with troops' &c. Don't mention the names of the commanders."[39] By contrast, three months later real rein-forcements in the form of most of Longstreet's corps of the Army of Northern Virginia did not receive newspaper space. Dire consequences would have befallen any editor who had published such news.

Finally, from time to time the provost were called upon to carry out tasks that defy classification. They can best be described as odd jobs which no one else cared to do or was available to do. One such task was burial of the dead. The only mention of the provost handling that unsavoury job was in the memoirs of a South Carolina colonel who recalled that at Second Manassas he had ordered provost to bury dead Yankees.[40]

A second miscellaneous task was responsibility for issuing transportation warrants. Only four references to such a duty were found. In his memoirs John Casler of the Stonewall Brigade noted that following leave at his home in the Shenandoah Valley he had reported to the Staunton provost marshal, who had furnished transportation to a railroad depot. Another reference describes the Richmond provost office, where the provost marshal "kept a blackboard on which he who ran it might read the names of the regiments sent to the Peninsula. It was a help to the sergeant who issued transportation." In September, 1863, Private Lawrence Daffen of the 4th Texas reported to the Richmond provost office and was provided transportation and rations to Resaca, Georgia. The mention of rations is interesting but inconclusive because this was the only reference that put the provost in the ration business. Finally, the provost office at Newberry, South Carolina, was still arranging transportation for soldiers as late as March, 1865.[41] The task of issuing transportation is much more likely to have been a permanent provost job than burials were. This assumption seems reasonable because the omnipresent provost offices throughout the South and the requirement that all travelers obtain passes from them would have made the provost the ideal choice to issue transportation warrants. Significant economies in manpower would have been achieved.

39. *OR,* Vol. XXIII, Pt. 2, p. 885.

40. Bond (ed.), *South Carolinians,* 53.

41. Casler, *Four Years in the Stonewall Brigade,* 248; Bill, *Beleaguered City,* 115; Obituary, *Confederate Veteran,* XV (1983), 184–86; C. C. Chambers, "The Coahoma Invincibles," *Confederate Veteran,* XXXI (rpr. 1983), 461–63.

This wide range of secondary duties, coupled with the major ones described earlier, indicate the worth of the provost to the army and the government. Many of these minor but necessary tasks would have been done badly or not at all if the provost had not been able to take them on. The effects would have been serious and debilitating, costing the country useful property, draining off manpower from the fronts and essential occupations, and turning the population against the government for its perceived failure to care, and be seen to care, that the normal services due the citizen were maintained.

The Paths of Glory

I shall however endeavor to do my duty and fight to
the last.

R. E. LEE

In addition to their duties in the field dealing with stragglers, deserters, and prisoners of war, Confederate provost were frequently committed to combat. The provost were often temporarily employed as infantry because they were the only troops immediately available to restore critical tactical situations. At other times they were called upon to act as advance and rear guards and to conduct reconnaissance to gain intelligence on enemy strength, dispositions, and intentions.

Not surprisingly, participation in combat or other operations put great strain on provost resources. Rapid tactical movements and engagement in frequent heavy battles inevitably created problems with stragglers, prisoners of war, and discipline. Normal provost duties could be taxing in themselves, but when the exhaustion caused by combat was added, the cumulative effect must have been enervating in the extreme.

It is ironic that many references categorize the provost as "noncombatants" and as a "nonfighting" branch. Such nomenclature must surely have bemused the many provost guardsmen who suddenly found themselves propelled into combat. Fighting often meant dying, and provost casualties were inevitable. One of the first was a Tennessee provost marshal killed in action at New Madrid on the Mississippi River in March, 1862.[1] The bullet that killed him was completely indifferent to his noncombatant status. It is unlikely that this officer would have noted any reluctance on the part of his superiors to insert him in the fighting. There would not have been any. Operational necessity demanded the participation in combat of any Confederate officer or man who was capable of bearing arms.

In the Union army provost strength was recorded separately from the num-

---

1. Moore, *Conscription and Conflict,* 111; Thomas G. Jones, "Last Days of the Army of Northern Virginia," *SHSP,* XXI (rpr. 1977), 88; *OR,* VIII, 128.

bers of men present for duty. For example, at Chancellorsville the seven corps of Joseph Hooker's army totaled 133,868 "effective strength present for duty," but after deducting "provost guard, artillery reserve and absent cavalry," the balance was 122,000. Jubal Early referred to this Union practice in his comparison of Union and Confederate strength at Gettysburg: "Thus we get the actual fighting force available, after eliminating all the general and staff officers, provost guard, engineer brigade, signal corps and guards and orderlies, at over 100,000 officers and men."[2]

As much as Early may have privately agreed with the theory that the provost did not belong in combat, he and other Confederate generals could not afford the luxury of leaving large numbers of men out of battle. In tabulating Confederate strength, Early therefore included "all general officers and their staff officers, including engineer officers, as well as the non-commissioned staff officers," less only "the staff officers, who, under no circumstances were required to get under fire." Union calculations of Confederate fighting strength at various times during the war all agree that "the rebels habitually put into battle nearly all of the extra duty men." Adam Badeau, Grant's military secretary, assessing Lee's strength during the 1864 campaign, stated that the "present for duty" column included the enlisted fighting men, plus those made available for fighting such as the provost guard. Southern writers took the opposite approach, deducting "detailed men in the medical, ordnance, quartermaster, subsistence, engineer and provost departments of Lee's own army, who were not included in his line of battle strength. . . . Any one conversant with the proportion that such details bear to the aggregate strength of an army will readily admit that this is a moderate estimate for the number of these non-combatants."[3]

Whether they were combatants or not, there is no disputing that the provost were many times fighters first and policemen second. In the parlance of the time, the Rebel provost "saw the elephant."[4] One of the earliest references to provost in combat concerned the unfortunate provost marshal killed in action at New Madrid. Other provost officers were luckier, surviving to win commenda-

---

2. Early, "Relative Numbers," 29.

3. David Gregg McIntosh, "The Campaign of Chancellorsville," *SHSP*, XL (rpr. 1979), 62; Early, "Relative Numbers," 29; Jones, "Last Days of the Army of Northern Virginia," 64, 88.

4. Sword, *Shiloh*, 158. "Seeing the elephant" was Civil War slang for being shot at in battle. The term originated from the common practice of small boys watering circus elephants so they could see the show free. As one veteran soldier put it, combat was the same: "You won't like it a bit."

tion and sometimes promotion for their conduct under fire. Colonel James Fuqua, provost marshal general of the District of the Mississippi, was one provost officer who performed well in combat. His opportunity came when General John Breckinridge launched his two small divisions against Union-held Baton Rouge in August, 1862. Fuqua, on the staff of General Daniel Ruggles during the action, earned praise for his efficiency, coolness, and gallantry throughout.[5] He may well have figured prominently for, although Confederate losses were remarkably light, Breckinridge lost one division and three brigade commanders. Fuqua, as an extra colonel, would have been useful indeed.

Another provost colonel, meantime, was earning similar praise west of the Mississippi. In mid-July, 1862, Colonel Charles Livenskiold, provost marshal at Corpus Christi, Texas, reported the arrival of Federal warships off the city and announced to General H. P. Bee, commanding the District of the Lower Rio Grande, that he was taking charge of the city. The reason for this unique assumption of command by a provost officer was, as he put it, "because of other officers' reluctance to assume command." Livenskiold's determination to hold Corpus Christi is evident in the energetic measures he immediately took to prepare the city's defenses, including the impressment of all available foodstuffs, clothing, and munitions for issue to the defenders. Commodities such as cotton and tobacco were sent to the interior well out of the way, and two ships in danger of capture were burned. Three other vessels filled with concrete were sunk in the ship channel to block the entrance to the bay. Livenskiold's city withstood three days of Federal bombardment in mid-August but in the absence of sufficient troops fell to the Federals in October. Just up the coast at Matagorda, another provost marshal, with the assistance of a squadron of cavalry, was doing his best to maintain law and order in face of the enemy threat.[6]

During the summer and autumn of 1862, provost officers in other commands in Virginia, South Carolina, and Kentucky were adding luster to the provost's combat record. Colonel Johnson Hagood, whose experiences as provost marshal of Charleston were related in Chapter 11, was another provost officer who came under fire. When enemy forces landed on James Island on June 3, Hagood and his assistant provost marshals joined the Confederate troops opposing the Federals. As it turned out, the initial engagement was brief and desultory but sufficient to give the party of military police officers a taste of a

5. Thompson, *History of the Orphan Brigade*, 133.
6. *OR*, IX, 610–13, 723; Delaney, "Corpus Christi," 6.

"heavy gunboat shelling and a night of picket duty accompanied by heavy rain, and the dropping of an occasional shell on the line."[7]

Provost at the battle of Groveton, Virginia, in late August got more than a taste. The 1st Virginia's list of twenty-six wounded included the names of eighteen provost privates and one provost sergeant. One officer, Lieutenant W. L. Nichols, assistant provost marshal at Cynthiana, Kentucky, received praise for acting with great gallantry on September 6. In Wade Hampton's cavalry brigade of the Army of Northern Virginia the provost guard of forty men under Captain J. F. Waring was commended in September when it "charged the enemy, scattered them in every direction, killing and wounding many, taking ten prisoners . . . and capturing a gun."[8]

Greater things awaited the cavalry and the provost. On October 9 Jeb Stuart, with eighteen hundred troopers and four guns, commenced his sensational second ride around McClellan. Riding with the expedition were Major J. P. W. Hairston, provost marshal of the division, and a number of provost guardsmen. Moving into Pennsylvania, Stuart occupied Chambersburg on the tenth, spending most of that day wrecking trains, machine shops, and depots and destroying any military equipment that could not be carried. He then headed south, crossing the Potomac on October 12. Hairston was expected to detain anyone the raiding party encountered to prevent information from reaching the enemy and to prevent straggling by the troops.[9]

The quickening pace of the war in both the eastern and western theaters in 1863 involved the provost even more heavily in combat. In the West it was obvious that the Federals were after Vicksburg and Port Hudson, the last two obstacles to their complete freedom of movement on the Mississippi. By May 21 both these bastions were under siege, Grant surrounding Pemberton in Vicksburg and Nathaniel P. Banks smashing at the doors of Port Hudson. Defending the latter was Major General Franklin Gardner with about 4,500 men, among them Colonel J. G. W. Steedman and his 1st Alabama. On May 24 Steedman moved his troops forward to determine the enemy's strength but by dusk had bumped into only a few pickets. His regiment, reinforced by a battalion each from the 1st Mississippi and 15th Arkansas and the "battalion of the provost guard, commanded by Captain J. R. Wilson," then returned to the main defensive line. The following morning Steedman put his 600 men in line

7. Hagood, *Memoirs*, 83.

8. Spence, "Reports," 262–64; *OR*, Vol. XVI, Pt. 1, p. 943; Vol. XIX, Pt. 1, pp. 822–23.

9. General J. E. B. Stuart, "Stuart's Report of His Expedition into Pennsylvania in October, 1862," *SHSP*, XIV (rpr. 1978), 480.

of battle to meet the advancing enemy, beating off an attack that, according to Steedman, was not seriously pressed. A second and more determined attack then forced him to withdraw to the main fortifications. After a brief respite the Federals launched a major attack on May 27. It is not known whether Wilson's provost battalion remained in the line during this attack. Steedman's casualty report listing some 225 killed, wounded, and missing, or a loss of one man out of every four engaged, makes no mention of provost casualties. With such a high rate of casualties it seems unlikely that the provost would have remained untouched had they been involved. It must be concluded, therefore, that Wilson and his men did not participate in the action.[10]

In the eastern theater the provost were actively involved in operations with the Army of Northern Virginia and in defense of various threatened localities. H. T. Parrish, provost marshal of Farmville, was ordered on May 3, 1863, by Secretary of War Seddon to prepare the defense of the town, although the enemy was not believed to be approaching it. Farther north, the beaten Federals were withdrawing toward U.S. Ford, having narrowly escaped total disaster during Lee's brilliant tactical success at Chancellorsville. No accounts of direct provost participation in this battle were found, although the 12th Georgia under Colonel Edward Willis spent part of May 3 as provost guard for Doles's Georgia Brigade. This temporary duty lasted only the afternoon, and by nightfall the 12th was again moving on Chancellorsville.[11]

In June the Army of Northern Virginia was on the march toward Pennsylvania and Gettysburg. This Southern offensive affords a number of examples of the operational duties the provost were assigned to carry out. Brigadier General John B. Gordon, commanding a brigade in Early's division, used his provost as an advance guard during the June 22 march from Gettysburg to York: "I moved directly through, having sent in front of the brigade a provost guard to occupy the city and take down the Federal flag."[12]

Reports from the cavalry that accompanied Lee to the North show that in at least one instance a provost officer participated in a cavalry charge. The officer rightly received more credit for his part in the affair than did the cavalry. The action occurred near Fairfield, Pennsylvania, on July 3, when the 7th Virginia

10. "Fortification and Siege of Port Hudson—Compiled by the Association of Defenders of Port Hudson," *SHSP*, XIV (rpr. 1978), 316.

11. *OR*, Vol. XXV, Pt. 2, p. 773; Francis T. Willis, "The Twelfth Georgia Infantry," *SHSP*, XVII (rpr. 1978), 179.

12. John B. Gordon, "Report of Brigadier-General John B. Gordon," *SHSP*, VII (rpr. 1977), 242.

Cavalry, part of W. E. Jones's brigade, charged the 6th U.S. Cavalry. Coming under flanking fire, the graycoats faltered and broke to the rear, where they failed to rally. According to Jones, the "blemish" was partly made up because "many officers formed noble exceptions," including "Lieutenant Simpson . . . on provost guard duty . . . in the thickest of the fight from first to last, capturing many more prisoners than he had men." Four days later, the 7th Virginia redeemed itself when it fell on the 6th U.S., scattering it and taking sixty prisoners: "The Sixth United States regular cavalry numbers among the things that were." Meantime, the provost marshal of Stuart's errant cavalry was earning a good report even if Stuart was not. "The untiring energy, force of character and devotion to duty . . . of Lieutenant G. M. Ryal [sic], C.S. Army, Provost Marshal," wrote Stuart, "deserves my special gratitude and praise."[13]

The gloom caused by Vicksburg and Gettysburg was lifted somewhat by Chickamauga in September. This sanguinary battle provides the largest number of reports describing the provost in action of any one battle of the war. Regimental and brigade commanders in three of Bragg's five corps referred specifically to the provost in their official accounts of the two-day battle.

Two such accounts were those of Brigadier Generals Z. C. Deas and A. M. Manigault, commanding brigades in Thomas Hindman's division, which for the battle was shifted from Leonidas Polk's to Simon Buckner's corps. These two brigades, advancing on Sunday, September 20, as part of Longstreet's left wing of the army, were soon heavily engaged. Manigault was almost immediately in trouble, the failure of the troops on his left to keep pace leaving him open to enfilade fire from that flank and forcing him to retire, losing one gun in the process. One of his regiments, the 28th Alabama, retrieved the gun. Deas, meantime, had pushed forward over the Union breastworks, as did Patton Anderson's brigade, which temporarily replaced Manigault's. The confusion that characterized the Battle of Chickamauga was already setting in, and staff officers were sent right and left to determine the positions of friendly troops and to assist in reforming the brigades that were in disorder. One of these staff officers was Lieutenant Edward Malone, Manigault's provost marshal. Manigault spoke of him as active and efficient in preventing straggling, "forcing many who were unwilling to face the heavy fire to which they had been exposed back into their proper positions." Colonel J. C. Reid, commanding the 28th Alabama, also spoke highly of Malone, expressing his obligations to the

13. General W. E. Jones, "Summer Campaign of 1863—Report of Gen'l. W. E. Jones," *SHSP*, IX (rpr. 1979), 116, 118; W. Gordon McCabe, "Major Andrew Reid Venable, Jr.," *SHSP*, XXXVII (rpr. 1979), 65.

provost marshal for rallying the troops "when they showed a disposition to falter."[14] Malone was no doubt also kept busy with the brigade's share of the eleven hundred prisoners captured by the division and custody of the captured equipment, which included fourteen hundred rifles, five caissons, a number of horses and wagons, and 165,000 rounds of ammunition.

Deas, too, had high praise for his provost marshal, Lieutenant Charles J. Michailoffsky, to whom he was "specially indebted for . . . willingness and gallantry in carrying out my orders on the field." The division commander, Thomas Hindman, made similar remarks regarding the conduct of the division provost marshal, Captain J. F. Walton.[15]

Bushrod Johnson, commanding a brigade in Hood's division, was instrumental in the Confederate victory. His command carried out one of the most spectacular movements of the war, the piercing of the Union center, and then, with Hindman, the shattering of the Union right wing. Colonel J. S. Fulton, commanding one of Johnson's three brigades, gave unstinting praise to his brigade provost guard:

> The provost guard under Lieutenants Ewing and Orr rendered invaluable service.
>
> I am pleased to note the conduct of Private Turner Goodall, of the provost guard, who, in the thickest of the fight on Sunday evening, seeing the men all so gallantly at work and hard pressed, came up with his gun and fought manfully through the hottest of the fight, and by words of encouragement to his fellow soldiers and example did his whole duty as a soldier and provost guard. . . . I would also mention Lieutenant Ewing of the provost guard, from the Seventeenth Tennessee Regiment, who, finding that the officers of his company had all been placed *hors de combat,* asked permission and returned to take command of his company on Sunday morning. He is a worthy and promising officer.[16]

Provost of the other corps (Buckner's) of Longstreet's left wing received their share of praise for meritorious conduct. William Bate's brigade of A. P. Stewart's division reported going into action with 1,055 riflemen and 30 provost guardsmen, presumably from the brigade provost guard. Colonel R. C. Trigg reported the exemplary conduct of his brigade provost guard to the

---

14. *OR,* Vol. XXX, Pt. 2, pp. 344, 350; Major-General T. C. Hindman, "Battle of Chickamauga," *SHSP,* XIII (rpr. 1978), 367–72.

15. *OR,* Vol. XXX, Pt. 2, p. 331; Hindman, "Battle of Chickamauga," 372.

16. *OR,* Vol. XXX, Pt. 2, p. 478.

division commander, Brigadier General William Preston. One of his regimental commanders, Colonel W. S. Dilworth, provided the details. "The provost guard, under Lieutenant J. G. Butler, Company A, Third Florida," Dilworth wrote, "was formed on the right of my regiment during the greater part of the day. They volunteered to go out as skirmishers early in the morning, much to the relief of my weary men, and in every place they served they did their duty faithfully and efficiently."[17]

In Polk's corps, too, the provost did their part in the fighting. Colonel S. S. Stanton, commanding the 28th Tennessee in Wright's brigade of Benjamin Cheatham's division, reported going into action with "308 men, including field and staff, infirmary corps, provost guard and etc." The brigade commander, M. J. Wright, commended the brigade provost guard and the provost marshal and, unique among the reports, mentioned that the provost had suffered casualties: one killed in action and two wounded.[18]

The year 1864 opened with a period of relative quiet both east and west, enlivened only by the small skirmishes that occurred almost daily. It was obvious, though, that while the Northern manpower and material advantage continued to accrue, the South was growing weaker economically and militarily. It was also obvious that when the weather broke and active campaigning resumed, the North would bring all her resources to bear, continuing her relentless pursuit of victory. In Virginia Lee's army was as ready to face Grant, the new Federal commander, as its smaller numbers and scant resources could make it.

At about 9 A.M., Wednesday, May 4, 1864, the Confederate signal station on Clark's Mountain on the southern bank of the Rapidan flashed the news that the Federals were on the march. By late in the day three of Grant's corps were over the river at Germanna and Culpeper Mine Fords, and with the fourth rapidly moving up, Grant had 122,000 men ready to tackle Lee. The latter, meantime, had been on the move shortly after the signaler's report; some 66,000 Rebels were marching rapidly eastward from the deserted camps in the Orange Court House–Gordonsville areas, Richard Ewell leading on the Orange Turnpike, A. P. Hill parallel to him on the Orange Plank Road, and James Longstreet coming up from Gordonsville. Lee's intent was to enmesh Grant in the dense and dark Wilderness, which would negate the superior Union artillery and conceal the inferior strength of the Army of Northern Virginia.

That night the Confederate columns bivouacked near Verdiersville, rising

17. *Ibid.*, 234, 386; McMurray, *History of the Twentieth Tennessee Infantry,* 289.
18. *OR,* Vol. XXX, Pt. 2, pp. 126, 121.

early on the morning of the fifth to continue the march to meet Grant. Late in the morning Ewell's 2d Corps ran into a strong force of Federals moving southeast toward the Orange Plank Road. The titanic struggle was on. Meantime, Henry Heth of A. P. Hill's 3d Corps had moved up, followed closely by C. M. Wilcox's division, which partially filled the gap between Heth's left and the right of Ewell's corps. The two Confederate corps now held a line of battle perpendicular to the Orange Plank Road, crossing it and the Orange Turnpike to the north.

Throughout the day the enemy repeatedly assaulted Heth's line, losing many men in each of seven separate attacks. Heth, feeling it time to counterattack, then launched his and Wilcox's division into a costly assault, which was repulsed. Even worse was a report that the Yankees were pushing into the gap between the 2d and 3d corps, which Wilcox had not been able to fill. This thrust threatened disaster unless it could somehow be stopped. The only troops immediately available, 125 men of the 3d Corps provost guard, the 5th Alabama Battalion, were occupied guarding prisoners. Quickly putting these in the care of several wounded men, the battalion commander, Major Albert Van De Graaff, deployed his little command in a skirmish line and with a wild Rebel yell drove forward, surprising the Federals and bringing them to a stumbling halt. The danger was over and night closed out the savage action.[19] Grave consequences for the army had been averted by the grit and élan of a single small provost battalion.

The war ground on in the East: at Spotsylvania Court House, North Anna River, Cold Harbor, and then the beginning of the siege of Petersburg in June, after which for two months the main front was relatively quiet, with the notable exception of the Battle of the Crater at the end of July. Not until mid-August did the siege heat up again when the Federal 5th Corps seized and held onto a section of the vital Weldon railroad running south from Petersburg, despite three Confederate attempts to retake it. In mid-September Southern spirits and appetites were gratified by Wade Hampton's rustling expedition, which cut almost twenty-five hundred fat beeves out from under Grant's nose and took them safely across the lines to the Confederate field kitchens. Hampton attributed the successful expedition to "Major Venable . . . and . . . Major Ryal [sic], Provost Marshal, who had been very efficient. . . . These officers discharged their duty admirably, and the successful manner in which the cattle were brought off is due very much to their zeal and enterprise."[20]

19. Foote, *Civil War*, III, 163.
20. McCabe, "Major Andrew Reid Venable, Jr.," 69–70.

In late September the 5th Alabama Battalion got a taste of trench warfare south of Petersburg. To fill the gap created by the movement of elements of A. P. Hill's 3d Corps north across the James River, Lee was forced to use detailed men, including cooks, clerks, and teamsters and reserve units from the city, and extend the frontages of regular brigades that remained in the area. The 5th Alabama, which was at 3d Corps headquarters at the time, and many of the provost from Petersburg were also inserted in the line on September 30. It is not known if the 5th remained overnight in the trenches.[21]

In the western theater the provost were engaged in operations both with the Army of Tennessee and in the rear areas. One of these, the northern part of Alabama, had become infested with deserters and Northern sympathizers who were making life hell for the inhabitants by pillaging and raiding. On April 14 Lieutenant Colonel John W. Estes, the provost marshal of the First District of Alabama, reported on his activities against the "tories" to Major Jules C. Denis, the provost marshal general of Polk's Department of Alabama, Mississippi, and East Louisiana. According to Estes, "Everything comparatively quiet. . . . The tory raids . . . are becoming less frequent. . . . I think I can break up the whole clan as soon as I can organize 100 good men."[22]

About three weeks later, Sherman started nearly a hundred thousand men on the road to Atlanta. Opposing them Joseph E. Johnston had sixty thousand men in good defensive positions at Dalton, but they were soon outflanked, causing him to evacuate Dalton on May 12 and fall back to new positions at Resaca. On the fifteenth Hood's corps was driven back by Joseph Hooker, and, realizing the danger with the Oostenaula River at his back, Johnston withdrew from Resaca during the night. Colonel James Nisbet's 66th Georgia, part of W. H. T. Walker's division, did not withdraw but instead was ordered to report to Colonel Benjamin Hill, provost marshal general of the army, for special duty. Reporting as ordered, Nisbet was told by Hill, "Johnston's army is going to fall back tonight; and after they are all over the river, I want you to take up the pontoon bridges and burn the railroad bridge." Toward morning, on being advised that the army was across the Oostenaula, Nisbet dealt with the bridges and then rejoined his brigade.[23]

21. Sommers, *Richmond Redeemed*, 186, 555. Elements of the 1st Virginia Battalion, the army provost guard, also saw action. One company of the battalion rejoined it in Petersburg within a few hours to assist in guarding more than thirteen hundred prisoners taken in the Confederate counterattack south of the city on September 30.

22. *OR*, Vol. XXXII, Pt. 3, pp. 782–83.

23. Nisbet, *4 Years on the Firing Line*, 186.

Meanwhile, in northern Mississippi Nathan Bedford Forrest was soon to wreck Samuel Sturgis' command at Brice's Cross Roads on June 10. There was little time to celebrate the event for on June 15 Forrest learned that another expedition under A. J. Smith was moving in a fresh attempt to destroy him. In face of this threat, Forrest concentrated as many men as possible, ordering General James Chalmers to bring his division as near as he could to Okolona. Other reinforcements in the form of an additional cavalry brigade reported to Forrest, while at the same time he organized a brigade of infantry at Tupelo from dismounted men. Not yet content, Forrest proposed to augment this dismounted brigade with a large number of "employees and detailed men, provost guards," which would increase the brigade to at least two thousand men.[24] These troops performed credibly at Tupelo, which, although a Federal victory tactically, did not destroy Forrest. Smith then withdrew to Memphis leaving Forrest free to continue his unceasing harassment of the Federals.

The evacuation of Atlanta on September 1 was a crushing blow to Confederate prospects, making Lincoln's reelection a virtual certainty and ending any hope of a negotiated settlement. Something had to be done to draw Sherman out of Georgia, and Hood, after conferring with President Davis, determined to do just that. Moving north to try to cut Sherman's lengthy supply lines, Hood struck the Western and Atlantic Railroad at Big Shanty and Kennesaw, forcing Sherman to send troops north from Atlanta, including George Thomas, who went to Nashville to prepare defenses against a possible invasion of Tennessee by Hood. Skirmishing along the railroad at Resaca, La Fayette, and Dalton continued during early October, but by the seventeenth Hood was moving toward Gadsden, Alabama, intent on marching into Tennessee. On November 9, having dispatched two corps to reinforce Thomas at Nashville, Sherman announced his decision to march to the sea.

Hood's subsequent mauling in Tennessee, resulting in the almost total destruction of his army, needs no recounting. The activities of his provost marshal general, Colonel Martin H. Cofer, during the debacle make fascinating reading and illustrate just how valuable Cofer was to the army. Ed Porter Thompson's *magnum opus* on the Kentucky Orphan Brigade makes it clear that Cofer commanded a provost "admirably organized and controlled, and more than usually efficient."[25] It was fortunate for Hood that this was so, for without the

24. Bearss, *Forrest at Brice's Cross Roads,* 162.
25. Thompson, *History of the Orphan Brigade,* 426.

assistance of the provost he might not have been able to break free of the Union pursuit after Nashville.

By all accounts Cofer was a first-class officer. Promoted to colonel in September, 1863, he became provost marshal general of the Army of Tennessee in August, 1864. Throughout Hood's Tennessee campaign Cofer performed yeoman service, but never more so than after the disaster at Nashville, when he was instrumental in saving the army's trains and putting the mobs of stragglers into some semblance of order. According to Thompson, Cofer's efforts played a very large part in getting the army back across the Duck River at Columbia and then across the Tennessee. Had it not been for Cofer "perfecting" the crossing of the latter, with the enemy in pursuit, the retreat might well have "become another march from Moscow, and the Tennessee the Beresina of the South."[26]

The *Official Records* confirm the meritorious conduct of one other provost marshal of the Army of Tennessee during Hood's fiasco. This officer, Captain T. C. Henderson of Major General S. G. French's division, was commended for "distinguished gallantry."[27]

One of the last operational tasks performed by the provost occurred during the evacuation of the Confederate capital in April, 1865. On April 2, Captain Clement Sulivane, an officer attached to the Local Defense Brigade, was ordered to establish defensive positions around Mayo's Bridge, the last remaining one over the James River, and hold it until the cavalry rear guard under Major General M. W. Gary could cross. Sulivane later recalled that Gary's cavalry appeared at the bridge around 7 A.M. on April 3, taking the better part of an hour to cross. Just before this, the city's remaining provost troops had been told to withdraw with the cavalry. As the last of the cavalry and the provost crossed over and the engineer officer on duty set fire to the bridge, Gary departed with the words, "All over, goodbye; blow her to hell." It seems fitting that the provost should have been among the last out of the burning capital, serving as the rear guard of a nation also blown to hell. Like Stonewall Jackson, the Confederacy was about to "cross over the river and rest under the shade of the trees."[28]

26. *Ibid.*, 427.
27. *OR*, Vol. XXXVIII, Pt. 3, p. 907.
28. Irvine, "Fall of Richmond," 390; Clement Sulivane, "The Fall of Richmond," in Robert Underwood Johnson and Clarence Clough Buel (eds.), *Battles and Leaders of the Civil War* (4 vols.; 1887; rpr. New York, 1956), IV, 725–26; Foote, *Civil War*, II, 319. These were Jackson's last words.

Another important operational duty of the provost was directing or actively participating in the collection of military intelligence. Sometimes the provost obtained valuable information because they were the sole military presence in many areas and people tended to report news and developments of a military nature to them. Less frequently the provost controlled the activities of scouts and spies, assigning them to obtain information and then forwarding any reports received to the appropriate officers. Provost efforts often provided commanders with accurate and timely knowledge of the size, composition, and intentions of enemy forces.

As early as the autumn of 1861, the provost in Virginia were involved in information gathering. In September, J. A. Totten, provost marshal of Brigadier General John Floyd's Army of the Kanawha, was reporting on enemy troop movements. This report and many others on Union movements in the Alleghenies were very useful to the Confederates. In the autumn of 1862, Lieutenant Colonel Robert P. Blount, provost marshal of Longstreet's 1st Corps, advised President Davis that he had "made use of every opportunity to get useful information . . . Burnside's army only consists of seven corps . . . much reduced by sickness, desertion. . . . I do not think their army will fight with confidence." Blount's estimate of the number of corps was close; Burnside actually had six, with a further two about twenty miles to the north, but he was badly awry on his prediction on Yankee fighting spirit. On December 13 the Union army launched repeated, determined, and, as it proved, costly assaults on the unbreakable Confederate line at Fredericksburg. Burnside failed miserably and withdrew beaten and humiliated. Another example of provost reporting on the enemy in Virginia occurred in October, 1864, when Major Cornelius Boyle, provost marshal at Gordonsville, advised Lee that Federal cavalry had partially destroyed a bridge over the Rapidan. Lee telegraphed this news to the president.[29]

There is evidence that in the western theater Confederate scouts customarily reported to provost marshals. Sam Davis, the celebrated Rebel scout, went to the gallows in November, 1863, after papers describing the Nashville defenses and the Union army in Tennessee, along with letters to his superiors, were found in his possession. One of these letters was addressed to Colonel Alex McKinstrey, provost marshal general of the Army of Tennessee, at Chat-

29. *OR*, V, 838; XII, Pt. 3, p. 937; Ser. II, Vol. IV, pp. 949–50; Douglas Southall Freeman and Grady McWhiney (eds.), *Lee's Dispatches: Unpublished Letters of General Robert E. Lee, C.S.A. to Jefferson Davis and the War Department of the Confederate States of America, 1862–65* (1915; rpr. New York, 1957), 300–301.

tanooga. Davis refused to divulge the source of his information and was executed, thereby becoming a Confederate martyr.[30]

Provost in Mississippi and Louisiana were also receiving and forwarding information on the enemy. In April, 1863, the provost marshal of Columbus, Mississippi, advised Brigadier General Daniel Ruggles, commanding the District of Mississippi and East Louisiana, that enemy forces were moving on Houston, about fifty miles northwest of Columbus, and were expected to reach that town within a few hours. The following month a report on the engagement between Federal gunboats and Fort Beauregard on the Ouachita River at Harrisonburg, Louisiana, made reference to information gathered by the provost: "G. Spencer Mayo . . . Provost Marshall [sic], at Trinity, and Superintendent of Scouts on Black River, brought me further information that four gunboats had laid up the night previous four miles above Major Beard's." Warned by this information, the local commander, Colonel George Logan, stood to his defenses and beat off the Federal assault. Mayo, according to Logan, "did good service."[31]

During the spring of 1864, the provost in Alabama were busy deploying scouts and passing on the information received from them. In March, Major Jules C. Denis, provost marshal general of the Department of Alabama, Mississippi, and East Louisiana, received a report from the chief of the department's scouts, which makes it clear that in Polk's command at least, the provost were directly responsible for controlling the activities of those seeking military intelligence for the Confederacy, in this case an unknown Southern Mata Hari:

> In compliance with instructions received from your office, I . . . completed such arrangements as will secure to the general commanding information from time to time of the forces, designs and movements of the enemy, as well as other information of general use to the Confederacy. I have also placed within the lines a person who will within the next few weeks traverse a large part of the West and North, gathering all the general movements of the enemy, their strength and future plans. . . . This person is a highly intelligent and observant lady. . . . I trust the letters forwarded to you . . . were useful.[32]

30. Ridley, *Battles and Sketches,* 259–66.

31. *OR,* Vol. XXIV, Pt. 1, pp. 550–51; Colonel George William Logan, "Official Report on the Engagement Between the Federal Gunboats and Fort Beauregard, on the 10th and 11th May, 1863," *SHSP,* XI (rpr. 1977), 497–501.

32. *OR,* Vol. XXXII, Pt. 3, pp. 633–34.

The chief provost marshal of the First District of Alabama, Lieutenant Colonel John W. Estes, also advised Denis of arrangements to obtain timely and accurate information on the strength and movements of the enemy in and around Decatur and Athens.[33] One last report is unique in that a cavalry officer detailed to lead a party of scouts was also specifically given what can only be described as military police duties. This officer, Captain Perry Evans of the 9th Texas Regiment, Lawrence Ross's brigade, was tasked to preserve order and protect the citizens, arrest all conscripts, and aid wherever possible in enforcing Confederate law.[34] It is possible that the intent was for Evans to act as a roving provost marshal to assist Captain Watkins, the division provost marshal.

All in all, the provost's operational and combat record was a good one, earning them some favorable recognition from an audience all too ready to carp and abuse. Their participation in combat gained them a measure of praise and perhaps some grudging respect from the front-line Johnny Reb, but it could not overcome the basic antipathy of the combat soldier toward those he perceived to be essentially noncombatants. As well, whatever their contribution to the war effort, the provost were never allowed to forget that they were members of a calling historically and universally despised. These feelings went beyond the army. Whatever good "press" was achieved did not travel well, nor could it counteract the widely expressed contempt that showered on the "riffraff" provost from all sides.

33. *Ibid.*, pp. 782–83.
34. *OR*, Vol. XXXIX, Pt. 2, p. 575.

14

Good Men and Bad

When I am right no one remembers,
When I am wrong no one forgets.

ANONYMOUS

It has been said that a staff officer is like a trouser button: "There are few to praise it while it goes on with its work, and very few to abstain from cursing it when it comes off."[1] This adage could also apply to the provost in the Confederate army. Many of the documented complaints about the provost, discussed in earlier chapters, condemned individual officers and men for alleged lack of character, integrity, or intelligence or for inefficiency, but others voiced criticism of the provost as a whole because of the unpopular duties they had to perform. Yet others were virulent outbursts against the very concept and existence of provost in the Confederacy. These complaints, some probably justified but many overstated and emotional, provide a good insight into the attitudes of citizens and soldiers toward the provost.

Many of those who condemned the military police questioned the validity of detailing able-bodied men to such noncombatant organizations when every bayonet was needed at the battle fronts. Such details were objects of much scorn and the infantryman's jibe, "Who ever saw a dead cavalryman?" applied even more to the provost guardsman. A number of Confederate general officers also subscribed to this opinion. As Brigadier General Johnson Hagood put it: "Detachment was so convenient a cloak for skulking that among the faithful soldiers in the ranks it was considered not much more creditable than absence without leave."[2]

Nor were combat troops the only ones to berate the provost. State governments, the press, the judiciary, and the ordinary citizen all weighed into the nefarious provost. Even the soldier who served with the military police was often unhappy and bitter with his lot, considering himself a useless parasite on the country. Being on the receiving end of so much abuse was not a pleasant

1. C. E. Montague, *Disenchantment* (London, 1968), 32.
2. Hagood, *Memoirs,* 318.

experience for the Rebel provost, those outrageous, insufferable "plug uglies" who were assigned a thankless task in life.

The antagonisms aroused by the provost and their activities and the low esteem in which they were held were very evident in Richmond, a city closely policed by the provost during the war. Her rapidly expanding population and the large number of transient soldiers who thronged the streets on their way to and from the front in northern Virginia necessitated a strong and vigorous military police. It was inevitable that this vigor and indeed the provost's very presence began to grate on the sensitivities of Richmond's citizens, unaccustomed as they were to restrictions on their liberties or daily life. Similarly, their regulating activities brought the provost into head-on conflict with a Southern soldiery that had no desire to be regulated by anyone, and most certainly not by the despised and low-class provost.

Right from the start the combat soldier displayed no reluctance in expressing his contempt for the Richmond military police. Basic hostility, aggravated by such things as the provost's enforcement of passport controls—a system that often caused great hardship to the soldier—soon developed into deep-seated hatred of the provost marshals and their guards. Men on furlough, for instance, were infuriated by the requirement to obtain passes, which cost them precious leave time. Even convalescents from the city's hospitals were not exempt:

> An unforeseen annoyance arose in the frequent disruptions which occurred between our Provost Marshal, General Winder, and the Examining Board of Surgeons, through whom the soldiers in a state of convalescence received furloughs. It was not infrequently the case, when a convalescent soldier succeeded in procuring from his surgeon a certificate upon which to ground an application for a furlough, and when not in a condition to return to his regiment for service in the field, that he was kept in Richmond . . . because General Winder had quarrelled with the Board, and there was no authority delegated to examine into and decide upon his case.[3]

Other soldiers on furlough and officers on leave were enraged by the passport office's limited hours, which increased the time required to obtain a pass and meant wasted hours in Richmond. Failure to obtain a pass or attempts to travel without one more often than not propelled "many a poor soldier with a few days leave into Winder's lockup."[4]

3. Putnam, *In Richmond During the Confederacy,* 161.
4. Bill, *Beleaguered City,* 205–206.

Winder became a hated figure and the object of vituperation, starting at the highest levels of government. Joseph E. Johnston, who said of Hood, "Confident language by a military commander is not usually regarded as evidence of competency," might well have applied the statement to Winder had it occurred to him in May, 1862. Certainly Winder did not have Johnston's confidence, as is evident from Johnston's complaints during the Seven Days' Battle on the leakage of military information from the Provost Marshal's Office. The leakage was apparently caused by carelessness in issuing passes to those wishing to visit within the army's lines. General Lee was also concerned about the inadequacy of Winder's system of checking the authenticity of those who requested passes, a feeling echoed by Assistant Secretary of War Campbell, who declared that "Winder's brown paper passes could be had for a hundred dollars apiece." Laxity in maintaining proper security is also obvious from a description in early 1862 of blackboards full of military information being left in public view in the Richmond Provost Marshal's Office. And this, at a time when Federal spies were believed to be everywhere, did little for the provost's credibility.[5]

At the War Department it was said the staff "hated" the provost marshal. John B. Jones, a clerk in the department, noted in his diary for October 29, 1862, exactly what he thought of Winder. "Yesterday," he wrote, "the whole bunch of 'Plug Ugly' policemen in the Provost Marshal's 'department,' were summarily dismissed by General Winder for 'malfeasance, corruption, bribery and incompetence.' These are the branches: the roots should be plucked up, and General Winder and his Provost Marshal ought to resign."[6]

Inevitably, many soldiers focused their energies on how best to circumvent the "elegant young assistant provost marshals" and their guards. Alexander Hunter of the 17th Virginia described one method of outwitting the "Melish" provost. The method, simplicity in itself, involved play-acting at being "Winder's pets," dropping the sham only when the real provost "creatures" chanced their way. Hunter had words for Winder, too, calling his appointment a "most unfortunate step," an opinion shared by Jeb Stuart, who could afford to be\ considerably more direct in confronting Winder and his guard. Out of patience with having his men locked up, Stuart determined to do his own policing of any cavalry troopers in the city. Winder reacted by threatening Stuart with arrest. Placing himself at the head of a squadron, Stuart rode the streets of Richmond "daring Winder to do his worst." There was good reason why Stuart did not

5. *OR,* Vol. XXXVIII, Pt. 5, p. 888; Bill, *Beleaguered City,* 115, 125, 205.
6. Bill, *Beleaguered City,* 125; Jones, *Rebel War Clerk's Diary,* 111–12.

want any of his men in the city's prisons; he much preferred to deal firmly but humanely with those who committed military offenses. Some of the prisons were notorious for alleged bad treatment of inmates. Castle Thunder, for one, had a particularly evil reputation, with stories circulating of cruel punishments such as barrel shirts and suspension by the thumbs. These tales gathered such credibility that in the spring of 1863 Congress ordered an investigation into the management and conduct of prison affairs.[7]

Civilians were equally hostile toward Richmond provost. Winder's thankless task, even when carried out with the best of intentions, met with constant disapproval from the majority of Richmonders, who summed up the provost as active but outrageous. Some credit accrued to them for their efforts in reducing the violence in the city, but this could not outweigh the infuriation cause by their interference with civil liberties. As some put it, "Evildoers were the only ones the police did not trouble." Others stated the corollary: the provost were "oppressive only to the . . . peaceful." Provost attempts to clean their own house served only to confirm the civilians' low estimate of the military police. The arrest of Augustus Simcoe, one of Winder's detectives, caused a sensation in the city. In October, 1863, Simcoe precipitated a ruckus in a brothel, and during the heated exchange that followed, he shot the madam of the establishment. The titillating spectacle of the wounded madam hurling abuse at Simcoe in a crowded Richmond courtroom did little to improve the provost's image or increase public confidence in the police administration. The city press, however, displayed no surprise: "It has long been understood that detectives are, in not a few cases, not only *habitués* of bawdy and gambling houses, but the allies of the keepers of such establishments."[8]

Winder's prestige fell to an all-time low in November, when he suffered the supreme indignity of having his home burgled. His misfortune delighted the good burghers of Richmond, who as early as the first imposition of martial law in March, 1862, had expressed their dislike for a man who "combined the more belligerent traits of the Military Police with the sterner qualities of the martinet." These qualities soon made him "the most unloved official on either side." The people loathed him, considering that the worst feature of life in

---

7. Hunter, *Johnny Reb and Billy Yank,* 599, 607; Bill, *Beleaguered City,* 205–206; Thomas, *Confederate State of Richmond,* 106. Castle Thunder was commanded by Captain Alexander, later assistant provost marshal of Richmond and then commandant of Salisbury prison.

8. Bill, *Beleaguered City,* 205; Bevier, *History of the First and Second Missouri Confederate Brigades,* 449; Thomas, *Confederate State of Richmond,* 154.

Richmond was the presence of his provost, "who interfered intolerably with citizens going about their lawful business." His overzealous method of combating crime won him no friends either; arbitrary arrests, often on the flimsiest of excuses, were deeply resented and led to a deluge of complaints. Similarly, the operation of the passport office, apparently a "filthy" establishment, manned by "rowdy" clerks who bullied the applicants, offended and angered the civilian as much as it did the soldier. Provost officers in the eyes of many were no better than their clerks. "Lords ascendant," wrote one citizen, "they loll and roll in their glory."[9]

Other irritants were the unbelievable arrogance displayed by the provost, the classic case being perhaps their forgeries of prescriptions for brandy and then arresting those who had sold it to them. The condemnation by Captain A. C. Godwin, provost marshal of the eastern district of Richmond, of the police for their "iniquitous" forgeries only highlighted the case in the public mind. Winder even had the effrontery to threaten to suspend publication of the Richmond *Examiner* for taking him to task over the activities of his police. Likewise, the city was incensed that Winder seemed to be doing nothing to eradicate the Yankee spies that were believed to infest Richmond; the "inefficiency, and worse than inefficiency, with which their activities were dealt with by Winder's police aroused general indignation." Some of the blame for this state of affairs was also laid at the government's door. "I must not criticize General Winder's inefficiency," said Jones in the War Department, "for he acts under the instructions of Mr. Benjamin." The City Council, entirely fed up with the galling annoyance of the provost and martial law, felt that the only solution was for the council to guard the public interest and provide the police services rather than leave them to the Confederate government.[10] Nothing came of this proposal.

Elsewhere in the Confederacy the assessment of the provost's intelligence, integrity, and efficiency was equally low. During the Sharpsburg campaign, while Brigadier General J. R. Jones was in Winchester arresting stragglers, he was of the opinion that the provost was of "little assistance." A few months earlier, Lieutenant J. M. Otey, a staff officer with Beauregard in Mississippi, concluded that the "delinquencies" of the provost were owing to the lack of "proper instructions as to what constitutes their duties rather than to a disposi-

---

9. Dowdey, *Experiment in Rebellion*, 89, 176; Bill, *Beleaguered City*, 97, 127.

10. Jones, *Rebel War Clerk's Diary*, 54, 70; Bill, *Beleaguered City*, 97, 104, 115; Manarin (ed.), *Richmond at War*, 280.

tion to shirk them, they being in most cases men of inferior intelligence."[11] "Palpable dereliction on the part of police officials," said Otey, made a mockery of attempts to impose proper military order on the railroads in Mississippi.

There seems to have been tacit agreement on the part of some commanding generals that all else failing, mediocre or incompetent officers could be absorbed by the provost, for they could do no harm in such an organization. Brigadier General Alfred Iverson was one such officer. He had led a brigade in Robert Rodes's division at Gettysburg, but because of "want of capacity in the field . . . was relieved of his command and assigned to provost guard duty." On the other hand, some generals, albeit only at brigade level, held up the provost as the example good soldiers should strive to emulate. Just before the Battle of Fair Oaks in April, 1862, Brigadier General W. H. C. Whiting congratulated Dorsey Pender's 6th South Carolina and as a "special mark of distinction" allowed the regiment to perform provost duty, with one of its own officers as provost marshal.[12]

That same summer the provost marshal of Atlanta was found wanting, not because of incapacity, but for his "social position," which did not "command confidence and respect sufficiently to insure the enrollment . . . of the citizens" into a home guard force for the city. It was suggested that this provost marshal, the "clever" Major George Washington Lee, be restricted to his police duties, while a more socially acceptable officer take charge of Atlanta's home defense. In August this new officer, Colonel M. H. Wright, was complaining to Brigadier General W. W. Mackall, chief of staff of the Army of Tennessee, that little good could be accomplished by putting guards on the trains running out of Atlanta because of "the class of men we are compelled to have to do the duty. They succeed pretty well in annoying all respectable travelers and letting all villains pass." As for Major Lee, Wright continued, "for the life of me I can get nothing from him. I want to get at the bottom, and commence the cleaning."[13] One wonders, the bottom of what? There is no indication of why Lee was socially unacceptable, although it may be surmised that his provost status caused the townspeople's antipathy to him.

It appears that the men of the Army of Tennessee also found the provost socially unacceptable. Arthur Manigault, a brigade commander in Johnston's army, noted at Dalton, Georgia, just before the start of the Atlanta campaign:

11. *OR*, Vol. XIX, Pt. 2, p. 629; Vol. X, Pt. 2, pp. 304–305.

12. William R. Cox, "Major-General Stephen D. Ramseur: His Life and Character," *SHSP*, XVIII (rpr. 1977), 239; A. L. Diket, *wha hae wi' [Pender] . . . bled* (New York, 1979), 28.

13. *OR*, Vol. XXIII, Pt. 2, p. 910; Vol. XXX, Pt. 4, p. 520.

As may be supposed, they [the provost] were not regarded with any very kindly feeling by the men, who never lost an opportunity of sneering at them, or letting off some witticism at their expense. On one occasion, I happened to be near a regiment, standing at ease, or resting, when the Provost Guard was passing near. My attention was attracted by hearing someone call out, "Look out, boys! Anybody with a pocketbook or plug of tobacco in his pocket, put his hand over it, for here comes the Provost Guard!" Of course, a number of his comrades immediately pretended to secure the supposed pocketbook, and a succession of remarks and humorous speeches flew along the line, although there was nothing of such a character, or so pointed, as to render it necessary that any officer should interfere. It was very amusing, and I laughed heartily, particularly as I was unobserved; and the scorn and contempt with which the Guard passed by, in the most profound silence, made it still more ludicrous, they not deigning a reply to the jokes which they knew were leveled at them, but looking as though they had mentally resolved to pay off this score whenever an opportunity offered itself of doing so, promising themselves that it would be no laughing matter then.[14]

The veterans of Lee's army were equally quick to point out, even to captured Yankees, the provost's lack of integrity. George Booth, a Maryland cavalry officer, refused to intervene when one of his troopers appropriated a prisoner's watch. The unfortunate Northerner, according to Booth, was bound to lose his possessions anyway because once he was turned over to the provost they would strip him of attractive items like timepieces.[15] Better a combat soldier should have the use of the watch.

Some general officers continued to view the provost askance. Just after Christmas of 1863 Lieutenant General Leonidas Polk, the newly assigned commander of what was then the Department of Mississippi and East Louisiana, forwarded his views on the department's provost to Secretary of War Seddon. "The military police . . . I find very defective," wrote Polk, "I propose a thorough reorganization. . . . The principal difficulty has been to secure a competent chief. Such a one I found in Major Denis, who is eminently qualified." During the Red River campaign Lieutenant General Richard Taylor also expressed his disgust with certain provost activities: "My attention was called about this time to the existence of a wide-spread evil. A practice had

---

14. Tower (ed.), *A Carolinian Goes to War,* 166.
15. Booth, *Personal Reminiscences,* 112.

grown up of appointing provost marshals to take private property for public use. . . . The land swarmed with these vermin, appointed without due authority, or self-constituted, who robbed the people of horses, mules, cattle, corn and meat."[16] Major General Lafayette McLaws, commanding the defenses of Savannah, Georgia, from May, 1864, indirectly gave as his opinion that the provost were not worth very much. "The reserve troops in the condition they are now," said McLaws, "will answer for provost guards, and for the city lines, but would not be reliable elsewhere."[17]

Civilian discontent with the provost was reflected in the columns of the Confederacy's newspapers. F. G. De Fontaine, a newspaperman in Charlotte, North Carolina, in an 1865 dispatch to the Southern Associated Press, spoke of provost abuses such as "illegal imprisonment, arrest of citizens without authority . . . the passport system," all matters that infuriated the people. The Jacksonville *Republican* suggested that unnecessary provost should be removed from areas where they were of little use except to bother orderly citizens for passes: "Every provost at a railway station must have a guard sufficient to do picket duty for a brigade. . . . Their officious meddling with quiet citizens is a burlesque upon military rule, an outrage as intolerable as it is offensive and annoying." The governors of the states, in October, 1864, expressed their disgust with the provost in similar terms, considering them of no use to the country.[18]

Soldiers who were employed as provost held conflicting viewpoints on their duties. Some men despised assignment to the provost, feeling that they were being asked to perform tasks beneath the dignity of real soldiers. Charles Loehr recalled that this was certainly the attitude of his regiment, the 1st Virginia Infantry, at Gettysburg. Following the failure of the assault on July 3, General Lee, probably because of the horrific casualties suffered by Pickett, assigned that division as provost guard, a step "but little relished by the men, most of them considering it as almost a disgrace to act as provost." Pickett's inspector general, Walter Harrison, was equally dismayed with provost service. "Pickett's Division," he said, "was at once degraded to the position of 'Provost Guard' of the Army of Northern Virginia; doubtless a post of honor we had merited from being so badly mauled." Nevertheless, the division escorted some four thousand prisoners safely back to Williamsport, where they were turned

16. *OR,* Vol. XXXI, Pt. 3, pp. 875–76; Taylor, *Destruction and Reconstruction,* 208.

17. *OR,* Vol. XXXV, Pt. 2, p. 522.

18. Freeman and McWhiney (eds.), *Lee's Dispatches,* 343; Moore, *Conscription and Conflict,* 94, 305–306; *OR,* Vol. XLII, Pt. 3, p. 1150.

over to General John Imboden, earning General Lee's thanks and his regret that he had temporarily "imposed" on the division "such service."[19]

Major Charles A. Davidson, later to command his unit, the 1st Virginia Battalion, remembered that early in his provost service, in June, 1861, when the unit was Stonewall Jackson's provost guard, it had experienced "quite an easy time." Others were happy to be on provost duty, thinking it relatively easy and a reasonably safe place to spend the war. One who saw some merit in being with the provost was Robert Moore of the 17th Mississippi, a regiment that performed provost duty several times between December, 1862, and May, 1863. Some of Moore's diary entries record the agreeable side of provost service: "comfortable" quarters, freedom to travel throughout the city "at our leisure," and being excused from parades and drill while on provost guard.[20]

John Hubbard, a private in Forrest's cavalry, likewise remembered the more pleasant side of provost duty: "I had not entirely recovered my health, and would have more privileges on the road, though no less responsible service." This responsible service was also hinted at by Private Ephraim Anderson of the 1st Missouri Brigade, who categorized provost duties as "very heavy" and recalled that a company from the 3d Texas Cavalry had been required to assist the 1st Missouri on provost guard. Another western soldier, R. M. Collins of the Texas Brigade of the Army of Tennessee, who spent time with his brigade on provost duty at Tuscumbia, Alabama, in December, 1864, recalled how the "boys" quickly obtained a good supply of pork and how they "enjoyed" the service.[21]

As the war dragged on, many began to find provost service increasingly frustrating and hard. Major Davidson of the 1st Virginia, which from Christmas of 1863 was the provost guard of the Army of Northern Virginia, recollected his dissatisfaction with provost service just before the 1864 campaign. "I am tired and disgusted," he wrote, "with being on Provost duty and should greatly prefer being with the Brigade where there is a chance for promotion and where I could feel I was performing some service." By the winter of 1864–1865 provost service, according to William Fulton of the 5th Alabama, was far less

19. Charles T. Loehr, "The 'Old First' Virginia at Gettysburg: Men Who Fought to the Bitter End in the Greatest of Battles. The Famous Pickett Charge and the Part the Old First Virginia Played in It," *SHSP*, XXXII (rpr. 1979), 38; Harrison, *Pickett's Men*, 105–107.

20. Turner, "Major Charles A. Davidson," 20; Moore, *A Life for the Confederacy*, 122, 129–30, 144–48.

21. Hubbard, *Notes of a Private*, 183; Anderson, *Memoirs*, 207; Collins, *Chapters from the Unwritten History*, 267–68.

than agreeable, offering "great hardships by reason of increased and laborious guard duty and a lack of food."[22]

Complaints about the provost by civilians, soldiers, and state governments were echoed by the Confederacy's legislators, who were determined to end the abuses of power by provost marshals. Between September, 1862, and February, 1865, Congress tabled at least three resolutions proposing the abolition of provost marshals in positions where they had authority over civilians or in areas distant from the operational theaters of the armies. The common element of these resolutions is the inordinate amount of invective against the provost they contained. A typical example categorized the provost and the passport system as "a great and growing evil . . . a source of almost boundless oppression . . . wholly incompatible with public liberty and that no time should be lost in removing this nuisance . . . a grievance so overgrown and intolerable."[23] Yet even Congress recognized the necessity for some provost marshals. In March, 1865, Bill S.191 "legalized" a system of army and department provost that had been in existence for over three years.

Not unexpectedly, given their dramatic impact on the daily life of the Confederate citizen and their generally ugly reputation in the army, there were few who had anything laudatory to say about military police. Most of the favorable references are to specific individuals, mainly officers, who in their staff capacity won the praise of their superiors. The majority of these, as they pertain to battlefield exploits, have been described in the previous chapter. Only two or three references made favorable mention of provost units or the provost as a whole, and these latter often merely by inference.

In the eastern theater of operations, provost officers were occasionally commended for the way they carried out their police duties. One instance is in the report of Brigadier General George H. Steuart, who in September, 1862, had been appointed to command at Winchester, Virginia, by General Lee. "The quiet and good order prevailing in the town," wrote Steuart, "is due to the provost marshal (John B. Brooke) and to that excellent soldier, Captain J. Louis Smith, commanding the provost guard." A similar report in October by Brigadier General Wade Hampton reflected his satisfaction with his provost marshal during the occupation of Chambersburg, Pennsylvania: "I . . . immediately

22. Turner, "Major Charles A. Davidson," 36 (Davidson obviously never read Napier's comment that the labor and dangers of staff and regimental officers are generally in inverse ratio to their promotion); Fulton, *War Reminiscences*, 107.

23. *Journal of the Confederate Congress*, VII, 312.

made dispositions to establish a rigid provost guard . . . under the command of Captain J. P. Macfie, Second South Carolina . . . I am happy to say that good order was maintained during the whole of our stay." Macfie later earned another accolade from Hampton for his performance during the Sharpsburg campaign: "I beg to commend the conduct of Captain Macfie as provost marshal." Jeb Stuart likewise warmly commended Lieutenant G. M. Ryals, his provost marshal, for his service during the 1863 invasion of Pennsylvania, expressing his "special gratitude and praise" for Ryals' "untiring energy, force of character and devotion to duty."[24]

One soldier who earned praise for his participation in combat was Private Turner Goodall. It was said of another provost private, Hampton Hammond of the 14th North Carolina: "Liked by his comrades and never failed them . . . looked after the camp and always favored a member of the Anson Guards [Hammond's original company]. Bore the hardship of the entire war and was numbered with those who stacked arms at Appomattox."[25]

The western theater also provides examples of provost officers who gained distinction for their conduct. Colonel James O. Fuqua, provost marshal general of the District of the Mississippi, was commended by General John Breckinridge for his gallantry during the Confederate attack on Baton Rouge, Louisiana, in August, 1862. As related in the preceding chapter, Colonel Martin H. Cofer, provost marshal general of the Army of Tennessee at Chickamauga, was likewise congratulated for the admirable manner in which he organized and led the army's provost. Lieutenant J. W. Cochran, provost marshal of Preston Smith's brigade in Benjamin Cheatham's division at Chickamauga, was praised for his promptness and efficiency in performing his duties. Similarly, Major General Sterling Price's report on his foray into Missouri in September, 1864, includes his thanks to his provost marshal general, Lieutenant Colonel John P. Bull, for the "able, energetic and efficient discharge of his duties."[26]

24. *OR*, Vol. XIX, Pt. 2, pp. 57–58, 664–65; Vol. XXVII, Pt. 2, p. 710; McCabe, "Major Andrew Reid Venable, Jr.," 65; General J. E. B. Stuart, "Report of Operations After Gettysburg," *SHSP*, II (rpr. 1977), 77; General J. E. B. Stuart, "The Gettysburg Campaign," *SHSP*, VII (rpr. 1977), 433.

25. W. A. Smith, *The Anson Guards: Company C Fourteenth North Carolina Volunteers, 1861–1865* (1914; rpr. Wendell, N.C., 1978), 333.

26. Thompson, *History of the Orphan Brigade*, 133, 427–28; *OR*, Vol. XXX, Pt. 2, p. 109; General Sterling Price, "The Missouri Campaign of 1864," *SHSP*, VII (rpr. 1977), 231.

Favorable references to provost units are harder to come by. In Chapter 13 the meritorious conduct of the 5th Alabama Battalion, A. P. Hill's provost guard at the Wilderness in 1864, was described. Another provost unit particularly distinguished itself during the Confederate rout at Winchester in the Shenandoah in October, 1864. According to Jubal Early, the only "organized" body that left the field was the provost guard, whose "imposing appearance" checked pursuing cavalry and saved the army. The guard even got off with over a thousand Union prisoners. The *Official Records* mention one other provost unit that was well regarded, although its conduct on one occasion left something to be desired. This regiment, the 55th Georgia, numbering about five hundred men, served as the provost guard at Knoxville, Tennessee, and was, according to the commander of the brigade to which it belonged, noted for discipline and efficiency, "though the men did ride their colonel on a rail, which he never resented, but on promise to them of better behavior, was allowed to resume his command."[27] One wonders, in view of the 55th's treatment of its colonel, what was the state of discipline of the other regiments at Cumberland Gap.

Laudatory comments about the provost as a genre are even more difficult to find, but buried in the plethora of abuse they endured there is the occasional nugget of praise. The sheer volume of the abuse is in itself a backhanded compliment to the provost's vigor in the performance of their duties. Coulter, for example, notes that the provost's record in the enforcement of the passport system and the control of railroad travel was such that they became generally regarded as "ubiquitous and efficient." The large number of arrests of soldiers who attempted to travel without the vital passports is evidence of the provost's efficiency in that regard. Many narratives by Confederate soldiers refer to the certainty of provost inspection of passes and how those without papers would scatter for fear of being arrested. The Reverend J. L. Burrows, a Richmond clergyman, attested to the provost's efficiency in the winter of 1864–1865: "To leave the city was to be picked up by a patrol; to remain was to be hunted down."[28]

All in all, the dime's worth of praise received by the provost was totally immersed in the dollar's worth of blame that was their lot. For the Confeder-

27. Booth, *Personal Reminiscences,* 157; *OR,* Vol. XXX, Pt. 2, p. 611.

28. Coulter, *Confederate States,* 396; Barrett (ed.), *Yankee Rebel,* 80–81; Nisbet, *4 Years on the Firing Line,* 80; Burrows, "Recollections of Libby Prison," 91; Casler, *Four Years in the Stonewall Brigade,* 60.

acy's military police seldom was it "the best of times." For them, it was almost always "the worst of times."[29]

29. The quote is taken from the first line of Charles Dickens' *A Tale of Two Cities*, published in 1859. Dickens was widely read in the South during the war (see Charles Roland, *The Confederacy* [Chicago, 1960], 158). That redoubtable Virginian Edmund Ruffin finished reading the book on December 31, 1859 (Scarborough [ed.], *Diary of Edmund Ruffin*, I, 385).

15

Finis

To the legion of the lost ones
to the cohort of the damned.
RUDYARD KIPLING

It has been estimated that the Confederate States put something in the order of 750,000 men in the field, an astonishing achievement for a nation with a total population of about 12 million. The members of this force, both volunteers and those forced into the ranks by the first conscription act in the Western Hemisphere, participated in some ten thousand military actions, ranging from great battles like Chancellorsville and Chickamauga down to the most minute skirmishes. War on such a scale demanded the systematic and comprehensive marshaling of the country's wealth, including agricultural, industrial, commercial, transport, and that most precious of all a nation's resources, her people.

Southerners, who showed their preference in 1860 and 1861 for states' rights by voting to leave a Union that had gradually become anathema to them, were a proud and highly sensitive people. Inhabitants of a violent society, they were, as individuals and as a culture, quick to resent and retaliate against perceived threat or slight. The doctrine of states' rights suited well the Southern temperament, particularly that streak of individualism and independence which had contributed so much to secession. These attitudes were to accompany those who marched in the gray columns of the new army.

These two factors, the scale of the war and the nature of those who fought it, made strict direction of the nation's war effort absolutely vital. There was an obvious need for an organization that could assist line officers in the establishment and maintenance of good order and discipline over the masses of hurriedly raised and untrained Confederate soldiers. Nor could these controls be confined to the immediate operational areas of the armies. They had also to extend into the rear areas of the Confederacy to control the movement of men and generally maintain internal security. To meet these requirements, so essential to the prosecution of the War for Southern Independence, the provost system came into being in the field armies and in the department commands. The basis for the system was the Articles of War, which, as adopted in March, 1861, provided for military courts and provost marshals in the army.

Almost at once the system raised doubts and apprehension about just how far it would go and to whom it would apply. Civilian fears regarding the extension and the perversion of the original provost mandate were justified, for as the war expanded and intensified so too did the scope of their activity. Soon the provost's power reached far beyond the mere preservation of good order in the armies. With martial law providing blanket authority for whatever actions they chose to take, the provost were in a position to monitor virtually every activity of both the soldier and the civilian. Even when martial law was lifted, or in areas where it never existed, the harsh realities of war enabled the provost pretty well to proceed as they saw fit. Their presence became oppressively obvious throughout the nation. They were everywhere, and to an unprecedented degree, before or since, they influenced the lives of ordinary citizens.

The high profile of the provost and their enforcement of measures which civilians and even some military leaders regarded as intolerable tyranny made them a hated feature of Confederate life. Their unpopularity was constant and increasing as the war went on, regardless of attempts to attract and hold the best possible officers and men in provost service and the occasional purge that aimed at ensuring that provost personnel would continue to set an example of high moral and professional standards. This was particularly true in the selection of provost officers, for it was realized that the virtue and efficiency, or inefficiency, of the provost would depend largely on the officers.

To a considerable extent the competence of the provost officer had significant impact on the army. One author, writing of the British officer corps during the colonial wars of the last half of the nineteenth century, noted that because the officers dominated the army, they determined its quality and character. They set its moral and social mores, its standard of discipline, its organization, tactics, and strategy, and, most important, its attitudes and opinions. This was equally true of the Confederate provost and, in fact, of the Confederate army as a whole. There is no doubt that the appalling and crippling casualties to the army's leadership had, by 1864, much reduced its competence and tactical efficiency, making it less sure and responsive on the battlefield.[1]

1. Bryan Farwell, *Queen Victoria's Little Wars* (New York, 1972), xviii. Sommers, in *Richmond Redeemed*, 117, 139–40, 148, gives several examples. One particularly striking one is the abortive Confederate attempt to retake Fort Harrison, south of Richmond, in late September, 1864. Sommers calls it a "disgusting example of how his [Lee's] army's once-vaunted tactical cohesion had fallen apart."

Inevitably there were failures in personnel selection, misfits incapable of command, incompetents who had been banished to the provost, men of low intelligence and capability, and the tactless martinets who so infuriated soldier and civilian alike. Foremost among the latter was the provost marshal general of the Confederacy, Brigadier General John H. Winder, who was universally loathed and who for many epitomized the shortcomings of the men and the provost system itself. For this reason, and others, proposals to limit the powers of the military police, and even to abolish the entire apparatus, soon found vociferous supporters in Congress, in the army, in the press, and among the civilian population. When their proposal for abolition failed, some state governors suggested that state management and control of the provost was far preferable to leaving the police mandate to the care of the central government. When they were stymied in their bid for direct control, the governors and their supporters then attempted to limit provost authority to the immediate operational areas of the armies, a restriction that admittedly would have prevented many abuses against the civilian population but that would also have worsened the increasingly precarious military situation. The controversy raged on, still a subject for debate as late as February, 1865, at which time legislation sanctified in arrears the appointments and activities of the provost marshals who had been designated by both the field and department commanders since the first year of the war.

Another protracted debate ensued over the sources of provost manpower. At first, to avoid too sudden a shock to civilians, prominent individuals were appointed as provost marshals, but by June, 1863, such appointments had been abolished, primarily because of complaints by the military, who felt that untrained civilians were not capable of meeting the demands of such positions. This appeared to leave commanders free to appoint whomever they wished, but that was not the case. The war's insatiable appetite for men, chewing up volunteers and conscripts alike, meant that provost duties, which were essentially noncombatant, had to be carried out by militia, disabled men, and those who were too young or too old for active field service. Use of such classes of men adversely affected the provost's performance by preventing the selection of those best qualified to act as military policemen. It also reduced police capabilities because of the sheer physical incapacity of the disabled, the young, and the elderly, and it made the provost a target for contempt and derision. This is not to say that the provost did not continue to employ large numbers of men who were liable to active service. From the conscription officer's point of view, the provost's determination to retain able-bodied men was contemptible and designed only to keep shirkers and "bomb-proofs" in the rear. What better evidence was there of the provost's uselessness and perfidy?

It is apparent that the provost was not, in fact or in theory, a separate and distinct corps of the army in the same way as the infantry or the cavalry. Provost duties were carried out by individual officers, soldiers, and units detailed for varying periods to perform police tasks. Most details were for extended periods of time, but conversely, units selected for provost duty generally performed police duties for only a few days or weeks. The notable exceptions are the 25th Georgia Battalion (Atlanta Provost Battalion), which was the only unit identified as bearing the "provost" designation, and the three infantry battalions that formed the provost guards of two of the corps of the Army of Northern Virginia and the army itself. These three infantry battalions were the 1st North Carolina, provost guard of the 2d Corps from June, 1863; the 5th Alabama, which took up provost duty in the 3d Corps shortly after Gettysburg; and the 1st (Irish) Virginia, which first served as provost in June, 1861. The provost service of the three is well documented, particularly the 1st Virginia, for which strength returns are complete for almost the whole of the last two years of the war.

Unfortunately, although they most probably existed, no units could be positively identified as the provost guards of the 1st Corps, Army of Northern Virginia, and the Army of Tennessee. Many other units were identified on provost service in the rear areas, thus proving conclusively that the provost system was in full operation in the departmental commands of the Confederacy.

Confederate provost performed basically the same duties that provost do now. The purely military duties such as measures against stragglers and deserters, the control of prisoners of war, and the maintenance of military discipline, plus additional duties associated with the passport system and martial law and a number of secondary tasks, were highly expensive in manpower, a commodity never in adequate supply. Faced with this multitude of demanding and widespread tasks, the provost's major problem was simply that there was not enough of them to do all the jobs that had to be done. As well, extra men were required to support the provost establishment: clerks and other administrative personnel, doctors, and ordnance and transportation staff added to the manpower bill. Some idea of the numbers involved is obvious even from the limited strength returns available. The Army of Northern Virginia, for example, had a provost establishment of about 1,700 officers and men in mid-1862. The Atlanta Provost Battalion in July and August, 1863, averaged over 170 officers and men, and nine months later the manpower available for provost duty in Richmond stood at over 1,200. Similarly, the nine provost districts within Leonidas Polk's Department of Alabama, Mississippi, and East Louisiana were a major consumer of manpower. In August, 1864, just six of the twenty-four posts in the department listed a total of 357 officers and men on provost duty. Extrapolating this figure, almost 1,500 men would have been on police duty in Polk's department alone.

Perhaps the primary duty of the grayclad provost was the maintenance of good order and discipline. The gentleman private of the Southern armies, with his "I'm as good as any man" attitude, had a constant tendency to ignore orders. This had a pronounced effect on many battles. Without the presence of the provost to ensure proper discipline, many of the tactical victories achieved by Confederate arms might have turned out otherwise. Resistance to regulation and control and frequent dedicated pursuit of loot, cards, wine, and women made direction of Johnny Reb's activities a major challenge for the provost.

What could happen when the provost were unable to enforce discipline is clearly illustrated by the aftermath of Pemberton's surrender at Vicksburg. His men having been relieved of their weapons, the provost could not prevent them leaving for their homes, thus breaking up the force which Pemberton had hoped to keep intact until such time as it was exchanged and could fight again. In spite of this event and other serious breakdowns of discipline, there is no doubt that the prodigious efforts of both the provost and commanders at all levels to impose discipline were remarkably successful. Brigadier General Arthur Manigault of the Army of Tennessee attested that a carefully selected and well-officered provost soon became "a terror to all evil-doers and triflers, and assisted much in the preservation of discipline."[2] The combat record of the Army of Northern Virginia is similarly indicative of provost success.

Provost efforts were unfortunately hampered by the weaknesses of the military judicial system, which was noted for its inconsistent and often lenient punishment of offenders. The initial court-martial system was found so ineffective that in October, 1862, legislation established field military courts, which, it was hoped, would be more responsive to the disciplinary needs of the army. But these courts, much to the consternation of senior field commanders such as Lee and Beauregard, often meted out the most inadequate sentences for such heinous offenses as desertion and violence against superiors.

The imprecise wording of the regulations pertaining to these courts and the mistaken impression on the part of some officers that civilians were subject to military courts and military arrest, created other problems for the provost.

2. Tower (ed.), *A Carolinian Goes to War,* 166.

Some of these were self-inflicted because of a lack of tact and discretion in enforcing the laws. In short order the issue became a major one, once again embroiling the military police and the army in acrimonious dispute with the state governments and with the population as a whole. There is no question that the provost were sometimes guilty of abusing their powers of arrest. Commissions established to investigate irregularities often set the provost's prisoners free. From 1862 on, in an attempt to prevent abuse, the provost were required to submit full reports of any arrests they made. This applied even during those infrequent periods when the president had been able to suspend the writ of *habeas corpus* and institute martial law.

Provost administration of martial law led to tremendous controversy both in and out of the army. Accusations of provost abuses such as the assumption of powers beyond the scope of martial law made the air thick with cries of usurpation, despotism, tyranny, and intolerable oppression. This was inevitable since martial law brought the provost into close and daily contact with civilians. The provost's power, which could so thoroughly monitor civilian activities, was distressing and disturbing, no matter how tactfully it was exercised. The courts, the civilian police, even the economy functioned as the provost wished, and the fact that these measures were instituted as a result of direct enemy threat did not mitigate civilian unhappiness with the regulations and those who had to enforce them. Rumors of ill treatment of civilians incarcerated in military prisons also led to investigations of the provost system, and even though prison officials were exonerated the bad press was not to the advantage of the provost. In sum, enforcement of martial law severely damaged the provost's image, and to some degree it tarnished that of the army as a whole. Even worse, military interference with the customary civil liberties brought the government into disrepute, a development the beleaguered Confederacy could ill afford.

Another major provost task was the control of movement, including that on the dilapidated rail network. This was accomplished by means of the passport system. Although only a temporary restriction under martial law, passports were to become a permanent feature of Confederate life, spreading an apparatus of provost checkpoints, stations, and units throughout the entire country. The initial purpose of the passport—"to restrain stragglers and deserters, prevent communication with the enemy and detect spies"—was thus perverted, leading to total control of the movement of soldiers and civilians.[3] The provost's vigor

3. Beers, *Guide to the Archives,* 260.

and diligence in the supervision of the passport system were notorious, and there are many accounts of the efficiency with which they enforced the regulations. In Richmond, for example, attempts to evade the constant passport checks were almost always futile, and those who tried to travel without the authority of a passport were bold indeed.

Unquestionably, the passport system was of great benefit to Confederate conduct of the war, but there were unfortunate side effects. Furloughed men, for example, often suffered the partial loss of much deserved leave because of the necessity to obtain passports. Controls also infringed on the liberties of the ordinary citizen, who could not see why the military should enjoy such powers. The inconvenience of obtaining passports and the arrogance of some of the provost left the civilian embittered and enraged, causing him to put the blame for the situation squarely on the shoulders of those who had to enforce the regulations. In the eyes of many, passports and the ever-present provost, many of them fit men who should have been at the front, were an "unnecessary annoyance . . . of no possible benefit to the country."[4]

Once the armies were in the field, the provost were forced to combat the colossal straggling and desertion. These offenses, which were quickly recognized as severe limitations on military strength and performance, proved extremely difficult to control, and in spite of the most rigorous measures, provost efforts were never truly adequate. Perhaps the classic example of the pernicious effects of straggling was the Battle of Sharpsburg, where it is estimated that fifteen thousand stragglers were absent from the thin line of battle, causing Lee deep concern for the future of his army. Provost guards enjoyed mixed success in checking the problem throughout the war. There were the good times like late 1862 and early 1863, when Confederate prospects were bright and there was a very perceptible falling off in straggling. This was only temporary, however, for as Southern hopes dimmed and then vanished, so too did more and more men from the armies.

It was not just temporary absence but determined intent to cease fighting that vastly complicated the provost's antideserter measures, for though straggling was localized to more or less the immediate operational areas of the armies, deserters had to be searched for throughout the vast Confederacy. The problem was absolutely immense; by the autumn of 1864 it was estimated that some hundred thousand men had seceded from the war, a figure which, as General Lee had warned, brought calamity.

4. *OR*, Vol. XLII, Pt. 3, p. 1150.

As might be expected, it was impossible for the provost to stem desertion, which after all was but a symptom of a deeper and more general cancer in the body of the Confederacy. To put it bluntly, the provost failed in their task—the arrest and return of deserters to their units—but to be fair, cure of the disease was beyond the capability of any one agency of the Confederate States. Inadequate and inconsistent punishment and obstruction by the various state political and judicial authorities of provost attempts to check it had been allowed to go on for too long. The situation, serious at first, became hopeless, and with this, came defeat.

The provost were more successful in controlling over two hundred thousand Federal prisoners of war. It was essentially a far simpler task, involving only escort and some custodial responsibility, but it was a vital chore and one that the provost performed to the satisfaction of all. A bonus for the provost was that their contact with the prisoners enabled them to glean information of military value, which, when passed to commanders, earned them some gratitude for their generally unappreciated efforts. Similarly, their efficiency in performing many of the secondary duties that fell to them earned the provost considerable praise. Their responsibility for such diverse tasks as control of Negroes, shipping, preventing trade with the enemy, executions, and the security of property are an indication of just how much the army and the government relied on the provost.

The devotion of provost officers and men to their country is evident in their active participation in combat against the Yankee invader. Inevitably there were provost guardsmen who gave their tomorrows for the Confederacy. The number of provost officers, and less frequently men and units, who received the commendation of their superiors for conduct under fire is noteworthy, particularly in view of provost status as a "nonfighting" branch of the army. Controversy over whether the provost were included in line-of-battle strength is immaterial; what is relevant is that when and where necessary the provost did their share of the fighting. Other provost operational activities, such as acting as advance and rear guards and the planning and execution of reconnaissance missions, were much to their credit.

Otherwise, however, the provost were singularly unappreciated. It seemed that whatever they did they were wrong, useless, and ineffective, never there when they were required, and yet, at the same time, they were guilty of unwarranted interference, skulking from the army, and much other intolerable behavior. This was the particular provost dilemma: there was no pleasing anyone; it was possible only to offend and annoy. The army, the press, the judiciary, the state governments, the Congress, and the people were unanimous—everyone loathed the corrupt, incompetent, cowardly, "plug-ugly" provost!

Regardless of the restrictions placed on their power, the criticism that frustrated and hampered their efforts, the chronic manpower shortage, and the necessity to use men pathetically unfit for police duties, it must be stated that the provost's performance was generally commendable. Within the limitations set by others, over which they had no control, and considering the masses of people that had to be controlled, with no historical precedent to guide them, the provost must rate high marks for efficiency. In short, their record borders on the amazing. That the Confederate States of America could maintain her armies in the field for four long years against an enemy vastly superior in every aspect, except perhaps fighting spirit, was in no small way creditable to the efforts of the Rebel watchdogs. Let Stonewall Jackson's words stand as their epitaph: "Duty is ours; consequences are God's."

Appendix I

Provost Personnel

This appendix lists provost personnel for whom substantive information was located; provost personnel merely mentioned by name in the various sources are not included. Sources following the descriptive data for each individual are for the benefit of those who may wish to read further about specific individuals. Ranks given are the highest that can be documented for each individual and not necessarily his rank while on provost duty. Dates given do not delineate the exact periods personnel were on provost service since in most cases only the date of appointment or detachment can be documented, and therefore the actual length of employment cannot be determined. Some entries do include "from-to" dates, but it is possible that personnel were on provost service after the dates shown.

Abbott, Captain Joel Houghton
  8th Virginia Cavalry. Provost marshal of the Department of Southwestern Virginia, May, 1862. Obituary, *Confederate Veteran,* XXXIV (rpr. 1983), 64.
Adams, Private J. M.
  C Company, 4th Texas. Detailed to Texas Brigade provost guard in April, 1863. Simpson, *Hood's Texas Brigade: A Compendium,* 113.
Aikens, Private James O.
  G Company, 4th Texas. Detailed to Texas Brigade provost guard in the winter of 1864. Simpson, *Hood's Texas Brigade: A Compendium,* 139.
Aldrich, Captain Edward
  Deputy provost marshal, Missouri State Guard, November, 1861. Bevier, *History of the First and Second Missouri Confederate Brigades,* 72.
Alexander, Captain G. W.
  Assistant provost marshal in Richmond in June, 1862, and still in that position in December, 1863. Also served as commandant of Castle Thunder in Richmond and then commanded the Salisbury, North Carolina, prison in May and June, 1864. Resigned December 31, 1864. *OR,* Ser. II. Vol. VI, p. 440; Thomas, *Confederate State of Richmond,* 154; Brown, *Salisbury Prison,* 168; Crute, *Confederate Staff Officers,* 212.
Alexander, Lieutenant J. P.
  Provost marshal of Ross's cavalry brigade at Deasonsville, Mississippi, in February, 1865. *OR,* Vol. XLIX, Pt. 1, p. 998.

Allnoch, Private William

F Company, 5th Texas. Detailed to Texas Brigade provost guard in September, 1862. Simpson, *Hood's Texas Brigade: A Compendium,* 212.

Alvis, Private William D.

I Company, 42d Virginia. Listed with division provost, Gordon's 2d Corps, at Appomattox. Brock (ed.), *Paroles,* 229.

Anderson, Lieutenant Colonel John H.

2d Battalion North Carolina Junior Reserves. Commanded provost guard at Weldon, North Carolina, Department of North Carolina and Southern Virginia, in September, 1864. *OR,* Vol. XLII, Pt. 2, p. 1226.

Armistead, Brigadier General Lewis A.

Appointed provost marshal of the Army of Northern Virginia on September 6, 1862, by General Order 103 for only a few days. *OR,* Vol. XIX, Pt. 2, pp. 592, 596; Duncan, "Marylanders and the Invasion of 1862," 185.

Armstrong, Captain F. M.

In May, 1864, Armstrong's unattached cavalry company was ordered to report to Lieutenant Colonel M. T. Polk, post commandant at Aberdeen, Mississippi, for provost duty. *OR,* Vol. XXXIX, Pt. 2, p. 611.

Austin, Private Frank

C Company, 4th Kentucky. Detailed to provost at Jonesboro, Georgia, in December, 1864, and remained on provost duty to the end of the war. Thompson, *History of the Orphan Brigade,* 639.

Ayers, Provost I. T.

I Company, 1st Virginia Regiment. On provost duty at the Battle of Groveton in August, 1862. Slightly wounded. Spence, "Reports of the First, Seventh and Seventeenth Virginia Regiments in 1862," 263.

Baker, Lieutenant Colonel T. H.

46th and 55th Tennessee. Permanently disabled from wounds suffered in July, 1863. Subsequently served as chief provost marshal of the Second District of Alabama with headquarters at Tuscaloosa. *OR,* Vol. XXXII, Pt. 3, pp. 611, 745–48, 824–25; Veterans Records, National Archives.

Bard, Captain Samuel

Appointed temporary provost marshal of Ascension Parish, Louisiana, on September 8, 1862. *OR,* XV, 805–806.

Beale, Major Richard Lee Turberville

Provost marshal at Camp Lee, Virginia, in December, 1861. *OR,* Vol. V, pp. 990–91, 996–97; Beale, *History of the Ninth Virginia Cavalry,* 11.

Berry, Private William

M Company, 6th Alabama. Listed with division provost, Grimes's division, 2d Corps, at Appomattox. Brock (ed.), *Paroles,* 244.

Birdsong, Private Washington F.

F Company, 21st Georgia. Detailed to provost guard, Doles-Cook Brigade, November, 1863. Thomas, *History of the Doles-Cook Brigade,* 426.

Blanc, Jules L.

Appointed as temporary provost marshal of St. Tammany Parish, Louisiana, September 8, 1862. *OR,* XV, 805–806.

Bledsoe, Private William H.

E Company, 1st Virginia Battalion. Listed as a clerk in the Provost Marshal's Department in the Appomattox roster. Brock, *Paroles,* 452.

Blount, Lieutenant Colonel Robert P.

Captain, F Company, 5th (later 9th) Alabama Battalion, August 20, 1861. In April, 1862, as a lieutenant colonel, Blount reported to General John C. Breckinridge at Corinth, Mississippi. In June he was with Beauregard at Baldwin, Mississippi. Blount was captured at Warrenton, Virginia, on October 1, and his parole listed him as lieutenant colonel on Longstreet's staff. On November 20, 1862, in a letter to President Davis, Blount signed himself as provost marshal of Longstreet's corps. In June, 1863, he was listed as the provost marshal at Hamilton's Crossing, Virginia. Correspondence of March, 1865, indicates that Blount was on duty at Mobile, Alabama, in the summer of 1864. *OR,* Vol. LI, Pt. 2, pp. 721, 1065; Ser. II, Vol. IV, pp. 949–50; Crute, *Confederate Staff Officers,* 123; Veterans Records, National Archives.

Bolen, Captain James N.

Commanded a dismounted cavalry company on provost duty at Jackson, Mississippi, in January, 1863. *OR,* Vol. XVII, Pt. 2, p. 819.

Bond, Captain Frank A.

1st Maryland Cavalry. Provost marshal of Gettysburg, July 1–3, 1863. Bond, "Company A, First Maryland Cavalry," 79.

Booth, Private Albert

G Company, 6th Alabama. Listed with 2d Corps provost guard in April, 1864. Brock (ed.), *Paroles,* 243.

Bowen, Private J. M.

K Company, 5th Texas. Assigned to Texas Brigade provost guard in April, 1864. Simpson, *Hood's Texas Brigade: A Compendium,* 244.

Bowie, Captain M. L.

6th Alabama. His regiment was on provost duty at Martinsburg, Virginia, in June, 1863. *OR,* Vol. XXVII, Pt. 2, p. 599.

Bowles, Private William Vincent

K Company, 44th Georgia. Wounded at Chancellorsville. Detailed to provost, Doles-Cook Brigade, November, 1863. Surrendered at Appomattox. Thomas, *History of the Doles-Cook Brigade,* 585.

Boyle, Major Cornelius

Provost marshal of Virginia forces at Camp Pickens, Virginia, from August 21 to November 14, 1861. On the latter date he signed himself "Provost Marshal, Army of the Potomac," in a letter to General Winder. In May, 1862, he was provost marshal at Gordonsville and was still there as late as March 27, 1865. General Lee, in correspondence of December 30, 1863, referred to Boyle as provost marshal of the Army of Northern Virginia. In a letter to Secretary of War Seddon from Gordonsville, dated August 26, 1864, Boyle signed as "Maj and Pro Mar, Army of Northern Virginia." See entry for Major Bridgford. *OR,* Vol. XII, Pt. 3, p. 894; Vol. XXV, Pt. 2, p. 664; Vol. XXVII, Pt. 3, pp. 891, 956; Vol. XLII, Pt. 3, pp. 1290–91; Vol. XLVI, Pt. 3, p. 1359; Ser. II, Vol. II, p. 1375; Ser. IV, Vol. III, pp. 604–606, 611–13, 615, 624; Mosby, "Stuart in the Gettysburg Campaign," 196; Freeman and McWhiney (eds.), *Lee's Dispatches,* 300; War Department, Collection of Confederate Records, Record Group 109, Chap. IX, Vol. 199½; Veterans Records, National Archives.

Bradfield, Major William

Provost marshal of Marshall County, Texas, in July, 1862. Heartsill, *Fourteen Hundred and 91 Days,* 81.

Bradford, Captain J. W.

Appointed provost marshal of Hood's Texas Brigade in July, 1862. Simpson, *Hood's Texas Brigade: A Compendium,* 7.

Bradford, Captain William K.

In a list of general and staff officers serving with the Department of South Carolina, Georgia, and Florida, dated January 27, 1864, Bradford was shown as provost marshal, District of Georgia. *OR,* Vol. XXXV, Pt. 1, p. 552.

Brenan, Lieutenant W.

Provost marshal at Weldon, North Carolina, on May 23, 1863. *OR,* Ser. II, Vol. V, p. 957.

Bridgford, Major David B.

Bridgford was a captain commanding B Company, 1st Virginia Battalion, in May, 1861, and was promoted to major in October, 1862. He and his unit were the provost marshal and provost guard respectively of Jackson's corps. Bridgford stated, "I served with Gen. T. J. Jackson as a Capt. up to the time I was commissioned Maj. of the 1st Va Bn, when I was ordered to him as Provost Marshal of his corps, in which capacity I served up to the time of his death." Bridgford continued, "I was then ordered to report to Gen R. E. Lee and have since . . . filled the position of Acting Provost Marshal, ANV, and commanding posts of the army." During the summer of 1863 Bridgford is shown variously as "commanding post" at Winchester, Culpeper Court House, and Orange Court House, Virginia. In December, 1863, Bridgford, signing as "Actg Pro Mar, A.N. Va.," wrote to President Davis asking the appointment of provost marshal. The request was recommended by Generals Ewell, A. P. Hill, Early, R. E. Rodes, E. Johnson, and C. M. Wilcox, but General Lee's comment was "Maj. Boyle has occupied this position and performed its duties and I know of no reason for a change." Throughout the winter of 1864–1865 Bridgford was referred to in correspondence as "On detached service Acting Provost Marshal Army of Northern Virginia." The Appomattox roster lists him as commanding the provost guard and provost marshal of the army. Although it appears that Major Cornelius Boyle (see entry above) was by title provost marshal of the Army of Northern Virginia, from all evidence he was not with the army in the field and his functions were carried out by Bridgford, the "acting" provost marshal. Douglas, *I Rode with Stonewall*, 98, photo of Bridgford, provost marshal, Jackson's Army of the Valley; Krick, *Lee's Colonels*, 59. An officer of the 1st Virginia said that Bridgford had "the gift of attracting the notice of superior officers, but . . . did not measure up"; Schenck, *Up Came Hill*, 229; Early, "Relative Numbers," 36; Brock (ed.), *Paroles*, 449, 453; Bidgood, "List of General Officers," 166; *OR*, Vol. XL, Pt. 3, p. 765; XXI, 635, 641–42, 1074; Vol. XXIX, Pt. 2, p. 899; Vol. XLII, Pt. 1, p. 870; Vol. XLII, Pt. 3, p. 1156; Vol. XLVI, Pt. 1, p. 1267; Vol. LI, Pt. 2, p. 721; Veterans Records, National Archives.

Brooke, Lieutenant F.

30th Virginia Infantry. With provost guard, Pickett's division. Bidgood, "List of General Officers," 176; Harrison, *Pickett's Men*, 192.

Brooke, Captain John B.

Provost marshal at Winchester, Virginia, in October, 1862. *OR*, Vol. XIX, Pt. 2, pp. 664–65; Howard, *Recollections*, 178.

Brooks, Lieutenant John E.

Deputy provost marshal, Missouri State Guard, November, 1861. Bevier, *History of the First and Second Missouri Confederate Brigades*, 72.

Brown, Colonel Alex H.

Appointed assistant provost marshal of Charleston, South Carolina, May 12, 1862. Brown, a prewar chief of police in Charleston, was described as an arbitrary and overbearing man. On June 9, 1862, he replaced Colonel Johnson Hagood as provost marshal and three days later was also commanding the provost guard, the Charleston reserve regiment. Beers, *Guide to the Archives*, 285; Hagood, *Memoirs*, 74, 76–80, 82–83.

Brown, Private David O.

I Company, 12th Georgia. Detailed to provost guard, Doles-Cook Brigade. Surrendered at Appomattox. Thomas, *History of the Doles-Cook Brigade*, 318.

Brown, Private Peter M.

27th North Carolina. Detailed to provost duty February, 1864. Sloan, *Reminiscences*, 121.

Bull, Lieutenant Colonel John P.

Appointed provost marshal general of the Army of Missouri about September 27,

1864, and served in that capacity until at least December 7, 1864. Price, "Missouri Campaign of 1864," 231; *OR,* Vol. XLI, Pt. 1, p. 648; Crute, *Confederate Staff Officers,* 158.

Bullock, Captain W. F.

Appointed assistant provost marshal general of the Department of Alabama, Mississippi, and East Louisiana by Provost Marshal General Colonel T. H. Taylor on July 8, 1864. War Department, Collection of Confederate Records, Record Group 109, Chap. II, Vol. 196.

Burthe, Judge Victor

Appointed provost marshal of Jefferson Parish, Louisiana, under authority of martial law on March 15, 1862. *OR,* VI, 857–58.

Butler, Lieutenant J. G.

A Company, 3d Florida. Commanded provost guard of Trigg's brigade, Preston's division, at Chickamauga. *OR,* Vol. XXX, Pt. 2, p. 234.

Butler, Private John B.

B Company, 1st Texas. On detached service with provost in July, 1863. Simpson, *Hood's Texas Brigade: A Compendium,* 21.

Butler, Major W. P.

Provost marshal, 1st Brigade, Confederate States Army of the Potomac at Fairfax Court House, Virginia, in July, 1861. Davis, *Battle at Bull Run,* xi.

Cabell, Lieutenant Colonel George Craighead

Major, 18th Virginia, May, 1861. Appointed provost marshal of Petersburg on October 1, 1863, replacing Lieutenant N. B. Hawes. Appointed provost marshal of the Department of North Carolina in January, 1864. Promoted to lieutenant colonel in July, 1864. *OR,* Vol. LI, Pt. 2, p. 771; Krick, *Lee's Colonels,* 68; Veterans Records, National Archives.

Calhoun, Private Andrew P.

H Company, 12th Alabama. Detached to provost, Grimes's division, 2d Corps, at Appomattox. Brock (ed.), *Paroles,* 245.

Cameron, Lieutenant Colonel John F.

Announced as provost marshal of Wheeler's cavalry corps on January 21, 1865. As a captain he was Wheeler's provost marshal after the evacuation of Atlanta. *OR,* Vol. XLVII, Pt. 2, p. 1035.

Capers, Brigadier General Ellison

Commanding officer, 24th South Carolina. On provost duty at Jonesboro, Georgia, in September, 1864. Promoted to colonel during the Atlanta campaign and brigadier general in March, 1865. *OR,* Vol. XXXIX, Pt. 2, p. 831; Warner, *Generals in Gray,* 43–44.

Capers, First Lieutenant J. H.

In the Appomattox roster listed as the adjutant of the provost guard of the Army of Northern Virginia. Brock (ed.), *Paroles,* 449.

Caperton, A. T.

Provost marshal, Monroe County, Virginia, in November, 1862. Younger (ed.), *Inside the Confederate Government,* 42–43.

Carley, Private Martin F.

G Company, 4th Texas. Detailed to Texas Brigade provost in December, 1863. Simpson, *Hood's Texas Brigade: A Compendium,* 140.

Carmack, Captain J. M.

Appointed deputy provost marshal of the Eighth District of Tennessee with headquarters at Athens on September 25, 1862. He was the provost marshal of Athens in January, 1862. *OR,* Ser. II, Vol. I, p. 878; Vol. IV, pp. 899–900.

Carnes, Private William C.

L Company, 1st Texas. Assigned to Texas Brigade provost guard in February, 1864. Simpson, *Hood's Texas Brigade: A Compendium,* 79.

Carrington, Lieutenant Colonel Isaac Howell

Major, 38th Virginia, June 12, 1861, but dropped during spring 1862 reorganization. Carrington was provost marshal of Richmond from July 14, 1863, to the evacuation. He was listed as commanding the post of Richmond in May, 1864. He was also assistant provost marshal under General Winder, and for a short time after Winder's death in February, 1865, he was acting provost marshal general of the Confederacy. Krick, *Lee's Colonels,* 73–74; Beers, *Guide to the Archives,* 281–82; Jones, "Roster," 7; Ewell, "Evacuation of Richmond," 248; Hunter, "Post-Bellum Mortality Among Confederates," 273; Manarin (ed.), *Richmond at War,* 571; Hesseltine, *Civil War Prisons,* 121; *OR,* Vol. XLII, Pt. 2, p. 1204; Vol. XLVI, Pt. 1, p. 1293; Ser. II, Vol. VII, pp. 422–23; Hoehling and Hoehling, *Day Richmond Died,* 112; Veterans Records, National Archives.

Carter, Provost C. C.

B Company, 1st Virginia. Seriously wounded when on provost duty at Groveton in August, 1862. Spence, "Reports of the First, Seventh and Seventeenth Virginia Regiments in 1862," 262.

Cary, Lieutenant Colonel John Baytop

Lieutenant colonel, 32d Virginia, July, 1861. Acting provost marshal at Yorktown in early 1862. Dropped at May reorganization. Krick, *Lee's Colonels,* 76.

Caton, Private H. W.

B Company, 4th Texas. Detailed as "division detective," Hood's division, on April 4, 1863. Simpson, *Hood's Texas Brigade: A Compendium,* 105.

Cecil, Captain Giles

Appointed deputy provost marshal of the Second District of Tennessee, with headquarters at Jonesborough, on September 25, 1862. *OR,* Ser. II, Vol. IV, pp. 899–900.

Chilton, Captain Frank B.

After the 1864 Louisiana campaign, in which Chilton was disabled by wounds, he was appointed provost marshal of Navasota, Texas. Polley, *Hood's Texas Brigade,* 292.

Chinn, R. H.

Provost marshal of Matagorda, Texas, in July, 1862. *OR, IX,* 724–26.

Chisholm, Colonel Ted

Provost marshal in northern Alabama in October, 1862. Hubbard, *Notes of a Private,* 68.

Chisholm, Private Thomas

E Company, 5th Alabama. With provost guard of Grimes's division, 2d Corps, at Appomattox. Brock (ed.), *Paroles,* 242.

Churchwell, Colonel William Montgomery

34th Tennessee. Appointed provost marshal of the Department of East Tennessee by Major General E. Kirby Smith on April 19, 1862. He was still in this appointment when he died on August 18, 1862. He was replaced by Colonel John E. Toole. *OR,* Vol. X, Pt. 1, pp. 636–37; Ser. II, Vol. I, pp. 883–88, 929; Ser. II, Vol. II, pp. 1423– 24, 1426; Ser. II, Vol. III, p. 876; Ser. II, Vol. IV, pp. 834–35; Veterans Records, National Archives.

Clack, Major Franklin Hulse

Commanded the Confederate Guards Response Battalion at Shiloh, where the battalion may have been on provost duty. *OR,* Vol. X, Pt. 1, p. 512.

Claiborne, Colonel Thomas

Provost marshal general of the Army of Tennessee under Albert Sidney Johnston. Obituary, *Confederate Veteran,* XXI (rpr. 1983), 302.

Cochran, Lieutenant J. W.

Provost marshal of Smith's brigade, Cheatham's division, at Chickamauga. *OR,* Vol. XXX, Pt. 2, p. 109.

Cochran, Lieutenant Colonel Thomas M.

2d Arkansas Cavalry. In March, 1864, provost marshal general on the staff of Brigadier General J. R. Chalmers, a division commander under Nathan Bedford Forrest. Crute, *Confederate Staff Officers,* 33.

Cockrill, Second Lieutenant D. H.

A Company, 2d Virginia. Provost marshal of Gordon's corps at Appomattox. Brock (ed.), *Paroles,* 84.

Cofer, Colonel Martin Harding

Commanding officer, 6th Kentucky. He was severely wounded at Shiloh. Cofer was appointed provost marshal general of the Army of Tennessee after Chickamauga in September, 1863, but returned to his unit in May, 1864. He was again appointed provost marshal general on August 29, 1864, relieving Lieutenant Colonel G. A. Henry. Cofer was announced as provost marshal general of Joseph E. Johnston's army in North Carolina on March 31, 1865, and served in that capacity until the surrender. Thompson, *History of the Orphan Brigade,* 423–27, photo of Cofer; Davis, *Orphan*

Brigade, 187, 204, 222; *OR,* Vol. XXXVIII, Pt. 5, pp. 988, 1000; Vol. XLVII, Pt. 3, p. 729; Veterans Records, National Archives.

Collins, J. H.

Appointed temporary provost marshal of East Feliciana Parish, Louisiana, on September 8, 1862. *OR,* XV, 805–806.

Colville, Captain W. E.

Appointed deputy provost marshal of the Ninth District of Tennessee, with headquarters at Washington, on September 25, 1862. *OR,* Ser. II, Vol. IV, pp. 899–900.

Corley, Sergeant Richard H.

B Company, 12th Alabama. With provost guard, Grimes's division, 2d Corps, at Appomattox. Brock (ed.), *Paroles,* 244.

Counts, Private George W.

E Company, 5th Texas. Wounded at Gaines' Mill, June 27, 1862, and detailed to provost in September, 1862. Simpson, *Hood's Texas Brigade: A Compendium,* 206.

Crabtree, Private J. W.

I Company, 4th Texas. Detached to provost duty April–June, 1863. Simpson, *Hood's Texas Brigade: A Compendium,* 156.

Craven, Reverend Doctor Braxton

Commandant of Salisbury prison in early 1862. Failed to receive a commission and returned to duties as president of Trinity College near High Point, North Carolina. Brown, *Salisbury Prison,* 40–41, 59, 168.

Crigen, Provost W. H.

B Company, 1st Virginia. Wounded at Groveton in August, 1862, while on provost duty. Spence, "Reports of the First, Seventh and Seventeenth Virginia Regiments in 1862," 262.

Crimm, Private Warren W.

G Company, 3d Alabama. With provost of Grime's division, 2d Corps, at Appomattox. Brock (ed.), *Paroles,* 240.

Croom, Captain Allen

Listed with provost guard, Second Subdistrict, Kinston, North Carolina, in January, 1865. *OR,* Vol. XLVI, Pt. 2, p. 1187.

Crow, Sergeant B. M.

One source noted that a "careful search of personnel service files . . . failed to reveal anyone serving as sgt by the name of Crow in the Richmond provost marshal's office. . . . Since extant records . . . give no clue . . . it is reasonable to assume that he was a civilian." It is known that a Sergeant Crow was in the provost office in November and December, 1862. Could he have been Sergeant B. M. Crow, 1st Virginia Regiment, who was wounded at Groveton in August, 1862, along with a number of other provost soldiers? Another source noted that a Sergeant Crow was in charge of a soldiers' home in Richmond at the time of the evacuation of the city. It was used to house soldiers who were in Richmond without leave. Worsham, *One of*

Jackson's Foot Cavalry, 92–93; Spence, "Reports of the First, Seventh and Seventeenth Virginia Regiments in 1862," 262; Sturgis, "About the Burning of Richmond," 474.

Cullen, Captain

Assistant provost marshal at Winchester, Virginia, in July, 1863. Park, "War Diary," 14; Park, "12th Alabama Infantry," 245.

Culley, Private Horace B.

H Company, 6th Kentucky. Following the evacuation of Atlanta, he was detached for service with Captain Cameron, provost marshal of Wheeler's cavalry corps, and surrendered with the guard at Greensboro, North Carolina. Thompson, *History of the Orphan Brigade,* 793.

Cuvellier, Adjutant P. C.

Relieved from duty in the Provost Marshal's Office at Mobile, Alabama, and appointed adjutant of the Provost Marshal's Office, Department of Alabama, Mississippi, and East Louisiana on January 27, 1864. War Department, Collection of Confederate Records, Record Group 109, Chap. II, Vol. 196.

Danley, Lieutenant Colonel Ben F.

3d Arkansas Cavalry. Appointed chief provost marshal, Trans-Mississippi Department, on July 10, 1862. He had previously been provost marshal of Pulaski County. *OR,* LIII, 811–12.

Davidson, Major Charles A.

Served with the 1st Virginia (Irish) Battalion, provost guard of Jackson's corps and then of the Army of Northern Virginia. He was commanding the battalion at the end of the war. Turner, "Major Charles A. Davidson," 16, 20, 36.

Davidson, F. G.

Appointed temporary provost marshal of Livingston Parish, Louisiana, in September, 1862. *OR, XV,* 805–806.

Deaderick, First Lieutenant William W.

Assigned to provost duty around April, 1863, because of severe wounds. Anderson, *Memoirs,* 578.

De Butts, J.

In the Appomattox roster listed as surgeon, provost guard, Army of Northern Virginia. Brock (ed.), *Paroles,* 449.

Deishler, Corporal Chris

K Company, 5th Alabama. Listed with provost guard, Grimes's division, 2d Corps, at Appomattox. Brock (ed.), *Paroles,* 242.

Denis, Major Jules Charles

Lieutenant colonel, 10th Louisiana, May, 1861. Resigned December, 1861. In July, 1863, Denis was temporarily commanding at Mobile, Alabama. He was appointed provost marshal general of the Department of Alabama, Mississippi, and East Louisiana on January 22, 1864, and was relieved at his own request by Colonel Thomas H. Taylor on June 24, 1864. Thereafter Denis served with the Bureau of Conscription in Mississippi. Krick, *Lee's Colonels,* 104; *Index,* III (August 27, 1863), 278; *OR,* Vol. XXXI, Pt. 3, pp. 875–76; Vol. XXXII, Pt. 3, pp. 611–12, 633–34, 710, 745–48, 782–83, 804–807; War Department, Collection of Confederate Records, Record Group 109, Chap. II, Vol. 196; Veterans Records, National Archives.

Desha, Captain Joseph

Appointed assistant provost marshal of Orange Court House, Virginia, on March 17, 1862. *OR,* Vol. LI, Pt. 2, pp. 504–505.

Dingle, W. E.

Dingle, a civilian, was in charge of the civilian passport office in May and June, 1862, while Charleston was under martial law. Hagood, *Memoirs,* 79.

Dodd, Lieutenant Thomas L.

Severely wounded and disabled from active service while serving with Forrest, he was in command of the provost at Covington, Georgia. He was recommended as provost marshal general of Georgia, but the war ended before he could be appointed. Thompson, *History of the Orphan Brigade,* 119–20.

Doggett, Captain H. S.

Provost marshal, Fredericksburg, Virginia, in January, 1865. *OR,* Ser. II, Vol. VIII, pp. 68–69.

Doswell, Captain

Provost marshal, Fredericksburg, Virginia, in March, 1862, and in March, 1865. Wilson, *Borderland Confederate,* 91.

Doughton, Private C. B.

H Company, 5th Texas. Detailed as a divisional guard in April, 1863. Simpson, *Hood's Texas Brigade: A Compendium,* 229.

Duff, Captain James

14th Texas Cavalry Battalion. In July, 1862, appointed provost marshal of a number of counties in West Texas by Brigadier General H. P. Bee. Kerby, *Kirby Smith's Confederacy,* 92.

Dufour, Cyprian

Appointed provost marshal of Second District, Orleans Parish, Louisiana, on March 15, 1862. *OR,* VI, 857–58.

Eastham, P. C.

In May, 1861, provost marshal on the staff of Brigadier General John McCausland in western Virginia. Crute, *Confederate Staff Officers,* 136.

Echols, Captain John H.

2d Alabama Reserves. Provost marshal at Greenville, Alabama, in August, 1863. Park, "War Diary," 15.

Elkins, Captain John L.

E Company, 23d Tennessee. Assigned to command provost guard of Buckner's division in October, 1863. In August, 1864, he was assigned to the Conscript Bureau in Alabama. Obituary, *Confederate Veteran*, XII (rpr. 1983), 450.

Elliott, Lieutenant Colonel W. M

Commanding the Richmond City Guard in March, 1864. Krick, *Lee's Colonels*, 116; *OR*, XXXIII, 1217.

Ervin, First Lieutenant R. H.

Alabama Mounted Rifles (later in 7th Alabama). Appointed provost marshal of Braxton Bragg's army at Pensacola, Florida, in April, 1861. Served at Bragg's headquarters for at least ten months. Spratley, "Alabama Mounted Rifles," 469.

Estes, Lieutenant Colonel John W.

Appointed chief provost marshal, First District of Alabama (headquarters Blountsville) in March, 1864, and was in that position in April. Throughout the autumn of 1864 he was in various hospitals suffering from a gunshot wound. *OR*, Vol. XXXII, Pt. 3, pp. 611, 782–83, 804–807; Veterans Records, National Archives.

Evans, Captain Perry

I Company, 9th Texas Cavalry. Detailed for special duty with scouts and provost of Jackson's cavalry division in Alabama in May, 1864. *OR*, Vol. XXXIX, Pt. 2, p. 575.

Evans, Captain Walter R.

Appointed deputy provost marshal of the Fourth District of Tennessee (headquarters Tazewell) on September 25, 1862. *OR*, Ser. II, Vol. IV, pp. 899–900.

Ewing, Captain Z. W.

17th Tennessee. With the provost guard of Bushrod Johnson's brigade at Chickamauga. *OR*, Vol. XXX, Pt. 2, p. 478; Ewing, Letter to Editor, 534.

Fackler, Lieutenant Wiley B.

In September, 1864, provost marshal on the staff of Brigadier General J. S. Marmaduke during Sterling Price's invasion of Missouri. Crute, *Confederate Staff Officers*, 132.

Farmer, Private Henry G.

E Company, 38th Georgia. With provost of Grimes's division at Appomattox. Brock (ed.), *Paroles*, 220.

Farra, A. K.

Appointed provost marshal of Adams County, Mississippi, on September 8, 1862. *OR*, XV, 805–806.

Fay, Sergeant Edwin H.

Detailed as provost marshal of a general court-martial at Camp Priceville near Tupelo, Mississippi, on June 18, 1862. Fay, *"This Infernal War,"* 89, 93.

Feild, Colonel Hume R.

Feild, commanding the 1st Tennessee, was relieved of provost guard duty at Shelbyville, Tennessee, on May 25, 1862, and ordered to return to the Army of Tennessee. *OR*, Vol. XXIII, Pt. 2, p. 851.

Figg, Private John O.

B Company, 1st Virginia. Slightly wounded while on provost duty at Groveton in August, 1862. Spence, "Reports of the First, Seventh and Seventeenth Virginia Regiments in 1862," 262.

Fisher, Private William S.

H Company, 4th Texas. Assigned to provost duty at Winchester, Virginia, in October, 1862. Simpson, *Hood's Texas Brigade: A Compendium*, 149.

Foreacre, Captain Green J.

Provost marshal of Atlanta in July, 1862. Replaced by Major G. W. Lee. *OR*, Vol. X, Pt. 1, pp. 636–39; Ser. IV, Vol. II, pp. 9–10.

Forrester, Colonel R. H.

In June, 1862, provost marshal on the staff of General J. B. Villepigue (Bragg's army). Appointed provost marshal of Yalobusha County, Mississippi, on September 8, 1862. *OR*, XV, 805–806; Crute, *Confederate Staff Officers*, 200.

Francis, Captain Thomas H.

4th Tennessee. Provost marshal at Auburn, Alabama, from July to September, 1864. *OR*, Vol. XXXVIII, Pt. 3, p. 974.

Frazer, Captain George Morton

Herbert's Arizona Battalion, Arizona Brigade. Provost marshal of Albuquerque, New Mexico, in late 1861, and announced as provost marshal general of the Confederate Territory of Arizona in January, 1862. Hall, *Confederate Army of New Mexico*, 354–55.

Frazier, Private Albert

K Company, 4th Kentucky. Detailed to provost duty at Savannah, Georgia, 1864. Thompson, *History of the Orphan Brigade*, 688.

Freret, William

Appointed provost marshal of the First District, Orleans Parish, Louisiana, on March 15, 1862. *OR*, VI, 857–58.

Fulkerson, Captain George Hardin

16th Mississippi. Lost an arm at Fredericksburg in December, 1862. After recovering, he became provost marshal at Macon, Georgia, serving in that capacity to the end of the war. Beers, *Guide to the Archives*, 286; Obituary, *Confederate Veteran*, X (rpr. 1983), 273.

Fuller, Private William B.

G Company, 44th Georgia. Detailed to provost, Doles-Cook Brigade, May, 1864. Served through the war. Thomas, *History of the Doles-Cook Brigade*, 558.

Fuqua, Colonel James O.

Judge advocate and provost marshal general of the District of the Mississippi, July to December, 1862. Thompson, *History of the Orphan Brigade*, 133; *OR*, XV, 805–806; Ser. II, Vol. IV, p. 894; Crute, *Confederate Staff Officers*, 169.

Galloway, Captain S.

Commandant of Salisbury Prison from December, 1863, to May, 1864. Brown, *Salisbury Prison*, 168.

Gammon, Captain A. L.

Appointed deputy provost marshal of the First District of Tennessee, headquarters at Blountsville, Tennessee, on September 25, 1862. *OR*, Ser. II, Vol. IV, pp. 899–900.

Garity, Private Michael

L Company, 1st Texas. Detailed to provost of Hood's division in 1862. Simpson, *Hood's Texas Brigade: A Compendium*, 80.

Gayer, Captain W. J.

Responsible for soldiers' passports during May and June, 1862, when Charleston was under martial law. He was provost marshal of the city from January to June, 1864. Hagood, *Memoirs*, 79; *OR*, XXXV, Pt. 2, p. 330; Ser. II, Vol. VII, p. 215.

Gee, Major John H.

Commandant of Salisbury Prison from August 24, 1864, to January, 1865. Brought to trial after the war on charges of neglect and murder but found not guilty. Brown, *Salisbury Prison*, 44 (photo), 168. There is considerable material on Gee throughout the book, including his pre- and postwar career and a physical description.

Gibbes, Captain Cooper

Provost marshal at Tallahassee, Florida, in February, 1864. Described as an "intelligent, zealous, and efficient officer." *OR*, LIII, 308–309.

Gibbs, Captain George C.

Commandant of Salisbury Prison January to June, 1862. Assigned to command of the prison at Macon, Georgia, on May 25, 1864, and was there as late as June 26. He also commanded Castle Thunder in Richmond for a time in 1862–1863. One authority shows him commanding Andersonville before the arrival of General Winder on June 8, 1864. Brown, *Salisbury Prison*, 41, 168; Burrows, "Recollections of Libby Prison," 89; Hesseltine, *Civil War Prisons*, 246; *OR*, Vol. XXXIX, Pt. 2, p. 625.

Gilmer, Colonel J. A.

Commandant, Salisbury Prison, June to August, 1864. Brown, *Salisbury Prison*, 47, 168.

Glenn, Provost Germain R.

I Company, 1st Virginia. On provost duty at Groveton in August, 1862. Severely wounded. Spence, "Report of the First, Seventh and Seventeenth Virginia Regiments in 1862," 263.

Godwin, Brigadier General Archibald Campbell

Assistant provost marshal, Libby Prison, Richmond, at the outbreak of war. Appointed provost marshal of the eastern district of Richmond on March 1, 1862. Commanded Salisbury Prison June to September, 1862, and then commanded the Richmond prisons. Commanded 57th North Carolina during and after the Battle of Fredericksburg. Appointed brigadier general on August 5, 1864. Killed at Winchester, Virginia, September 19, 1864. Brown, *Salisbury Prison*, 43, 168; Thomas,

Confederate State of Richmond, 81; Richardson (ed.), *Messages,* I, 221; Jones, *Rebel War Clerk's Diary,* 70; *OR,* Ser. II, Vol. III, p. 890; Crute, *Confederate Staff Officers,* 71; Warner, *Generals in Gray,* 108.

Goff, First Lieutenant J. M.
Provost marshal, Rodes's division, Army of Northern Virginia, in February, 1864. Yearns and Barrett (eds.), *North Carolina Civil War Documentary,* 99.

Goodall, Private Turner
Served with provost of Johnson's brigade at Chickamauga. *OR,* Vol. XXX, Pt. 2, p. 478; Ewing, Letter to Editor, 534.

Goodwin, Captain John
Provost marshal general of Forrest's corps, April to December, 1864. *OR,* Vol. XXXII, Pt. 3, p. 797; Vol. XLV, Pt. 2, p. 682; Vol. XXXII, Pt. 1, p. 619; Vol. XXXIX, Pt. 1, p. 227.

Gossett, First Lieutenant I. W.
2d South Carolina. Served with provost of Pickett's division. Bidgood, "List of General Officers," 176; Crute, *Confederate Staff Officers,* 151; Harrison, *Pickett's Men,* 192.

Gossett, Lieutenant John R.
Appointed provost marshal on Pickett's staff in the Department of North Carolina on September 24, 1863, and as provost marshal general of the department on October 1. *OR,* Vol. LI, Pt. 2, pp. 769, 771.

Gourdin, Lieutenant Colonel Robert Newton
On the staff of the Charleston passport office in May and June, 1862, when the city was under martial law. He was also a lieutenant colonel with the Charleston Reserves, which were called out as provost on June 12. Hagood, *Memoirs,* 79, 82.

Green, Lieutenant Colonel Allen J.
Lieutenant colonel, 23d South Carolina, November, 1861. Dropped at reorganization. Served with the Conscript Bureau and was provost marshal at Chester, South Carolina, in April, 1865. Krick, *Lee's Colonels,* 150; *OR,* Vol. XLVII, Pt. 3, p. 762.

Griswold, Major Elias
Provost marshal in Richmond from May, 1862, to at least December, 1863. Manarin (ed.), *Richmond at War,* 177; Crute, *Confederate Staff Officers,* 213.

Griswold, Captain John B.
Provost marshal of the First Subdistrict, Department of North Carolina, Goldsboro, September 1, 1864, to January 31, 1865. His guard consisted of one company of senior reserves. *OR,* Vol. XLII, Pt. 2, p. 1225; Vol. XLVI, Pt. 2, p. 1186.

Hagood, Brigadier General Johnson
Commanding 1st South Carolina. Appointed provost marshal of Charleston on May 5, 1862, relinquishing the appointment to Colonel Alex Brown on June 9. Tracy, "Operations Before Charleston," 544; Hagood, *Memoirs,* 89; *OR,* XIV, 492.

Hairston, Major J. P. W.

11th Mississippi. Provost marshal of the Army of Northern Virginia cavalry division during Stuart's 1862 ride around McClellan. Stuart, "Expedition into Pennsylvania in October, 1862," 480.

Hamilton, Major Daniel Heyward
13th North Carolina. Provost marshal at Columbia, South Carolina, November, 1864, to January 31, 1865. *OR*, XLIV, 876; Vol. XLVII, Pt. 2, p. 1073; Obituary, *Confederate Veteran*, XVII (rpr. 1983), 89.

Hamilton, Lieutenant Colonel Jones P.
Provost marshal general of the District of East Louisiana in May, 1864. Probably appointed in March, 1864. *OR*, Vol. LII, Pt. 2, p. 703; Vol. XXXII, Pt. 3, p. 611.

Hammond, Captain George H.
Provost marshal, Williamsport, Maryland, February, 1864. *OR*, XXXIII, 1160.

Hampton, Lieutenant Colonel Frank
On provost guard at Charleston, May and June, 1862. Afterward lieutenant colonel, 2d South Carolina Cavalry. Killed at Brandy Station. Hagood, *Memoirs*, 80; Krick, *Lee's Colonels*, 159.

Hamsteg, Corporal William
E Company, 3d Alabama. With provost of Grimes's division, 2d Corps, at Appomattox. Brock (ed.), *Paroles*, 240.

Hand, Private Thomas B.
G Company, 5th Alabama. Detached to provost guard, 2d Corps, at Appomattox. Brock (ed.), *Paroles*, 242.

Hanlon, Lieutenant Colonel Joseph
Appointed chief provost marshal of the Third District of Mississippi (headquarters Columbus), on March 10, 1864. *OR*, Vol. XXXII, Pt. 3, pp. 611, 710.

Hardee, D. C.
Appointed provost marshal of East Feliciana Parish, Louisiana, on September 8, 1862. *OR*, XV, 805–806.

Harkreader, Lieutenant William H.
7th Tennessee. Lost an arm at Second Manassas. Commanded a conscript camp at Knoxville, Tennessee, and then became provost marshal at Marietta, Georgia. Captured there in June, 1864, and spent the remainder of the war as a prisoner of war. Obituary, *Confederate Veteran*, XXI (rpr. 1983), 453.

Harlett, Captain S. T.
C Company, 21st Georgia. Commanded the provost guard of the 2d Corps at Appomattox. Brock (ed.), *Paroles*, 185.

Haslett, Private George H.
C Company, 21st Georgia. Served in Ewell's provost guard throughout the war. Thomas, *History of the Doles-Cook Brigade*, 395.

Haslett, Captain Samuel D.
C Company, 21st Georgia. Detailed as provost marshal of the 2d Corps in 1864.

Listed as provost marshal of the 2d Corps at Appomattox. Brock (ed.), *Paroles*, 189; Thomas, *History of the Doles-Cook Brigade*, 369, 392.

Hawes, Lieutenant Napoleon B.

Listed in Appomattox roster as an acting assistant provost marshal. May have been provost marshal of Petersburg in October, 1863. Relieved by Major G. C. Cabell. *OR*, Vol. LI, Pt. 2, p. 771.

Hawk, Private Thomas H.

Disabled and detailed to provost of Doles-Cook Brigade. Surrendered at Appomattox. Thomas, *History of the Doles-Cook Brigade*, 168.

Henderson, Captain T. C.

Provost marshal with Major General French's division of Hood's army in December, 1864. *OR*, Vol. XXXVIII, Pt. 3, p. 907.

Henry, Lieutenant Colonel Gustavus A.

Relieved Colonel Benjamin Hill as provost marshal general of the Army of Tennessee on August 24, 1864. Relieved by Colonel M. H. Cofer on August 29. Probably resumed duties as assistant adjutant general of the army. *OR*, Vol. XXXVIII, Pt. 5, p. 1000.

Hicks, Captain W. J.

Appointed deputy provost marshal of the Seventh District of Tennessee (headquarters London) on September 25, 1862. *OR*, Ser. II, Vol. IV, pp. 899–900.

Hill, Major General A. P.

Provost marshal of Carlisle, Pennsylvania, on July 1, 1863. Nisbet, *4 Years on the Firing Line*, 121.

Hill, Brigadier General Benjamin Jefferson

Hill led his regiment, the 5th, later 35th, Tennessee, in forty-two skirmishes and battles before being appointed provost marshal general of the Army of Tennessee in late 1863. Relieved August 24, 1864, by Lieutenant Colonel Henry and became brigadier general of cavalry on November 30. Nisbet, *4 Years on the Firing Line*, 186; Ridley, *Battles and Sketches*, 514, 516 (photo); *OR*, Vol. XXXII, Pt. 3, pp. 681–82, 867; Vol. XXXVIII, Pt. 5, p. 988; Ser. II, Vol. VII, p. 616; Carter, *Siege of Atlanta*, 148, 274; Crute, *Confederate Staff Officers*, 85; Warner, *Generals in Gray*, 135–36; Veterans Records, National Archives.

Hinds, Howell

Appointed provost marshal of Jefferson County, Mississippi, on September 8, 1862. *OR*, XV, 805–806.

Hinton, Captain W. E.

Served with provost of Dearing's brigade in December, 1864. Transferred to 10th Virginia Cavalry. *OR*, Vol. XLII, Pt. 3, p. 1276.

Holland, Private William T.

I Company, 42d Virginia. Listed with divisional provost, 1st Corps, at Appomattox. Brock (ed.), *Paroles*, 229.

Hopkins, Private Frank M.

G Company, 1st Texas. Assigned to provost duty in summer, 1863. Simpson, *Hood's Texas Brigade: A Compendium,* 53.

Hopper, Private Booker W.

E Company, 38th Georgia. Provost at Appomattox. Brock (ed.), *Paroles,* 220.

Howard, Major T. B.

On provost duty at Columbus, Georgia, in March, 1864. *OR,* Ser. IV, Vol. III, p. 460.

Howdson, Sergeant Dabney R.

C Company, 13th South Carolina. With provost, Wilcox's division, 3d Corps, at Appomattox. Brock (ed.), *Paroles,* 374.

Hubbard, Private John Milton

Served with provost at Selma, Alabama, in March, 1865. Hubbard, *Notes of a Private,* 185.

Hundley, Captain

Provost marshal on the staff of Brigadier General J. K. Jackson in the Army of Tennessee. Relieved March 5, 1865. Crute, *Confederate Staff Officers,* 95.

Hunter, R. A.

Appointed provost marshal of Baton Rouge, Louisiana, on September 8, 1862. *OR,* XV, 805–806.

Hurtel, Captain Alphonse

Served with provost in Atlanta in January, 1863. Myers, *Children of Pride,* 1559.

Hyllested, Major Waldemar

Major, Louisiana Zouave Battalion, March, 1861. Appointed provost marshal of Yorktown, Virginia, on December 23, 1861, and then provost marshal of the Peninsula until March, 1862. In June Hyllested was at Richmond and on July 12 was ordered to report to General Magruder at Jackson, Mississippi. On December 2 he was appointed provost marshal general of the District of Texas, New Mexico, and Arizona. He was still in this appointment in October, 1864, and probably remained in it until the end of the war. Krick, *Lee's Colonels,* 187; Beers, *Guide to the Archives,* 292.

Ives, Colonel Samuel Spencer

Commanded 35th Alabama guarding prisoners at Newburg, Alabama, in April, 1864. *OR,* Vol. XXXII, Pt. 1, p. 662.

Jackson, Private John F.

B Company, 6th Alabama. Detached to provost at Appomattox. Brock (ed.), *Paroles,* 242.

James, Lieutenant Colonel George Shorter

Appointed provost marshal of Third Military District, Department of South Carolina and Georgia, on May 17, 1862. Killed at South Mountain in September. Krick, *Lee's Colonels,* 189; *OR,* XIV, 505.

Johnson, Private A. C.

K Company, 26th Georgia. On provost duty at Appomattox. Brock (ed.), *Paroles,* 217.

Johnson, Private John N.
F Company, 4th Texas. Detailed to Texas Brigade provost guard in spring, 1863. Simpson, *Hood's Texas Brigade: A Compendium,* 134.

Jordan, Private J. C.
I Company, 4th Texas. Detailed to Texas Brigade provost guard in spring, 1864. Simpson, *Hood's Texas Brigade: A Compendium,* 158.

Keen, W. S.
Provost marshal of Alleghany County, Virginia, in April, 1863. Escott, *After Secession,* 112.

Keenan, Private W. A.
D Company, 5th Texas. Detailed to Texas Brigade provost guard in January, 1863. Simpson, *Hood's Texas Brigade: A Compendium,* 200.

Kelley, Lieutenant H. C.
Provost marshal at Shubuta, Mississippi, in July, 1864. *OR,* Vol. XXXIX, Pt. 2, pp. 736–37.

Kelly, Private Solomon P.
G Company, 4th Texas. Detailed to Texas Brigade provost guard in April, 1864. Simpson, *Hood's Texas Brigade: A Compendium,* 142; Veterans Records, National Archives.

Kerr, Lieutenant Henry C.
Deputy provost marshal, Missouri State Guard, November, 1861. Bevier, *History of the First and Second Missouri Confederate Brigades,* 72.

Knight, Captain George N.
4th Texas. Appointed provost marshal of Columbus, Georgia, in the winter of 1863–1864. Retired for disability in September, 1864. Simpson, *Hood's Texas Brigade: A Compendium,* 93.

Knight, Sergeant Martin G.
H Company, 26th Georgia. With provost at Appomattox. Brock (ed.), *Paroles,* 217.

Lahey, Private John
B Company, 5th Texas. Detailed to Texas Brigade provost guard in spring, 1864. Simpson, *Hood's Texas Brigade: A Compendium,* 186.

Lamb, Lieutenant Wilson G.
17th North Carolina. Provost marshal of Major General Robert Hoke's division at Petersburg in 1864. Obituary, *Confederate Veteran,* XXX (rpr. 1983), 268.

Lancaster, Private Ben H.
F Company, 4th North Carolina. With 2d Corps provost at Appomattox. Brock (ed.), *Paroles,* 255.

Lartigue, Captain G. B.
Appointed assistant provost marshal of Charleston and assigned to supervision of the

guards on May 12, 1862. Afterward quartermaster of Hagood's brigade to the end of the war. Hagood, *Memoirs,* 74, 76–77.

Lee, Lieutenant Colonel George Washington

Lee, as a major, was provost marshal of Atlanta from October, 1862, to at least October, 1863. Krick, *Lee's Colonels,* 214; Yearns and Barrett (eds.), *North Carolina Civil War Documentary,* 289; *OR,* Vol. XXX, Pt. 4, pp. 520, 748; Vol. XVI, Pt. 2, pp. 979–80; Vol. X, Pt. 1, pp. 635–39; Vol. XXIII, Pt. 2, p. 910.

Leftwich, Private John R.

E Company, 1st Virginia Battalion. Listed in the Appomattox roster as a clerk in the Provost Department. Brock (ed.), *Paroles,* 452.

Litty, Second Lieutenant P. B.

H Company, 43d North Carolina. Listed with 2d Corps provost at Appomattox. Brock, *Paroles,* 185.

Livenskiold, Colonel Charles G.

Provost marshal of Corpus Christi, Texas, in July, 1862. Assumed command of the city and organized its defense. *OR,* IX, 610–13; Delaney, "Corpus Christi," 6.

Logan, Private James E.

D Company, 21st Georgia. Detailed to Ewell's provost guard. Surrendered at Appomattox. Thomas, *History of the Doles-Cook Brigade,* 407.

Macfie, Captain J. P.

2d South Carolina Cavalry. Commanded Wade Hampton's provost guard at Chambersburg, Pennsylvania, in October, 1862. *OR,* Vol. XIX, Pt. 2, pp. 57–58.

Malone, Lieutenant Edward

24th Alabama. Appointed provost marshal of Manigault's brigade, Hindman's division, Army of Tennessee, on September 20, 1863. Manigault singled him out for praise because of his conduct at Chickamauga. Hindman, "Battle of Chickamauga," 367–72; *OR,* Vol. XXX, Pt. 2, p. 344; Crute, *Confederate Staff Officers,* 131; Tower, *A Carolinian Goes to War,* 166.

Marchman, Lieutenant James (Joseph?)

Provost marshal of L. L. Lomax's cavalry brigade from at least April, 1863 until September, 1863. Bidgood, "List of General Officers," 171; Crute, *Confederate Staff Officers,* 122.

Marsh, Captain E.

Commanded E Company, 40th Alabama, on provost duty at Jackson, Mississippi, in January, 1863. *OR,* Vol. XVII, Pt. 2, p. 819.

Martin, Judge G. W.

Appointed provost marshal of St. Helena Parish, Louisiana, on September 8, 1862. *OR,* XV, 805–806.

Martin, Lieutenant Colonel Rawley White

53d Virginia. Severely wounded and captured at Gettysburg. Exchanged in April, 1864. Appointed provost marshal of "the portion of Virginia lying north of the York

River." At this time Martin was in the Invalid Corps. Krick, *Lee's Colonels*, 244; *OR*, Vol. XLVI, Pt. 2, p. 1240.

Massie, Major Josiah C.

9th Texas Cavalry. Provost marshal at Galveston in September, 1862. *OR*, Ser. II, Vol. IV, p. 890.

Maynard, Captain J. C.

Appointed provost marshal of the western district of Richmond on March 1, 1862. Thomas, *Confederate State of Richmond*, 81.

Mayo, G. Spencer

Provost marshal at Trinity, Louisiana, and superintendent of scouts on the Black River in May, 1863. Logan, "Official Report on the Engagement Between the Federal Gunboats and Fort Beauregard," 497.

McAnerney, Colonel John

Commanded 3d Regiment, Local Defense Troops, on provost duty in Richmond in February, 1865. Krick, *Lee's Colonels*, 227; *OR*, Vol. XLVI, Pt. 2, p. 1237.

McCampbell, Captain William

Appointed deputy provost marshal, Third District of Tennessee (headquarters Morristown) on September 25, 1862. *OR*, Ser. II, Vol. IV, pp. 899–900.

McClatchey, Lieutenant W. T.

9th Texas Cavalry. Appointed provost marshal of Ross's Cavalry Brigade, Lexington, Mississippi, March 20, 1865. *OR*, Vol. XLIX, Pt. 2, p. 1134; Crute, *Confederate Staff Officers*, 168.

McCown, Captain Jerome B.

Appointed provost marshal of Mesilla, New Mexico, at the end of the New Mexico campaign. Hall, *Confederate Army of New Mexico*, 187.

McCoy, Captain Henry

Commandant, Salisbury Prison, September 28, 1862, to October, 1863. Brown, *Salisbury Prison*, 168.

McGee, Captain H. L. P.

Commanded provost guard of Jackson's division of Stephen D. Lee's cavalry in the Department of Mississippi and East Louisiana in November, 1863. *OR*, Vol. XXXI, Pt. 3, pp. 727, 746.

McKie, Dr. M. J.

Appointed provost marshal of Madison Parish, Louisiana, on September 8, 1862. *OR*, XV, 805–806.

McKinstrey, Colonel Alex

32d Alabama. McKinstrey was on court-martial duty during the latter half of 1862 and then served as provost marshal general of the Army of Tennessee during 1863. In 1864 he was again a member of a military court. Ridley, *Battles and Sketches*, 260; *OR*, Vol. XXIII, Pt. 2, p. 885; Crute, *Confederate Staff Officers*, 22; Veterans Records, National Archives.

McQueen, Archibald A.

Assistant surgeon, provost guard, 2d Corps, at Appomattox. Brock (ed.), *Paroles,* 185.

Meanley, Provost George L.

D Company, 1st Virginia. Wounded when on provost duty at Groveton in August, 1862. Spence, "Reports on the First, Seventh and Seventeenth Virginia Regiments in 1862," 262.

Meanly, Provost John A.

H Company, 1st Virginia. Severely wounded when on provost duty at Groveton in August, 1862. Spence, "Reports on the First, Seventh and Seventeenth Virginia Regiments in 1862," 263.

Mebane, Lieutenant Samuel R.

Appointed chief provost marshal of the District of Indian Territory, Fort Towson, March 15, 1864. He was also the chief enrolling officer of the district. *OR,* Vol. XXXIV, Pt. 2, pp. 1045–46.

Meeks, Private Nacy

Detailed to provost of Jackson's cavalry division in 1864. Fay, *"This Infernal War,"* 456.

Messick, Colonel Otis M.

11th Texas Cavalry. In December, 1864, as a major, he was provost marshal at Waynesboro, South Carolina. On January 21, 1865, he was appointed provost marshal of Wheeler's cavalry corps. Dodson (ed.), *Campaigns of Wheeler and His Cavalry,* 398; *OR,* Vol. XLVII, Pt. 2, p. 1035.

Michailoffsky, Lieutenant Charles J.

Provost marshal of Deas's brigade, Hindman's division, Army of Tennessee, at Chickamauga. *OR,* Vol. XXX, Pt. 2, p. 331; Crute, *Confederate Staff Officers,* 49.

Miles, C. Richardson

Appointed assistant provost marshal of Charleston on May 12, 1862, and assigned to duties with the provost marshal's court. Hagood, *Memoirs,* 74, 76–77, 80.

Miller, John C.

Appointed provost marshal of Port Hudson, Louisiana, on September 8, 1862. *OR,* XV, 805–806.

Moodie, Private John R.

F Company, 5th Texas. Assigned to the division provost guard in June, 1863. Simpson, *Hood's Texas Brigade: A Compendium,* 215.

Moore, Second Lieutenant Cleon

K Company, 2d Viriginia. Listed on duty with Provost Battalion, 2d Corps, at Appomattox. Brock (ed.), *Paroles,* 84.

Moore, Private Robert A.

17th Mississippi. On provost duty at Fredericksburg, Virginia, from December 9,

1862, to April 29, 1863, and from May 5 to June 2, 1863. Moore, *A Life for the Confederacy,* 122, 129, 130–38, 144–48.

Morehead, Lieutenant G. W.

Assistant provost marshal at Lynchburg, Virginia, in December, 1864. *OR,* Ser. II, Vol. VII, p. 1270.

Morfit, Major Mason

Commanded Confederate prison, Danville, Virginia, March–April, 1864. *OR,* XXXIII, 1217, 1300.

Morris, Private Robert

D Company, 5th Texas. Detailed to Hood's Brigade provost guard on April 6, 1864. Simpson, *Hood's Texas Brigade: A Compendium,* 201.

Morton, Provost Tazewell S.

D Company, 1st Virginia. On provost duty at Groveton, Virginia, in August, 1862. Slightly wounded. Spence, "Reports on the First, Seventh and Seventeenth Virginia Regiments in 1862," 262.

Moseley, Lieutenant Alexander M.

G Company, 9th Kentucky. Wounded and disabled for further service in July, 1864. Assigned to provost duty in the autumn of 1864 and served until the surrender. Thompson, *History of the Orphan Brigade,* 838.

Mullins, First Lieutenant John

Ordered to report for provost duty with General Winder in July, 1861. *OR,* Ser. II, Vol. III, p. 687.

Munford, Major W. P.

1st Virginia, 1861. Later served as paymaster and in the Richmond Provost Marshal's office. Krick, *Lee's Colonels,* 262.

Murchison, Captain D. J.

Provost marshal of Neely's brigade, Forrest's cavalry, in May and June, 1864. *OR,* Vol. XXXIX, Pt. 2, p. 631.

Nichols, Private G. W.

61st Georgia. On provost guard at New Market, Virginia, in November, 1864. Nichols, *Soldier's Story,* 202.

Nichols, Lieutenant W. L.

Assistant provost marshal at Cynthiana, Kentucky, in September, 1862. *OR,* Vol. XVI, Pt. 1, p. 943.

Nickelson, Private George W.

K Company, 44th Georgia. Detailed to provost, Doles-Cook Brigade in January, 1864. Captured at Spotsylvania, May, 1864. Surrendered at Appomattox. Thomas, *History of the Doles-Cook Brigade,* 589.

Nunn, Lieutenant J. R.

Provost marshal at Harrisonburg, Virginia, in March, 1864. *OR,* Ser. II, Vol. VI, pp. 1119–20.

Nutzell, Lieutenant Conrad

15th Tennessee. During the battle of Corinth (October, 1862) Nutzell was assigned to the staff of Colonel Benjamin Hill, provost marshal at Dalton, Georgia. Obituary, *Confederate Veteran*, XIII (rpr. 1983), 86–87.

Ogden, Colonel H. D.

Appointed provost marshal of Fourth District, Orleans Parish, Louisiana, on March 15, 1862. *OR*, VI, 857–58.

Oggden, Provost L. W.

B Company, 1st Virginia. Wounded when on provost duty at Groveton, Virginia, in August, 1862. Spence, "Reports on the First, Seventh and Seventeenth Virginia Regiments in 1862," 262.

O'Hara, Captain Theodore

Ordered to report to General Winder for provost duty in July, 1861. Krick, *Lee's Colonels*, 269; *OR*, Ser. II, Vol. III, p. 687.

Orr, Lieutenant Samuel

On provost guard at Chickamauga. *OR*, Vol. XXX, Pt. 2, p. 478.

Otey, Captain Van R.

Provost marshal at Lynchburg, Virginia, in December, 1864. *OR*, Ser. II, Vol. VII, p. 1270.

Pannill, Captain William

Appointed provost marshal of Petersburg on March 8 and was still there until at least April 18, 1863. Richardson (ed.), *Messages*, I, 222; *OR*, Ser. II, Vol. IV, p. 801; XVIII, 998; Vol. XI, Pt. 3, pp. 495–96, 502; Vol. LI, Pt. 2, p. 493; War Department, Collection of Confederate Records, Record Group 109, Chap. II, Vol. 236.

Parham, Colonel W. A.

41st Virginia. As a lieutenant, Parham was provost marshal of Norfolk, Virginia, in March, 1862. In October, 1864, as a colonel, he was ordered to report to Richmond for duty as provost marshal on the line of the Blackwater River south of Richmond. Krick, *Lee's Colonels*, 273; *OR*, Vol. LI, Pt. 2, p. 491; Vol. XLII, Pt. 3, p. 1136.

Parker, Provost Calvin Lee

I Company, 1st Virginia. Slightly wounded when on provost duty at Groveton in August, 1862. Spence, "Reports on the First, Seventh and Seventeenth Virginia Regiments in 1862," 263.

Parker, G. M.

Provost marshal at Mobile, Alabama, in January, 1863. *Index*, III (August 27, 1863), 278.

Parker, Captain N. P.

Provost marshal at Augusta, Georgia, in January, 1864. Abraham Lincoln Book Shop, *Catalogue 105, Americana*, Item 281.

Parrish, Colonel H. T.

Colonel, 16th Virginia, January, 1862, but dropped in May, 1862, and became provost marshal of Farmville, Virginia, where he remained at least until May, 1863. Krick, *Lee's Colonels,* 274; *OR,* Vol. XXV, Pt. 2, p. 773.

Passmore, Private John L.

C Company, 6th Alabama. With 2d Corps provost at Appomattox. Brock (ed.), *Paroles,* 243.

Peacock, Sergeant C. L.

2d Battalion Georgia Sharpshooters. Served with this unit as provost at Chattanooga in late 1862 to early 1863. Peacock, "Conscription in the Mountains," 171.

Peden, Captain Charles W.

Appointed deputy provost marshal of the Tenth District of Tennessee on September 25, 1862. During the Battle of Murfreesboro he was provost marshal of Shelbyville. Peden was provost marshal of Murfreesboro in January, 1863. Anderson, Letter to Editor, 72; Parole of Federal Prisoner, 42; *OR,* Ser. II, Vol. IV, pp. 899–900, 910; V, 789.

Pendleton, Lieutenant Robert

Provost marshal of Brigadier General W. H. Payne's cavalry brigade in 1865. Bidgood, "List of General Officers," 175; Crute, *Confederate Staff Officers,* 146.

Phillips, Colonel James J.

9th Virginia. Ordered to Ivor Station on the Norfolk and Petersburg Railroad on October 1, 1863, to be provost marshal on the line of the Blackwater River south of Richmond. Krick, *Lee's Colonels,* 280; *OR,* Vol. LI, Pt. 2, p. 771.

Plummer, Private F. W.

A Company, 5th Texas. Wounded at Gaines' Mill in June, 1862, and detailed to brigade provost guard. Simpson, *Hood's Texas Brigade: A Compendium,* 179.

Pomroy, Private Chancey A.

F Company, 3d Alabama. With 2d Corps provost at Appomattox. Brock (ed.), *Paroles,* 240.

Porter, Private Benjamin

I Company, 6th Alabama. With 2d Corps provost at Appomattox. Brock (ed.), *Paroles,* 243.

Porter, Provost G. T.

D Company, 1st Virginia. Badly wounded when on provost duty at Groveton in August, 1862. Spence, "Reports on the First, Seventh and Seventeenth Virginia Regiments in 1862," 262.

Porter, Lieutenant J. R.

29th Mississippi. In May, 1864, Porter commanded the provost guard of Hindman's division of the Army of Tennessee. *OR,* Vol. XXXVIII, Pt. 3, pp. 640, 806.

Porter, Colonel John

Appointed provost marshal of Richmond, March 1, 1862. Thomas, *Confederate State of Richmond,* 81.

Priddy, Provost Ezekiel

I Company, 1st Virginia. Slightly wounded when on provost duty at Groveton in

August, 1862. Spence, "Reports on the First, Seventh and Seventeenth Virginia Regiments in 1862," 263.

Pritchard, Lieutenant Hoskiner
A Company, 5th Virginia. With 2d Corps provost at the surrender. Brock (ed.), *Paroles*, 185.

Radcliffe, Provost I. W.
B Company, 1st Virginia. On provost duty at Groveton in August, 1862. Wounded and subsequently died of wounds. Spence, "Reports on the First, Seventh and Seventeenth Virginia Regiments in 1862," 262.

Ragland, Private Samuel Beaufort
B Company, 1st Virginia Battalion. In Appomattox roster listed as a clerk in the Provost Marshal's Office. Brock (ed.), *Paroles*, 451.

Randolph, Major Peyton
Lieutenant of infantry, January, 1862. Assistant adjutant general to Robert Rodes and then provost marshal with Lewis A. Armistead in September, 1862. Captain and engineer officer with Armistead in May, 1863. Major, 1st Confederate Engineers in April, 1864. Krick, *Lee's Colonels*, 289.

Ratcliffe, Captain W. H.
Commanded a small provost guard (fourteen men) at Athens, Georgia, in February, 1865. *OR*, Vol. XLIX, Pt. 1, pp. 974–76.

Ratterree, Private Robert
I Company, 3d Arkansas. Detailed to provost June, 1863. Simpson, *Hood's Texas Brigade: A Compendium*, 310.

Reed, Captain W. Shelby
Assigned as provost marshal and commander of provost guard at Andersonville on June 22, 1864. *OR*, Ser. II, Vol. VII, pp. 397, 518.

Reese, Lieutenant George
A Company, 44th Alabama. Commanded provost guard of Law's brigade, Hood's old division, at Petersburg in 1864. Reese, "What Five Confederates Did at Petersburg," 286.

Reynolds, Private William M.
C Company, 3d Arkansas. Detailed to provost duty in the spring of 1862. Simpson, *Hood's Texas Brigade: A Compendium*, 273.

Rhea, Robert A.
Deputy provost marshal at Blountsville, Tennessee, in May, 1862. *OR*, Ser. II, Vol. I, p. 888.

Rice, Private A. R. ("Old Pontoon")
B Company, 4th Texas. Detailed to provost duty in the spring of 1863. Simpson, *Hood's Texas Brigade: A Compendium*, 109.

Richardson, Lieutenant W. L.

Provost marshal of Wright's brigade, Cheatham's division, at Chickamauga. *OR,* Vol. XXX, Pt. 2, p. 121; Crute, *Confederate Staff Officers,* 217.

Ritter, Captain Wade

Commanded 3d Corps provost guard (5th Alabama Battalion) from January, 1865, to the surrender. *OR,* Vol. XLVI, Pt. 1, p. 1272, Pt. 2, p. 1182.

Rives, Lieutenant George S.

Listed in Appomattox roster as provost marshal of Beale's cavalry brigade. Brock (ed.), *Paroles,* 10.

Roberts, M.

F Company, 3d Florida. On provost duty at Mobile, Alabama, from May to July, 1862. Roberts, "Third Florida Regiment," 355.

Robinson, James H.

Assistant deputy provost marshal at Greeneville, Tennessee, in February, 1863. *OR,* Ser. II, Vol. V, pp. 831–32.

Rogers, Captain M. M.

Provost marshal, Munford's cavalry brigade, in 1864. Bidgood, "List of General Officers," 174; Crute, *Confederate Staff Officers,* 144.

Roland, Private Hugh B.

H Company, 6th Alabama. With Grimes's provost guard at the surrender. Brock (ed.), *Paroles,* 243.

Ruffin, Captain James

D Company, 4th Mississippi Cavalry. Commanded provost guard of Major General Stephen D. Lee's cavalry from July to September, 1863. *OR,* Vol. XXIV, Pt. 3, p. 1042; Vol. XXX, Pt. 4, pp. 517, 656; Vol. XXXI, Pt. 3, p. 865.

Ruggles, Brigadier General Daniel

Replaced General Winder as commissary general of prisoners in February, 1865. Amann (ed.), *Confederate Armies,* 176.

Ryals, Major G. M.

Provost marshal of the cavalry corps of the Army of Northern Virginia from July, 1863, to the end of the war. Stuart, "Report of Operations After Gettysburg," 77; Stuart, "Gettysburg Campaign," 433; Cardwell, "A Brilliant Coup," 152; Bidgood, "List of General Officers," 180; Opie, *Rebel Cavalryman,* 186; *OR,* Vol. XXVII, Pt. 2, p. 710; Crute, *Confederate Staff Officers,* 77, 189.

Sanford, Colonel John W. A.

60th Alabama. On provost duty in Richmond in June, 1864. Krick, *Lee's Colonels,* 307; *OR,* Vol. XL, Pt. 2, p. 670.

Sanford, Lieutenant R. H.

Provost marshal in Mississippi in August, 1864. May have been with Chalmer's cavalry brigade under Forrest. *OR,* Vol. XXXIX, Pt. 2, p. 773.

Savery, Major Phineas M.

Appointed provost marshal of Sterling Price's army in August, 1861. *OR*, VIII, 784; LIII, 728; Bevier, *History of the First and Second Missouri Confederate Brigades*, 72.

Scott, Captain

Provost marshal of Stonewall Jackson's corps sometime in 1863 before the Battle of Chancellorsville. Oates, *War Between the Union and the Confederacy*, 144.

Sharp, Captain John J. A.

Commanded a company of the 23rd Georgia on provost duty in Florida in April, 1864. *OR*, Vol. XXXV, Pt. 2, p. 441.

Sharpe, Private E. Tonkey

B Company, 27th North Carolina. On March 25, 1864, he was detailed to provost duty by order of Major General Henry Heth. The roster of the 27th gives the date as April 26. Surrendered at Appomattox. Sloan, *Reminiscences*, 77, 116, 128.

Shepard, First Lieutenant Philo B.

K Company, 6th Georgia Cavalry. Provost marshal at Augusta, Georgia, until its surrender in 1865. Shepard, Letter to Editor, 238.

Sherrard, Major John Broome

13th Virginia. Detailed as provost marshal of Stonewall Jackson's division from Second Manassas to Sharpsburg (August to September, 1862). Resigned and joined the recruiting service. Obituary, *Confederate Veteran*, XXI (rpr. 1983), 301.

Shivers, Colonel W. R.

Provost marshal at Shreveport, Louisiana, December, 1863. Heartsill, *Fourteen Hundred and 91 Days*, 187.

Sibert, Captain M. M.

Commandant of post and provost marshal at Harrisonburg, Virginia, in April, 1862. *OR*, Ser. II, Vol. III, p. 839.

Simms, J. H.

Appointed provost marshal of Wilkinson County, Mississippi, on September 8, 1862. *OR*, XV, 805–806.

Simpson, Lieutenant Samuel Jefferson

7th Virginia Cavalry. On provost duty with W. E. Jones's cavalry brigade during the 1863 summer campaign. Jones, "Summer Campaign of 1863," 116.

Sinskoe, Provost Joseph

I Company, 1st Virginia. Severely wounded when on provost duty at Groveton in August, 1862. Spence, "Reports of the First, Seventh and Seventeenth Virginia Regiments in 1862," 263.

Skeer, W.

Provost marshal of Alleghany and commanding the post at Covington, Virginia, in August, 1862. *OR*, Vol. XII, Pt. 3, p. 937.

Smith, Provost I. H.

I Company, 1st Virginia. On provost duty at Groveton in August, 1862. Badly wounded and later died of wounds. Spence, "Reports of the First, Seventh and Seventeenth Virginia Regiments in 1862," 263.

Smith, Captain J. Louis

Commanded the provost guard at Winchester, Virginia, in October, 1862. *OR*, Vol. XIX, Pt. 2, pp. 664–65.

Smith, J. S.

Deputy provost marshal, Atlanta, Georgia, March, 1863. Hallock, "The Hidden Way to Dixie," 496.

Smith, Corporal James P.

G Company, 5th Texas. Assigned to provost duty May, 1863. Simpson, *Hood's Texas Brigade: A Compendium*, 218.

Sneed, Lieutenant Thomas E.

Commanding San Antonio, Texas, provost guard in March, 1864. Kerby, *Kirby Smith's Confederacy*, 271.

Soule, Pierre

Appointed provost marshal of Third District, Orleans Parish, Louisiana, on March 15, 1862. Morgan, *Recollections*, 75; *OR*, VI, 857–58.

Sparks, Major J. H.

Provost marshal at Austin, Texas, in March, 1864. Kerby, *Kirby Smith's Confederacy*, 271.

Spofford, H. M.

Provost marshal at New Orleans in April, 1862. *OR*, LIII, 802.

Stanfield, Private Thomas B.

A Company, 4th Texas. Detailed to provost duty May, 1863. Simpson, *Hood's Texas Brigade: A Compendium*, 102.

Steel, Private John

K Company, 5th Alabama. With 2d Corps provost guard at the end of the war. Brock (ed.), *Paroles*, 242.

Steger, Provost A. G.

D Company, 1st Virginia. Wounded when on provost duty at Groveton in August, 1862. Spence, "Reports of the First, Seventh and Seventeenth Virginia Regiments in 1862," 262.

Stewart, Alcee William

13th and 20th Louisiana. Appointed provost marshal at Marietta, Georgia, in December, 1863, serving there until its evacuation in 1864. Obituary, *Confederate Veteran*, XXVI (rpr. 1983), 123.

Stone, Lieutenant William R.

Assistant provost marshal with Major Cornelius Boyle in October, 1863. Anderson, *Brokenburn*, 60, 81.

Straber, Provost W. A.

B Company, 1st Virginia. Wounded at Groveton in 1862. Spence, "Reports of the First, Seventh and Seventeenth Virginia Regiments in 1862," 262.

Stringfield, Captain W. W.

Appointed deputy provost marshal of Sixth District of Tennessee on September 25, 1862. *OR,* Ser. II, Vol. IV, pp. 899–900.

Stuart, James D.

Appointed provost marshal of Jackson and Hinds counties, Mississippi, September 8, 1862. *OR,* XV, 805–806.

Stuart, Provost Robert G.

G Company, 1st Virginia. Wounded at Groveton in 1862. Spence, "Reports of the First, Seventh and Seventeenth Virginia Regiments in 1862," 263.

Swan, Private T. B.

C Company, 4th North Carolina. With division provost at Appomattox. Brock (ed.), *Paroles,* 255.

Swindler, Private James E.

C Company, 5th Texas. Detailed to provost duty December, 1863. Simpson, *Hood's Texas Brigade: A Compendium,* 194, 546.

Sykes, William

Provost marshal at Murfreesboro, Tennessee. On staff of A. P. Stewart in the summer of 1863. Ridley, *Battles and Sketches,* 475.

Tate, Colonel Fred

Appointed provost marshal general of the Department of Southern Mississippi and East Louisiana on June 26, 1862. *OR,* XV, 772, 1121; Crute, *Confederate Staff Officers,* 199.

Tatum, Private A. Randolph

F Company, 21st Virginia. Assigned to duty with General Winder in February, 1862. Worsham, *One of Jackson's Foot Cavalry,* 205.

Taylor, Captain C. A.

Appointed provost marshal of Vicksburg and Warren counties, Mississippi, on September 8, 1862. *OR,* XV, 805–806.

Taylor, Private Canty M.

F Company, 3d Alabama. With Grimes's division provost guard, 2d Corps, at Appomattox. Brock (ed.), *Paroles,* 240.

Taylor, J. R.

Deputy provost marshal of Bradley and Polk counties, Tennessee, in May, 1862. *OR,* Ser. II, Vol. II, p. 1423.

Taylor, Colonel Thomas H.

1st Kentucky. Appointed provost marshal of Orange Court House, Virginia, on March 17, 1862. Was provost marshal on Pemberton's staff at Vicksburg. Became provost marshal general of the Department of Alabama, Mississippi, and East Louisiana, replacing Major J. C. Denis, on June 24, 1864. On September 16 Taylor was appointed commandant at Mobile, Alabama. *OR,* Vol. XXXIX, Pt. 2, pp. 664, 736–37; Vol. LI, Pt. 2, pp. 504–505; Crute, *Confederate Staff Officers,* 119, 191; Warner, *Generals in Gray,* 300–301; War Department, Collection of Confederate Records, Record Group 109, Chap. II, Vol. 196; Veterans Records, National Archives.

Taylor, Washington

Entered the Confederate army at age fourteen in August, 1862. Appointed courier to the provost marshal at Petersburg, Virginia, where he served until 1864, when he became a lieutenant and adjutant of a local defense battalion. Obituary, *Confederate Veteran,* XII (rpr. 1983), 130.

Teel, Captain Trevanion Theodore

Appointed provost marshal before the evacuation of Arizona. Hall, *Confederate Army of New Mexico,* 337.

Thomas, Captain J. D.

Appointed deputy provost marshal of the Fifth District of Tennessee (headquarters Jacksborough) on September 25, 1862. *OR,* Ser. II, Vol. IV, pp. 899–900.

Tichenor, Captain George H.

2d Tennessee Cavalry. Appointed provost marshal of Canton, Mississippi, in January, 1864, after wounds led to his discharge. "Thrilling Experiences by Dr. Tichenor," 67–69.

Todd, First Lieutenant David H.

Ordered to duty with General Winder in July, 1861. *OR,* Ser. II, Vol. III, p. 687.

Toole, Colonel John E.

39th Tennessee Mounted Infantry. On June 1, 1862, Toole was detailed to report for duty with Colonel W. M. Churchwell, provost marshal general of the Department of East Tennessee. Toole was a captain and assistant provost marshal of the department from August 12 to September 1, when he was appointed provost marshal general, replacing Churchwell, who died on August 18. Toole served in this capacity until July, 1863, when he was made redundant by the merger of the Department of East Tennessee with the Department of Tennessee. On September 2, 1863, Toole was appointed provost marshal of Simon Buckner's corps. In January, 1864, Toole was provost marshal at Bristol, Tennessee. It appears Toole had no further service with the provost after that. Heartsill, *Fourteen Hundred and 91 Days,* 128; *OR,* Ser. II, Vol. I, p. 878; Ser. II, Vol. IV, pp. 899–900, 910; Vol. XXIII, Pt. 2, p. 731; Vol. XXX, Pt. 2, p. 443; Ser. II, Vol. V, pp. 831–32; Veterans Records, National Archives.

Totten, J. A.

Provost marshal, Army of the Kanawha, September, 1861. *OR,* V, 838.

Trepagnier, Captain Norbert

Appointed provost marshal of Algiers, Louisiana, on March 15, 1862. *OR,* VI, 857–58.

Truehart, Captain Henry Martyn

Appointed assistant provost marshal of Galveston, Texas, on its recapture in January,

1863. He was not keen on provost service; his opinion was that every able-bodied man was required at the front. He joined J. E. B. Stuart in Virginia. Obituary, *Confederate Veteran,* XXII (rpr. 1983), 521.

Truly, Private Bennet R.

A Company, 3d Arkansas. Detached to provost duty in the spring of 1862. Simpson, *Hood's Texas Brigade: A Compendium,* 262.

Tunnard, Willie H.

3d Louisiana. Provost marshal of a general court-martial at Fayetteville, Arkansas, in December, 1861. Tunnard, *A Southern Record,* 119.

Turnham, Private R. C.

G Company, 5th Texas. Detailed to Texas Brigade provost guard in February, 1864. Simpson, *Hood's Texas Brigade: A Compendium,* 226.

Tyler, H. C.

Appointed provost marshal of Yazoo County, Mississippi, on September 8, 1862. *OR,* XV, 805–806.

Tyler, Brigadier General Robert C.

15th Tennessee. Wounded at Shiloh. Appointed provost marshal general of Bragg's army at Tullahoma, Tennessee, on November 15, 1862, and was in that appointment in April, 1863. Tyler then rejoined his regiment until he was incapacitated for further field service by wounds suffered at Missionary Ridge. Assumed command of West Point, Georgia. Appointed brigadier general in February, 1864. Killed in action at West Point, Georgia, April 16, 1865. Warner, "Who Was General Tyler?" 15; *OR,* Vol. XX, Pt. 2, p. 404; Crute, *Confederate Staff Officers,* 312–13; Veterans Records, National Archives; Faust (ed.), *Historical Times Illustrated Encyclopedia of the Civil War,* 767–68.

Van De Graaff, Major Albert Sebastian

Captain, 5th Alabama Battalion, May, 1861; major, June, 1862. Commanded the battalion (Hill's 3d Corps provost guard) throughout most of the war. Krick, *Lee's Colonels,* 354; *OR,* Vol. LII, Pt. 2, p. 378.

Vaughan, Lieutenant Alexander H.

11th Tennessee. Provost marshal at Tazewell, Tennessee, in the autumn of 1861. Killed while trying to arrest members of his regiment for "depredations" against the citizens. Of the three men arrested for the murder, one was court-martialed and shot. Schultz, "Lieut. A. H. Vaughan, Killed in the War," 518.

Wade, Private John G.

B Company, 1st Virginia Battalion. In Appomattox roster listed as a clerk in the Provost Marshal's Office. Brock (ed.), *Paroles,* 451.

Walker, Captain David C.

F Company, 6th Kentucky. Walker lost his left arm at Resaca in 1864 and on recovery became the provost marshal of Americus, Georgia, where he served to the end of the war. Thompson, *History of the Orphan Brigade,* 504.

Walker, Colonel H. H.

Commanded seven companies of Richmond City Guard in May, 1863. *OR,* XVIII, 1059.

Walshe, Captain Blayney Townley

6th Louisiana. Severely wounded at Gaines' Mill in June, 1862. Appointed chief of the Richmond passport office and subsequently provost marshal of the parishes of Livingston, St. Tammany, and Washington, Louisiana. In December, 1863, he was provost marshal of Lake Shore District, Louisiana, with headquarters at Covington. He eventually became chief provost marshal on the staffs of several commanders of the District of Southern Mississippi and East Louisiana. In February, 1865, he was appointed commander of the Lake Shore Subdistrict. Both Lieutenant General Richard S. Ewell and Major General H. T. Hays spoke of Walshe as "gallant and efficient." *OR,* Vol. XXVI, Pt. 2, pp. 558–59; "Captain B. T. Walshe," 575–76.

Walton, Captain J. F.

Provost marshal of Hindman's division at Chickamauga. Hindman, "Battle of Chickamauga," 372; *OR,* Vol. XXX, Pt. 2, p. 306; Crute, *Confederate Staff Officers,* 88.

Wardlow, Major W. A.

An officer in the regiment of Charleston Reserves, which was called out on June 12, 1862, for provost duty in Charleston. Hagood, *Memoirs,* 82.

Waring, Captain J. F.

Jeff Davis Legion. Commanded Wade Hampton's provost guard in September, 1862. *OR,* Vol. XIX, Pt. 1, pp. 822–23.

Watkins, Captain

Provost marshal of Jackson's division, Forrest's cavalry, in December, 1864. *OR,* Vol. XLV, Pt. 2, p. 682.

Watts, Colonel William M.

Watts commanded the Richmond City Guard in April, 1864. Krick, *Lee's Colonels,* 362; *OR,* XXXIII, 1300.

Weisensee, Sergeant Charles P.

K Company, 4th Texas. Assigned to provost duty in the spring of 1864. Simpson, *Hood's Texas Brigade: A Compendium,* 165.

West, Captain

Provost marshal. Killed in action at New Madrid, Missouri, in March, 1862. *OR,* VIII, 128.

West, Captain James Nephew

On April 16, 1863, appointed provost marshal of military courts in the Department of East Tennessee; stationed successively at Knoxville, Bristol, and Abingdon. Myers, *Children of Pride,* 1723–24.

Wharton, Major Rufus Watson

Commanded the 1st North Carolina Battalion (2d Corps provost guard). In March,

1864, he was appointed to command the 67th North Carolina. Early, *War Memoirs,* 253; Krick, *Lee's Colonels,* 264; Veterans Records, National Archives.

Whiting, Major Henry Augustine

Provost marshal of Rodes's division, 2d Corps, Army of Northern Virginia, September to November, 1864. Garnett, "Diary," 8, 15.

Williams, Major J. J.

Provost marshal of the Western Department, June, 1862. Beers, *Guide to the Archives,* 300; *OR,* Ser. II, Vol. II, pp. 1398–99.

Willis, Colonel Edward

12th Georgia. Provost marshal at Greencastle and Chambersburg, Pennsylvania, during the Gettysburg campaign. Coddington, *Gettysburg Campaign,* 163–64; Krick, *Lee's Colonels,* 373; Power, "Young and Full of Promise," 25.

Wilson, Captain

Provost marshal of the Army of the Mississippi at Tupelo in May, 1862. Anderson, *Memoirs,* 203.

Wilson, Captain J. R.

Commanded the provost guard at Port Hudson, Louisiana, during the siege in May and June, 1863. "Port Hudson," 316.

Wilson, Lieutenant LeGrand J.

42d Mississippi. On provost duty with the 42d in Richmond in June, 1862. Wilson, *Confederate Soldier,* 88–89, 93.

Winder, Brigadier General John H.

Appointed provost marshal of Richmond in June, 1861. Was provost marshal general of the city in 1862. On July 26, 1864, he was made responsible for all prison camps in Georgia and Alabama and on November 21 was appointed commissary general of prisoners. Was also provost marshal general of the Confederacy. Died February 7, 1865, at Florence, South Carolina. Putnam, *In Richmond During the Confederacy,* 113, 161; Jones, "Roster of General Officers," 7; McCabe, "Graduates of the United States Military Academy," 41; Browne, "Stranger Than Fiction," 184; Beers, *Guide to the Archives,* 247; Dowdey, *Experiment in Rebellion,* 89, 176; Bill, *Beleaguered City,* 96–97, 104–105, 115, 127, 205–206; Warner, *Generals in Gray,* 340–41; Hunter, *Johnny Reb and Billy Yank,* 566; Jones, *Rebel War Clerk's Diary,* 53–54, 69–70, 111–12; *OR,* XVIII, 1059, 1061–62; XXXIII, 1160, 1216; Ser. II, Vol. III, pp. 683, 685, 700, 703–705, 711; Ser. II, Vol. VII, pp. 205, 501; Vol. XI, Pt. 3, pp. 516, 576–77, 643, 503, 506, 514, 639; Vol. LI, Pt. 2, p. 482; Crute, *Confederate Staff Officers,* 212; Warner, *Generals in Gray,* 340; Veterans Records, National Archives.

Winstead, Captain Thomas Henderson

Badly wounded at Dallas, Georgia, during the Atlanta campaign. In the autumn of 1864 he was assigned to duty with the provost marshal general of the Army of Tennessee, Colonel Cofer, and remained on provost duty to the end of the war. Thompson, *History of the Orphan Brigade,* 631.

Wirz, Captain Henry

Madison Infantry, Louisiana Volunteers. Ordered to report to General Winder in August, 1861. Commanded the prison at Tuscaloosa, Alabama, in November, 1861, as a sergeant. Later commanded Andersonville Prison. *OR,* Ser. II, Vol. III, p. 711; IV, 901.

Wood, Lieutenant Carroll

Deputy provost marshal, Missouri State Guard, November, 1861. Bevier, *History of the First and Second Missouri Confederate Brigades,* 72.

Woodham, Private Nelson

H Company, 3d Alabama. Detached to Grimes's division provost, 2d Corps, at Appomattox. Brock (ed.), *Paroles,* 240.

Woodson, Captain Charles H.

Commanded a company of eighty men on provost duty at Harrisonburg, Virginia, in February, 1864. *OR,* XXXIII, 1192.

Young, Private James

K Company, 3d Alabama. With Grimes's division provost guard, 2d Corps, at Appomattox. Brock (ed.), *Paroles,* 241.

Appendix II

Units on Provost Duty

This appendix lists units for which information, in some cases complete rosters, was located. Generally the sources show only that a specific unit was on provost duty at a specific time, although for some it can be stated when the unit assumed such duties and when they ended.

ALABAMA

Regiments (Infantry)

6TH ALABAMA

On provost duty at Martinsburg, Virginia, in June, 1863. *OR*, Vol. XXVII, Pt. 2, p. 599.

7TH ALABAMA

On provost duty at Chattanooga, Tennessee, in November, 1861. *OR*, IV, 248–50.

16TH ALABAMA

Guarding prisoners at Shiloh in 1862. *OR*, Vol. X, Pt. 1, p. 597.

32D ALABAMA

On provost duty at Chattanooga, August to October, 1862. Ives, "The Record That We Made," 334.

35TH ALABAMA

Guarding prisoners at Newburg, Alabama, in April, 1864. *OR*, Vol. XXXII, Pt. 1, p. 662.

40TH ALABAMA

E Company under Captain Marsh was on provost duty at Jackson, Mississippi, in January, 1863. *OR*, Vol. XVII, Pt. 2, p. 819.

60TH ALABAMA

Commanded by Colonel John W. A. Sanford. Ordered to Richmond as provost in June, 1864, to replace the 25th Virginia (City) Battalion. Ordered to the front August to September, 1864. *OR,* Vol. XXXVI, Pt. 3, p. 902; Vol. XL, Pt. 2, p. 670; Vol. XLII, Pt. 2, pp. 1237–40.

Battalions (Infantry)

5TH ALABAMA

Designated 5th Alabama Battalion on December 2, 1861, at Dumfries, Virginia, the battalion consisted of the companies of Captains Thomas Bush, E. T. Smyth, A. S. Van De Graaff, Dickinson, Davis, and Smith. There was some confusion over the numerical designation for on October 22, 1862, Richmond ordered that "the battalion of Alabama Volunteers under the command of Capt. A. S. Van De Graaff, heretofore known . . . as the 8th, will be hereafter known as the 5th." At Gettysburg the 5th lost half of its 200 men and was then placed on provost duty in A. P. Hill's 3d Corps. During the Wilderness battles in 1864 the 125 men of the battalion, still under Van De Graaff, prevented Federal penetration between the 2d and 3d corps. Strength returns for August 31, 1864, show 14 officers and 151 men and for September 10, 14 officers and 145 men. By January, 1865, Captain Wade Ritter was in command. According to the Appomattox roster, the following were present at the surrender:

Third Corps
Fifth Alabama Battalion—Provost Guard
Wade Ritter, Capt, Co. A, Com'd'g Battalion

Serg't-Major B. L. Roberts	Hosp'l Steward J. M.
Q.M. Serg't W. A. Wayne	Turk

A Company

1st Lieut. Richard Payne	J. T. Dandridge
Serg't M. B. Holland	G. W. Denton
W. S. Hale	John Domon
L. T. Ormond	E. L. Fargo
J. H. Long	J. B. Freeman
Corp'l J. F. Ormond	2d Lieut. W. F. Fulton
D. O. McKinley	Private T. J. Gilbert
Taylor Bradshaw	Y. W. Harris
	Peter Hart
Private J. T. Barns	J. N. Hitt
J. R. Bradshaw	W. T. Ivy
Wm. Cashman	W. B. Jones
Peter Clark	E. N. Kring
L. L. Clary	B. B. Little
R. W. Clary	Seth Little
F. M. Crooks	Courier with private horse
F. W. Cox	T. M. Long

A Company (*continued*)

Private Robt. Markham
Barney McDevitt
W. M. Milenn
S. C. More
Charles Myers

J. T. More
B. D. Nance
W. A. Newton
J. D. Tureman

B Company

1st Lieut. J. R. Willson
Serg't J. P. Crow
A. W. Bryant
Corp'l J. F. White
T. M. Kirkpatrick
Private —— Bartlett
Martin Beal
J. W. Bishop
John Bullock
S. S. Carter
R. S. Craft
J. S. Craft
J. J. Dial
Wm. Dial
T. J. Dixon
John Goins
J. N. Head
I. C. Hill
W. B. Hill
E. D. Henson
John Hollingsworth
W. L. Hollingsworth

2d Lieut. D. C. Turner
Private John Johnson
T. B. Johnson
A. B. Logan
Wm. Loften
J. N. McCaghren
P. W. McCaghren
W. F. McCaghren
G. W. Manning
E. J. Mattison
A. J. Mount
R. C. Mount
Wm. Mount
T. H. Owens
W. G. Parnell
J. M. Pettitt
J. C. Shell
Thos. Sullivan
F. M. Vincent
Walter Whiteside
D. B. Willson
J. B. C. White

C Company

1st Lieut. T. A. Kerr
2d Lieut. W. E. Clay
Serg't W. J. Cambrin
V. M. Thackerson
Corp'l W. M. Glenn
Private James Alred
J. W. Burns
J. B. Burns
J. E. Bolton
James Bridges
J. W. Bray
J. W. Clay
E. W. Colson
E. J. Cambrin
Albert Cambrin
H. Gipson
M. Glenn
W. R. Hillburn

Jr 2d Lieut. W. L. Bray
Private A. J. Jennings
J. H. King
T. B. Logan
G. W. McKerley
W. F. McKaskle
John Noblet
Jasper Stedman
L. M. Segers
W. R. Smith
C. H. Smith
A. W. Smith
E. F. Saunders
J. Thomason
P. M. Watson
L. M. Wiggins
R. H. Yarbrough
Alex. Jones

Tucker, "Death of General A. P. Hill," 569; Brock (ed.), *Paroles,* 271–73; Taylor, *General Lee and His Campaigns,* 274; Katcher, *Army of Northern Virginia,* 35; Hassler, *A. P. Hill,* 191; *OR,* Vol. XLII, Pt. 2, pp. 1214, 1219, 1243; Vol. XLVI, Pt. 1, pp. 1272, 1278; Vol. XLVI, Pt. 2, p. 1182; Vol. LI, Pt. 2, p. 401; Vol. LII, Pt. 2, pp. 378–79; Evans, *Confederate Military History,* VII, 239–40; Fulton, *War Reminiscences,* 156–60.

FLORIDA

Regiments (Infantry)

3D FLORIDA

A Company of the 3d may have been on provost duty at Chickamauga. *OR,* Vol. XXX, Pt. 2, p. 234.

4TH FLORIDA

On provost duty at Chattanooga, August to October, 1862. Ives, "The Record That We Made," 334.

GEORGIA

Regiments (Infantry)

18TH GEORGIA

On provost duty with Longstreet's corps at Bean's Station, Tennessee, winter 1863–1864. Polley, "Texans Foraging for Christmas," 362.

23D GEORGIA

A company of the 23d under Captain John J. A. Sharp was on provost duty in Florida in April, 1864. *OR,* Vol. XXXV, Pt. 2, p. 441.

55TH GEORGIA

On provost duty at Knoxville, Tennessee, in November, 1864. On March 29, 1865, a detachment that had been at Salisbury, North Carolina, and Andersonville, Georgia, was ordered to report to Joseph E. Johnston. The detachment was relieved by reserves. *OR,* Vol. XXX, Pt. 2, p. 611; Vol. XLVII, Pt. 3, p. 713.

61ST GEORGIA

A detachment of the 61st was on provost duty at New Market, Virginia, in November, 1864. Nichols, *Soldier's Story,* 202.

64TH GEORGIA

On June 19, 1864, the 64th, part of Colquitt's brigade, was ordered to Petersburg for service as provost. *OR,* Vol. XL, Pt. 2, p. 669.

65TH GEORGIA

During the Atlanta campaign the 65th under Colonel R. H. Moore was guarding prisoners. *OR,* Vol. XXX, Pt. 2, p. 443.

66TH GEORGIA

Spent a few days as provost in the Army of Tennessee in May, 1864. Nisbet, *4 Years on the Firing Line,* 185–87.

Battalions (Infantry)

2D SHARPSHOOTERS

On provost duty at Chattanooga in late 1862 to early 1863. Participated in antideserter operations south of the city in early 1863. Peacock, "Conscription in the Mountains," 171.

25TH GEORGIA (ATLANTA PROVOST BATTALION)

The 25th, commanded by Lieutenant Colonel G. W. Lee, was disbanded on June 24, 1864. *OR,* Vol. XXIII, Pt. 1, pp. 585–86, Pt. 2, pp. 920, 941, 945, 957; Vol. XXX, Pt. 4, p. 519; Vol. XXXVIII, Pt. 4, p. 789; Veterans Records, National Archives.

27TH GEORGIA

Under Major T. B. Howard the 27th was on provost duty at Columbus, Georgia, in March, 1864. Its strength was 161 men. *OR,* Ser. IV, Vol. III, 460.

KENTUCKY

Regiments (Infantry)

1ST KENTUCKY

Two hundred men of the 1st, under Captain Joseph Desha, were on provost duty at Orange Court House, Virginia, in March, 1862. The regimental commander, Colonel T. H. Taylor, was the provost marshal there. *OR,* Vol. LI, Pt. 2, pp. 504–505.

LOUISIANA

Regiments (Infantry)

1ST LOUISIANA

The 1st was on provost duty for "some time" at Murfreesboro, Tennessee, before leaving for the front on December 29, 1862. "Daily Rebel Banner," 344.

3D LOUISIANA

Two companies were on provost duty at Fayetteville, Arkansas, from December, 1861, to the spring of 1862. One company participated in antideserter operations in Mississippi in April, 1864. Tunnard, *A Southern Record,* 110; *OR,* Vol. XXXII, Pt. 3, pp. 819–22.

Battalions (Infantry)

9TH LOUISIANA

Three companies participated in antideserter operations along the Pearl River, Mississippi, in April, 1864. *OR,* Vol. XXXII, Pt. 3, pp. 819–22.

MISSISSIPPI

Regiments (Cavalry)

4TH MISSISSIPPI

D Company (Captain James Ruffin) was the provost of Stephen D. Lee's cavalry from July to December, 1863. *OR,* Vol. XXIV, Pt. 3, pp. 1042; Vol. XXX, Pt. 4, pp. 517, 656; Vol. XXXI, Pt. 3, p. 865.

Regiments (Infantry)

6TH MISSISSIPPI

Participated in antideserter operations along the Pearl River in Mississippi in April, 1864. *OR,* Vol. XXXII, Pt. 3, pp. 819–22; Howell, *Going to Meet the Yankees,* 210–17.

17TH MISSISSIPPI

On provost duty at Fredericksburg, Virginia, from December 9, 1862, to April 29, 1863, and from May 5 to June 2, 1863. Moore, *A Life for the Confederacy,* 122, 129–38, 144–48.

42D MISSISSIPPI

On provost duty at Richmond in June, 1862, providing one officer and twenty men daily for duties. Companies rotated through the duties. Wilson, *Confederate Soldier,* 88–89, 93.

Battalions (Infantry)

1ST RESERVES

A battalion of underage men raised for provost duty. Obituary, *Confederate Veteran,* XXXIV (rpr. 1983), 104.

MISSOURI

Regiments (Infantry)

2D MISSOURI

G Company acted as provost for the Army of the Mississippi starting on June 9, 1862, near Tupelo, Mississippi. Its provost duty ended July 29, 1862. Anderson, *Memoirs,* 203, 212, 500.

NORTH CAROLINA

Regiments (Infantry)

32D NORTH CAROLINA

C Company guarded prisoners at the Confederate prison in Danville, Virginia, in March and April, 1864. *OR,* XXXIII, 1217, 1300.

45TH NORTH CAROLINA

D and G companies assisted the 32d (above). *OR,* XXXIII, 1217, 1300.

46TH NORTH CAROLINA

A detachment was on provost guard at Camp Lee, Virginia, in March, 1864. *OR,* XXXIII, 1217.

53D NORTH CAROLINA

C Company of the 53d guarded prisoners at the prison in Danville, Virginia, in March and April, 1864. *OR,* XXXIII, 1217, 1300.

Battalions (Infantry)

1ST NORTH CAROLINA

Detached from Hoke's brigade, Early's division, before June 20, 1863, and assigned as provost of the 2d Corps, Army of Northern Virginia. The 1st consisted of two companies commanded by Major R. W. Wharton. At Appomattox the battalion was listed with R. D. Johnston's brigade, Early's division, 2d Corps. The roster shows the following men:

First North Carolina Battalion

A Company

1st Serg't J. G. Reavis
Corp'l M. C. Sheek
Private A. A. Anderson
John Brooks
S. J. Brooks
J. H. Brown
E. W. Crews
Hiram Childress
Isam Cook
Wilson Carter
Martin Davis
Arch. Farris
J. W. Hobson
T. C. Hobson

Private J. F. Hembrick
J. B. Jones
O. C. Jones
Lee Lawrence
N. G. Montgomery
Giles Reavis
W. D. Reece
J. A. Shugart
Perry Shermar
Thomas Tanner
M. S. Woodhouse
Wm. Whitehead
Benjamin Williamson

B Company

1st Serg't J. J. Welch
4th Serg't J. N. Idol
1st Corp'l J. H. Wilson
2d Corp'l G. E. Nissen
Private A. B. Butner
E. H. B. Cassel
J. R. B. Cassel
H. L. B. Cassel
W. J. Cooper
Y. D. Close
N. Crowder
C. N. Boll
T. B. Douthit
Wash. Denney
Theof. Essic
W. L. Fuller
Elwood Fisher
W. T. Henshaw
C. E. Houser

Private Amos Hege
Lee Hendrix
A. M. Idol
J. A. Kiger
S. G. Keesler
J. T. Lewis
Wm. Loman
C. S. Mack
Robt. Murphy
John Newsom
C. T. Phillips
Thos. Ring
E. A. Shouse
J. A. Williamson
S. A. Waugh
Wm. Houser
Fred Standerford
A. L. Welch
J. H. Lewis

I certify, on honor, that of the number of men on these rolls only forty-six (46) were armed on the morning of the 9th instant.

R. W. WOODRUFF,
1st Lt. Com'd'g First N.C. Batt.

Early, *War Memoirs*, 253; Haythornwaite, *Uniforms of the American Civil War*, 190; Early, "Relative Numbers," 36; Brock (ed.), *Paroles*, 204–205.

SOUTH CAROLINA

Regiments (Infantry)

1ST SOUTH CAROLINA

Provided the guard at Charleston while the city was under martial law in May and June, 1862. Hagood, *Memoirs,* 80.

24TH SOUTH CAROLINA

Ordered under its commanding officer, Colonel E. Capers, to Jonesboro as provost, probably relieving the 6th Tennessee of Cheatham's division. *OR,* Vol. XXXIX, Pt. 2, p. 831.

Battalions (Cavalry)

HAMPTON'S BATTALION

Under Major Frank Hampton was on provost duty at Charleston in May and June, 1862. Hagood, *Memoirs,* 80.

Reserves

CHARLESTON RESERVE REGIMENT

Under Colonel Alex H. Brown the regiment was called out for provost duty in Charleston in May and June, 1862. Hagood, *Memoirs,* 82.

TENNESSEE

Regiments (Infantry)

1ST TENNESSEE

Under Colonel H. R. Feild the 1st served as provost at Shelbyville, Tennessee, in May, 1863, and again at the end of 1863. *OR,* Vol. XXIII, Pt. 2, p. 851; Obituary, *Confederate Veteran,* XIX (rpr. 1983), 131.

8TH TENNESSEE

On provost duty at Atlanta in March, 1864. *OR,* Vol. XXXII, Pt. 3, p. 657.

15TH TENNESSEE

Relieved the 1st Louisiana as provost at Murfreesboro, Tennessee, on December 29, 1862. "Daily Rebel Banner," 344.

20TH TENNESSEE

On provost duty starting the day after the Battle of Franklin, Tennessee. McMurray, *History of the Twentieth Tennessee,* 144.

28TH TENNESSEE

Relieved the 1st Tennessee as provost guard at Shelbyville on May 25, 1863. The 28th fought at Chickamauga and in March, 1864, was on provost duty in Atlanta. *OR,* Vol. XXIII, Pt. 2, p. 851; Vol. XXXII, Pt. 3, p. 657; Vol. XXX, Pt. 2, p. 118.

35TH TENNESSEE

Ordered to report to the provost marshal general of the Army of Tennessee on April 30, 1864. *OR,* Vol. XXXII, Pt. 3, p. 867.

TEXAS

Regiments (Cavalry)

3D TEXAS

A company assisted the 2d Missouri on provost duty near Tupelo, Mississippi, in May and June, 1862. Anderson, *Memoirs,* 207.

Battalions (Cavalry)

WALLER'S

On provost duty for part of the 1864 Red River campaign. Noel, *Campaign from Sante Fe to the Mississippi,* 140.

VIRGINIA

Regiments (Cavalry)

7TH VIRGINIA

On provost duty during part of the Gettysburg campaign. Jones, "Summer Campaign of 1863," 116.

Battalions (Cavalry)

39TH VIRGINIA

D Company of the 39th was on provost guard at Camp Lee, Virginia, in March, 1864. *OR*, XXXIII, 1217.

Regiments (Infantry)

2D VIRGINIA

The 2d, part of the Stonewall Brigade, was on provost guard at Winchester, Virginia, in May, 1862. Howard, *Recollections*, 112.

3D VIRGINIA

D Company of the 3d was guarding prisoners at the Confederate prison at Danville, Virginia, in March and April, 1864. *OR*, XXXIII, 1217, 1300.

9TH VIRGINIA

In October, 1863, the 9th, commanded by Colonel J. J. Phillips, was ordered to Ivor Station on the Norfolk and Petersburg Railroad for provost duty along the line of the Blackwater River. A Company of the 9th was on provost duty at Camp Lee, Virginia, in March and April, 1864. *OR*, XXXIII, 1217; Vol. LI, Pt. 2, p. 771.

12TH VIRGINIA

I Company of the 12th was guarding prisoners at the Confederate prison at Danville, Virginia, in March, 1864. *OR*, XXXIII, 1217.

18TH VIRGINIA

G Company of the 18th was guarding prisoners at the Confederate prison at Danville in March and April, 1864. C Company was part of the City Guard in Richmond. *OR*, XXXIII, 1217, 1300.

20TH VIRGINIA

Two companies of the 20th were on provost guard in Richmond in May, 1862. *OR*, Vol. XI, Pt. 3, p. 542.

21ST VIRGINIA

F Company of the 21st was on provost guard at Harpers Ferry, Virginia, during the Gettysburg campaign. The company commander was Captain W. A. Pegram. Worsham gives a complete list of company personnel, *One of Jackson's Foot Cavalry,* xxi, 100–101.

28TH VIRGINIA

I Company was guarding prisoners at the Confederate prison, Danville, Virginia, in March and April, 1864. The rest of the 28th was with the Richmond City Guard. *OR,* XXXIII, 1217, 1300.

32D VIRGINIA

Relieved of provost duty at Fredericksburg, Virginia, by the 17th Mississippi in January, 1863. The 32d had been on provost probably from mid-December, 1862. Moore, *A Life for the Confederacy,* 129.

36TH VIRGINIA

A detachment of the 36th was on provost guard at Camp Lee, Virginia, in March, 1864. *OR, XXXIII,* 1217.

54TH VIRGINIA

On provost duty at Knoxville, Tennessee, from January to August, 1863. Obituary, *Confederate Veteran,* X (rpr. 1983), 323.

Battalions (Infantry)

1ST VIRGINIA (IRISH)

The 1st was organized in state service in May, 1861, and was mustered into Confederate service on June 30, 1861. The companies were enlisted for three years. It was known as the Irish Battalion and after 1861 as the 1st Battalion Virginia Regulars and was designated at times as the 1st Virginia Battalion of the Provisional Army, C.S. At the end of the war the battalion was serving as the provost guard, Army of Northern Virginia. A brief summary of the companies and commanders of the battalion is as follows:

Munford, Major John D., 1861–1862
Seddon, Major John
Leigh, Captain Benjamin, commanding 1862
Davidson, Lieutenant C. A., commanding 1862

Bridgford, Captain D. B., commanding 1862; major 1863–1865

A Company. Benjamin W. Leigh's company, organized in state service in May, 1861; enlisted for three years. Captains B. W. Leigh (commanding battalion in 1862), Thomas R. Dunn.

B Company. D. B. Bridgford's company, organized in state service in May, 1861; enlisted for three years. Captains D. B. Bridgford (promoted to major, 1863), William Overton.

C Company. J. P. Thom's company, organized in state service in May, 1861; enlisted for three years. Captains J. P. Thom, George B. Horner.

D Company. John Seddon's company, organized in May, 1861; enlisted for three years. Captains John Seddon, O. C. Henderson.

E Company. J. Y. Jones. Organized in May, 1861; enlisted for three years. Captains J. Y. Jones, J. A. Turner, C. A. Davidson.

For most of the war the 1st was the provost guard of the Army of Northern Virginia. In June; 1861, it was the provost guard of Jackson's command. There is some doubt as to the exact date the 1st became provost guard of the army. In a letter from General Lee to General Cooper dated December 20, 1862, the 1st is listed as belonging to the 2d Corps. According to Major D. B. Bridgford, the battalion commander, the battalion was on provost duty from December 12, 1862, on. Bridgford signed his report "Chief Provost Marshal, HQ Provost Marshal Second Corps," and its content indicates that he was reporting to the 2d Corps. The commandant of one of the Richmond military prisons in a letter dated January 30, 1863, noted that the 1st Virginia Battalion was provost guard for General Jackson's corps. He had this information from Lieutenant B. E. Coltrane of E Company of the battalion. Other sources state that around December 17 the battalion was detached from the 2d Corps and made provost guard of the Army of Northern Virginia, but it was not until June, 1863, that the 1st was detailed "temporarily" as the army provost guard. Rosters from June 20, 1863, show the battalion as the army provost guard. Field returns from January to April, 1864, show an average strength of 20 officers and 260 men. Figures for the period October to December show 22 officers and 211 men, dropping to 21 officers and 202 men for January and February, 1865. The Appomattox roster shows the following personnel at the surrender:

First Virginia Battalion Infantry
Noncommissioned Staff

Ordnance Serg't Henry Lentz   Color Serg't Jos. Collins
Q.-M. Serg't George Baskerville

A Company

1st Serg't Geo E. Coghill   Private Wm. M. Agee
3rd Serg't G. N. Hancock   Burwell Butler
4th Serg't W. J. Traylor   Frank Cosgrove
Drummer Wm. Ashburn   Jere. Daily

Private J. A. Garnett
 J. B. Harrison
 Tim Hurly
 J. H. Johnson
 Jno Kennedy
 John Sullivan
 Marcellus Sax
 E. N. Lynham
 James Maley
 B. S. Oliver

 Thomas H. Peters
 Wm Powers
 Jno. Roberts
 William Roberts
 Dan'l Shea
 P. R. Vest
 Wm. Welsh
 Bird Roop
 F. M. White

B Company

1st Serg't Jeremiah Dilworth
2d Serg't E. F. Driskill
3rd Serg't P. H. Caldwell
4th Serg't Dan'l Colman
1st Corp'l Nathaniel Prewitt
2d Corp'l C. A. Woodson
Private Hugh Cassidy
 G. M. Cumbee
 P. R. Driskill
 Patrick Horn
 W. S. Hodges
 James Kevan
 Joseph Kinsley
 L. H. Kefarever
 Thos Lawler

Private C. M. Pettus
 John Powers
 Charles Patton
 Eli Polk
 Robt. Prewitt
 Pat. Reilley
 J. H. Stevens
 J. G. Sharitz
 J. W. Thompson
 J. H. Tucker
 Sam'l B. Ragland, clerk in
  office of provost marshal
 John G. Wade, clerk in
  office of provost marshal

C Company

2d Serg't Humphrey Jeffers
3d Serg't John A. Ryan
Corp'l Richard Dunnovan
Private R. T. Bradshaw
 John Collins
 Jno Cannon
 Sidney Crosby
 Carn S. Carter
 Andrew Dodson

Private G. W. Elam
 J. W. Jenkins
 Michael Kinney
 William Martin
 P. G. Johnson
 J. H. Overstreet
 W. D. Thompson
 R. A. Williamson
 R. H. Wilkes

D Company

Serg't George W.
 Morecock
 Chambers Driskill
Corp'l P. H. Harlow
Private W. B. Blankenship
 Benj. Butcher
 Jno Cline
 James Clowdis
 Patrick Donlan
 Estis Mark

Private Benj. Farmer
 Laikey Grant
 Theod'k Jackson
 James McMahan
 J. B. Pleasants
 Wm. Stewart
 Robert Wade
 Jos. Ward

E Company

Corp'l E. G. Hankla	Private H. E. Harkrader
Private John Brassey	Wm. Harman
P. T. Burruss	W. S. Jones
Tyree Bowman	Dan'l McCarty
C. S. Bolt	Pat. McCarty
John Kountz	Levi Nuam
Wm. Childress	I. N. Suits
Jere. Caton	Owen Sweeney
Robt Dogan	David Staley
Benj. Estill	Wm. Whaley
Wm. Flannegan	David Gordon
M. B. Glover	Austin Lawler
John Heller	

John R. Leftwick, clerk P.M. Dep't.
Wm H. Bledsoe, clerk P.M. Dep't.
Wm M. Netherland, office orderly
Walter Farrell, office orderly

Wallace, *Guide to Virginia Military Organizations,* 296; Early, "Relative Numbers," 18, 36; Brock (ed.), *Paroles,* 449–52, 457; Bidgood, "List of General Officers," 166; Katcher, *Army of Northern Virginia,* 34; Worsham, *One of Jackson's Foot Cavalry,* 95; Turner, "Major Charles A. Davidson," 16, 20, 36; *OR,* XXI, 641–42, 1074; Vol. XXIX, Pt. 2, p. 899; Vol. XLVI, Pt. 1, p. 1267; Vol. LI, Pt. 2, p. 721; War Department, Collection of Confederate Records, Record Group 109, Chap. IX, Vol. 199½.

44TH VIRGINIA

At the surrender B Company was on provost duty with the 1st Virginia. A roster of B Company is as follows:

Serg't R. F. Charles	Private E. Saunders
Private Able Bates	W. F. Kennon
Julius Branch	L. J. Wren
J. H. Moore	W. T. Wilkerson

Katcher, *Army of Northern Virginia,* 34; Brock (ed.), *Paroles,* 447; *OR,* Vol. XLVI, Pt. 1, p. 1267; Obituary, *Confederate Veteran,* XXXIV (rpr. 1983), 109.

RESERVES AND LOCAL TROOPS

Regiments

3D REGIMENT, LOCAL DEFENSE TROOPS

The 3d, commanded by Colonel John McAnerney, was assigned to guard duty in Richmond in February, 1865. *OR,* Vol. XLVI, Pt. 2, p. 1237.

19TH VIRGINIA MILITiA

Ordered on guard duty in Richmond in January, 1865. *OR*, Vol. XLII, Pt. 2, pp. 1237–40; Vol. XLVI, Pt. 2, p. 1140.

1ST REGIMENT, 2D CLASS MILITIA

Ordered on guard duty in Richmond in January, 1865. *OR*, Vol. XLII, Pt. 2, pp. 1237–40; Vol. XLVI, Pt. 2, p. 1140.

Battalions

1ST BATTALION, VIRGINIA RESERVES

Guarding prisoners at Belle Isle, Richmond, in September, 1864. Commanding officer was Lieutenant Colonel Richard T. W. Duke. *OR*, Vol. XLII, Pt. 2, pp. 1237–40.

2D BATTALION, VIRGINIA RESERVES

This battalion of seven companies commanded by Major J. H. Guy was organized in Richmond on February 27, 1865. It was on provost guard the night Richmond was evacuated. *OR*, Vol. XLVI, Pt. 2, pp. 1262–63.

25TH BATTALION, VIRGINIA VOLUNTEERS (RICHMOND CITY BATTALION), LOCAL DEFENSE TROOPS

Officially designated as the 25th Battalion Virginia Volunteers, but better known as the Richmond City Battalion. Organized on August 15, 1862, for six months' service in and around Richmond, it consisted of five companies (A to E), with F, G, and H companies being added later. In January and February, 1863, the battalion was remustered for the war. Its commanding officer to the end of the war was Major, later Lieutenant Colonel W. M. Elliott. The companies were as follows:

A Company. John H. Greener's company. Enlisted July 1, 1862, for six months, reenlisted January 1, 1863, for the war. Some members of the company had prior service in the 1st Virginia Regiment. In September, 1862, some of the men were transferred to the Maryland Line. Captain John H. Greener.

B Company. Louis J. Bossieux's company. Enlisted July 21, 1862, for six months, reenlisted January 21, 1863, for the war. A note appended to a muster roll in January stated that on reenlistment the men were transferred to Camp Lee and to other organizations. Captains L. J. Bossieux, John W. Fisher.

C Company. Enlisted for six months on July 28, 1862, and reenlisted for the war on February 9, 1863.

D Company. Enlisted for six months on July 26, 1862, and reenlisted for the war

in January or February, 1863. Captain John F. C. Potts (resigned March 1, 1865).
E Company. William L. Maule's company. Enlisted August 27, 1862, for six
months and reenlisted for the war on January 30, 1863. Captains W. L. Maule, F.
M. Boykin.

F Company. Cyrus Bossieux's company. Enlisted March 3, 1862, for one year as
Co. H/K, 3d Regiment, Virginia Artillery, Local Defense Troops, but disbanded
in May, 1862, and reorganized as infantry. Assigned to duty guarding prisoners
in Richmond. After a short time with the 59th Virginia Infantry the company
joined the 25th Battalion. Captain C. Bossieux (retired March 30, 1865).

G Company. President's Guard. Enlisted March 7, 1862, for the war. Served a
short time with the 28th Battalion Virginia Infantry and with the 59th and was
assigned to the 25th Battalion on March 5, 1863. The company consisted of boys
sixteen to eighteen years of age. Captains William S. Reed, Robert G. Portlock,
Lucien L. Bass.

H Company. William H. Allison's company. Organized June 4, 1863.

I Company. Captain Aston's company.

Captain Alexander B. Guigon's company Light Artillery. Mustered in on March
13, 1862, and performed guard duties in Richmond and at Confederate prisons.

In 1862 during the Seven Days' Battle, the 25th Battalion was called out on provost
duty. In 1864 it was replaced as provost guard by the 60th Alabama. A complete roster
of the battalion's officers is as follows:

Wyatt M. Elliott, Major and Lt. Col.
Louis J. Bossieux, Major
Thomas L. Bondurant, Assistant Surgeon and Surgeon
Oscar R. Hough, Adjutant
Jesse P. Hope, Surgeon
Joseph A. Baden, Assistant Surgeon
Henry C. Shent, Assistant Surgeon
Thaddeus B. Starke, Assistant Quartermaster
Benjamin F. Cocke, Acting Adjutant
John E. Bradley, Ensign

A Company

John H. Greaner, Capt.	George Bell, 2d Lt.
James T. Vaughan, 1st Lt.	Robert E. Mills, 2d Lt.
Oscar R. Hough, 2d Lt.	James B. Newberry, 2d. Lt.
John Poe, 2d Lt.	

B Company

Louis J. Bossieux, Capt. and Major	George P. Bondurant, 2d Lt. and 1st
John W. Fisher, 1st Lt. and Capt.	Lt.
John La Touche, 2d Lt. and 1st Lt.	John W. Beard, 2d Lt. and 1st Lt.
	Robert P. Nixon, 2d Lt. and 1st Lt.

C Company

William Wirt Harrison, Capt.	John Randolph, 2d Lt. and 1st Lt.

William H. Allison, 1st Lt., promoted Capt., H Company

Charles D. Anderson, 2d Lt., 1st Lt.,
and Capt.

Robert A. Stephenson, 2d Lt. and
1st Lt.

Edward P. Sheppard, 2d Lt. and 1st
Lt.

D Company

John F. C. Potts, Capt.

William A. Jenkins, 1st Lt.

Henry T. Miller, 2d Lt. and 1st Lt.

Rigdon McCoy McIntosh, 2d Lt. and
1st Lt.

N. R. Motley, 2d Lt. and 1st Lt.

Charles H. Erambert, 2d Lt. and 1st
Lt.

E Company

William L. Maule, Capt.

F. M. Boykin, 1st. Lt. and Capt.

James L. Bray, 2d Lt. and 1st Lt.

William A. Garrett, 2d Lt.

Thomas H. Harris, 2d Lt.

William G. Herrington, 2d Lt.

R. L. Scott, 2d Lt.

F Company

Cyrus Bossieux, Capt.

John McCawley, 1st Lt.

Peter C. Willis, 2d Lt. and 1st Lt.

Virginius Bossieux, 2d Lt.

Robert G. W. Dillard, 2d Lt.

G Company

William S. Reed, Capt.

R. G. Portlock, 1st Lt. and Capt.

Lucien L. Bass, 2d Lt., 1st Lt., and
Capt.

William U. Bass, 2d Lt. and 1st Lt.

W. L. Moody, 2d Lt.

F. S. Dalton, 2d Lt.

H Company (organized June 4, 1863)

William H. Allison, Capt.

Benjamin F. Cocke, 1st Lt.

Robert H. Gillian, 2d Lt.

Samuel A. West, 2d Lt.

Artillery Company Attached

A. B. Guigon, Capt.

George P. Bondurant, 1st Lt.

Wallace, *Guide to Virginia Military Organizations,* 218–19; "Roster of Officers of
City 25th Battalion (Richmond)," 323–25; Manarin (ed.), *Richmond at War,* 186–
87; *OR,* Vol. XVIII, 1059; Vol. XLII, Pt. 2, pp. 1237–40.

MISCELLANEOUS

J. R. JONES'S BRIGADE (OF JACKSON'S DIVISION)

Acted as provost in Frederick City, Maryland, in September, 1862. *OR,* Vol. XIX, Pt.
1, pp. 1006–1007.

1ST REGIMENT ENGINEERS

Was on guard duty in Richmond in March, 1864. *OR,* XXXIII, 1217.

14TH CONFEDERATE CAVALRY REGIMENT

Participated in antideserter operations along the Pearl River in Mississippi in April, 1864. *OR,* Vol. XXXII, Pt. 3, p. 819.

1ST CONFEDERATE INFANTRY BATTALION

A Company was relieved of provost duties in Atlanta on May 30, 1864, and ordered to Virginia to rejoin its parent battalion. *OR,* Vol. XXXVI, Pt. 3, p. 850.

CONFEDERATE GUARDS RESPONSE BATTALION

Under Major F. H. Clack may have been provost at Shiloh. *OR,* Vol. X, Pt. 1, p. 512.

CAPTAIN F. M. ARMSTRONG'S MISSISSIPPI CAVALRY COMPANY

This unattached company of cavalry was ordered to Aberdeen, Mississippi, on provost duty on May 15, 1864. It was composed of men seventeen to eighteen and forty-five to fifty years of age. *OR,* Vol. XXXIX, Pt. 2, p. 611.

CAPTAIN JAMES N. BOLEN'S DISMOUNTED KENTUCKY CAVALRY COMPANY

On provost guard with E Company, 40th Alabama at Jackson, Mississippi, in January, 1863. *OR,* Vol. XVII, Pt. 2, p. 819.

PROVOST GUARD, MERCER COUNTY, VIRGINIA LOCAL DEFENSE TROOPS

Commanded by Captain A. B. Calfee. He enlisted in this company on September 25, 1862, for three years. Wallace, *Guide to Virginia Military Organizations,* 225.

CAPTAIN JOHN AVIS' COMPANY, PROVOST GUARD, STAUNTON, VIRGINIA

Enlisted July 12, 1862, for the war. Some of the men were disabled soldiers from other units, temporarily detailed to the company for light duty. Company rolls show that a detachment of the company was mounted and paid as cavalry. Wallace, *Guide to Virginia Military Organizations,* 198.

CAPTAIN WILLIAM HENDRICK'S COMMAND

The men of this command were on special service by the day under the direction of the Richmond provost marshal by order of General John H. Winder. Hendrick was "acting captain." Most of the men served only part time during July, 1862. Wallace, *Guide to Virginia Military Organizations,* 198.

IST LIEUTENANT J. F. CECIL'S COMPANY, LOCAL DEFENSE TROOPS

A company of nonconscripts and exempts acting as provost guard at Wytheville, Virginia. Wallace, *Guide to Virginia Military Organizations,* 221.

CAPTAIN W. B. MALLORY'S COMPANY, LOCAL DEFENSE TROOPS

Organized June 27, 1863. Provost guard at Charlottesville, Virginia. It was enlisted specifically as provost guard and included no detailed men, as was usually the case. Wallace, *Guide to Virginia Military Organizations,* 223.

CAPTAIN J. S. MOORMAN'S COMPANY, LOCAL DEFENSE TROOPS

Organized September 5, 1863. Provost guard at Dublin, Virginia. Some members of the company were later conscripted into regular Virginia units. Wallace, *Guide to Virginia Military Organizations,* 223.

CAPTAIN CHARLES H. WOODSON'S PARTISAN COMPANY

This company of about eighty men served as provost with Brigadier General John D. Imboden's Northwest Virginia Brigade. In May, 1864, the Confederate Congress thanked the company for its resolution to serve for forty years or the war. "General Information," 157; *OR,* XXXIII, 1192, 1363; Vol. XXXVIII, Pt. 3, p. 1008; Vol. XLIII, Pt. 1, p. 89, Pt. 2, p. 826; Vol. XLVI, Pt. 2, p. 309; Vol. LI, Pt. 2, p. 1061.

Bibliography

Manuscripts

Brown, Colonel Alexander Haskell. M-91 Record Book. Southern Historical Collection, University of North Carolina Library, Chapel Hill.

Carrington, Major I. H. Papers. William R. Perkins Library, Duke University, Durham, N.C.

Davis, Robert. Diary. Robert W. Woodruff Library, Emory University, Atlanta, Ga.

List of Officers and Employees in Provost Marshal Office, Richmond, April 5, 1864. Department of Archives and Manuscripts, Louisiana State University, Baton Rouge.

Veterans Records. National Archives and Records Service. Washington, D.C.

War Department. Collection of Confederate Records. Record Groups 109, 232, 236, 250, National Archives, Washington, D.C.

Winder, Brigadier General J. H. Papers. Southern Historical Collection, University of North Carolina Library, Chapel Hill.

Government Documents

Beers, Henry Putney. *Guide to the Archives of the Government of the Confederate States of America.* Washington, D.C., 1968.

Confederate States War Department. *Regulations for the Army of the Confederate States, 1863.* Richmond, 1863.

Journal of the Congress of the Confederate States of America, 1861–1865. 7 vols. Washington, D.C., 1904–1905.

The War of the Rebellion: A Compilation of the Official Records of the Union and Confederate Armies. 130 vols. Washington, D.C., 1880–1901.

Microfilm

Henry Hotze. *The Index: A Weekly Journal of Politics, Literature, and News. Devoted to the Exposition of the Mutual Interests, Political and Commercial, of Great Britain and the Confederate States of America.* 5 vols. London, 1862–65.

Books

Abraham Lincoln Book Shop. *Catalogue 105, Americana.* Chicago, 1983.

Alexander, E. P. *Military Memoirs of a Confederate: A Critical Narrative.* New York, 1907.

Amann, William Frayne, ed. *The Confederate Armies.* New York, 1961.

Anderson, Ephraim McD. *Memoirs: Historical and Personal; Including the Campaigns of the First Missouri Confederate Brigade.* 1868; rpr. Dayton, 1972.

Anderson, John Q., ed. *Brokenburn: The Journal of Kate Stone, 1861–1868.* Baton Rouge, 1972.

Antrim, Earl. *Civil War Prisons and Their Covers.* New York, 1961.

Barrett, John G. *The Civil War in North Carolina.* Chapel Hill, 1963.

————, ed. *Yankee Rebel: The Civil War Journal of Edmund DeWitt Patterson.* Chapel Hill, 1966.

Barron, S. B. *The Lone Star Defenders: A Chronicle of the Third Texas Cavalry, Ross' Brigade.* 1908; rpr. Waco, 1964.

Bartlett, Napier. *Military Record of Louisiana, Including Biographical and Historical Papers Relating to the Military Organizations of the State.* 1874; rpr. Baton Rouge, 1964.

Beale, R. L. T. *History of the Ninth Virginia Cavalry in the War Between the States.* 1899; rpr. Amissville, Va., 1981.

Beals, C. *War Within a War: The Confederacy Against Itself.* New York, 1965.

Bearss, Edwin C. *Forrest at Brice's Cross Roads and in North Mississippi in 1864.* Dayton, 1979.

Bernard, George S., ed. *War Talks of Confederate Veterans.* 1892; rpr. Dayton, 1981.

Bettersworth, John K. *Confederate Mississippi: The People and Policies of a Cotton State in Wartime.* 1943; rpr. Philadelphia, 1978.

Bevier, R. S. *History of the First and Second Missouri Confederate Brigades, 1861–1865.* 1879; rpr. N.p., 1985.

Bill, Alfred Hoyt. *The Beleaguered City: Richmond, 1861 1865.* New York, 1946.

Black, Robert C. *The Railroads of the Confederacy.* Chapel Hill, 1952.

Boatner, Mark Mayo. *The Civil War Dictionary.* New York, 1959.

Bond, Natalie Jenkins, and Osmun Latrobe Coward, eds. *The South Carolinians: Colonel Asbury Coward's Memoirs.* New York, 1968.

Booth, George Wilson. *Personal Reminiscences of a Maryland Soldier in the War Between the States, 1861–1865.* 1898; rpr. Gaithersburg, Md., 1986.

Bragg, Jefferson Davis. *Louisiana in the Confederacy.* Baton Rouge, 1941.

Bridges, Hal. *Lee's Maverick General: Daniel Harvey Hill.* New York, 1961.

Broadfoot, Thomas W., ed. *Civil War Books: A Priced Checklist.* Wendell, N.C., 1978.

Brock, R. A., ed. *Paroles of the Army of Northern Virginia, R. E. Lee, Gen., C.S.A., Commanding, Surrendered at Appomattox C. H., Va., April 9, 1865, to Lieutenant-General U. S. Grant, Commanding Armies of the U.S., Southern Historical Society Papers,* XV (1887; rpr. 1977).

Brown, Louis A. *The Salisbury Prison: A Case Study of Confederate Military Prisons, 1861–1865.* Wendell, N.C., 1980.

Bryan, Thomas Conn. *Confederate Georgia.* Athens, Ga., 1953.

Carter, Samuel. *The Siege of Atlanta, 1864.* New York, 1973.

Casler, John O. *Four Years in the Stonewall Brigade.* 1893; rpr. Dayton, 1971.

Chambers, Lenoir. *The Legend and the Man to Valley V.* New York, 1959. Vol. I of Chambers, *Stonewall Jackson.* 2 vols.

Chesnut, Mary Boykin. *A Diary from Dixie.* 1905; rpr. Edited by Ben Ames Williams. Boston, 1949.

Clark, Walter, ed. *Histories of the Several Regiments and Battalions from North Carolina in the Great War, 1861–'65.* 1901; rpr. 5 vols. Wendell, N.C., 1982.

Coddington, Edwin B. *The Gettysburg Campaign: A Study in Command.* New York, 1968.

Coker, James Lide. *History of Company G, Ninth S.C. Regiment, Infantry, S.C. Army and of Company E, Sixth S.C. Regiment, Infantry, S.C. Army.* Greenwood, S.C., 1979.

Collins, R. M. *Chapters from the Unwritten History of the War Between the States; or, The Incidents in the Life of a Confederate Soldier in Camp, on the March, in the Great Battles, and in Prison.* 1893; rpr. Dayton, 1982.

Confederate Historical Society *Journals.* 10 vols. London, 1962–72.

Connelly, Thomas Lawrence. *Army of the Heartland: The Army of Tennessee, 1861–1862.* Baton Rouge, 1967.

———. *Autumn of Glory: The Army of Tennessee, 1862–1865.* Baton Rouge, 1971.

Coulter, E. Merton. *The Confederate States of America, 1861–1865.* 1950; rpr. Baton Rouge, 1968.

———. *Travels in the Confederate States: A Bibliography.* Norman, 1948.

Crute, Joseph H. *Confederate Staff Officers, 1861–1865.* Powhatan, Va., 1982.

Cummings, Charles M. *Yankee Quaker Confederate General: The Curious Career of Bushrod Rust Johnson.* Cranbury, N.J., 1971.

Cunningham, S. A., and Edith D. Pope, eds. *Confederate Veteran.* 1893–1933; rpr. 40 vols. Wendell, N.C., 1983–84.

Dabney, Virginius. *The Last Review: The Confederate Reunion, Richmond, 1932.* Chapel Hill, 1984.

Dame, William Meade. *From the Rapidan to Richmond and the Spotsylvania Campaign.* Baltimore, 1920.

Davis, Jefferson. *The Rise and Fall of the Confederate Government.* 1881; rpr. 2 vols. New York, 1958.

Davis, Varina. *Jefferson Davis, Ex-President of the Confederate States: A Memoir by His Wife.* 2 vols. New York, 1890.

Davis, William C. *Battle at Bull Run: A History of the First Major Campaign of the Civil War.* New York, 1977.

———. *The Orphan Brigade: The Kentucky Confederates Who Couldn't Go Home.* New York, 1980.

————, ed. *Fighting for Time.* New York, 1983. Vol. IV of Davis, *The Image of War, 1861–1865.* 6 vols.

————, ed. *Touched by Fire: A Photographic Portrait of the Civil War.* Vol. II of 2 vols. Boston, 1986.

Dawson, Francis W. *Reminiscences of Confederate Service, 1861–1865.* 1882; rpr. Baton Rouge, 1980.

Diket, A. L. *wha hae wi' [Pender] . . . bled.* New York, 1979.

Dodson, William Carey, ed. *Campaigns of Wheeler and His Cavalry, 1862–1865.* Atlanta, 1899.

Donnelly, Ralph W. *The History of the Confederate States Marine Corps.* Washington, N.C., 1976.

Douglas, Henry Kyd. *I Rode with Stonewall.* 1940; rpr. Chapel Hill, 1968.

Dowdey, Clifford. *Experiment in Rebellion.* New York, 1947.

Dowdey, Clifford, and Louis H. Manarin, eds. *The Wartime Papers of R. E. Lee.* Boston, 1961.

Duke, Basil W. *A History of Morgan's Cavalry.* Bloomington, 1960.

————. *Reminiscences of General Basil W. Duke, C.S.A.* 1911; rpr. Freeport, N.Y., 1969.

Early, Jubal Anderson. *Autobiographical Sketch and Narrative of the War Between the States.* Philadelphia, 1912.

————. *War Memoirs.* 1867; rpr. Bloomington, 1960.

Elliott, Joseph Cantey. *Lieutenant General Richard Heron Anderson: Lee's Noble Soldier.* Dayton, 1985.

Escott, Paul D. *After Secession: Jefferson Davis and the Failure of Confederate Nationalism.* Baton Rouge, 1978.

Evans, Clement A., ed. *Confederate Military History.* 1899; rpr. 12 vols. New York, 1962.

Farwell, Bryan. *Queen Victoria's Little Wars.* New York, 1972.

Faust, Patricia L., ed. *Historical Times Illustrated Encyclopedia of the Civil War.* New York, 1986.

Fay, Edwin Hedge. *"This Infernal War": The Confederate Letters of Sgt. Edwin H. Fay.* Edited by Bell Irvin Wiley. Austin, 1958.

Fletcher, William Andrew. *Rebel Private Front and Rear.* Austin, 1954.

Foote, Shelby. *The Civil War: A Narrative.* 3 vols. New York, 1958, 1963, 1974.

Freeman, Douglas Southall. *Lee's Lieutenants.* 3 vols. New York, 1942.

————. *R. E. Lee, A Biography.* 4 vols. New York, 1942.

————, and Grady McWhiney, eds. *Lee's Dispatches: Unpublished Letters of General Robert E. Lee, C.S.A. to Jefferson Davis and the War Department of the Confederate States of America, 1862–65.* 1915; rpr. New York, 1957.

Fulton, William Frierson II. *The War Reminiscences of William Frierson Fulton II 5th*

Alabama Battalion Archer's Brigade A. P. Hill's Light Division A.N.V. N.d.; rpr. Gaithersburg, Md., 1986.

Gallagher, Gary W. *Stephen Dodson Ramseur: Lee's Gallant General.* Chapel Hill, 1985.

——, ed. *Extracts of Letters of Major General Bryan Grimes . . . Together with Some Personal Recollections of the War.* 1883; rpr. Wilmington, 1986.

Govan, Gilbert E., and James W. Livingood. *A Different Valor: The Story of General Joseph E. Johnston, C.S.A.* Westport, Conn., 1975.

Hagood, Johnson. *Memoirs of the War of Secession.* Columbia, S.C., 1910.

Hale, Laura Virginia, and Stanley S. Phillips. *History of the Forty-Ninth Virginia Infantry C.S.A., "Extra Billy Smith's Boys."* Lanham, Md., 1981.

Hall, Martin Hardwick. *The Confederate Army of New Mexico.* Austin, 1978.

Hall, Winchester. *The Story of the 26th Louisiana Infantry, in the Service of the Confederate States.* 1890?; rpr. Gaithersburg, Md., 1984.

Harrison, Walter. *Pickett's Men: A Fragment of War History.* 1870; rpr. Gaithersburg, Md., 1984.

Hartje, Robert G. *Van Dorn: The Life and Times of a Confederate General.* Nashville, 1967.

Harwell, Richard B. *The Confederate Reader.* New York, 1957.

——. *In Tall Cotton: The 200 Most Important Confederate Books for the Reader, Researcher and Collector.* Austin, N.C., 1978.

Hassler, William Woods. *A. P. Hill: Lee's Forgotten General.* Richmond, 1962.

Haythornwaite, Philip J. *Uniforms of the American Civil War.* Poole, Dorset, Eng., 1975.

Heartsill, W. W. *Fourteen Hundred and 91 Days in the Confederate Army.* 1876; rpr. Edited by Bell I. Wiley. Jackson, Tenn., 1954.

Heinl, Robert Debs. *Dictionary of Military and Naval Quotations.* Annapolis, Md., 1966.

Henderson, Colonel G. F. R. *Stonewall Jackson and the American Civil War.* 1898; rpr. New York, 1943.

Hermann, I. *Memoirs of a Veteran Who Served as a Private in the 60's in the War Between the States.* 1911; rpr. Lakemount, Ga., 1974.

Hesseltine, William B. *Civil War Prisons: A Study in War Psychology.* New York, 1964.

Hill, Daniel Harvey. *Bethel to Sharpsburg.* 2 vols. Raleigh, N.C., 1926.

Hoehling, A. A., and Mary Hoehling. *The Day Richmond Died.* New York, 1981.

Hoke, Jacob. *The Great Invasion.* 1887; rpr. New York, 1959.

Hood, J. B. *Advance and Retreat: Personal Experiences in the United States and Confederate States Armies.* New Orleans, 1880.

Horn, Stanley F. *The Army of Tennessee.* Norman, Okla. 1941.

315

Howard, McHenry. *Recollections of a Maryland Confederate Soldier and Staff Officer Under Johnston, Jackson and Lee.* 1914; rpr. Dayton, 1975.

Howell, H. Grady. *Going to Meet the Yankees: A History of the "Bloody Sixth" Mississippi Infantry, C.S.A.* Jackson, Miss., 1981.

Hubbard, John Milton. *Notes of a Private.* 1909; rpr. Bolivar, Tenn., 1973.

Hubbell, John T., ed. *Battles Lost and Won: Essays from Civil War History.* Westport, Conn., 1975.

Hunter, Alexander. *Johnny Reb and Billy Yank.* New York, 1905.

Johnson, Robert Underwood, and Clarence Clough Buel, eds. *Battles and Leaders of the Civil War.* 4 vols. 1887–88; rpr. New York, 1956.

Johnston, Joseph E. *Narrative of Military Operations Directed, During the Late War Between the States.* 1874; rpr. Bloomington, 1959.

Jones, John B. *A Rebel War Clerk's Diary.* 1866; rpr. Edited by Earl Schenck Miers. New York, 1958.

Jones, Terry L. *Lee's Tigers: The Louisiana Infantry in the Army of Northern Virginia.* Baton Rouge, 1987.

Jordan, Thomas, and J. P. Pryor. *The Campaigns of Lieut.-Gen. N. B. Forrest, and of Forrest's Cavalry.* 1868; rpr. Dayton, 1973.

Katcher, Philip R. N. *The Army of Northern Virginia.* Reading, Berkshire, Eng., 1975.

Kerby, Robert L. *Kirby Smith's Confederacy: The Trans-Mississippi South, 1863–1865.* New York, 1972.

Krick, Robert K. *Lee's Colonels: A Biographical Register of the Field Officers of the Army of Northern Virginia.* 1979. Rev. ed. Dayton, 1984.

———. *Parker's Virginia Battery, C.S.A.* Berryville, Va., 1975.

Livermore, Thomas Leonard. *Numbers and Losses in the Civil War in America.* 1901; rpr. Bloomington, 1957.

Loehr, Charles T. *War History of the Old First Virginia Infantry Regiment, Army of Northern Virginia.* 1884; rpr. Dayton, 1970.

Long, A. L. *Memoirs of Robert E. Lee.* 1887; rpr. Secaucus, N.J., 1983.

Long, E. B. *The Civil War Day by Day: An Almanac, 1861–1865.* New York, 1971.

Longstreet, James. *From Manassas to Appomattox: Memoirs of the Civil War in America.* 1896; rpr. Edited by James I. Robertson. Bloomington, 1960.

Lonn, Ella. *Desertion During the Civil War.* New York, 1928.

Lord, Francis A. *Civil War Collector's Encyclopedia.* Harrisburg, 1963.

McBrien, Joe Bennett. *The Tennessee Brigade.* Chattanooga, 1977.

McCarthy, Carlton. *Detailed Minutiae of Soldier Life in the Army of Northern Virginia, 1861–1865.* Richmond, 1882.

McClendon, W. A. *Recollections of War Times By an Old Veteran While Under Stonewall Jackson and Lieutenant General James Longstreet.* 1909; rpr. San Bernardino, 1973.

McGuire, Judith W. *Diary of a Southern Refugee During the War.* Richmond, 1889.

McKim, Randolph Harrison. *The Numerical Strength of the Confederate Army.* New York, 1912.

McMurray, Richard M. *John Bell Hood and the War for Southern Independence.* Lexington, Ky., 1982.

McMurray, W. J. *History of the Twentieth Tennessee Regiment Volunteer Infantry, C.S.A.* 1904; rpr. Nashville, 1976.

Manarin, Louis H., ed. *Richmond at War: The Minutes of the City Council, 1861–1865.* Chapel Hill, 1966.

Military Analysis of the Civil War: An Anthology by the Editors of Military Affairs. Millwood, N.Y., 1977.

Miller, Francis T., ed. *The Photographic History of the Civil War.* 1911; rpr. 5 vols. New York, 1957.

Montague, C. E. *Disenchantment.* London, 1968.

Moore, Albert Burton. *Conscription and Conflict in the Confederacy.* New York, 1924.

Moore, Robert Augustus. *A Life for the Confederacy.* Edited by James W. Silver. Jackson, Tenn., 1959.

Morgan, James Morris. *Recollections of a Rebel Reefer.* London, 1918.

Myers, Robert Manson, ed. *The Children of Pride: A True Story of Georgia and the Civil War.* New Haven, 1972.

Nevins, Allan, James I. Robertson, Jr., and Bell I. Wiley, eds. *Civil War Books: A Critical Bibliography.* 2 vols. Baton Rouge, 1967.

Nichols, G. W. *A Soldier's Story of His Regiment (61st Georgia) and Incidentally of the Lawton-Gordon-Evans Brigade Army Northern Virginia.* 1898; rpr. Kennesaw, Ga., 1961.

Nichols, James L. *Confederate Engineers.* Tuscaloosa, 1957.

Nisbet, James Cooper. *4 Years on the Firing Line.* 1914; rpr. Edited by Bell Irvin Wiley. Jackson, Tenn., 1963.

Noel, Theophilus. *A Campaign from Sante Fe to the Mississippi: Being A History of the Old Sibley Brigade . . . 1861–1864.* 1904; rpr. Edited by Martin Hardwick Hall and Edwin Adams Davis. Houston, 1961.

Oates, William C. *The War Between the Union and the Confederacy and Its Lost Opportunities.* 1905; rpr. Dayton, 1974.

Opie, John Newton. *A Rebel Cavalryman with Lee, Stuart and Jackson.* 1899; rpr. Dayton, 1972.

Owen, William Miller. *In Camp and Battle with the Washington Artillery of New Orleans.* 1885; rpr. Gaithersburg, Md., 1983.

Owsley, Frank Lawrence. *State Rights in the Confederacy.* 1925; rpr. Gloucester, Mass., 1961.

Parks, Joseph H. *General Leonidas Polk C.S.A.: The Fighting Bishop.* Baton Rouge, 1962.

317

Paxton, John Gallatin. *The Civil War Letters of General Frank "Bull" Paxton, C.S.A., A Lieutenant of Lee and Jackson.* 1905; rpr. Hillsboro, Texas, 1978.

Polk, William M. *Leonidas Polk, Bishop and General.* 2 vols. New York, 1915.

Polley, J. B. *Hood's Texas Brigade: Its Marches, Its Battles, Its Achievements.* 1910; rpr. Dayton, 1976.

Putnam, Sallie A. *In Richmond During the Confederacy.* 1867; rpr. New York, 1961.

Richardson, James D., ed. *The Messages and Papers of Jefferson Davis and the Confederacy, Including Diplomatic Correspondence, 1861–1865.* 1905; rpr. 2 vols. New York, 1966.

Ridley, Bromfield Lewis. *Battles and Sketches of the Army of Tennessee.* 1906; rpr. Dayton, 1978.

Riley, E. S. *"Stonewall Jackson": A Thesaurus of Anecdotes of and Incidents in the Life of Lieut.-Gen. Thomas Jonathan Jackson, C.S.A.* Annapolis, Md., 1920.

Roland, Charles. *The Confederacy.* Chicago, 1960.

Scarborough, William Kauffman, ed. *The Diary of Edmund Ruffin.* Vol. I. Baton Rouge, 1972.

Schenck, Martin. *Up Came Hill: The Story of the Light Division and Its Leaders.* Harrisburg, 1958.

Sears, Stephen W. *Landscape Turned Red: The Battle of Antietam.* New Haven, 1983.

Shaver, Lewellyn A. *A History of the Sixtieth Alabama Regiment.* 1867; rpr. Gaithersburg, Md., 1983.

Simpson, Harold B. *Hood's Texas Brigade: A Compendium.* Hillsboro, Tex., 1977.

———. *Hood's Texas Brigade: Lee's Grenadier Guard.* Waco, 1970.

Sloan, John A. *Reminiscences of the Guilford Grays, Co. B, 27th N.C. Regiment.* 1883; rpr. Wendell, N.C., 1978.

Smith, W. A. *The Anson Guards: Company C Fourteenth Regiment North Carolina Volunteers, 1861–1865.* 1914; rpr. Wendell, N.C., 1978.

Sommers, Richard J. *Richmond Redeemed: The Siege at Petersburg.* New York, 1981.

Sorrel, Gilbert Moxley. *Recollections of a Confederate Staff Officer.* 1905; rpr. Edited by Bell Irvin Wiley. Jackson, Tenn., 1958.

Southern Historical Society Papers. 52 vols. 1876–1959. Rpr. Edited by J. William Jones *et al.* New York, 1977–80.

Stiles, Robert. *Four Years Under Marse Robert.* New York, 1903.

Sword, Wiley. *Shiloh: Bloody April.* New York, 1974.

Tanner, Robert G. *Stonewall in the Valley.* New York, 1976.

Taylor, Richard. *Destruction and Reconstruction.* New York, 1879.

Taylor, Walter H. *General Lee His Campaigns in Virginia, 1861–1865, with Personal Reminiscences.* 1906; rpr. Dayton, 1975.

Thomas, Emory M. *The Confederate Nation, 1861–1865.* New York, 1979.

———. *The Confederate State of Richmond: A Biography of the Capital.* Austin, 1971.

Thomas, Henry W. *History of the Doles-Cook Brigade Army of Northern Virginia, C.S.A.* 1903; rpr. Dayton, 1981.

Thomas, Wilbur D. *General James "Pete" Longstreet, Lee's "Old War Horse," Scapegoat for Gettysburg.* Parsons, W.Va., 1979.

Thompson, Ed Porter. *History of the Orphan Brigade.* 1898; rpr. Dayton, 1973.

Thucydides. *History of the Peloponnesian War.* Translated by Rex Warner. Harmondsworth, Eng. 1954.

Tower, R. Lockwood, ed. *A Carolinian Goes to War: The Civil War Narrative of Arthur Middleton Manigault, Brigadier General C.S.A.* Columbia, S.C., 1983.

Tucker, Glen. *Chickamauga: Bloody Battle in the West.* New York, 1961.

Tunnard, W. H. *A Southern Record: The History of the Third Regiment Louisiana Infantry.* 1866; rpr. Dayton, 1970.

Vandiver, Frank E. *Mighty Stonewall.* New York, 1957.

Wakelyn, Jon L. *Biographical Dictionary of the Confederacy.* Westport, Conn., 1977.

Wallace, Lee A. *A Guide to Virginia Military Organizations, 1861–1865.* Richmond, 1964.

Warner, Ezra J. *Generals in Gray: Lives of the Confederate Commanders.* Baton Rouge, 1959.

Watkins, Samuel R. *"Co. Aytch" Maury Grays First Tennessee Regiment or A Sideshow of the Big Show.* 1900; rpr. Jackson, Tenn., 1952.

Welch, Spencer Glasgow. *A Confederate Surgeon's Letters to His Wife.* 1911; rpr. Marietta, Ga., 1954.

West, John C. *A Texan in Search of a Fight.* 1901; rpr. Waco, 1969.

Wicker, Tom. *Unto This Hour.* New York, 1984.

Wiley, Bell I. *The Life of Johnny Reb: The Common Soldier of the Confederacy.* New York, 1943.

Wilson, LeGrand James. *The Confederate Soldier.* Memphis, 1973.

Wilson, William Lyne. *A Borderland Confederate.* Edited by Festus P. Summers. Pittsburgh, 1962.

Winters, John D. *The Civil War in Louisiana.* Baton Rouge, 1963.

Wise, George. *History of the Seventeenth Virginia Infantry C.S.A.* 1870; rpr. Arlington, Va., 1969.

Wolseley, Field Marshal Viscount. *The American Civil War: An English View.* Charlottesville, Va., 1964.

Wormser, Richard. *The Yellowlegs: The Story of the United States Cavalry.* Garden City, N.Y., 1966.

Worsham, John H. *One of Jackson's Foot Cavalry.* 1912; rpr. Jackson, Tenn., 1964.

Wyeth, John Allan. *Life of General Nathan Bedford Forrest.* New York, 1899.

Yearns, W. Buck, and John G. Barrett, eds. *North Carolina Civil War Documentary.* Chapel Hill, 1980.

Young, J. P. *The Seventh Tennessee Cavalry (Confederate): A History.* 1890; rpr. Dayton, 1976.

Younger, Edward, ed. *Inside the Confederate Government: The Diary of Robert Garlick Hill Kean.* New York, 1957.

Articles

Alexander, E. P. "Sketch of Longstreet's Division." *Southern Historical Society Papers,* IX (rpr. 1977), 512–18.

Anderson, John. Letter to Editor, *Confederate Veteran,* II (rpr. 1983), 72.

Armstrong, William M. "Cahaba to Charleston: The Prison Odyssey of Lt. Edmund E. Ryan." *Civil War History,* VIII (June, 1962; rpr. 1972), 218–27.

Baxter, Alice. "Battle Flag of the Third Georgia." *Southern Historical Society Papers,* XXXVIII (rpr. 1977), 210–16.

Bidgood, Joseph V. "List of General Officers and Their Staffs in the Confederate Army, Furnished by Virginia, As Far as I Have Been Able to Get Them." *Southern Historical Society Papers,* XXXVIII (rpr. 1977), 156–83.

Bond, Frank A. "Company A, First Maryland Cavalry." *Confederate Veteran,* VI (rpr. 1983), 78–80.

Brown, B. F. "A Unique Experience." *Confederate Veteran,* XXXI (rpr. 1983), 100–101.

Browne, W. B. "Stranger Than Fiction: Capture of United States Steamer Maple Leaf, Near Cape Henry, Half a Century Ago." *Southern Historical Society Papers,* XXXIX (rpr. 1979), 181–85.

Burrows, J. L. "Recollections of Libby Prison." *Southern Historical Society Papers,* XI (rpr. 1977), 83–92.

Byrne, Frank L., ed. "A General Behind Bars: Neal Dow in Libby Prison." *Civil War History,* VIII (June, 1962; rpr. 1972), 164–83.

Calkin, Homer L. "Elk Horn to Vicksburg." *Civil War History,* II (March, 1956; rpr. 1963), 7–43.

"Captain B. T. Walshe, A Gallant Confederate." *Confederate Veteran,* VI (rpr. 1983), 575–76.

Cardwell, Colonel D. "A Brilliant Coup: How Wade Hampton Captured Grant's Entire Beef Supply." *Southern Historical Society Papers,* XXII (rpr. 1977), 147–56.

Chambers, C. C. "The Coahoma Invincibles." *Confederate Veteran,* XXXI (rpr. 1983), 461–63.

Cox, William R. "Major-General Stephen D. Ramseur: His Life and Character." *Southern Historical Society Papers,* XVIII (rpr. 1977), 217–60.

Crocker, W. A. "The Army Intelligence Office." *Confederate Veteran,* VIII (rpr. 1983), 118–19.

"The Daily Rebel Banner." *Confederate Veteran,* IV (rpr. 1983), 344.

Davis, Jefferson. "Address of the President to the Soldiers of the Confederate States." *Southern Historical Society Papers,* XIV (1978), 466–68.

Delaney, Norman C. "Corpus Christi—The Vicksburg of Texas." *Civil War Times Illustrated,* XVI (July, 1977), 4–9, 44–48.

Duncan, Richard R. "Marylanders and the Invasion of 1862." In John T. Hubbell, ed., *Battles Lost and Won.* Westport, Conn., 1975.

Early, J. A. "Relative Numbers—General Early's Reply to Count of Paris." *Southern Historical Society Papers,* VI (rpr. 1977), 12–36.

Ewell, R. S. "Evacuation of Richmond." *Southern Historical Society Papers,* XIII (rpr. 1978), 247–52.

Ewing, Z. W. Letter to Editor, *Confederate Veteran,* XV (rpr. 1983), 534.

"Fortification and Siege of Port Hudson—Compiled by the Association of Defenders of Port Hudson." *Southern Historical Society Papers,* XIV (rpr. 1978), 305–48.

Freeman, Douglas Southall. "An Address." *Civil War History,* I (rpr. 1963), 7–15.

Garnett, Captain James M. "Diary of Captain James M. Garnett, Ordnance Officer of Rodes' Division, 2d Corps, Army of Northern Virginia, from August 5th to November 30th, 1864, Covering Part of General J. A. Early's Campaign in the Shenandoah Valley." *Southern Historical Society Papers,* XXVII (rpr. 1977), 1–16.

"General Information." *Confederate Veteran,* XXXIV (rpr. 1983), 157.

Goldsborough, W. W. "Grant's Change of Base: The Horrors of the Battle of Cold Harbor, from a Soldier's Notebook." *Southern Historical Society Papers,* XXIX (rpr. 1978), 285–91.

Gordon, John B. "Report of Brigadier-General John B. Gordon." *Southern Historical Society Papers,* VII (rpr. 1977), 241–44.

Greer, George H. T. "All Thoughts Are Absorbed in the War." *Civil War Times Illustrated,* XVII (December, 1978), 30–35.

Hallock, Charles. "The Hidden Way to Dixie." *Confederate Veteran,* XXIV (rpr. 1983), 494–96.

Hill, D. H. "Address." *Southern Historical Society Papers,* XIII (rpr. 1978), 259–76.

Hindman, Major General T. C. "Battle of Chickamauga." *Southern Historical Society Papers,* XIII (rpr. 1978), 367–72.

"Historical Sketch of the Rockbridge Artillery, C.S. Army, by a Member of the Famous Battery." *Southern Historical Society Papers,* XXIII (rpr. 1977), 98–158.

Horsley, A. S. "Reminiscences of Shiloh." *Confederate Veteran,* II (rpr. 1983), 234.

Hunter, R. M. T. "Post-Bellum Mortality Among Confederates." *Southern Historical Society Papers,* XVI (rpr. 1978), 270–76.

Hyman, Harold M. "Deceit in Dixie." *Civil War History,* III (rpr. 1963), 65–82.

Irvine, Dallas D. "The Fall of Richmond: Evacuation and Occupation." In *Military Analysis of the Civil War: An Anthology by the Editors of Military Affairs,* 383–93. Millwood, N.Y., 1977.

Ives, W. M. "History Fourth Florida Regiment." *Confederate Veteran,* III (rpr. 1983), 102–103.

———. "The Record That We Made." *Confederate Veteran,* XXXI (rpr. 1983), 334.

Johns, John. "Wilmington During the Blockade." *Civil War Times Illustrated,* XIII (June, 1974), 34–44.

Johnson, B. R. "Operations from the 6th to the 11th of May, 1864." *Southern Historical Society Papers,* XII (rpr. 1977), 274–82.

Johnson, B. T. "Memoir of the First Maryland Regiment. Paper No. 4: The Battle of Winchester." *Southern Historical Society Papers,* X (rpr. 1977), 97–109.

Jones, Charles C. "A Roster of General Officers, Heads of Departments, Senators, Representatives, Military Organizations, &C., &c., in Confederate Service During the War Between the States." *Southern Historical Society Papers,* I (rpr. 1977), 5–31.

Jones, J. William. "Reminiscences of the Army of Northern Virginia. Paper No. 4— Capture of Winchester and Rout of Banks's Army." *Southern Historical Society Papers,* IX (rpr. 1977), 233–37.

———. "Reminiscences of the Army of Northern Virginia. Paper No. 5—How Fremont and Shields 'Caught' Stonewall Jackson." *Southern Historical Society Papers,* IX (rpr. 1977), 273–80.

Jones, Thomas G. "Last Days of the Army of Northern Virginia." *Southern Historical Society Papers,* XXI (rpr. 1977), 57–103.

Jones, W. E. "Summer Campaign of 1863—Report of Gen'l W. E. Jones." *Southern Historical Society Papers,* IX (rpr. 1979), 115–19.

Lane, J. H. "Glimpses of Army Life in 1864." *Southern Historical Society Papers,* XVIII (rpr. 1977), 406–22.

Ledbetter, M. T. "With Archer's Brigade." *Southern Historical Society Papers,* XXIX (rpr. 1978), 349–54.

Leinbach, Julius. "Regiment Band of the 26th North Carolina." Edited by Donald McCorkle. *Civil War History,* IV (rpr. 1963), 225–36.

Lewis, P. F. Letter to Editor, *Confederate Veteran,* II (rpr. 1983), 332.

Loehr, Charles T. "The 'Old First' Virginia at Gettysburg: Men Who Fought to the Bitter End in the Greatest of Battles. The Famous Pickett Charge and the Part the Old First Virginia Played in It." *Southern Historical Society Papers,* XXXII (rpr. 1979), 33–40.

Logan, Colonel George William. "Official Report on the Engagement Between the Federal Gunboats and Fort Beauregard, on the 10th and 11th May, 1863." *Southern Historical Society Papers,* XI (rpr. 1977), 497–501.

Longstreet, James. "Causes of Lee's Defeat at Gettysburg." *Southern Historical Society Papers,* V (rpr. 1977), 54–85.

Lord, Francis A. "Badges of Civil War Provost Guards." *Military Collector and Historian,* XXIII (Fall, 1971), 91–92.

M'Amy, C. D. "Brave P. E. Drew and His Fate." *Confederate Veteran,* II (rpr. 1983), 85.

McCabe, Captain W. Gordon. "Graduates of the United States Military Academy at

West Point, N.Y., Who Served in the Confederate States Army, with the Highest Commission and Highest Command Attained." *Southern Historical Society Papers,* XXX (rpr. 1977), 34–76.

————. "Major Andrew Reid Venable, Jr." *Southern Historical Society Papers,* XXXVII (rpr. 1979), 61–73.

McIntosh, David Gregg. "The Campaign of Chancellorsville." *Southern Historical Society Papers,* XL (rpr. 1979), 44–100.

M'Neilly, James H. "With the Rear Guard." *Confederate Veteran,* XXVI (rpr. 1983), 338–40.

Mindler, F. T. "Levi Strauss, the Spy." *Confederate Veteran,* XVI (rpr. 1983), 17–18.

Mosby, Colonel John S. "Stuart in the Gettysburg Campaign: A Defense of the Cavalry Commander." *Southern Historical Society Papers,* XXXVIII (rpr. 1977), 184–96.

Obituaries. *Confederate Veteran* (all vols. rpr. 1983), X, 273, 323; XII, 130, 450; XIII, 86–87; XV, 184–86; XVII, 89; XIX, 131; XXI, 301, 302, 453; XXII, 521; XXVI, 123; XXX, 268; XXXIV, 64, 104, 109.

"Organization of the Army of Northern Virginia, (General R. E. Lee Commanding), August 28 to September 1, 1862." *Southern Historical Society Papers,* X (rpr. 1977), 555–60.

Owens, Thomas. "Penalties for Desertion." *Confederate Veteran,* II (rpr. 1983), 235.

Park, Captain Robert Emory. "The 12th Alabama Infantry, Confederate States Army." *Southern Historical Society Papers,* XXXIII (rpr. 1979), 193–296.

————. "War Diary, January 28th, 1863–January 27th, 1864." *Southern Historical Society Papers,* XXVI (rpr. 1977), 1–31.

Parole of Federal Prisoner. *Confederate Veteran,* VI (rpr. 1983), 42.

Peacock, C. L. "Conscription in the Mountains." *Confederate Veteran,* XXIII (rpr. 1983), 171.

Philpot, G. B. "A Maryland Boy in the Confederate Army." *Confederate Veteran,* XXIV (rpr. 1983), 312–15.

Poindexter, James E. "General Armistead's Portrait Presented: An Address Delivered Before R. E. Lee Camp No. 1, C.V., Richmond, Va., January 29, 1909." *Southern Historical Society Papers,* XXXVII (rpr. 1979), 144–51.

Polley, J. B. "Concernin' of a Hog." *Confederate Veteran,* V (rpr. 1983), 56–59.

————. "Texans Foraging for Christmas." *Confederate Veteran,* III (rpr. 1983), 362–65.

Power, J. Tracey. "Young and Full of Promise." *Civil War Times Illustrated,* XVIII (April, 1979), 22–27.

Pressley, Major John G. "The Wee Nee Volunteers of Williamsburg District, South Carolina, in the First (Hagood's) Regiment." *Southern Historical Society Papers,* XVI (rpr. 1978), 116–94.

Price, General Sterling. "The Missouri Campaign of 1864." *Southern Historical Society Papers,* VII (rpr. 1977), 209–31.

"Proceedings of First Confederate Congress, End of Second Session, Third Session in Part." *Southern Historical Society Papers,* XLVII (rpr. 1980), 18–19, 31–32, 46–47, 72–73, 75–76.

"Proceedings of First Confederate Congress, First Session Completed, Second Session in Part." *Southern Historical Society Papers,* XLV (rpr. 1980), 224–26, 249.

"Proceedings of First Confederate Congress, Second Session in Part." *Southern Historical Society Papers,* XLVI (rpr. 1980), 103, 104, 225–26.

"Proceedings of Second Confederate Congress, First Session, Second Session in Part, 2 May–14 June 1864, 7 November–14 December 1864." *Southern Historical Society Papers,* LI (rpr. 1980), 18–19, 28.

"Proceedings of Second Confederate Congress, Second Session in Part, December 15, 1864–March 18, 1865." *Southern Historical Society Papers,* LII (rpr. 1980), 29–30, 35, 334–35, 372, 383, 416–17.

"Proceedings of the First Confederate Congress, Third Session in Part, January, 29–March 19, 1863." *Southern Historical Society Papers,* XLVIII (rpr. 1980), 224.

Reese, George. "What Five Confederates Did at Petersburg." *Confederate Veteran,* XII (rpr. 1983), 286–87.

Reese, James, "Private Soldier Life—Humorous Features." *Confederate Veteran,* XVI (rpr. 1983), 161–66.

Ridley, B. L. "Camp Scenes Around Dalton." *Confederate Veteran,* X (rpr. 1983), 66–68.

Roberts, Albert. "I'm Conscripted, Smith, Conscripted." *Confederate Veteran,* III (rpr. 1983), 245.

Roberts, M. "Third Florida Regiment." *Confederate Veteran,* X (rpr. 1983), 355.

Rodgers, Robert L. "Roster of the Battalion of the Georgia Military Institute Cadets in the Confederate Army Service in the Civil War from May 10th, 1864, to May 20th, 1865." *Southern Historical Society Papers,* XXXIII (rpr. 1979), 306–19.

"Roster of Officers of City Battalion, Richmond, Va., the Twenty-fifth Battalion of Infantry." *Southern Historical Society Papers,* XXXI (rpr. 1979), 323–25.

Rutherford, Philip. "The Great Gainesville Hanging." *Civil War Times Illustrated,* XVII (April, 1978), 12–20.

Schultz, B. F. "Lieut. A. H. Vaughan, Killed in the War." *Confederate Veteran,* VIII (rpr. 1983), 518.

Shepard, Philo B. Letter to Editor, *Confederate Veteran,* XXII (rpr. 1983), 238.

Shoup, Brigadier General F. A. "Dalton Campaign—Works at Chattahoochee River—Interesting History." *Confederate Veteran,* III (rpr. 1983), 262–65.

Simmons, J. W. "Conscripting Atlanta Theater in 1863." *Confederate Veteran,* XI (rpr. 1983), 279.

Spence, E. Leslie. "Reports of the First, Seventh and Seventeenth Virginia Regiments in 1862." *Southern Historical Society Papers,* XXXVIII (rpr. 1977), 262–67.

Spratley, Major James Walter. "Alabama Mounted Rifles." *Confederate Veteran*, XVIII (rpr. 1983), 469.

Stiles, John C. "Mr. Commissary Banks." *Confederate Veteran*, XXIV (rpr. 1983), 496.

Stuart, General J. E. B. "The Gettysburg Campaign—Full Report of General J. E. B. Stuart." *Southern Historical Society Papers*, VII (rpr. 1977), 400–434.

———. "Report of Operations After Gettysburg." *Southern Historical Society Papers*, II (rpr. 1977), 65–78.

———. "Stuart's Report of His Expedition into Pennsylvania in October, 1862." *Southern Historical Society Papers*, XIV (rpr. 1978), 477–84.

Sturgis, H. H. "About the Burning of Richmond." *Confederate Veteran*, XVII (rpr. 1983), 474.

Sulivane, Clement. "The Fall of Richmond." In Robert Underwood Johnson and Clarence Clough Buel, eds., *Battles and Leaders of the Civil War*. 4 vols. 1887–88; rpr. New York, 1956. Vol. IV, pp. 725–28.

Taylor, Walter H. "The Battle of Sharpsburg." *Southern Historical Society Papers*, XXIV (rpr. 1977), 267–74.

Thompson, Captain John H. "Historical Address of the Former Commander of Grimes Battery." *Southern Historical Society Papers*, XXXIV (rpr. 1979), 149–55.

"Thrilling Experiences by Dr. Tichenor." *Confederate Veteran*, IX (rpr. 1983), 67–69.

Timberlake, W. L. "The Last Days in Front of Richmond." *Confederate Veteran*, XXII (rpr. 1983), 303.

———. "Last Days in Front of Richmond, 1864–65." *Confederate Veteran*, XX (rpr. 1983), 119.

Tracy, Colonel Carlos. "Operations Before Charleston in May and July, 1862." *Southern Historical Society Papers*, VIII (rpr. 1977), 541–47.

Tucker, G. W. "Death of General A. P. Hill." *Southern Historical Society Papers*, XI (rpr. 1977), 564–69.

Turner, Charles W., ed. "Major Charles A. Davidson: Letters of a Virginia Soldier." *Civil War History*, XXII (March, 1976), 16–40.

Walker, John C. "Reconstruction in Texas." *Southern Historical Society Papers*, XXIV (rpr. 1977), 41–57.

Warner, Ezra J. "Who Was General Tyler?" *Civil War Times Illustrated*, IX (October, 1970), 14–19.

West, Colonel Douglass. "'I am Dying, Egypt, Dying!' and Its Author, a Touching Incident of the War." *Southern Historical Society Papers*, XXIII (rpr. 1977), 82–94.

Willis, Francis T. "The Twelfth Georgia Infantry." *Southern Historical Society Papers*, XVII (rpr. 1978), 160–87.

Index

Covington, Virginia, 282
Crater, Battle of the, 202, 226
Crew's Prison, Richmond, 171*n*19
Crow, B. M., 78, 78*n*11
Culpeper Court House, Virginia, 94, 129, 258
Cumberland Gap, Kentucky, 244
Cumberland River, Tennessee, 190
Curtis, Samuel, 142
Cynthiana, Kentucky, 221, 227

Daffen, Lawrence, 216
Dallas, Georgia, 288
Dallas *Herald,* 142
Dalton, Georgia, 36, 58, 86, 87, 92, 137, 159, 227, 228, 238, 278
Danville, Virginia, 29, 156, 173
Danville Prison, Virginia, 171*n*19, 277, 296, 300, 301
Davidson, Charles A., 44–45, 44*n*42, 241
Davis, Jefferson: and martial law, 178–81, 185, 190, 192, 194; mentioned, 7, 8, 10, 15, 20, 21, 22, 29, 46, 47, 60, 62, 66, 67, 71, 74, 80, 102, 121, 125, 133, 150, 151, 161, 197, 198, 208, 212, 228, 230
Davis, Sam, 230–31
Davis, Thomas A., 42*n*36
Deas, Zachariah Cantey, 223–24
Deasonville, Mississippi, 255
Decatur, Alabama, 99, 232
De Fontaine, F. G., 240
Demopolis, Alabama, 36, 170
Denis, Jules Charles, 9, 40, 97, 99, 170, 205, 211, 227, 231, 239
Desertion, Confederate: causes, 146, 147–49; statistics on, 146–57 *passim,* 252; combating, 30, 33, 49, 51, 52, 87, 147, 149–62 *passim,* 194, 196, 227, 249, 252, 253; mentioned, 3, 6, 10, 30, 81, 83, 100, 253
Desertion, Union, 207–208
Desha, Joseph, 108
Deshler, James, 135
Dickinson, Captain, 42*n*36
Dilworth, William S., 225
Dingle, W. E., 87
Dodd, Thomas L., 19
Dow, Neal, 173

Drewry's Bluff, Virginia, 203
Dublin, Virginia, 309
Duck River, Tennessee, 229
Duke, Basil, 57, 59
Duke, Richard T. W., 213
Dumfries, Virginia, 42*n*36

Early, Jubal, 12, 44, 62, 83, 95, 119, 219, 222, 244
East Feliciana Parish, Louisiana, 263, 270
East Florida, District of, 209
East Louisiana, District of, 270
East Tennessee, Department of: provost system, 41; movement controls, 76, 84–85; under martial law, 194–95; mentioned, 14, 67, 68, 262, 285, 287
East Tennessee, District of, 171
Elkhorn Tavern, Arkansas, 142
Elliot, Wyatt M., 37
Elzey, Arnold, 156
Estes, John W., 9*n*14, 22, 97, 227, 232
Evans, Nathan, 121
Evans, Perry, 232
Ewell, Richard S., 23, 30, 46, 61, 72, 129, 130, 176, 213–14, 225–26
Ewing, Z. W., 224

Fairfax Court House, Virginia, 260
Fairfield, Pennsylvania, 222
Fair Oaks, Battle of, 109, 238
Falmouth, Virginia, 57
Farmville, Virginia, 222, 279
Farragut, David Glasgow, 83, 190, 192
Fauntleroy, James Henry, 84
Fay, Edwin H., 65
Fayetteville, Arkansas, 41, 50, 65, 286
Fisher's Hill, Virginia, 133
Florence, Alabama, 84
Florence, South Carolina, 171*n*19, 288
Florida, military units of:
—Infantry regiments: 3d, 260, 281, 293; 4th, 39–40, 293
Floyd, John, 230
Foote, Henry S., 7
Foreacre, Green J., 85–86, 195
Forrest, Nathan Bedford: and straggling, 140; mentioned, 11, 19, 35, 40, 64*n*1, 93, 136, 138, 159, 170, 171, 202, 205, 228, 241

Maney, George, 35
Manigault, Arthur: on provost duties, 52;
  mentioned, 136, 223, 238–39, 250
Marietta, Georgia, 19n21, 137, 172n19,
  270, 283
Marshall, Humphrey, 106, 184
Marshall County, Texas, 210, 258
Martial law: controversy over, 178–80,
  193, 197–99, 251
Martinsburg, Virginia, 35, 257, 290
Maryland military units: 1st Cavalry Reg-
  iment, 257; 1st Infantry Battalion, 154;
  1st Infantry Regiment, 167, 214
Matagorda, Texas, 209, 211, 220, 262
Maury, Dabney, 210
Maynard, J. C., 182
Mayo, G. Spencer, 231
Mayo, Joseph Carrington, 18, 60, 213
Mebane, Samuel R., 27, 88
Mechanicsville, Virginia, 42
Memphis, Tennessee, 35, 84, 96, 172,
  192, 194, 211, 228
Mercer County, Virginia, 308
Meridian, Mississippi, 91, 174
Mesilla, New Mexico, 275
Michailoffsky, Charles J., 224
Millen, Georgia, 171n19
Milroy, Robert Huston, 129
Missionary Ridge, Tennessee, 20, 136,
  286
Mississippi: District of the, 66, 68, 83,
  141, 220, 243, 267; Third District of,
  9n14, 211, 270
Mississippi, military units of:
—Cavalry regiments: 4th, 31, 31n53, 40,
  281, 295; Jeff Davis Legion, 287
—Cavalry brigades: Walthall's, 204
—Infantry battalions: 1st, 221
—Infantry regiments: 1st, 221; 6th, 295;
  11th, 270; 16th, 59, 267; 17th, 241,
  276, 295; 18th, 59; 27th, 56; 29th, 36,
  279; 42d, 80, 80n14, 96, 173, 288, 296
—Reserve battalions: 1st, 23, 296
Mississippi and East Louisiana: District of,
  231; Department of, 239, 275
Missouri, military units of:
—Cavalry regiments: 1st, 35, 84
—Cavalry brigades: 1st, 5, 75, 106, 164,
  241

—Infantry regiments: 1st, 52, 106; 2d, 40,
  84, 84n25, 296, 299
—State Guard, 41, 255, 259, 273, 289
Mobile, Alabama, 40, 84, 92, 171n19,
  172, 205, 257, 264, 278, 281, 285
Mobile Bay, Alabama, 92
Monroe County, Virginia, 261
Montgomery, Alabama, 56, 86, 96,
  172n19
Moore, R. H., 171
Moore, Robert A., 241
Moore, Samuel, 208–209
Moore, Thomas, 66, 68, 190, 192, 193–
  94
Morgan, James, 193
Morgan, John Hunt, 35, 57, 59
Morristown, Tennessee, 275
Mosby, John Singleton, 93
Munfordville, Kentucky, 134
Murfreesboro, Tennessee, 134, 279, 284,
  295, 299

Nashville, Battle of, 35, 138
Nashville, Tennessee, 35, 134, 140, 228,
  229
Navasota, Texas, 26, 262
Neufville, Edward, 65, 65n3
Newbern, North Carolina, 159
Newberry, South Carolina, 216
Newburg, Alabama, 272, 290
New Madrid, Missouri, 194, 218, 219,
  287
New Market, Battle of, 23, 62
New Market, Virginia, 277, 293
New Mexico: provost in, 41; campaign,
  275
New Orleans, Louisiana: passport controls
  in, 83; under martial law, 190–92; men-
  tioned, 15, 47, 79, 87, 171n19, 172,
  185, 193, 196, 201, 210, 211, 215, 283
Niblett's Bluff, Texas, 202
Nisbet, James, 58–59, 82, 201, 227
Norfolk, Virginia: under martial law, 15,
  53, 180–81; mentioned, 278
North Anna River, Virginia, 226
North Carolina, Department of: provost es-
  tablishment in, 38–39; First Subdistrict,
  269; mentioned, 47n51, 260